LION CITY NARRATIVES

It takes a good geographer to put the past in its place. Professor Savage has pursued seven centuries of contemporary writings about Singapore to seek distinctive Western perspectives about the island at the heart of the Malay World that became a modern city-state. He reminds us that when the geographer has immersed himself in centuries of images and reflections, he makes the past visible and enriches all our senses. This is that kind of book, and anyone who wants to know what Singapore stands for will find a multifaceted answer to just about any question he may ask.

Wang Gungwu
University Professor, National University of Singapore

This is a remarkable book. Associate Professor Victor Savage opens a field which will grow other scholars to follow. Its main elements were known, but much scattered. Tumasik/Singapura/Singapore's history goes back to the Indianised thalassic kingdoms of Sri Vijaya, Palembang, and the Malacca sultanate. This historic background apart, its special theme is in the Western colonisers' descriptions in over many chapters, of what Raffles founded in 1819. Savage has brought these descriptions together, showing the fascinating full impact and value. To him, "Tropical nature and the Oriental landscape were powerful frames that captured the Western mental pictures of Singapore — the settings within which were placed all other experiences of the place". The richly varied lives of the colonised — native Malays, immigrant Chinese and Indians — fascinated White resident colonisers and visitors including Kipling and Conrad. The many writings intrigue. They were able to observe and occasionally participate in Singapore's bustling Asian life. They were not separated by walls.

What we have starts with the *Sejarah Melayu* and ends with Dennis Bloodworth. We look forward to Associate Professor Savage's concluding volume, on our Singapore.

Edwin Thumboo
Emeritus Professor, National University of Singapore

Singapore's bicentennial, in 2019, has inspired the publication of several new books. This book by Dr. Victor Savage is to be warmly welcomed. He has gone through the enormous literature on Singapore written by Western scholars and observers, and analysed their perceptions into this compelling volume. The Western view of Singapore will always be different from our own view. This was brought home to me recently, when two Western scholars described the ruling People's Action Party's performance in General Election 2020, as a "disaster" and a "humiliating defeat". It is, nevertheless, important for us to understand how others view us. We should also have an open mind and be prepared to learn from others.

Tommy Koh
Professor of Law, National University of Singapore, and Ambassador-at-Large, Ministry of Foreign Affairs, Singapore

LION CITY NARRATIVES

SINGAPORE THROUGH WESTERN EYES

LION CITY NARRATIVES

SINGAPORE THROUGH WESTERN EYES

VICTOR R. SAVAGE

NEW JERSEY · LONDON · SINGAPORE · BEIJING · SHANGHAI · HONG KONG · TAIPEI · CHENNAI · TOKYO

Published by

World Scientific Publishing Co. Pte. Ltd.
5 Toh Tuck Link, Singapore 596224
USA office: 27 Warren Street, Suite 401-402, Hackensack, NJ 07601
UK office: 57 Shelton Street, Covent Garden, London WC2H 9HE

Library of Congress Control Number: 2021931304

British Library Cataloguing-in-Publication Data
A catalogue record for this book is available from the British Library.

Cybil Kho is the designer of the book cover and the chapter opening illustrations.

LION CITY NARRATIVES
Singapore Through Western Eyes

Copyright © 2022 by Victor R. Savage

All rights reserved.

ISBN 978-981-122-915-2 (hardcover)
ISBN 978-981-123-176-6 (paperback)
ISBN 978-981-122-916-9 (ebook for institutions)
ISBN 978-981-122-917-6 (ebook for individuals)

For any available supplementary material, please visit
https://www.worldscientific.com/worldscibooks/10.1142/12068#t=suppl

Desk Editors: Jayanthi Muthuswamy/Karimah Samsudin/Thaheera Althaf

Typeset by Stallion Press
Email: enquiries@stallionpress.com

To the memory of the many Singaporeans (my friends, neighbours, classmates, working colleagues, artists, and the varsity buddies) with whom I have been fortunate to share precious time:

Aileen Lau, Alice Swan-Koh, Alvin Foo Kiam Hiong, Anthony Chin, Ben D'Souza, Bernard Fong, Betty Cheah, C.P. Pow, Charles Tan, David Cham Tshoong Mun, Dudley de Souza, Faisal Francis Fernandez, Gerard 'Gerry' de Souza, J. Nathan, James Pakiam, Jeremy Ong Kah Meng, Brother Joseph McNally, Lim Meng Kin, M. S. Maniam, Michael Sweet, Ng Choon Hwa, Ng Eng Teng, Ong Chit Chung, Ooi Giok Ling, P. Naidu, Pakir Singh, Palakrishnan, Reverend Peter Lim, Philip Ariken, Rocky Yan Fook Sun, S. Namasivayam, Salleh bin Osman, Seah Lim Soon, Siva Choy, Susie Soh, Sylvester Raj, Tan Chuan Kiat, Tan Guat Whye, Tang Ah Ying, Thai Quang Trung, Tony Greer, Victorine Chen-Toh, Viji Menon, Vincent Wong Kok Kee, William Lau Tan Meng, and Winnah Rodé.

CONTENTS

List of Illustrations   xiii

About the Author   xxi

With Gratitude   xxiii

Foreword   xxvii

Preface   xxix

Chapter 1   Lion City Narratives   3
   I. Introduction   3
   II. The Setting   7
   III. Unfolding History: The *Longue Durée*   9
   IV. Lion City in Retrospect   11
   V. Other Interpretations, Cultural Distillations   12
   VI. Raffles to Lee: The Colonial Heritage   16
   VII. What Lies Ahead   20

Chapter 2   What is the Narrative of Western Perceptions?   27
   I. Defining Western Perceptions   27
   II. What Influenced Western Views   31
      a) Western Culture and Civilisation   31
      b) Long 19th Century, Tempestuous 20th Century   32
      c) The Evolving Colonial Statement   35
   III. The Value of Western Perceptions   39

IV. Alternative Western Perspectives	42
a) The Urban Biography	43
b) Temporal Insights	44
V. Summing Up: The Conceptual Statement	47

Chapter 3 Tumasik: Surrogate Kingdom in the *Alam Melayu*   51

I. Unfolding the Historical Processes	51
II. What's in a Name: The Mythological Toponym	55
III. The Thalassic Kingdom Remembered	60
IV. Geopolitical Tussle by Regional Hegemons	63
V. The Tumasik Legacy	67
VI. Summing Up: Tumasik's Historical Watershed	74

Chapter 4 One Man's Vision: Raffles' Singapore 'Child'   79

I. Singapore: The Raffles Gamble	79
II. The Raffles Vision	89
III. Entrepôt Singapore: Free Trade	98
IV. *Mission Civilisatrice*: The Educational Institution	101
V. Colonial City Foundations: Ethnic Segregation	102
VI. Land Tenure: Colonisation and Capitalisation of Land	109
VII. Summing Up: The Raffles Legacy	112

Chapter 5 Tropical Nature and the Agricultural Mania   117

I. The Historical Background	117
II. Tropical Experience: The Singapore Experiment	119
III. The Torrid Tropical Climate	121
IV. Coastal Scenery	123
V. Tropical Nature's Plenitude and Diversity	125
VI. Salubrious Singapore	129
VII. Miasma Fevers: The Singapore Deduction	131
VIII. The Tiger Menace	132
IX. The Agriculture Mania	135
a) Why Agriculture?	136
b) European Agricultural Enterprise	138
c) Chinese Gambier	143
d) Tropical Fruit	145
e) Enter Rubber	146
X. Summing Up: Singapore's Changing Landscape	147

List of Illustrations   149

Chapter 6 Urban Morphology: Street Life and Iconic Places	175
I. Defining Singapore's Urban Morphology	175
II. European and Asian Towns	179
III. The Sense Landscape	182
IV. The Roadside Narratives	186
V. The Singapore River and Keppel Harbour	189
VI. Chinatown	191
VII. Change Alley	196
VIII. Commercial Square: Raffles Place	197
IX. Iconic Landscapes that Surprised and Disturbed	200
a) Bugis Street: Bewildering Nights of Passage	200
b) Red-Light Areas	201
c) Sago Lane Death Houses	204
X. Summing Up: A Planned City of Contrasts	206
Chapter 7 Singapore's Imageability	211
I. Formulating Urban Impressions	211
II. Imageable Singapore	213
a) Singapore Lights	215
b) The Beehive of Activity	218
c) The Amorphous City	220
d) Shifting Cultural Landscapes	221
III. The Great Entrepôt	224
a) Singapore's Port: Product Diversity	226
b) Explaining Singapore's Entrepôt Success	228
c) The 20th-Century Trade	230
d) Capitalism Operationalised	232
IV. Singapore's White 'Society'	234
V. Landscapes of Vice: Opium, Gambling, and Prostitution	240
VI. Urban and Cultural Change	245
VII. Summing Up: The Making of Cosmopolitan Identity	246
Chapter 8 Asia's Navel: Cultural Pluralism	251
I. The Makings of Pluralism	251
II. Polyglot Society	254
III. Sexual Inequality: Domestic 'Boys'	256
IV. Colours of Culture	258
V. Ethnic Characteristics	260
a) The 'Malays' in the *Alam Melayu*	263
b) Chinese from the Celestial Empire	272

c) The Indians: Klings and Kalinga	280
d) The Arabs	282
VI. Cultural Distancing: 'We' and 'They'	284
VII. Summing Up: Reflections on the Developmental Software	289

Chapter 9 Colonialism Challenged: Stirrings of Independence ... 295
  I. *'Orang Putehs'*: Colonialism in Doubt ... 296
  II. Colonialism Questioned: The Sepoy Uprising and the Japanese Occupation ... 299
  III. The Cusp of Independence: Changing Perceptions ... 303
  IV. The Enright Affair: East-West Cultural Conflict ... 308
  V. The Chinese Question: The Threat of Communism ... 312
  VI. Summing Up: The Colonial Inheritance ... 319

Chapter 10 Reflections and Recollections ... 327
  I. Something Borrowed, Something Learnt ... 327
  II. Ethnic Insights, Cultural Revelations ... 330
  III. Operationalising Colonialism: People, Economy, and Society ... 335
  IV. Biography of the City through Other Eyes ... 339
  V. The Tropical Laboratory: Western Experiences ... 346
  VI. Singapore: The Meeting of East and West ... 348
  VII. Raffles' Vision, Lee's Audacious Impact ... 354

Glossary ... 363

References and Selected Bibliography ... 377

Index ... 407

LIST OF ILLUSTRATIONS

The following list indicates the original names and dates for the images from pages 149 to 172, and where relevant, additional information about their content provided through their copyright owners, as well as about alterations to the original images which appear in this book. The original images may be accessed either through the website of the National Archives of Singapore, or at Antiques of the Orient, Singapore.

Plate 1. Animal specimens and faunistic curiosities in the Raffles Museum. Source: *Interior View of Raffles Museum.* 1920s. Lim Choo Sye Collection. Courtesy of National Archives of Singapore. Image recoloured and significantly cropped.

Plate 2. Children of the ubiquitous *orang laut*, or sea gypsies at play. Source: *Malay Village. Orang laut* boys from a Malay village. 1890s. Lim Kheng Chye Collection. Courtesy of National Archives of Singapore. Image recoloured and significantly cropped.

Plate 3. Panorama of the Padang, with Raffles' house on Government Hill, later renamed Fort Canning Hill. Source: *Vue du temple protestant à Singapour.* c. 1852. Courtesy of Antiques of the Orient. Image recoloured and significantly cropped.

Plate 4. *Portrait Painting of Sir Thomas Stamford Raffles* (1781–1826). Source: Courtesy of National Archives of Singapore. Image retouched, recoloured, and significantly cropped.

xiv *Lion City Narratives: Singapore through Western Eyes*

Plate 5. The 1822 Raffles Town Plan which formed the spatial outline of the colonial city, as mapped out by Lt. Philip Jackson. Source: *Plan of the Town of Singapore by Lieut. Jackson.* 1828. Courtesy of Antiques of the Orient. Image cropped.

Plate 6. An 1839 version of George Coleman's map of Singapore town, based on an actual field studies survey. Source: *Map of the Town and Environs of Singapore from an Actual Survey by G. D. Coleman.* 1839. Courtesy of Antiques of the Orient. Image significantly cropped.

Plate 7. A European lady dressed unsuitably for the hot humid tropics posing before a colonial bungalow house. Source: *Untitled.* Courtesy of Antiques of the Orient. Image retouched and cropped.

Plate 8. The first Christian cemetery at Fort Canning, with the eastern part of the town in the background. Source: *Fort Canning View.* View of coast from Fort Canning, Christian cemetery in foreground, steeples of Cathedral of the Good Shepherd and Convent of the Holy Infant Jesus in background. c. 1950s. George Tricker Collection. Courtesy of National Archives of Singapore. Image retouched and significantly cropped.

Plate 9. Istana Kampong Glam before recent refurbishment. Built by Coleman in 1840, it remains a key part of Singapore's Malay-Muslim community. Source: *Istana Kampong Glam at Sultan Gate.* September 1, 1990. Courtesy of National Archives of Singapore. Image retouched, recoloured, and significantly cropped.

Plate 10. Fullerton Road with trolley buses and rickshaws heading toward Anderson Bridge and Fullerton Building, originally housing the General Post Office. Source: *Trolley Buses at Empress Place, Singapore.* c. 1930. Andrew Tan Collection. Courtesy of National Archives of Singapore. Image retouched, recoloured, and significantly cropped.

Plate 11. A Chinese hunter with the prize tiger, taken when tiger hunting was considered a sport. Source: *Tiger Hunt, 1930.* Members of the Straits Hunting Party; from left, Tan Tian Quee (vice-president), Ong Kim Hong (shooter), and Low Peng Hoe (president). Courtesy of Antiques of the Orient. Image recoloured and significantly cropped.

List of Illustrations xv

Plate 12. A favourite spot in the Botanic Gardens off Orchard Road, with its waterlily pond which Europeans enjoyed. Source: *Botanical Gardens*. Courtesy of Antiques of the Orient. Image recoloured and significantly cropped.

Plate 13. With agriculture becoming an economic activity, both Westerners and Asians were avidly involved in plantations. Here is a pepper plantation. Source: *Pepper Plantation*. 1890s. Gretchen Liu Collection. Courtesy of National Archives of Singapore. Image retouched, recoloured, and significantly cropped.

Plate 14. At the turn of the 20th century, Chinese market gardens growing popular local vegetables thrived around the colonial town. Source: *Chinese Farmer, Singapore*. Working on a vegetable farm, 1911. Robert Feingold Collection. Courtesy of National Archives of Singapore. Image recoloured and significantly cropped.

Plate 15. Gambier cultivation was a major Chinese activity that changed Singapore's landscape. This atap-roof shed is part of a gambier processing cottage industry. Source: *Gambier Manufacturing*. 1890s. Gretchen Liu Collection. Courtesy of National Archives of Singapore. Image recoloured and significantly cropped.

Plate 16. After 'Mad Ridley's' promotion of rubber, Singapore would have many plantations owned by both Chinese and European companies. Lim Nee Soon is visiting his rubber estate. Source: *Lim Nee Soon Visits His Rubber Estate, Singapore*. November 11, 1909. Courtesy of National Archives of Singapore. Image recoloured and significantly cropped.

Plate 17. Flanked by shophouses, early 20th-century Orchard Road was busy with motor cars and rickshaws. Source: *Orchard Road, Singapore*. Courtesy of Antiques of the Orient. Image cropped and extended.

Plate 18. 'Koek's Bazaar' at Orchard Road was an agglomeration of itinerant multiethnic food hawkers servicing the colony's cosmopolitan population. Source: *Scene of a Market, Singapore*. Hawkers at 'Koek's Bazaar' at Orchard Road and Cuppage Road before the construction of the brick façade in 1909. On the right stands Orchard Road Market. c. 1905. Courtesy of National Archives of Singapore. Image recoloured, significantly cropped, and extended.

xvi   *Lion City Narratives: Singapore through Western Eyes*

Plate 19.   Chinese food hawkers referred to as 'travelling kitchens' catering to the huge bachelor coolie population. Source: *Travelling Restaurant Serving Soup & Stew*. Courtesy of Antiques of the Orient. Image recoloured and cropped.

Plate 20.   The picturesque Singapore River with its motley bumboats and sampans was for decades Singapore's port; hence the nearby godowns that processed the import-export trade. Source: *Singapore River, c1880s*. Morgan Betty Bassett Collection. Courtesy of National Archives of Singapore. Image recoloured and significantly cropped.

Plate 21.   A unique engraving of Keppel Harbour which seems like a scene from the Arabian Nights, with camels ferrying goods and minarets in the background. Source: *Sincapore*. Singapore, 1861. Courtesy of Antiques of the Orient. Image recoloured, cropped, and spatially manipulated.

Plate 22.   This Chinatown scene best captures the framing of the street and its pedestrian traffic by the ubiquitous shophouses with their laundry hanging from windows. Source: *Chinatown Street Scene with View of Rickshaws*. 1900s. Lee Kip Lin Collection. Courtesy of National Archives of Singapore. Image retouched, recoloured, and significantly cropped.

Plate 23.   Singapore's multireligious society is on display in this Hindu procession of deities on a chariot pulled by bulls. The procession celebrates Queen Elizabeth II's 1953 coronation. Source: *A Float from the Indian Community on Parade during the Coronation of Queen Elizabeth II*. June 6, 1953. Ministry of Information and the Arts Collection. Courtesy of National Archives of Singapore. Image recoloured and significantly cropped.

Plate 24.   The most famous retail street 'Change Alley', in Raffles Place, was a Westerner's shopping paradise where one could tailor suits and buy small souvenirs. Source: *Change Alley*. c. 1950s. George Tricker Collection. Courtesy of National Archives of Singapore. Image retouched, recoloured, and significantly cropped.

Plate 25.   Commercial Square, later baptised as Raffles Place, was the upmarket shopping area of White residents. Featured is the big department store of John Little which lasted 174 years. Source: *John Little and Company Limited at Raffles Place, Singapore*.

1895–1900. Gretchen Liu Collection. Courtesy of National Archives of Singapore. Image recoloured and significantly cropped.

Plate 26. Here is a transvestite who 'entertained' tourists on Bugis Street after midnight. Source: *A Portrait of a Transvestites [sic] in Bugis Street (late 1980s)*. Singapore Tourist Promotion Board Collection. Courtesy of National Archives of Singapore. Image retouched, recoloured, and significantly cropped.

Plate 27. A wildly comic scene at seedy Bugis Street, a landmark of night entertainment. Here three foreign sailors try to mount a trishaw, much to the bewilderment of the trishawman. Source: *Bugis Street*. 1960s. RAFSA Collection. Courtesy of National Archives of Singapore. Image recoloured and significantly cropped.

Plate 28. Mourners outside a death house. Sago Lane was perhaps the most depressing sight in Singapore for Westerners viewing sickly old Chinese on their deathbeds with their coffins awaiting them. Source: *Death House in Sago Lane*. January 2, 1962. Courtesy of National Archives of Singapore. Image retouched and recoloured.

Plate 29. An elaborate early 20th-century Chinese funeral, complete with mourners, pallbearers, and monks. Source: *Chinese funeral party, Singapore*. 1900s. Royal Tropical Institute Collection. Courtesy of National Archives of Singapore. Image recoloured and significantly cropped.

Plate 30. As an entrepôt, Singapore had several luxury hotels, amongst them the Grand Hotel de l'Europe at the site of the current National Gallery Singapore. Source: *Hotel de l'Europe*. c. 1906. Courtesy of National Archives of Singapore. Image retouched, recoloured, and significantly cropped.

Plate 31. The minority Armenians were wealthy traders in the European Town north of the river. Here they are at their landmark 1835 church. Some intermarried and became part of the Eurasian community. Source: *Armenians, a Prosperous Minority in the Eurasian Community*. 1930s. Armenian Church Trust Collection. Courtesy of National Archives of Singapore. Image retouched, recoloured, and significantly cropped.

Plate 32. The Singapore Cricket Club, one of the island's oldest recreational clubs, was for most of its history exclusively for

Whites. The scene shows a New Year's Day outing in the 1880s. Source: *Cricket Pavilion New Year's Day*. 1880s. Lim Kheng Chye Collection. Courtesy of National Archives of Singapore. Image recoloured, significantly cropped, and spatially manipulated.

Plate 33. Opposite the cricket club was the Eurasians' Singapore Recreation Club, whose location north of the Singapore River demonstrated that they had something in common with the White community. Source: *Singapore Recreation Club, Singapore*. Courtesy of Antiques of the Orient. Image recoloured and significantly cropped.

Plate 34. Though Whites married locals to form the Eurasian community, the British, unlike the Spanish and Portuguese, never encouraged mixed marriages. This photo typifies late 19th-century Eurasians who dressed like Europeans. Source: *Eurasian Family*. 1880–1930. Boden-Kloss Collection. Courtesy of National Archives of Singapore. Image retouched, recoloured, and significantly cropped.

Plate 35. Hiring ayahs or servants who looked after children was an established practice, although these Indian ladies were only found amongst wealthy European and local families. Source: *Indian Servant and Child*. 1890s. Boden-Kloss Collection. Courtesy of National Archives of Singapore. Image retouched, recoloured, and significantly cropped.

Plate 36. Malays lived in coastal fishing villages and later, inland rural areas. A typical Malay village with its children and a hawker, all dressed in customary Malay outfits. Source: *Malay Hawker*, Singapore. 1900s. Lim Kheng Chye Collection. Courtesy of National Archives of Singapore. Image recoloured and cropped.

Plate 37. Chinese, Malay, and Indian coolies formed the backbone of Singapore's bustling port. Without machines, man was the beast of burden. Source: *The Steamer Travancore Taking in Cargo at Singapore*. 1873. Courtesy of Antiques of the Orient. Image significantly cropped.

Plate 38. The Peranakans came mainly from Malacca and Penang. This photo shows gender differences in clothing: males followed European styles while women were attired in Malay outfits. Source: *Photograph of a Peranakan family (c. 1900s)*. Mohd

	Amin Bin Kadarisman Collection. Courtesy of National Archives of Singapore. Image recoloured and significantly cropped.
Plate 39.	Hoo Ah Kay, often referred to by Whites as *Whampoa*, was an outstanding symbol of a mid-19th century Chinese *towkay*. Source: *Hoo Ah Kay (Whampoa)*. c. 1850s. Courtesy of National Archives of Singapore. Image recoloured and significantly cropped.
Plate 40.	Street hawkers and onlookers showing a male-dominated multiracial gathering: Chinese, Indians, Malays and Indian Muslims. Source: *Street Scene*. Courtesy of Antiques of the Orient. Image retouched and recoloured.
Plate 41.	After three-and-a-half years of Japanese Occupation, the British liberation in 1945 was a momentous occasion of joy for locals as seen by the attendance at this victory parade. Source: *Victory Parade along North Bridge Road near Elgin Bridge after the Japanese Surrender*. October 10, 1945. David Ng Collection. Courtesy of National Archives of Singapore. Image retouched, recoloured, and significantly cropped.

ABOUT THE AUTHOR

Victor R. Savage is an Adjunct Senior Fellow at the S. Rajaratnam School of International Studies, Nanyang Technological University, Singapore. He was the former Head of the Department of Geography and Coordinator of the Southeast Asian Programme at the National University of Singapore. He was also Deputy Chair of the Master of Science in the Environment Management programme (MEM) at the NUS School of Design and Environment. Among Dr. Savage's books are *Western Impressions of Nature and Landscape in Southeast Asia* (1984), Singapore University Press; and with Brenda Yeoh, *Singapore Street Names: A Study of Toponymics*, Marshall Cavendish, 4th edition in press.

WITH GRATITUDE

This book has been possible because of the help of many friends, colleagues, and associates. Though I began writing in 2019, the research for it had been ongoing for several years. I am most grateful to my boss, Ambassador Ong Keng Yong of RSIS, for mooting and supporting the idea of this work. Without his interest, it would never have seen the light of day. Even though the book was targeted for the bicentennial of Raffles' founding of colonial Singapore, the objective was to provide foreign readers with an introduction and some overall perspective of narrative threads in modern Singapore's history. Rather than being a further instance of Western historians and academics writing about Singapore's history, my endeavour represents a local narrative of the colonial experience. It was not intended to make another statement on the bicentennial, but more to spur reflection on Singapore based on the varied views about it in colonial times. I am also grateful for the time given to complete the book though it overran the bicentennial year.

Gratitude goes to my many friends for reading through different draft chapters: Arun Bala, Juliana Lim, Mano Sabnani, Silva Kandiah, Mushahid Ali, Daniel Tan, and the late Viji Menon. Most of all I have been fortunate to have two great friends who early on meticulously read through the first draft of the whole manuscript, and gave their insightful comments and edits: Irene Khng and Dr. Kenneth Corey. Your time, sharp eyes, patience, pertinent advice, and critique are much appreciated, Irene and Ken.

My thanks go also to various colleagues at RSIS for their kind help in matters relating both to the book and otherwise. They include Chris Lim

Hang-Kwang, Mohd Jaffar Bin Tandang, Tng Eng Cheong, Sandy Yeo, Shruthi Bhaskar, Maureen Lee, Pradumna Rana, Tan Seng Chye, Yang Razali Kassim, and Lawson Lau Kang Seng. Thank you, too, to the Events Management team headed by Scott Lai and many others who have been involved but have not been mentioned in these pages. Whether named or unnamed, you all provided practical help and moral support in a range of ways.

To the daily lunchtime usual suspects, comprising Chris Lim, Seng Chye, Pradumna, Han Fook Kwang, and further punctuated with guest artist appearances by Henrick Tsjeng, Vincent Mack, Mushahid, and Leonard Sebastian, thank you for the stimulating discussions.

Thanks are in order as well to my senior colleague Adrian Tan for making available the administrative and editorial support for the book's production. I am indebted to Tan Ming Hui for her continual help in many areas. She was my 'runner' for library books, copy editor, research helper, and administrative assistant for the book. She also contributed by doing the background research for the artwork for the chapter headings, in obtaining the illustration plate images, and with the academic referencing, and proofreading, and the useful advice on the book production and publication processes. My thanks go also to Kenneth Yeo for help with getting library books and photocopying material.

I have been fortunate to have at the second part of this endeavour Rachel Lucy Choo, my editor, who assisted me in more ways than I could define. She helped by discussing the text, editing, getting illustrations for the book, liaising with my designer and the publisher, providing art direction, being a research assistant and proofreader.

I am also grateful to my former student and designer, Cybil Kho, for her painstaking and beautiful work in researching and creating the front cover of the book and the many drawings for the 10 chapter headings.

To my friend Julie Yeo of Antiques of the Orient, thanks for kindly allowing me to reproduce several pictures and maps as illustration plates in the book. The National Archives of Singapore, too, graciously permitted me to use many of the images in their collection, including one from Singapore Tourism Board. To the staff of both those organisations for all their related help, *terima kasih*.

A great deal of appreciation is due naturally to the diverse and specialised members of the team at World Scientific, in particular, Jayanthi M. (Book Editor, India), Thaheera Althaf (Editor, Social

Sciences, Singapore), Khoo Yee-Hong (Director of Marketing), Teo Sze-Anne (Marketing Executive).

Finally, I thank Professors Edwin Thumboo (Singapore's poet laureate), Tommy Koh (the Ambassador par excellence), and Wang Gungwu (the consummate historian) for endorsing my book. I could not have asked for more esteemed people to provide encouragement for my work.

Victor R. Savage
S. Rajaratnam School of International Studies
Nanyang Technological University
Singapore
February 2021

FOREWORD

Singapore, if reckoned from its colonial founding in 1819, is not old. Thanks to recent archaeology and historical research, initiated by experts like RSIS colleague Kwa Chong Guan, we are increasingly aware that Singapore's history extends back many centuries. This wide-ranging book by Dr. Victor R. Savage illuminates a major way that story could be told — through Western observers, whose interest in Singapore began before the British envisaged it as a colonial possession — and affirms the value of exploring past Singapore narratives.

From the precolonial forays into Southeast Asia until Singapore's departure from British rule in the 20th century, Dr. Savage makes the point that even a tiny island might be a fulcrum of international attention. Such attention focused on the classical conceptions of Singapore as a backwater of Indianised kingdoms in the region; the 19th-century westernising economic and 'civilising' vision of Thomas Stamford Raffles for the island; the natural bounty and environmental challenges encountered during colonial development; the distinctiveness of the colony's burgeoning urban, commercial, and social scenes; its ethno-religious heterogeneity; and the upending of Western political assumptions surrounding the durability of colonial rule. Above all is the understanding that these views were what they were because of *whom* the viewers were: Westerners, each with particular interests related to Singapore at a given historical time.

Singaporeans reading outsider views on their own antecedents might respond to this book with familiarity, surprise, wonderment, amusement, agreement, horror, scepticism, pride, nostalgia, and more. Western or foreign readers might feel any of the same, and quite possibly for very different reasons.

Thus, this work should be read by Singaporeans and foreigners alike. At some point the divide between them might even prove artificial, since today's globalised Singapore has enlarged upon the conditions described in the book. Singapore may be for readers a microcosm of global society. Singaporeans can read this volume to understand our historic place in world currents, and perhaps glean a sense of where we are now and how we might shape our own future, given the manner we have previously been viewed. Others may peruse it to discern patterns, evolutions, and ruptures in what it has meant to be Singapore and of Singapore, as a path to better engaging with matters Singaporean. Particularly useful is the summing up in the relevant chapters, thereby reinforcing what readers take away.

The book is also a useful geo-historic window on multiple dimensions of local, regional, and global encounters between small polities and great powers, cultures and civilisations, the religious and the secular, the commercial and the civic, the human and the natural, the respectable and the seedy, and the socio-cultural and the political, all of which still play out throughout our world today.

As a Singaporean, a Eurasian, an academic, and a geographer, Dr. Victor R. Savage is very well placed to convey the complexities of colonial Singapore as it appeared to Westerners, from the combined vantage points of a Singaporean insider and scholar, a prominent member of one of its ethnic minorities, and a scion of the East-West meeting with which this lively work is wholly concerned. I commend both the work and its author to you.

Ambassador Ong Keng Yong
Executive Deputy Chairman
S. Rajaratnam School of International Studies
Nanyang Technological University
Singapore
July 2021

PREFACE

I had toyed with the idea of writing a book to commemorate the 200th anniversary of Singapore for several years. Unfortunately, in 2017 I became unwell and so the idea was shelved. But as fate had it, my project was revived when my boss Ambassador Ong Keng Yong, the Executive Deputy Chairman of the S. Rajaratnam School of International Studies, Nanyang Technological University, asked if I would be willing to write a book on Singapore. After reading my revised manuscript of *Western Perceptions of Southeast Asia*, he enquired whether I could use the same paradigm on Singapore. The idea here was not to write another chronological history of Singapore's founding, but to highlight what Westerners perceived the Lion City to be over the decades of British colonialism. The objective was to give new sojourners and visitors to modern Singapore some background to the city-state's development, and the things which had sparked the curiosity of past Western residents and sojourners about Singapore. So much has been written about the 50 years of Singapore's independent city-state, but much less is known about how the Lion City got to where it is today. And yet by global standards, Singapore's modern history is short if one uses 1819 as the date which initiated its continuous development till the present.

Writing this book has been both a challenging and pleasurable exercise. It has been challenging because there was no preconceived thesis of what the book would be about. The plan, however, was to record how Western visitors, sojourners, and residents felt about their impressions of Singapore, hence the subject matter was diverse, contradictory at times, subjective, and often biased. Trying to find suitable themes by which to frame these White optics of the evolving Lion City was thus not easy. But these personal perspectives at different points in time made for interesting insights about what was appealing or intriguing in their Singapore experiences. There were many parallel themes expressed, and other researchers have delivered their own interpretations.

One angle of the book situates the Western perceptions of Singapore within an ongoing academic context and discussion on varied pertinent issues raised. In this way, the book bridges the Western existential experiences in Singapore over 145 years with historians' interpretations and social science concepts, theories, and ideas that complement the distillations of White perceptions. Many of the ideas which Westerners elaborated on concerning their Singapore experiences were not new, though few ascribed them to earlier Western philosophers and academicians. Clearly, the centuries of Western thought were embedded in their thinking and became second nature in their descriptions of Singapore.

Though this metanarrative covers one-and-a-half centuries of Singapore's existence, it is not written as a purely historical or chronological narrative. The book is organised along a thematic structure, highlighting what caught the eyes of Western residents and travellers. Some of these themes were cross-sectional, appearing only at particular periods in Singapore's colonial history. They remain temporal benchmarks that identify dates, such as years or decades, which signify the coalescing of human activities at points in time. Other themes covered long stretches, and remained at the forefront of Western perceptions throughout the colonial era. These recurring themes in a way transcend history and time, and provide a master narrative of Singapore's colonial development.

Researching and writing this book has been a personally rewarding journey. I learnt a lot about Singapore's historical events and processes. Since I was not going to 'write' a 'history' of Singapore, I was not restricted by academic protocols in which a set trajectory and outcome are demanded. I wanted the Western writings to speak for themselves. I accepted that there were not necessarily any 'facts', only interpretations, viewpoints, and debates. Hence, the term *narratives* in the title is meant to underscore the open-ended nature of Western impressions of Singapore. From hindsight and 'contingent' historical developments, it seems easy to filter out contradictions and 'false' or inaccurate interpretations. In this book, I make no apologies nor offer personal 'corrections' to what White sojourners thought about in their deliberations on Singapore. What becomes obvious is that there were always alternative viewpoints, criticisms, and self-inspection of even sacrosanct White administrative policies. This was an evolving colonial city in the making: it had no precedent to emulate, no hard rules to follow. Therefore much of its success as a mercantile port and trading emporium was predicated on people on the ground — administrators, professionals, traders, entrepreneurs, bankers, and community leaders. Events unfolded with a fair share of administrative hiccups, political indecision, and questionable outcomes. Singapore was the paragon of British colonial power and the colonial city was fortunate in the 19th century to have Britain, the global hegemon, as its political patron.

While the turn of the 20th century brought rapid change to Singapore, the mindset of its migrant population was still subservient and somewhat reverential to White colonial rule. The scientific and technological changes in Europe in the 19th century were unprecedented and colonialism was the agency of diffusion of cultural change around the world. In many ways, the White superiority complex was emboldened and the divergence between White and the native populations widened. This explains the lingering White beliefs that Europe was dynamic, and Asia, stagnant and never-changing.

European views of a subservient Asian population, mired in age-old customs and traditions, and bedevilled by unfathomable secretive behaviour, were shattered by the Japanese Occupation in the Second World War. Singapore, the apex of colonial military power, was devastated by the Japanese. Then a new China was born in 1949, and communism became the plague of the region and Singapore. The political effervescence in the post-war years in Singapore was audible in White recordings. Singapore's docile and by then native Asian population had awoken and the White resident community members were agitated, fearful, and disturbed. They were puzzled at how the Chinese, whom they had previously often depicted as timid 'boys' in domestic services, exploded in the 1950s as belligerent high school rioters and demonstrators.

At the end of the day, the East-West dialogue centred on the vexing question of whether development was a White preserve, a culturally Western domain, and an environmental liability for tropical countries. This was the ultimate academic question in the post-war years facing the developing world: specifically, whether local Asian societies were capable of progress as in the West. To me the whole colonial legacy and its dominant Western narrative became the crusading challenge for the leaders of independent Singapore. What makes the Singapore economic miracle so outstanding is that it debunked all the earlier Western theories, myths, and perceptions that the tropics could not spawn civilisation, or that Asians had not the innovative culture, and Whites were racially destined for developmental superiority. This was the reason why the founding father of independent Singapore, Lee Kuan Yew, titled his book *From Third World to First*, to underscore Singapore's spectacular rise. Singapore became the 'poster state' of the developing world because it broke the Western myth that no developing country could reach developed status. How the Lion City achieved this has been a story told many times over and my interpretation might lead to a sequel to this book.

Victor R. Savage
S. Rajaratnam School of International Studies
Nanyang Technological University
Singapore
February 2021

1
Lion City Narratives

Chapter 1

LION CITY NARRATIVES

I. Introduction

> Singapore is such an interesting place, so little understood outside and so little appreciated inside, that it really is worth writing about. For my part, I have only attempted to give you a background against which you can paint your own picture; but the place does merit one really good book, and some day that book will be written, some unknown Kipling will rise in our midst and tell the world (R. Braddell 1935, 201).

The year of 1819 was auspicious for Singapore's foundation. It was the year of Queen Victoria's birth, and Singapore was always referred to as 'Her Birthday Isle'. In January 2019, the Singapore government launched its year-long commemoration of the 200th anniversary of Sir Thomas Stamford Raffles' founding of the British colonial city of Singapore. Yet, modern Singapore's genesis is froth with political controversy and embroiled with academic debate. Hence the official endorsement of the colonial origins of the city-state did not go down well with certain segments of Singapore's society. The government's tacit recognition of Raffles' founding brought three perspectives to the making of Singapore. Firstly, the authorities have acknowledged Singapore's colonial heritage; secondly, they have embraced the roots of modern Singapore's history in 1819 as part of its national narrative; and thirdly, Singaporeans have a definitive birth and continuous life span for their country's modern national history that is well documented and transparent.

This study, however, is not meant to make a political statement out of colonialism, but rather to define a convenient time frame in which Singapore developed from a tiny Malay village fiefdom in the Riau Archipelago and blossomed into a modern cosmopolitan city.

Though based on written records, this account is less concerned with the 'factual accuracy' of narratives or the historical interpretation of events. Rather, this analysis is grounded in the way Westerners wrote about their personal experiences and sojourns in the colonial city. These experiences can be understood within the broad context of personal 'perceptions', to which the expression 'Western eyes' refers essentially. Academically, the term 'perception' has had a long history in Western thought and has since the post-World War II period been amplified in a multi- and interdisciplinary manner.

In writing about colonial Singapore through Western eyes, three qualifications have to be borne in mind. Firstly, while the colonial period has been chosen for this analysis, this is not an attempt to give an endorsement of colonialism, nor is it an attempt to make a definitive evaluation of colonialism in Singapore's historical development. I leave this to historians, even if at various junctures I do point out certain benefits which could be said to have accrued to Singapore through colonialism. I have chosen 1819 as a starting point in this analysis because it marked Raffles' founding of the 'factory' for the East India Company (EIC) in Singapore. This was a significant event in British colonial history as well as a master stroke of geopolitical strategy. Contrary to some historians' trajectories, Raffles found a greenfield place of extraordinary location and the birth of modern Singapore became an entrepreneurial exercise.

Admittedly, much debate continues about Singapore's genesis. Revisionist historians are pushing Singapore's historical origins to the 13th century, some 700 years ago, when Tumasik (or *Singapura*, the Lion City) made a significant footnote in the annals of regional and Chinese historical documentations. This goes down better with those of nationalist inclination, who view an indigenous development as more politically correct than a Singapore which is purely the product of Western colonialism. Despite its short blip in history, Tumasik no doubt was an important thalassic kingdom in the region, that is, one bearing an important relation to the sea. The regional myths surrounding its existence still resonate because it was a key geopolitical interlude between the end of the Sri Vijayan empire and the rise of Malacca in the 15th century.

The *Alam Melayu* or Malay World[1] centred around the Straits of Malacca, and the three thalassic kingdoms of Sri Vijaya, Tumasik-Singapura, and Malacca were pivots of a great international trading ecosystem that spread Malay as the lingua franca of commerce in the Southeast Asian region. Malay cultural identity received its fertilisation from the successes of these three thalassic kingdoms and the Malay World was formulated as a result of the trading ecosystem that developed.

What nourished these three kingdoms over a period of 10 centuries, one might enquire? Historians have provided different explanations, but my take is that they commanded an exceptional location in the narrow Straits of Malacca which governed East-West and regional trade. The political mantra that Singapore has had no natural resources to depend on to explain its extraordinary development is incorrect — if one counts one's exceptional location as such a resource. In this, the colonial city and then city-state has had a geographical resource that is infinite: location, location, location. The bicentennial narrative which is in this book credits Raffles' astute perception of the locational importance that has formed the bedrock of Singapore's success story for 200 years.

Secondly, Western perceptions of Singapore's early development, its significant events, and urban biography are not meant to provide an ideological statement on Western colonial administration in Singapore. Rather, Western views of Singapore were chosen because White sojourners' insights on the colonial city formed a continuous and well-developed record of Singapore's historical processes over the 145 years of British colonialism. There is no such parallel documentation from non-Western perceptions of Singapore. This is not to say that indigenous views of the region's history were non-existent. Two compendia of indigenous perceptions of the region are contained in Harry J. Benda and John A. Larkin's (1967) *The World of Southeast Asia*, and Anthony Reid and David Marr's (1979) *Perceptions of the Past in Southeast Asia.*

The European impressions of Singapore's colony were made up of the accounts of residents as well as visitors who comprised Caucasians of varied nationalities (Dutch, French, Americans, Scots, Spaniards,

---

[1] The term *Alam Melayu* is used loosely to cover the region of variations of the spoken Malay language, which for our purpose includes present-day southern Thailand, Malaysia, Indonesia, and the southern Philippines, and which according to Geoffrey Benjamin's (2002) complex definition of the term, refers to the Malayic societal region where Malay culture is the practised paradigm.

Germans, and so on) and different professions, including EIC and colonial administrators, as well as merchants, traders, and non-government officials. The European views (and in this book the term *European* is used more or less interchangeably with *White*, *Caucasian*, and *Western*) thus came from a variety of perspectives: some critical of colonial government policies and others providing encouraging comments. Certainly, the colonial experience was subject to Western criticism, prejudicial perception, and varied suggestions.

Singapore was a colonial start-up which had no parallel in the region. Hence, the EIC administrators were sensitive to how European and Asian residents viewed colonial policies, especially with respect to trade and business development. Since there were no elections, the colonial authorities were not answerable to the resident population, but Singapore's survival as an entrepôt and its sustainability as a free port were not givens. The viability of the port had to be managed carefully. Had the British authorities not provided the right economic conditions of trade, commerce, and entrepreneurship, the trading community of Whites and Asians would have evaporated. Singapore's economic sustenance was dependent on the external environment; it was a 'relational' city of the region where changes in the external environment had severe repercussions on Singapore's trade and business.

Thirdly, this narrative of Western perspectives of Singapore's development is not meant to be a historical statement. Western perceptions were subjective, opinionated, and based on personal prejudices. There were many levels of cultural influence that shaped the European mindset. In a way, these subjective, prejudicial motivations provide new fodder for analysis in the understanding of history as being made up of processes. This study shows a gamut of these social and cultural interventions in the form of East-West civilisational contrasts, colonial smugness, Edward Said's (1979) 'we' and 'they' differentiations ('we' being the European colonial masters and 'they' being the subject peoples), White-native stereotyping, cultural relativity, and the 19th-century 'divergence' between the Western and other worlds. These subjective White perceptions capture the Western cognition of the Singapore landscape at three levels: (1) through on-site events that were witnessed and documented; (2) as etic (outsider) perspectives on Asian cultures; and (3) as unadulterated personal testimonies and reflections upon commonplace Singapore landscapes caught in time and space. The goal of Westerners' vivid descriptions was to give the European public back home an insight to foreign cultures and landscapes. But they were far from objective, and often infused with personal hyperbole. Given that most visitors from the 19th century onwards travelled through several countries and cities, their perceptions of the Lion City were always comparisons to other places visited or to their European homes.

II. The Setting

One of the great challenges in writing this book was to find a thesis and theme that capture holistically the varied Western perceptions of Singapore. That was a difficult aim as I did not want to impose a structure to bind the varied impressions. In this narrative, Westerners were given free expression of their feelings, views and ideas about the varied Singapore landscapes, cultural events, and diverse peoples who fascinated them. The verbatim quotes speak for themselves. Whatever repeatedly drew White commentary about the Lion City has been identified and reproduced. This book thus is a candid representation of what Whites over the decades of British rule recorded of their Singapore experiences: it contains the good, bad, and ugly.

At the end of the day, it is hoped that readers may acquire a snapshot of what Singapore was in the past. These perspectives carry three variables. First, Western culture served to provide a contrast to how Singapore as an Asian city was distinctive, through the lenses of White sojourners. Hence, it is not by accident that cultural contrasts are highlighted in European impressions. Many viewed Singapore through their own cultural prisms and formed distinctive opinions of the city and its peoples.

Second, given the relatively long span of time on which this study was based, it captures temporal events at various levels. There are events described here which in a later study could contribute to cross-sectional history of a period in time (an event, a month, a year, or decade) that captures situations on the spot which are key to understanding that period. One might call my book instantaneous documentation and recording to further serve the purposes of history-writing. Given the decades of colonial rule at a time of momentous global developments, one can capture Singapore's changing landscapes over time through these methods. Such changes over periods of time are best articulated in cultural and spatial diffusion studies (such as those about the spread of house-types, cultural artefacts, religious beliefs, fashion, and fads). Did colonial rule usher in evolutionary or revolutionary changes in the colonial city? Reading Noel Barber, Donald Moore, and other Western biographers of Singapore, it would seem that the colonial period before World War II registered slow change despite the frenzied economic activity. With two-thirds of the world's land area under colonial rule, the Second World War was, as Keith Lowe (2017) argues, a watershed event that changed the world. After the war, political changes in Singapore picked up rapidly. The postcolonial era became a reality, but not without its train of political instability in the form of racial riots, labour strikes, communist disturbances, and student demonstrations.

Third, colonialism has left a bad aftertaste amongst scholars and in political circles in developing countries. Colonialism is often viewed within the East-West debate, with the subtext of Western exploitation in colonies and mistreatment of natives. The works by Kenneth Pomeranz (2000) and Joel Mokyr (2017), however, demonstrate the major changes in the 19th century. Through the differences in natural endowments such as European coal, and ecology, demographic change, science and technology, the Industrial Revolution, and the culture of progress the West radically altered the East-West equation. Western civilisation had the upper hand due to profound intellectual changes in Europe and one might see colonialism in a broader light as a conduit for varied forms of cultural, social, and economic diffusion from the West. Singapore's birth and maturation as an entrepôt, free port, and colonial city in the 19th century was no accident. It was a narrative of British colonial audacity and a project in which merchants and traders, both White and Asian, took on risks and chances to make wealth, not only for the colony's coffers but more so for their own interests. The city rode on the coat-tails of British superpower status and the rest might be left to historical interpretation.

Alternatively, colonialism was a grand global process for the diffusion of ideas, techniques, methods, and new scientific instruments which flowed from the West to the four corners of the earth. It was the yeast that levelled up development. Colonialism carried the seeds of both westernisation and modernisation. In looking back retrospectively at Singapore's colonial development, it was, however, also a unique situation where immigrants formed the bulk of the city's population. This was a city where the cosmopolitan migrant population was the major catalyst and driver of the city's development. And it is still a unique place, as the only fully-recognised independent political entity outside China to have a majority Chinese population.

As colonialism ended in 1963, a new political entity would arise. The birth of Singapore as an accidental but successful city-state remains a wonder for developing countries to emulate. It is a story told many times. But the success of modern Singapore was not born out of ashes. The legacy of colonialism, its successes and failures, were lessons that were imbibed by the torchbearers of independent Singapore's phenomenal development. After all, these political leaders were products of colonialism.

III. Unfolding History: The *Longue Durée*

Singapore's history goes back before Raffles' 1819 founding. To put the development of Singapore's modern city-state in perspective, one should point out that modern Singapore reflects the culmination of three macro-periods: (1) the Indianised Malay World which established thalassic or maritime kingdoms in the Straits of Malacca; (2) the Western colonial impact over 450 years that engulfed the whole of what is today's Southeast Asia, save Thailand; and (3) the rise of 11 independent states after the colonial era, of which Singapore is one of the few city-states in the world today. It is thus a unique political entity.

This study has taken the birth of Singapore as 1819, based on the British historian C. Mary Turnbull's (1977) dating of her history of modern Singapore. This birth was a product of monetary transactions executed on behalf of the EIC. Unlike other regional colonial territories that were seized by annexation or colonised by military means, Singapore was an economic commodity. The modern Singapore narrative was launched when the EIC purchased the rights of property and sovereignty from a "native prince" (Crawfurd 1830, 2:395).

Singapore's 200-year history remains a constant reminder of the entrepreneurial idea of Raffles and the commercial importance of the city's port. Succeeding Singapore governors and bureaucrats had to keep in mind the colonial city's unique commercial enterprise and ensure that its traders, merchants, money-lenders, businessmen, and entrepreneurs were looked after, and their views heard, registered, and attended to. Unlike Tumasik, which had been the ceremonial centre of the Buddhist cosmos in the 14th century, Singapore was a secular and economic centre of the British-led globalising world of the 19th century. The Lion City gave the newly-initiated entrepôt three important qualities: (1) it had a peaceful takeover; (2) it was sealed by commercial transaction that defined Singapore's economic nature from henceforth; and (3) there was a certain respect for the Malay custodians and rulers of the fiefdom who remained in their own ethnic enclaves. Both the sultan and *temenggong* had their own territories of residence in the British colony.

While historians and academics have recounted, interpreted, and analysed various aspects of Singapore's history and components of its economic, political, social, and cultural *fabric*, this monograph is based on the Western *perceptions* of Singapore over its colonial history. It is certainly not about the political history of Singapore which has been the preserve of historians. Here, the on-site perceptions of Western residents and travellers are focused more on the changing social, economic, and cultural *landscape* of the colonial city. Academic interpretations of Singapore might state issues from hindsight as history and objective fact, but Western impressions captured over real time reveal many variables, based on speculation, conjecture, and uncertainty.

The Western resident population was small in the first 70 years of Singapore's British colonisation but their perceptions in shaping the colony were pivotal. This in some ways is their narrative of the Singapore story as a British colony. The colonial city went through several political incarnations between 1819 and the Japanese Occupation of the Second World War. It began as an EIC factory (a small area of the island leased from its Malay rulers), then the whole island became the undisputed property of the EIC after the 1824 treaty with the sultan and the *temenggong*. In the same year, the Anglo-Dutch Treaty ensured that Singapore came within the British geopolitical sphere. In 1867, the British government took over Singapore from the EIC and ruled it as a Crown Colony till 1942.

The British had earlier amalgamated three political entities (Penang, Malacca, and Singapore) to form the Straits Settlements. Like other Asian cities under Western rule, Singapore developed as a colonial city, but then later more particularly as a British Crown Colony. With the construction of the causeway in 1923, Singapore was linked to the Malay Peninsula and became its major trading outlet, educational capital, missionary headquarters, and defence outpost for the British.

Present-day Singapore, with its predominantly Chinese population, is hardly accepted by its Malay neighbours as an integral part of the Malay World. For them it is better defined as a Chinese city. As if history had conspired, arguably even Singapore's animal totem, the lion, lends itself as much to Chinese culture (as with lion dances, for example) as it originates in pre-modern Indianised Malay culture. Nonetheless, the belief in Singapore's mythical origin rooted in the legend of Sang Nila Utama's alleged sighting of a lion on the island still continues today with the invention of a new icon, the Merlion, half lion and half fish, to signify the unusual admixture that is Singapore. The Merlion could symbolise many things: Singapore's terraqueous geography that has to do with land and water, its maritime importance as entrepôt, and its mythical history reincarnated. Singapore's global and First World status might be a celebration for the tropical post-colonial world, although in the Malay regional community there is muted reticence.

IV. Lion City in Retrospect

Singapore's history of 700 years is manifest in many forms. Augmenting the Western written and published reflections of the colonial city has been its steady documentation through maps, charts, sketches, paintings, and more recently, archaeological artefacts. Given the Western interest in cartography since Greek times, Singapore has been relatively well documented in the cartographic sense. The early references to Singapore in 15th- and 16th-century Western maps of the region were basically pinprick locations in southern Johore.[2] Western cartographers were oblivious to the exact location of Singapura, knowing only that it was a port-kingdom in regional history. The first outlines of the island were recorded by the Portuguese Eurasian Godinho de Erédia's 1604 Map of 'Sincapura'.

It would take a couple of centuries before a well-documented outline of the island became cartographic knowledge in the Western world, with the publication of Capt. James Franklin's Plan of the British Settlement of Singapore. It appeared in John Crawfurd's (1830, vol. 2) *Journal of an Embassy from the Governor-General of India to the Courts of Siam and Cochin China*. This first complete map of Singapore Island with the surrounding islets, revealed the Malay or *orang laut* influence in the coastal place names, with 31 local names being identified.

---

[2]*Johore* may be taken as the old spelling for the area which is today the modern Malaysian state of Johor.

The descriptive account of this round-the-island survey had been first published in the *Singapore Chronicle* in November 1825 and would be later republished in J. H. Moor's (1837) *Notices*. The Crawfurd publication also carried the famous 1822 Raffles Town Plan of Singapore drafted by Lt. Philip Jackson, alternatively known as the Jackson Plan. Once the British established their secure footing in Singapore, several maps produced in the 19th century would provide expanding documentation of the colonial city. The Raffles or Jackson Plan provided an ideal, drawing-board spatial layout of the British factory. Decades later, the maps by John Thomson would document the on-the-ground configuration of the expanding town, an amalgamation of the 1822 conceptual plan and the realistic, up-to-date, spatial expansion of the colonial city.

Complementing the cartographic documentation were the visual scenes of the new colony. The earliest graphic representation of the Singapore town was a sketch by Jackson in 1823 with predominantly plank and *atap* structures (Teo and Savage 1991). Some of the earliest paintings of the fledgling British entrepôt were from the French maritime artist Barthélemy Lauvergne (1805–1871), who painted five scenes of Singapore. Lauvergne visited Singapore twice, first in 1830 on board *La Favorite*, and again as an exhibition artist on board *La Bonite* in 1837. It was on his 1837 stopover that Lauvergne gave us five first-hand glimpses of early Singapore. In addition to Lauvergne's paintings were those of another 19th-century artist, Charles Andrew Dyce (1816–1853), whose 16 sketches and watercolour paintings captured the historical landscapes of the colonial city between 1843 to 1847. Dyce was both a resident at Kampong Glam and Monk's Hill, and was heavily involved in the civic affairs of the colony (I. Lim 2003, 13–15).

V. Other Interpretations, Cultural Distillations

Given that this monograph on Singapore is partly intended to mark the 200th anniversary of Raffles' 1819 founding, the following brief overview of possible contributions to Singapore's historical narrative is meant to aid and not distract readers' contextualisation of the Singapore story as told by foreign observers and local interpreters.

Considering its relatively new origins from the point of view of its colonial founding, Western residents tried to write an encyclopaedic overview of the region, with Singapore being featured in these presentations, what might be termed in the 20th century as 'regional geographies'. Three of these 19th-century overviews were viewed by their writers as 'descriptive dictionaries'. It began with John Crawfurd's (1856) *A Descriptive Dictionary of the Indian Islands and Adjacent Countries*, which included an insertion on Singapore. John Thomson (1849a, 1849b, 1850a, 1850b) wrote a rather longer piece of Singapore that appeared across two volumes of the *Journal of the Indian Archipelago and Eastern Asia* (*JIAEA*). Towards the end of the 19th century, N. B. Dennys' (1894) *A Descriptive Dictionary of British Malaya* provided a detailed account of Singapore's modern development. Using various subheadings such as location, history, geology, climate, botany, topography, government, establishments, and population, these geographical descriptions were meant to give itinerant visitors and transient sojourners thumbnail sketches of Singapore. Summarising other previous studies, each presentation gave more up-to-date versions of Singapore's development.

As Singapore developed over the 19th century, many Western residents tried to document its history since its modern foundation as a British colony. The first compendium of Singapore's historical processes, personalities, and events was Charles Burton Buckley's (1902) two-volume *An Anecdotal History of Old Times in Singapore*. Buckley's first 40 years of Singapore's development was chronologically listed based on various anecdotes he had marshalled together, but without themes or conceptual arguments. In anticipation of the centennial celebration of Raffles' 1819 founding, G. M. Reith's (1892) *Handbook to Singapore*, which tried to sum up Singapore's development for easy reference, was revised by Walter Makepeace (1907). To mark the same anniversary, Makepeace, Gilbert E. Brooke, and Roland St. J. Braddell (1921) published *One Hundred Years of Singapore*. As though to complement Buckley's Western perspective of Singapore's history and the centennial publications, Song Ong Siang (1923) wrote his encyclopaedic tome *One Hundred Years' History of the Chinese in Singapore* from a Chinese perspective to, among other aims, underscore the Chinese contributions to colonial Singapore's development. Despite British colonial power, Song's book cast Singapore as a Chinese city and demonstrated the full weight of Chinese economic contributions. For a long time, these publications, put together by residents, remained the main historical overviews of Singapore's development as a colonial city.

To celebrate Singapore's 150th anniversary in 1969, more publications were released. The *Journal of the Malaysian Branch of the*

Royal Asiatic Society did a commemorative reprint of important articles to mark the anniversary, which it later repeated in 1982 (Sheppard 1982). The British entrepreneur Donald Moore and his wife Joanna (1969) wrote their review of the anniversary, filled with pertinent documentation and photographs. A new publication by two academics, geographer Ooi Jin Bee and historian Chiang Hai Ding (1969), compiled a series of articles from various disciplines, marking the development of *Modern Singapore*. Despite the many historical overviews of the region and Singapore by non-historians, it would take some time, however, before professional historians decided to legitimise the city-state's history.

It took over a century from Singapore's colonial founding when a historian finally provided a perspective of Singapore. C. M. Turnbull's (1977) *A History of Singapore 1819–1975* was the first attempt to view Singapore's history in a comprehensive and cohesive manner through a historian's lens. A second historical overview of Singapore from a multidisciplinary viewpoint was edited by two historians: Ernest C. T. Chew and Edwin Lee's (1991) *A History of Singapore*. Several decades after Turnbull's original *History*, the latter Singaporean historian made his own attempt to write an interpretation of Singapore's history. Edwin Lee's (2008) *Singapore: The Unexpected Nation* was written in the traditional historical-chronological manner.

Over the decades, many European nationalities have tried to legitimise their claims in the creation of the Singapore historical narrative. Each European nationality has documented interesting snippets, anecdotes, personalities, monuments, landscape mementoes, toponyms, and educational, missionary, and cultural contributions. It would seem that each nationality engaged in Singapore's early development has felt a sense of pride in wanting to associate with its modern origins. This has seen a string of national reflections on Singapore's history: Nadia Wright's (2003) *Respected Citizens: The History of Armenians in Singapore and Malaysia*, Jim Baker's (2005) *The Eagle in the Lion City: America, Americans and Singapore*, Rosemary Lim's (2008) *An Irish Tour of Singapore*, Maxime Pilon and Danièle Weiler's (2011) *The French in Singapore: An Illustrated History (1819–Today)*, Andreas Zangger's (2013) *The Swiss in Singapore*, and Graham Berry's (2015) *From Kilts to Sarongs: Scottish Pioneers of Singapore*.

The astounding rapid progress of Singapore after its political independence in 1965 brought about other publications, including some local and other Western ones which are worth mentioning, for providing a postscript to the earlier colonial era narratives. These have been less about the city-state's history than about trying to explain Singapore's success as an independent city-state against varying odds. Such perspectives taken from hindsight, or what historian Prasenjit Duara (1995) calls 'contingent history', might be seen as ephemeral historical perspectives. Compared to the articles compiled in 1969 by Ooi and Chiang, which were cautionary, tentative, and expressive of trepidation about the city-state's future, the current Singaporean narratives reflect confidence, expound reasons for Singapore's success, and in some cases distil a certain arrogance about why other states fail.

The main emphasis in the new overviews of Singapore has appeared to be on how Singapore has managed its political policies and success. In 1989, the Institute of Southeast Asian Studies produced a multi-authored book, *Management of Success: The Moulding of Modern Singapore* (Sandhu and Wheatley 1989). This was followed up 20 years later with Terence Chong's (2010) edited book *Management of Success: Singapore Revisited*. The titles are indicative of how Singapore is likened to a company and its politicians are viewed as 'managers'.

Another body of literature is obsessed with the nation's success as a political end-goal: *Singapore: Struggle for Success* (Drysdale 1984); *Singapore: Re-engineering Success* (Mahizhnan and Lee 2002); *Singapore's Success: Engineering Economic Growth* (Ghesquière 2007). No other state has made as public its obsession with national success as Singapore. Part of this focus has to do with the pangs of a young nation seeking economic stability, national identity, and global political legitimacy. Certainly, the most authoritative source of Singapore's success is none other than its first Prime Minister Lee Kuan Yew, whose two volumes of autobiography, *The Singapore Story* (1998) and *From Third World to First* (2000), provide in-depth accounts of how Singapore's leadership arrived at decisions, managed problems, and planned future trajectories.

Singapore in the 21st century has come of age, punching beyond its weight, and Westerners have been curious about its style of leadership and national strategies. Singapore is likened to a national product, marketed to a global audience. Foreign academic interest has returned to the country. Kent E. Calder's (2016) *Singapore: Smart City, Smart State* likens the city-state to a laboratory in which information technology and efficient data collection and analysis provide political leaders with the methods for innovative and adaptive governance. John Curtis Perry's (2017) *Singapore: Unlikely Power* provides shades of Joseph Nye's power conceptual framework and traces the survival of the thalassic city, colonial city, and city-state over history. Different rulers have made deft use of power to ride the uncertain waves of externality: "Singapore is a survival tale of overcoming periodic, even life-threatening crisis" (Perry 2017, xvii).

While foreign interest is focused on local political rule and achievements of the city-state, revisionist historians and academics have decided that Singapore's history needs a longer historical berth, a broader geopolitical perspective, and a greater regional cultural grounding in the *Alam Melayu*. Singapore's history is being stretched over 700 years to emphasise its important historical links to the golden age of Malay power, from Sri Vijaya to the Malacca sultanate. The historians Kwa Chong Guan, Derek Heng, and Tan Tai Yong (2009) in *Singapore: A 700-Year History* have tried to defend Singapore's historical links over centuries, despite its distinct phases. Karl Hack, Jean-Louis Margolin, and Karine Delaye's (2010) *Singapore from Temasek to the 21st Century* provides the first account of Singapore's historical metamorphosis by integrating the genesis of Tumasik, and its crystalline phase as colonial city, with the blossoming as an independent city-state. Given China's Belt and Road Initiative (BRI) and the revitalisation of the old Silk Road, the archaeologist John Miksic (2013) has attempted to frame Singapore's precolonial history within the context of a regional maritime Silk Road. Unlike the many historical accounts and interpretations, Miksic's thesis relies heavily on archaeological evidence, thereby providing important evidence of Tumasik's regional emporium and its Indianised cultural influence.

Despite its youthful age in the community of nations, the Singapore story had finally to be told from its own perspective. Mark Ravinder Frost and Yu-Mei Balasingamchow's (2009) *Singapore: A Biography* sums up its coming of age. The encyclopaedic account of the city (thalassic cosmic kingdom, colonial city, and city-state) underscores the importance of Singapore as idea, imagination, and ideal.

VI. Raffles to Lee: The Colonial Heritage

Donald and Joanna Moore (1969) believed that Singapore's history has been defined by two men: Stamford Raffles and Lee Kuan Yew. They were leaders at the right time who shaped its destiny, taking possession of Singapore as their personal concern under different situations. While Raffles spawned the idea of modern Singapore, Lee orchestrated its development as an able conductor. Raffles' dream of Singapore was not delivered personally, he had William Farquhar and John Crawfurd to thank for realising his vision. Lee on the other hand had a whole phalanx of political colleagues and bureaucrats to realise his objectives of his metropolitan state.

Whether Raffles' colonial endeavour in 1819 was deliberate, anticipated, and largely the vision of one person, the birth of the city-state of Singapore was a product of a political accident, and governed by externalities. In 1987, Prime Minister Lee said of its birth as an independent city-state that it was "a very unlikely country" (E. Lee 2008, 597), while historian Edwin Lee (2008) has called it an "unexpected nation". Despite its tenuous and unpredictable birth, Singapore's outstanding development over 50 years as a nation-state has become an ideal for many developing countries. Yet, one needs to be reminded that the history of modern Singapore did not begin in 1959 (self-government), 1963 (merger with Malaysia), nor 1965 (full independence). The British government had planted the seeds of modern Singapore by making it the 'primate city' of Malaya. Without the long, secure administrative sedimentation of the colonial city, Singapore's take-off as a dynamic city-state might have been even more rocky and difficult.

On a broader ideological plane, the East-West oscillating power relationships dominated Western perceptions in the 20th century and Singapore was caught in between. The Lion City, the custodian of Western civilisation in the Orient, was also the symbol of the demise of Western power when the Japanese captured the fortress in 1942. The fall of Singapore, a massive blow to Western military supremacy, heralded the end of colonialism. With it the British forfeited the right to rule Singapore. While the historian and Raffles Professor C. Northcote Parkinson (1963) made East-West relations the central concept in his book, the British foreign correspondent Dennis Bloodworth brought to life the economic and political significance of the East-West tug-of-war in his window onto events and issues in Southeast Asian relations. Alluding to Rudyard Kipling's famous words, Bloodworth (1970, 14) saw even more problematic fault lines: "East and West do not speak the same language, even when it is English".

The birth of communist China in 1949 had a serious impact on Western perceptions of the Orient and the Chinese diaspora in the region.

Singapore, as a result of its predominantly Chinese population, had often been referred to as a Chinese city since the mid-19th century, but this only really became a subject of serious Western attention and speculation as the Cold War intensified. A series of books by both European residents and external commentators in the 1950s and 1960s widened the East-West divide, and Victor Purcell's (1962) elaboration of the 'Yellow Peril' defined the Western fear of the inscrutable East and the Chinese. Meanwhile in 1960, Singapore's domestic governing People's Action Party (PAP) leaders took political umbrage against English professor D. J. Enright's (1969) criticism of the ban on 'yellow culture' (embodied, for example, by jukeboxes and rock and roll) that opened a Pandora's box on postcolonial national identity. Externally, Karl Wittfogel's (1957, iv) book *Oriental Despotism* condemned Asia as a region of despots and despotic governments, and sullied communist China's birth as a "peculiarity of Chinese economics as part of a peculiar Chinese (and 'Asiatic') society". For the European observer, any reference to despotism and totalitarianism was a nail in the coffin of democracy and liberalism; an unacceptable political proposition that stiffened East-West differences and made the Cold War an ideological confrontation.

The current plethora of academic interest in Singapore represents the city-state's achievements to date and every academic interpretation of the island's historical lifespan. For most of the country's post-independence history, it has been the conventional preference of the ruling PAP to have Singapore's official historical narrative begin in 1959, when self-governance was given, or 1965, when Singapore gained its independence, with those dates being used as guidelines within which to fit and develop the Singapore story. It is a historical narrative that is intertwined with the political longevity story of the PAP; but other politicians, historians, and academics have proposed different inception dates for Singapore's independence.

Despite the radical transformation of Singapore over the 50 years since independence (1965–2015), it would be difficult to deny the colonial foundations that have influenced the city-state's current economic, political, and social trajectory. In some ways, the recorded public Western perceptions of Singapore during its colonial history were a pervasive global advertisement and image for Singapore. Without independent comparative objective assessments and rankings, the anecdotal assessments of White visitors and residents gave the colonial city on balance a positive image. The goodwill they created could not be replaced. The nature of these perceptions is at the heart of this treatise.

Singapore became an iconic reference to different things. The colonial city was a place name in the mid-20th century Hollywood film series *Road to ...*, with Singapore constituting one episode. Singapore's name remained a referral of defence for the British during their century as a global power, a word resonating with British naval might and majesty. The fall of Singapore to the Japanese was one of the most humiliating defeats for the Western world in the Second World War. Another of the most unsavoury depictions of the city in transition from a colony to a modern city-state was Paul Theroux's (1973) novel *Saint Jack*, which was turned into a movie with the same name. While the book seemed obscure and uneventful to readers, the movie set in real time in Singapore gave the Western public a glimpse of an Oriental city on the cusp of modernisation. Despite having been written after Singapore gained independence, Theroux captured the last vestiges of an impotent colonial era caught in the Cold War polemics of the raging Vietnam War. The movie, banned in Singapore for many decades, gave a close-up seedy perspective of the newly independent state, where American GIs did their R&R during the Vietnam War. Theroux, an English lecturer and author, was familiar with Serene House — next to the university in Bukit Timah — the centre of the American GI activities during the 1960s and early 1970s.

The Western impressions of Singapore can be distilled from a variety of sources spanning the British development of the colonial city from 1819 to 1963, when Singapore joined Malaysia and became independent of colonial rule. These sources have been mainly the numerous writings (books, diaries, letters, journals, articles) of Western travellers, sojourners, missionaries, naturalists, and residents who penned first-hand accounts of their experiences in Singapore. This study may be based on historical data but it is not a historical study per se which is based on static issues. One might best see in it the French historian Marc Bloch's view of history as "a thing of movement" (Bastin 1960, 8). This is a study that documents the *processes* of history. And while it is tempting to extrapolate patterns of human behaviour and experiences from the past, one must be reminded that "every age interprets the past by its own standards; every age writes its own history" (Bastin 1960, 8). Caught in time, Western experiences in Singapore reflected the daily activities; the impressions that they created were documented as they were formed.

As the city-state passes yet another milestone, the 200th anniversary of Raffles' founding, a proliferation of publications is likely to document more of Singapore's history; some repetitions, a few refreshing additions, new interpretations, and more aspirations for the city-state. At the back of the minds of intellectuals and Singapore's political elite, however, are burning questions about whether its golden age will continue, if city-states are more vulnerable in the volatile age of globalisation, and if small states like Singapore will survive the fourth industrial revolution of information technology, big data, and digitisation.

VII. What Lies Ahead

There are nine more chapters unfolding the Singapore narrative through Western eyes. Each chapter is more or less self-contained around a particular theme.

Chapter 2 is meant to provide the conceptual underpinnings of what comprised Western 'perceptions'. This is not meant to be an exhaustive distillation of the concept of 'perceptions' (used interchangeably with terms such as *impressions, cognition, feelings, experiences, views, lenses,* and *eyes*), which itself takes part in a wider, rich, multidisciplinary academic dialogue. Instead, the chapter hopes to broadly guide the reader as to the major influences which shaped Western cultural perceptions. These would be the East-West divide, dialogue, and debates. Colonial Singapore operationalised Said's (1979) political, social, and cultural distinctions between 'us' (Whites) and 'them' (natives). While it lasted only 145 years of the 19th and 20th centuries, the experience of colonial Singapore was significant for occurring at a time of tremendous global change.

Chapter 3 gives the reader a peek into the 14th-century precolonial period of Singapore as the Indianised thalassic kingdom of Tumasik, later renamed as *Singapura*. Despite its short history of about 90 years, it was an important historical interlude between two great trading kingdoms in the Straits of Malacca: the Sri Vijayan-Palembang empire and the Malacca sultanate. Though there were few eyewitness accounts of the trading emporium, its importance in the Malay World outlived its short blip in history. Tumasik-Singapura, the Lion City, was magnified historically in four ways: (1) in Malay mythology, folk tale, and legend concerning its greatness; (2) in indigenous historical account, through the *Sejarah Melayu* or *Malay Annals*, which glorified Singapore's links with two of the greatest maritime kingdoms in Southeast Asia; (3) through the royal symbolic significance of the sacred hill, Fort Canning, as the direct link with the spiritual hill of Seguntang of Sri Vijaya in Palembang, from whence the genealogy of royal power emanated; and (4) by the attention it received from Western writers from the beginning of European involvement in Southeast Asia.

In Chapter 4, attention is focused on the 'perceptions' of Singapore's colonial creator, Thomas Stamford Raffles. Despite all the attempts to discredit Raffles' single-handed founding of Singapore, a chorus of Western biographers and historians has showered him with accolades and praises for his bold enterprise and percipient undertaking for the EIC. Singapore was his 'child'. Raffles was one of the early colonial scholar-administrators, who was influenced by well-heeled friends, academics, administrators, and on-the-ground botanists. Without the knowledge of Malay and the *Sejarah Melayu*, it seems unlikely that he would have been as determined about his choice of Singapore for the location of the EIC factory as he had been.

The Singapore narrative of mainly 19th-century Western residents, travellers, and sojourners further unfolds through perceptions of tropical nature and agricultural landscapes in Chapter 5. Compared to the vast region of Southeast Asia, Singapore is a small place, but its size belies the importance it had and still has in tropical biodiversity. No less than Raffles, the consummate naturalist Alfred Russel Wallace praised the island for its surprising diversity and plenitude of tropical nature. While often hailed for its salubrious climate, Singapore became notoriously feared for its roaming tigers, to which many local lives fell prey annually. White entrepreneurs acted upon their perceptions of nature through risky cash crop undertakings. Besides simply admiring tropical nature, Western residents also turned much of the island into functional holdings for economic crops. Singapore was the site of experimental garden crops, market gardens, and plantations.

Chapter 6 provides a Western insight into the urban morphology (form or appearance) of the Singapore colonial town. The most enduring aspect of Singapore's morphology which remains till today has been that of the 1822 Raffles Town Plan which spatially divided the city into two entities: the European Town north of the Singapore River, and the local or Asian Town south of the river. The two sectors repeatedly drew contrasting characterisations from Europeans: a sedate, quiet, orderly, residential European landscape of bungalows and gardens, versus a bustling, chaotic, energised Asian landscape of pedestrians, hawkers, noise, motley smells, travelling kitchens, varied foods, cultural ceremonies, and cottage industries.

In Chapter 7, we see Singapore's 'imageability' through Western optics. Using Kevin Lynch's concept of imageability which refers to a city's ability to demonstrate a distinctive character, the chapter identifies the salient aspects of colonial Singapore, including both the positive and negative features: the entrepôt merchant town, the bustling economic city, the enclosed, high-caste White 'society', and the landscapes of vice (gambling, prostitution, and opium dens). The colonial city was epitomised by its 'open', free-wheeling identity, from its trading, mercantile economy, through to its notoriety for economically profitable illicit activity.

Singapore's cultural legacy was always dichotomised in White eyes between its being 'cosmopolitan' and polyglot on the one hand, and a Chinese city on the other; the main theme in Chapter 8. For the Western sojourner, Singapore was a one-stop destination to sample the variety of Asian cultures, their peculiar ethnic ceremonies, distinctive religious festivals, and *genre de vie* or way of living. This city was the 'navel' of Asia as well as the pivot of the Malay World. Whites had much to say about the native or Asian community that they employed as servants, gardeners, drivers, and office staff. One recurring theme amongst the Western views of local society was the wide sexual imbalance between males and females amongst the Chinese. This led to the employment of Chinese 'boys' as domestic helpers in White homes. Stereotypes of the Malay, Bugis, Chinese, Indian, and Arab were continually the butt of Western discourse, ridicule, criticism, and praise that highlighted in many ways Said's (1979) conceptual distinction between 'us' and 'them'. Arising from post-war academic debates about the future of developing countries, the other preoccupation of the Western perceptions of native society was whether the Asian communities could develop like Western states.

In Chapter 9, an attempt is made to capture the changing geopolitics of the region and its impact on Singapore as a result of World War II and its aftermath, including the rise of Japan and China, the communist uprising, the Cold War, the 'Enright Affair', decolonisation, and the cultural differences between the Chinese-speaking and English-educated Chinese. As indigenous Singapore leaders prepared for independence, the British government eased the process with the *Malayanisation Report*, which projected how locals might take over the reins of colonial administration. Western residents had a great deal to say about the future independence of the colony. Some were optimistic while others drew the seemingly foregone conclusion that Singapore would end up in the Chinese communist camp.

Chapter 10 is meant to evaluate Western perceptions during the colonial period. What did White perspectives illustrate? The concluding chapter outlines six themes in the colonial legacy. These include: ethnic insights and cultural revelations; the operationalising of colonialism with regard to diverse peoples, economic activities, and society; the provision of an urban biography of Singapore; the documenting of White experiences in Singapore's tropical laboratory; the reflections upon East-West relationships; and finally, what was passed on by Raffles to the founder of independent Singapore, Lee Kuan Yew.

— 2 —
What is the Narrative of Western Perceptions?

Chapter 2

WHAT IS THE NARRATIVE OF WESTERN PERCEPTIONS?

This book captures the moments in history rather than its definitive outcomes from hindsight. If there is a storyline to this narrative, it is how colonialism unfolded and changed due to perceived domestic needs and external variables. Singapore is one of the few political entities in Asia which was developed from relatively virgin territory in the 19th century. The British administration operated with an entity which was a near-blank slate, and literally grew the colony with liberal immigration policies, enlightened economic administrative incentives, and a willingness to invest in the Lion City. While the Singapore colony might have been originally Raffles' idea, its development was a product of its many Western and Asian residents who believed they had found their El Dorado for personal gain.

I. Defining Western Perceptions

Over the centuries within the region, travellers have alluded to the nature of 'perceptions'. The British explorer and secretary of the Admiralty, Sir John Barrow (1764–1848) (1806, vi) observed that every traveller can provide accurate information of places he visits: with "a proper use of his eyes and his ears, much knowledge may be collected within the sphere of his observations, in the course of a very few days". In short, Western cognition was derived from sense perceptions of Singapore based on visual, aural, taste, olfactory, and tactile experiences, or in most cases, the combination of these sensory attributes. The perceptions could range from the stereotypical to culturally-biased impressions, from the whimsical to hyperbolic expressions, and from the emotional to the candid interpretations of events, landscapes, and peoples. Western perceptions became the widely-held images which people would have of places, street scenes, tropical nature, urban morphology (the forms taken by the city's growth), or society in general. Singapore was a city in the making, and Westerners who had traversed its landscapes had ideas, views, and perspectives which provide for interesting reading and reflection.

The renowned Movement poet D. J. Enright classified authors in the East in two categories. There were the authors who wrote factual, statistical, political-scientific, or sociological analysis that lacked the "specific taste of life". The other group of writers were the travelogical, impressionistic, and patronisingly congratulatory, with accounts full of quaint customs and ancient instances which provided the "local technicolours" (Enright 1969, 161), and whose writing was aimed at people who had no intent on travelling to foreign countries. The Singapore narratives by Western residents and sojourners emerged from both groups of writers. The Harvard professor Arthur Lovejoy (1936) classified writers in two other categories, major and minor writers. Major writers have universal appeal for all time and they would include the great writers. The minor writers would be those dealing with local issues and better portraying the culture, customs, and social issues of a particular period and place. The European writers of colonial Singapore were likely to have been Lovejoy's minor writers who captured its particular culture and society.

If there is a conceptual frame to this study, I would refer to it as a historical-geography narrative in that it discusses events in time which happened in a particular place, in relation to each other. My narrative provides clues to the way Western thinking developed over specific events and processes in Singapore. It is not historical in the way that a historian would attempt to impose an interpretation on a series of events, and select episodes or facts which help to argue for a particular conclusion he is driving towards, while discarding those which do not further his argument. My narrative is more open-ended in that it seeks not a particular conclusion, but presents a variety of Western views and leaves it to others to later draw conclusions where they may. As a perceived bastion of colonialism and more than any other city in the region, the Lion City entertained an endless motley of Western residents and passing visitors.

In the process, they left their opinions and imprints of their stay, and offered regional generalisations and comparisons with other cities and colonies. This narrative gives us an informal disclosure of how Westerners thought, their personal revelations of challenges faced, their cultural prejudices and biases, and their candid admission of likes and dislikes.

By and large, the Western perceptions of Singapore's landscapes were confined to what the renowned landscape authority John Brinckerhoff Jackson defined as the "vernacular" landscape. These were landscapes which connoted "immediate and temporary" usage in contrast to the elite's landscapes of status and permanence (J. B. Jackson 1984, xxx–xxxi). The "vernacular" refers to daily, commonplace activities, the shifting scenes, and the informal cultural landscapes which Westerners experienced. The cultural landscapes (street scenes, itinerant hawkers, coolie gangs, market scenes, and people jostling) were not meant to define the universal, but rather, scenes of the localised, utilitarian, and to the Westerner, the unconventional, from the point of view of what one was accustomed to seeing in the West. This vernacular character made the landscape experiences unique to Westerners in two ways: personally, to them, as well as peculiar to Singapore.

The area of greatest cultural interest for Westerners had to do with their insights into native peoples, their cultures, customs, traditions, religious practices, and behaviour. Singapore was a haven for such observations. To a large extent, Westerners captured local ceremonies and native festivals simply because they were around at the right place and time. Charles Wilkes (1845), the American explorer, was in Singapore during Chinese New Year in 1842, and he was able to witness and record the festivities first-hand.

For Europeans sampling 19th-century multiethnic and multireligious Singapore, it was like the bar scene in the Star Wars film — the variety of cultures and babel of languages were jaw-dropping and bewildering. Most Europeans thus spent much time describing different ethnic groups and their cultural habits, behaviours, and beliefs as they unfolded in Singapore. Today, such descriptions of people would be seen as impolite, stereotypical, and better discussed in private or held personally or confidentially. The cultural differences were manifestly more distinct at a time when globalisation and cosmopolitanism were circumscribed, and hence Westerners were openly frank in ventilating their opinions. They had to share their experiences with the public audience back home. By and large, the opinions reflected cultural stereotypes, cultural relativity, and cultural norms.

Manuel Castells (2010) wrote a three-volume work on the information age and its various impacts on society. His thesis was very much based on modern information technology and its galvanising impact on social movements, globalisation, international capitalism, nationalism, and cultural identity. My study, however, is based mainly on the information derived and diffused by the print media, from before the era of instantaneous 24/7 information, when books, newspapers, and journals remained for several centuries the principal forms of mass communication. The colonial city of Singapore was fortunate from its early inception to have had a series of newspapers over various intervals that carried views and news of its residents and visitors. The published vehicle was a White preserve for disseminating news of the entrepôt. Singapore's business community was thirsty for regional and international news that could affect its trade and businesses. Benedict Anderson (1991) has appropriately referred to newspapers as "print capitalism". Within this entrepôt, newspapers were an integral part of providing information on the externalities of trade for Singapore entrepreneurs and merchants. Singapore's affair with the printed press began with the *Singapore Chronicle* (1824–1837), *The Singapore Free Press* (1835–1862), *The Straits Times* (1845–present), *Straits Intelligence* (1883–1886), *Eastern Daily Mail* (1905–1906), and *The Malaya Tribune* (1914–1951). Despite its small resident White population, the production of varied local newspapers showed that the British factory and trading port were significant enough to warrant the medium. Westerners articulated frank criticisms about the administration, reflected on activities, documented important milestones and benchmarks of the resident White population, and at times, betrayed their inner feelings which provide us with glimpses into cultural values and moral differences.

The focus of this study is not to highlight the odd and exceptional viewpoints per se, but to provide the popular, repetitive themes of the Western cognition of Singapore. These themes were culled from Europeans who had written about their visits or residencies in the British colony during the period under review. The Western perceptions are thus on-the-ground reflections, based on personal experiences and eyewitness accounts. Like those of field anthropologists and geographers, the White accounts reflect objective details of a scene, capture moving activities in time, and reveal White prejudices and preconceived interpretations of native behaviour and rituals. Occasionally, an attempt is made to interpret local behaviour, traditions, and activities within cultural lenses, environmental influences, and historical precedents.

Though this study focuses on Western perceptions of Singapore, this is not an analysis of European or national cultures. Many books have been written on those and there is no need to reinvent the wheel. For this study, 'Westerner' refers to a person from Europe, North America, Australia, or New Zealand, one who is a product of Western civilisation, a Caucasian by race, White by stereotyping, and an Occidental of British, Dutch, German, French, Swedish, Danish, Spanish, Belgian, Portuguese, Italian, Greek, Armenian, American, or Canadian nationality. The Italian journalist Luigi Barzini (1984) decades ago wrote his witty and interesting book *The Europeans*, which defines 'European' behaviour with ethnic characteristics, national cultural traits, and some level of stereotyping. Despite the British founding of modern Singapore, the colonial city was a product of many nationalities (Western and Asian) contributing to its early development. No attempt is made here to define these Western perceptions as exclusive or dominant.

Though the first 50 years of Singapore's founding saw a small Western population, their contributions to Singapore's development was outstanding. Without their faith in the success of the colonial city, its development would have been short-lived and handicapped. As with all cities, Singapore's historical development was filled with apprehension and doubt as well as periods of optimism.

II. What Influenced Western Views

The three macro influences that undergirded Western perceptions of Singapore were the impact of Western culture and civilisation; the unfolding historical events of the 19th and first half of the 20th centuries; and the operationalisation of colonialism in Singapore.

a) *Western Culture and Civilisation*

One might argue that despite the varied personal influences, there were broad temporal, civilisational, and cultural influences that shaped the Western perceptions of Singapore. Using the qualifying term *Western* clearly underscores an important common ingredient in the perceptions — be they British, Scottish, Dutch, Swedish, French, Spanish, German, and so on.

The term *Western* is heavily loaded and I do not attempt to get into a debate over definitions. Essentially, all Westerners were Europeans (emanating from Europe), often seen as sharing a common historical classical Graeco-Roman heritage, a spiritual Christian lineage, and a commonality of historical experience (the Middle Ages, the Crusades, the Renaissance, the Enlightenment, the Industrial Revolution, and the Romantic period). Defining Westerners in some way assumes that they share some civilisational traits. Many Western historians identify significant time periods that they believe have created an indelible imprint on the Western psyche.

The European identity has been shaped by both internal and external factors. Yet, for most of history, Europe was not internally a monolithic cultural entity. It was a fragmented place of varying nationalities and its history was shaped by conflicts, contestations, and competitions. Europe was not the sort of arguably cohesive cultural entity as viewed today. The Christian influence was only developed as a pan-European tradition in the first millennium. The historian Victor Lieberman (2009) has noted that in the 15th century, there were 500 political entities all jostling for power and identity. By the 19th century, the 500 satrapies had been reduced to 26 nation-states. Up to the 20th century, Europe was still the epicentre of two bloody World Wars, a continent of political instability. To understand the Western perceptions of Singapore in the 19th century is to realise the deep nationalistic competitions in Europe and how this translated to other parts of the world through colonialism. The colonial land-grabbing tradition was spurred by developing European nation-states seeking to embellish their national coffers, define and extend their political power, and deny or restrict other European competitors from having their own colonies. Colonisation was a badge of national military prowess. By the end of the 19th century, the British reigned supreme in the colonial race, while South America had become a Spanish- and Portuguese-speaking continent.

b) *Long 19th Century, Tempestuous 20th Century*

The German historian Jürgen Osterhammel's (2014*) The Transformation of the World: A Global History of the Nineteenth Century* gives us an erudite cross-sectional history of the 19th century, as a period of global political, economic, and cultural transformation. The Italian sociologist Giovanni Arrighi (2010) on the other hand argues that the long 20th century shaped our contemporary world, developing "organised capitalism" and providing the genesis of state formations. Both the

19th- and 20th-century perspectives frame Singapore's rise as a major entrepôt and trading mecca under the formative decades of British colonialism.

Conversely, did the Westerners' perceptions of Singapore shape the overall Western definition of the Orient and Asia? The Western images of Oriental court eunuchs, ostentatious court rituals, and despotic satrapies were set up as being culturally and diametrically opposed to Western culture. Yet, in their management of local societies, senior Western bureaucrats like John Crawfurd (1820, 3:27) and Raffles (S. Raffles 1830) had no compunction in advocating despotism as the right form of colonial political rule in Java and Sumatra. John Steadman (1969) has argued that the West defined its culture partly by contrasting it with Oriental culture. Singapore was a prism of Oriental culture in Western eyes but it was defined by different cultural attributes from the ones usually associated by Westerners with an Oriental society. On the one hand, the Western experiences in Singapore were a form of operationalising "cultural relativity" (Lach 1965). They were the means by which Westerners came to accept that there could be views of any culture, Eastern or Western, and this allowed for greater sophistication because of the understanding that cultures could be seen in relative terms to one another and not as absolutes in themselves. On the other hand, Western experiences in Singapore were about defining an 'Oriental ethos' or 'Asiatic sociology' (Osterhammel 2018, 389–392). This involved understanding a foreign culture on its own terms rather than trying to compare it with any Western culture.

The multicultural composition of Singapore society was a perennial subject of Western interest and fascination, with ethnic comparisons being made and prejudices formulated. In their descriptions of local ethnic identities, Westerners used different parameters for defining local behaviour. They ranged from pure cultural stereotypes to environmental determinism, and from experiences born out of relationships to ethnically-biased perceptions. Singapore over the decades of British rule was a continuing colonial city project in motion. This was a British city that was shaped by the ideological dictates of many colonial governors and the feedback from numerous European elite residents. Unlike other colonial cities in the region, Singapore had no counterpart; it had no hinterland, no relative historical legacy to defend, and no large indigenous population to foster. In many ways, the British administration had a politically free ruling mandate to encourage migrants and finally turn its colonial city into a 'Chinese city', as Western travellers opined it to be. This ethnic distinction would become a bone of contention in the region as Singapore became a nation-state. Amongst the colonial narratives of the region, Singapore was a unique creation. As British global power grew, Singapore was developed as its bastion of defence, colonial power, and strategic interest. Singapore was the pride of Britain, rather than being viewed as the pivot of Asia. It was meant to express the success of British colonialism and not a changing modern Asia.

The construction of Singapore and Western perceptions of its development took place at a time when historical change was at its most expressive, effective, and explosive. Singapore was the product of two historical processes. It developed during the eventful long 19th century as well as at a time when colonialism was at its zenith. The 19th and 20th centuries (especially the period of high colonialism, 1870–1940) were particularly concerned with White views of the Oriental *genre de vie*. In Southeast Asia, Western colonialists and historians viewed those 70 years as the apogee of colonialism in the region. This period might be associated with the *Belle Époque* (1880–1914, the so-called golden age in Europe). According to Osterhammel (2018, 432–434), the spirit of awareness of cultural differences led to the birth of sociology. One might add that cultural relativity also gave rise to the science of anthropology. Indeed, the first descriptions of 'native' society and cultural practices and beliefs were documented by the scholar-administrators, many of them holding high official posts as Residents in Singapore: Sir Hugh Low, Sir William Maxwell, and Sir Hugh Clifford.

The 19th century was a time when Romanticism was influencing Western perceptions. Westerners saw the virtues of native societies, and were laudatory about local cultures and religious practices. The spell of the Oriental mystique and fabled Orient had not yet been broken in some Western minds. Through the eyes of romantic administrators, naturalists, and travellers, we have some of the most interesting perspectives of tropical nature and cultural landscapes of early Singapore and the region. Some residents like Singapore's government surveyor from 1841 to 1853, John Thomson, produced several detailed maps of Singapore. In his book *Some Glimpses into Life in the Far East*, he concentrated on describing people and characters he had interacted with (Thomson 1865). He gave detailed descriptions of Governor William Butterworth, the Jewish merchant Abraham Solomon, Capt. William Scott, Capt. Samuel Congalton, Thomas Duncan, Capt. Donker, and the Chinese merchant Whampoa (Hoo Ah Kay). Thomson might be the individual referred to by

Desmond Morris (2002) as a "people watcher", for he provided vivid descriptions of the Malay and Chinese societies in Singapore. Globetrotting professional writers like W. Somerset Maugham, Rudyard Kipling, and Joseph Conrad lent their unmistakable names to Singapore's fame as a legendary meeting place of travellers, merchants, professionals, and colonial administrators. Their short stories and novels provided the background of Singapore's colourful landscapes to the popular imagination and added more Oriental romance to Western perceptions of the East.

Singapore was a cauldron of British might and power. Externally-driven developments provided the catalyst for Singapore's domestic changes. If Singapore's labour, entrepreneurs, and power elite had not been able to capitalise on these changes, the colonial city would have been viewed in a different light by its many Western visitors and residents. Despite colonialism having created a Western superiority complex over Oriental peoples and a sense among many that the colonies would never rise from their state of backwardness, the general European perceptions of how Singapore was faring under British rule were positive, encouraging, and befitting of the great times of change. This was especially so considering how the colonies of other Western powers around the region were doing under their respective masters. And indeed, albeit unexpectedly to the Westerners, the colonial legacy in a way prepared Singapore for its take-off as an independent city-state. Despite the many historical debates about the importance of the indigenous role versus the Western influence in Asian history, one needs to be reminded by the historian John Bastin (1960, 24) that it would be foolhardy to regard the Western influence in Asian history as "extraneous".

c) *The Evolving Colonial Statement*

This narrative of Singapore's colonial biography does not promise to throw up new ideas or propose alternative frameworks. What it can do is provide more grounded interpretations of varying socio-cultural, economic, and political changes; shed some light on the way Western merchants, professionals, and colonial administrators confronted challenges; and provide thought on how unexpected externalities, such as the regional competition between different Western colonial powers, or potentially momentous world events, were interpreted and addressed by different sectors of the European community. We might debate endlessly over whether Singapore was lucky to have had a British nursemaid for a century of its modern existence. After weaning off colonial patronage, one can now reflect on whether the colonial upbringing was balanced, adequate, and responsible. Through the eyes of its White caretakers, one can see whether their inputs were positive or negative, whether their prejudices coloured their judgements, and whether on the whole, the Singapore narrative by Western tenants, capitalists, and administrators delivered a Lion City-state for its own good.

Many Western historical, political, and economic overviews of the Malay Archipelago, although not specific to Singapore, included the colonial city in the regional assessments. With competing colonies in the region, it was often difficult to derive 'objective' assessments of places and cities. British diplomats, bureaucrats, and militia of the 19th century were frequent ardent critics of the Dutch, French, and Spanish colonial administrators. One caveat that needs to be emphasised is that the use of Western perceptions of Singapore's first 145 years is in no way an attempt to endorse an "imposition of a Western structural framework" (Bastin 1960, 17) on Singapore's history. I leave the historical interpretations to historians and other savants. Academics have tried to organise historical processes into many classifications: modern and postmodern, and colonial and postcolonial. Singapore's colonial incubation might very well fit into some of these classifications if one distils its historical data. Timothy Harper's (1999) *The End of Empire and the Making of Malaya* is a daring attempt by a British historian to obtain the "clearer perception" of the "colonial form" and the social and cultural forces which shaped nation-building in Malaya. The irony of the "colonial inheritance" is that it not only laid the foundations of institutionalised political and economic goods of the colonial state, but also gave birth to national challenges and uprisings to colonial rule and government.

Western perceptions of Singapore over 145 or so years (1819–1963) came at the tail end of the 450-year-old colonial engagement in the region. Since its beginning, however, four metanarratives (or grand narratives) had governed Western colonial experience and engagement in Southeast Asia. First is the geographical metanarrative of East-West relationships. Since ancient times, the Orient has developed an identity of fables, fantasy, opulence, and mythology in Western perceptions. The biblical idea of Paradise located in the East, the three wise kings from the Orient making offerings at Jesus' birth, and Solomon's Ophir located in the East influenced Western perceptions of a fabled Orient (Steadman 1969). The explorations of Alexander the Great in India, the Ptolemaic cartographic reference to the *Aurea Khersonese* or golden peninsula in Southeast Asia (Wheatley 1961; Ptolemy 1932), and Marco Polo's (1871) adventures in China kept the opulent Oriental mystique alive in the West. It was later augmented by the lure of spices from the Maluku Islands, or the Moluccas. Before its current name, the South China Sea was known by Westerners as the Spice Sea or the Philippine Sea (Bowring 2019), thus reflecting the importance of the location of spices or their proximity to the Philippine Islands.

The East was therefore not only a cardinal reference point, it was according to Steadman (1969) a cultural antipode to Western culture. Westerners down to the 21st century have found Asia to be filled with strange practices, exotic rituals, and mysterious traditions. This underscores how Westerners in Singapore viewed the polyglot Asian population and its many cultural beliefs, religious customs, and eating habits. The general historical-philosophical spectacle of East and West was embedded in the Western perceptions of Asia, the Orient, and Singapore.

Second, the Western perceptions document an important part of the growing colonial engagement of the Western powers in various parts of the world. Singapore developed as a colonial city during the 19th century when colonialism was attaining its fullest expression in the region, the period of high colonialism. Singapore became what geographers call a 'primate city' under colonialism, the apex city in the hierarchy of towns and cities in the Malay Peninsula. The colonial city was the centre of British administration, security and defence, economic activity, education, and cultural activity for the whole of British colonial Malaya.

Internally, colonialism created a single framework whereby Western colonialists and elites of Asian society shared similar concepts concerning what Osterhammel (2018, 384) calls "the primacy of political power". By this, it was recognised that it was Western colonial power which held sway, and that limited advancement in economic, social, intellectual, and other spheres would be achieved without the acknowledgement of a positive role which could be played by that power. If we accept Edward Said's argument that imperialism engendered geographical violence and territorial rape (Jacobs 1996, 150), we also have to expand our biased horizons to acknowledge that colonial powers wanted to invest and develop successful colonies for their own sake. Hence, while the Dutch turned Java into a diverse agricultural granary, the British developed Singapore, its successful colonial administrative capital, as an entrepôt. Raffles laid down the first principles for his new factory — the suppression of crime, the security of property, and the encouragement of the "free growth of moral and mental gifts in the whole population" (Cross 1921, 59). Most of all, it would have a port that was free and open to all. It would seem that Singapore was fortunate in having been a British colony. The history of colonialism in the region produced different national outcomes, some positive, and others of lasting negativity.

Malayan colonialism was thus managed, executed, and translated from the primate city of Singapore. To put it in Benedict Anderson's (1991) framework, colonialism rested on three pillars and Singapore exemplified them: (1) colonial states introduced periodic population censuses (the first Singapore census was in 1824) to give the colonial administrators an understanding of whom they were governing; (2) it was engaged in cartography and surveys of the colony and region (the survey and map of the island and town by James Franklin and Philip Jackson were executed in the early 1820s); and (3) it developed a respectable museum (Singapore's Raffles Museum created in 1874 under Governor Sir Andrew Clarke) tracing both the flora and fauna of the region, and the prehistory and history of people of the colony and its immediate hinterland. Colonial administrators were interested in developing an indigenous historical narrative and the museum was meant to showcase the indigenous cultural developments. Despite the Western ideological influence in colonialism, the British colonial bureaucracy was still, to a recognisable extent, concerned with preserving the indigenous prehistorical and historical narratives of the region and Singapore.

Third, as colonialism became the norm for many states in the region, the cultural gap between the West and East grew. Since the Renaissance and the Age of Sail, the West had been exposed to a global ecumene or inhabited world from which foreign knowledge fertilised the European mind. This was further augmented by the Scientific (17th century) and Industrial (19th century) Revolutions that widened knowledge inequality between Europe and Asia. The downside of this led to what Said (1979) has called Orientalism that manifested itself in the Age of Colonialism. Said's central thesis was how Westerners distinguished themselves, 'we' (Whites), from 'others' (non-Whites and Asians) in descriptions of populations, cultures, and human landscapes. Hence, it is not surprising to find Western perceptions of native culture and local practices in Singapore carrying smugness, racial prejudice, derogatory opinion, and biased perception.

Finally, Western perceptions and assessments of Singapore for much of its colonial history were for the most part the only means of judging the city's successes and failures. Unlike the current quantitative measurements and assessments of countries, states, and cities around the world, the value of personal perceptions is not as great now as it was in the past. Today, one has real-time assessments and live views of places via television and the internet. A century ago, assessments and previews of places came largely from word descriptions of travellers. Fortunately, there were many bureaucrats, naturalists, businessmen, missionaries, and travellers who visited different cities, ports, and kingdoms in the region, and were able to make interesting and insightful comparisons of places. The traveller Horace Bleackley, for example, compared Saigon to Singapore and observed that the liveliness of Singapore's business activities had no equal in Saigon. He stayed in Singapore's Grand Hotel de l'Europe, which to him was one of the best hotels in Asia (Bleackley 1928, 121). The composite picture of the Singapore of the past was thus pieced together from numerous descriptions of places and landscapes from various Western travellers, residents, and sojourners.

III. The Value of Western Perceptions

In Asia, Westerners have not traditionally been portrayed positively — the Chinese for centuries referred to them as *hongmaofan* or red-haired barbarians, with the Hong Kong Cantonese viewing them as *hongmohkwai* or red-haired devils. The Japanese call Whites *gaijin* (an often derogatory reference to foreigners), the Thais called them *farang* (a corruption of the name of the Greek advisor to King Narai, Phaulkon), and Malays colloquially named them *orang puteh* (White people).

Despite these derogatory references, Westerners became the colonisers of Asia for nearly 500 years, and left an indelible imprint on Asian societies and culture. The legions of White administrators, naturalists, entrepreneurs, and missionaries also left an unparalleled written, cartographic, and visual (sketches, drawings, paintings, and photographs) record of the changing Asian landscapes which they visited, managed, explored, and traded with. It would seem short-sighted for Asian researchers to overlook the vault of data that Western travellers and residents left behind. No other civilisation has had such a profound and lasting impact on the world than the West. As academics and politicians debate the pros and cons of Western civilisation, one needs to be reminded by Arnold Toynbee's (1971, 58) historical reflection that civilisation is not an end product: "Civilization, as we know it, is a movement and not a condition, a voyage and not a harbor".

Western civilisation has bequeathed a treasure trove of historical, scientific, and documentary material that gives us insights into Asia's changing past, its significant events, historical personalities, and social and cultural signifiers. These signifiers derive from life-cycle occurrences like marriage or death, or the way people's lives were lived (through ritual or mundane daily practices), and conveyed social or cultural meaning. One is reminded by the leading historians of the region that 'perceptions' are also relevant in understanding the past, its processes, events, and personalities; and in the quest for origins, because of how perceptions themselves have determined uses (Reid and Marr 1979; Wang 1979) and thus affected history by being acted upon.

Western perceptions have been used in this study for six important methodological reasons. Firstly, Westerners provide a rich and continuous record of their travels and sojourns in Singapore which can be easily tapped and analysed. We are reminded by Bastin (1960, 17) that "often the richest sources for the study of modern Southeast Asian history tend to be Western". The story of Singapore's economic success was woven from many Western narratives.

Secondly, the founding of Singapore by a British administrator was significant, given that Britain at that time was one of the most powerful nations. The rise of British power in the 19th century would boost Singapore's fortunes. In some ways, Singapore's simultaneous rise throughout that century was bolstered by Britain's naval power and its international geopolitical dominance. It was dependent on its regional hinterland and it developed in relation to how it managed and exploited its economic catchment area. Since its 1819 founding, Singapore drew people from all over Asia and the West. It lived up to Raffles' perception as an ideal trading location between East and West. As Singapore's success as an entrepôt developed over the decades, Raffles' name would become synonymous with its success.

Thirdly, the documentation of Singapore as a thriving entrepôt, successful trading centre, and entrepreneurial nexus could only have been done by endless Western merchant and resident perceptions of the growing port. The varied perceptive European documentations reinforced the city's economic importance, its trading acumen, its entrepreneurial flair, and its globalising attraction. The undergirding of the growing economic globalisation of Singapore, as a historian has noted, has been as much about "states of mind and changes in behaviour, and about perceptions of challenges, problems, and opportunities, as it is about ratios, growth curves, and absolute and relative curves" (Coclanis 2006, 15).

Fourthly, Singapore was a prized economic and military outpost for the British and hence, a Western curiosity, and focus of intense Western speculation and subjective points of view. Singapore's founding and subsequent development as the main strategic British military base east of Suez made it an important city in regional affairs. It was a centre of British geopolitical strategy in global terms. Thus, when Singapore fell to the Japanese in the Second World War it made headline news around the world. The British surrender to the Japanese in Singapore was a historical watershed. It shattered the hitherto extant perception of the invincible British military power and demonstrated the ending of Western hegemony by an Asian power.

It was evident that from a defensive strategy, the British had placed emphasis on beach defences and an anticipated attack from the south. None other than Lt. Gen. Arthur Percival (1977, 285–287), who surrendered Singapore, demonstrated his wrong judgment in his earlier 1937 lecture on "The Strategical Problems of Singapore". His fundamental mistake was his misguided strategies of beach defence when in fact the Japanese came overland from Peninsula Malaya via the causeway. Percival's perceptions about the island's defence were unfortunately maritime oriented. Noel Barber (1978, 119) was strident in his criticisms of the British naval defence: "And in all this story of equivocation, of ineptitude, of the myth so assiduously fostered, nothing can match in grim irony the fact that when the moment of destiny finally did arrive, the base was valueless and impotent". As historians note, that was a fatal error when the Japanese invaded Singapore through Malaya.

Countless historians have tried to decipher the reasons for the fall of Singapore. Colonialism was brought to its knees and White racial supremacy became questionable in native eyes. This emboldened indigenous aspirations for independence and paved the way for a postcolonial era of independent states. Singapore thus had historic significance: first as a pioneering type of colonial city, a thriving entrepôt and bastion of British military power, and then as the symbol of the end of Western colonialism in the region.

Fifthly, another variable that makes the study of Western perceptions of Singapore, or for that matter Asia, an interesting exercise is the durability and elaboration of certain Western ideas even as the West developed. Despite its many constituent and even competing nationalities, Europe as the birthplace of the West has not disappeared but rather held together as it enlarged itself as a civilisation for over 2,000 years, sharing many cultural commonalities and historical epochs (Rabb 2006; Stark 2005; Spencer 2016). Nick Spencer's (2016) *The Evolution of the West* enumerates what he views as the software of Western civilisation — rule of law, welfare, humanism, human rights, nationhood, secularism, ethics, and democracy. While Laura Nader's (2015) *What the Rest Think of the West* is a brave attempt to reverse the dominant Western perspectives through other lenses, the so-called Occidentalism (or viewing of the West through non-Western eyes) remains a fragmentary means through which many culturally distinct perspectives are channelled: Middle Eastern, Indian, Chinese, and Japanese. She acknowledges that "Occidentalism is not a mirror image to Orientalism. No such academic hegemony comes from the East" (Nader 2015, xxiii).

Finally, Western perceptions leave us interesting insights at two levels. Foremost, as foreigners, Westerners provided an etic approach (outsiders' view) to Singapore's multicultural festivities, religious practices, and ethnic activities. At the same time, they were ringside eyewitnesses to Singapore's changing landscapes, and hence gave first-hand, opinionated, and candid perspectives which could be the fodder for historical interpretations of Singapore's development. They documented their personal perceptions of a colonial city on the one hand and an Oriental landscape on the other. While the truth of these first-hand accounts might be subjective, they provide us with the public thinking and general flavour of what Singapore was to Westerners at various points. In many cases, it was the public perceptions that influenced personal decisions, governed prejudices, and dictated general and individual behaviour.

IV. Alternative Western Perspectives

The Western views on the evolving Lion City were multifaceted, hence one could use varied themes to tease them out. In this study, Singapore also manifests itself in other sub-themes such as the shaping of an urban narrative (viewed in terms of the colonial city; the 1822

Raffles Town Plan and urban planning; urban slums and squatters; and urban imageability) and the temporal narrative (evolutionary change; cross-sectional history; historical events) of the British colony's development.

a) *The Urban Biography*

This book may represent a biography of an evolving city, but with some qualifications. The urban biography of Singapore is reflected in the personal experiences of Westerners who lived in and sampled the city. In a way, these are the common reflections of how Westerners viewed Singapore, its strengths and weaknesses, its negative and positive vibes, its iconic features, its societal warts and above all, its Lynchian 'imageable' landscapes, which were those that formed the holistic image of a city in their minds. The Westerners who wrote about their experiences in Singapore were not only box seat witnesses of events, changing landscapes, and societal interactions, they were indeed the actors in the city's developments.

We have to be grateful to the 74 male Europeans who were in Singapore at the 1824 census, many of whose names are still to be found in place names (Spottiswoode, Balestier, Crawford, Pearl, Scott) and known business enterprises (Boustead, Behn, Meyer, Guthrie, Little, Syme, Fraser, McAlister, Peterson, Simons, Gilfillan, Diethelm, Drew, Napier) (E. Brown 2007, 40–41). Aside from the male entrepreneurs and bureaucrats, some of the astute social and cultural observations of the developing colonial city have come from women. The most revealing 19th-century social observations are recorded in Richard Hale's (2016) wonderful book, *The Balestiers.* In her letters to her sister, relatives, and friends, Maria Balestier, the wife of US Consul Joseph Balestier, left us some of the most detailed observations of life in the colony between 1834 and 1847. Her nuggets of information about remuneration, the subaltern locals, Chinese funerals, food, religious practices and beliefs, the types of transport (*gharries*), and the lives of expatriates are a treasure trove for researchers. Many of the 19th-century books by the likes of such as Isabella Bird, Wilkes, and Crawfurd did not deal with Singapore exclusively. Usually, the colonial city made up some chapters in books on travel around and outside the region.

Singapore is an evolving story and many Westerners played their parts in narrating it, weaving varying personal components of the city's biography. Since its inception as a factory and entrepôt, many private individuals had faith in Singapore's success. They were the builders of Singapore's foundations. Each trader, merchant, and entrepreneur who invested in the colonial city in its early decades provided a vote of confidence in the entrepôt's survival, sustainability, and stability. After Singapore's success was deemed secure, Raffles' founding of 1819 thus came to be seen as modern Singapore's birth and its definitive birthday for celebration. Singapore's relatively short history as a British colony from 1819 to 1963 allows for a more manageable continuous biography of its travails and triumphs as told by the men and women who made it possible.

Singapore was a unique type of primate colonial city, which was Britain's colonial pride and strategic base east of Suez. It was not built within fortifications unlike the region's older colonial cities, nor far from a local centre of power. It was simply a town underscoring spatial segregation between Westerners and Asians. Both groups lived in relative closeness to each other and welcomed newcomers from elsewhere. Today, as an independent country, the city-state of Singapore is a political prodigy which punches above its weight. It has drawn comparisons with the glorious period of city-states in Renaissance Europe. Its success begs the question of whether the current halcyon days of its success, as one of the richest countries in the world, will continue. The economic prowess of Singapore and its abetting of capitalism have always been dogged by an underlying criticism of whether the Singapore spirit is overly material and lacking in soul. The sociologist Joseph Tamney's (1996) *The Struggle over Singapore's Soul* gives Singaporeans much food for thought about the future of their society: "Does Singapore represent the future?" With so much talk of the Asian Century and Asianism (Frey and Spakowski 2016), one wonders if Singapore is prepared to take on new challenges. Is Singapore society sufficiently cosmopolitan in outlook to adapt to globalisation? Or should Singapore define uniquely its Asian national character? The tide against globalisation and multilateralism, as championed by US President Donald Trump, provides an antidote to Singapore's historical narrative of free trade, laissez-faire economy, cosmopolitan population, international orientation, and global city-statehood.

b) *Temporal Insights*

The recorded Western perceptions of Singapore provide us with insights into three temporal dimensions of the city's development. First, at different slices of time (say 1830, 1860, 1890, 1910, or 1942), one might glean information with which to derive a further cross-sectional history of each of those slices that reflects important events defining certain years. Osterhammel's (2014) study of the global history of the 19th century, a slice of cross-sectional history based on a century, is written in this vein. An example of how illuminating a cross-sectional approach can be is in the way the notable French historian Fernand Braudel (1981) traced the development of much of Western table manners by observing the introduction and provision of different cutlery (spoons, knives, and forks), and explaining how their appearance in art pictorially and visually depicted the rise of Western capitalism. Simon Schama (1987) used the 17th century to demonstrate the Dutch *Embarrassment of Riches* during its mercantile phase. His book noted the Dutch display of riches was not centred around money, jewellery, nor material possessions, but rather on paintings of foods and feastings. The good life was demonstrated in having lots of good fare, including cheese, wine, and fruit. His emphasis on food showed how the Dutch, as had the rest of Europe in hard times, suffered from hunger and lack of nourishment, but also that the perception of riches varied from culture to culture.

The second dimension is best summed up in J. B. Jackson's (1984) 'vernacular landscape' concept, which deals with the immediate, local variety of sedimentary cultural influences rather than long periods. Vernacular culture is based on quotidian, functional activities, and as one will see, Singapore was defined by vernacular landscape scenes. Westerners captured the city's development at various stages of its evolution. They applauded what they approved of, and criticised and condemned what they believed was unsatisfactory or demeaning. Given that many Westerners were travelling to Asia or residing in an Oriental landscape for the first time, everything they perceived became unique, different, and culturally shocking. Most of all, what is today ethnically common in a globalised cosmopolitan environment was, in the 19th century, a new revelation. An assignment in Southeast Asia was like a posting in the outer realms of another world. For the British administrator Clifford (1929, 79), there was wonderment, excitement, and romance in working on the frontiers of the empire: "Until you have served your apprenticeship on the outskirts of the empire, breathed frontier air, heard frontier talk, dreamed frontier dreams, you cannot realise the splendour, the magic, the thrill of that idea". Singapore in the early 19th century was certainly a frontier colonial location in the British empire.

The third historical understanding of Western impressions of Singapore is found in Braudel's (1972, 1973) concept of the *longue durée*. One can capture the evolution of living and lifestyles over decades of perceptions. One notable change Westerners observed, for example, was the removal of Chinese 'pigtails' over the century, from which one might infer certain modifications in thinking among the Chinese. One might also state whether change was evolutionary or revolutionary. In an article on changes in Singapore's land use, I have argued that the colonial phase of history was marked by evolutionary change, whereas the independent period of the city-state was dictated by revolutionary change (Savage 1992). Development in the colonial city remained evenly paced, as manifested for example by the slowness with which the British authorities addressed the problems of the city's centre.

Up to the early 1970s, the bulk of Singapore's population was confined in the spatial area of the 1822 Jackson Plan. The Raffles Town Plan, as it was named alternatively, covered a mere 1.2 per cent of the colony but housed 60 per cent of its population. The Singapore shophouse suffered from residential involution, as it was ingeniously subdivided into many rooms to house the expanding population. Barrington Kaye (1960) wrote about the crammed living conditions in shophouses in *Upper Nankin Street Singapore*. The shophouse became ubiquitous with slum dwellings in Chinatown, the place of much communicable disease. The colonial administration had produced the *Simpson Report* in 1907 to deal with these unhealthy conditions. It would seem that while Westerners had for centuries written about various environmental conditions leading to malarial fever, few thought that crammed urban housing conditions could produce fatal disease. Brenda Yeoh's (1996) *Contesting Space, Power Relations and the Urban Built Environment in Colonial Singapore* demonstrates how a city planned by Westerners was inhabited by non-Westerners, and thus contestations, conflicts, and collisions between coloniser and colonised became recurrent issues. Unfortunately, these were often hidden from depictions of colonial Singapore.

The Second World War certainly changed colonialism in the region, and implanted the idea that the local population was capable of ruling itself. The first hint of this came when the British authorities were considering upgrading Raffles College to university status after World War II. The British commission ruled in favour of the change upon being impressed that the Singapore General Hospital during the Japanese

Occupation had been successfully managed and manned by local doctors, nurses, and orderlies.

As decolonisation got underway after the war, many of the expatriate faculty in the then University of Singapore deliberated about Singapore's future. Historian C. Northcote Parkinson (1963) wrote about the changing East-West winds, Patrick Anderson (1955) reflected on Singapore's evolving multicultural base, Paul Theroux (1973) wrote about Singapore's seedy culture during the Vietnam War, and Enright (1969), then head of the English Literature department, topped it all off with his defiant debate with the new Singapore leaders about the 'cultural spring-cleaning' and its attempts to replace 'yellow culture' with a national culture. The geographer and acting vice-chancellor, E. H. G. Dobby, got the brunt of the local anti-colonial venom, when his 'colonial'-themed speech to students in 1957 created a furore and forced him to leave the university in haste (Savage 2003). Later, the *Final Report of the Malayanisation Commission* (Malayanisation Commission 1956, 1–6), written by locals, would provide an endorsement that Singaporeans were ready to take control of local governance and the civil service.

V. Summing Up: The Conceptual Statement

This chapter has been written to provide the conceptual underpinnings of the book, such as the definitions of 'White', Western civilisation, colonialism, Western perceptions, the historical-geographical narrative, and temporal and landscape themes. Western perceptions themselves consisted of amalgamations of various ideas, which would evolve over time into critical thought about colonialism. They would also be the basis for contemplating urban change and development, and the influence of the landscape on the Westerner.

Singapore's early foundations as a British colony were well documented both in colonial government records (*Notices*) as well as in the informal optics of Western residents and travellers who continually penned their personal views of their experiences in the developing city. These documentations gave insights into the temporal changes that the colony was undergoing and the influences that shaped changes on the one hand. And on the other, Western perceptions provided a cross-sectional view of the history of Singapore at different points in time (a year, a decade, a century). We have on record the internal policies that created landscape modifications, as well as the externalities that influenced those policies and changes. Singapore is an interesting case study of a colonial city in the tropics because it did not have an integral hinterland of its own, yet by location, it became the locus and verve of trade in the region.

While Europeans were championing nationalism and nation-state building back home, in Singapore and other colonies in the region they unwittingly allowed the development of plural societies and multiethnic populations for their own economic purposes. Colonialism was an experiment and experience that European bureaucrats were defining, hence the varying views of the colonial mandate we have from different White masters. These historical developments left behind a bitter aftertaste when states in the region gained independence, where samples of ethnic cleansing, genocide, and racial riots became an unfortunate legacy. It is hoped that this chapter gives the reader a broad understanding of the issues at stake which influenced the Whites' perceptions of the peoples, activities, and cultural landscapes of a colonial city in the making. In the following chapters, the operationalisation of White perceptions of Singapore unfolds.

3

Tumasik: Surrogate Kingdom in the *Alam Melayu*

Chapter 3

TUMASIK: SURROGATE KINGDOM IN THE *ALAM MELAYU*

I. Unfolding the Historical Processes

Singapore would seem to have at least three possible origins or starting points: (1) Tumasik[1] or Singapura, 1299; (2) the British colony, 1819; or (3) the independent city-state, 1965. Thus, it is necessary to ensure there is no confusion in the historical narrative. The ancient thalassic kingdom of Singapura was glorified in Malay myths and fables, and continued to stir the Western imagination long after its demise. The romance of the past and Singapore's ancient origins were continuing staples in Western perceptions of the Orient. Singapore's mythological past had been embedded in the European ideas of a 'fabled Orient' for centuries. However, according to German historian Jürgen Osterhammel (2018), with the Enlightenment and secular developments in Europe, came the Western "unfabling of the East". The 19th-century British colonial period of Singapore reflected a marked contrast to the earlier historical processes of Tumasik which were immersed in local myths, legends, and fables. Nonetheless, this chapter provides the preceding context to Western views of Singapore during the island's colonial era, particularly the beginnings of Western thinking about Singapore and their fascination with the Malay foundations of Tumasik.

---

[1]The historical name for the ancient port-kingdom of Tumasik is spelt variously as *Temasek*.

The historian Prasenjit Duara (1995) coined the term 'contingent history' to underscore the view that most historical narratives are written with a current perspective in mind, and that such a perspective is generally based on hindsight. Singapore's current success as an economically viable global city calls for finding past attributes that have led to its pivotal importance. The book *Singapore from Temasek to the 21st Century*, edited by Karl Hack, Jean-Louis Margolin, and Karine Delaye (2010) is a prime example of contingent history. It would be a different history if Singapore had faded into oblivion after Stamford Raffles' founding. Historians would be seeking explanations for its failure, or it might never even have become a subject of academic attention. Certainly, there would have been less attention paid to Singapore's history had the current city-state not blossomed.

Those who argue that colonialism conferred certain benefits will place the start of Singapore's history with Raffles' 1819 founding, and the associated aura of British rule, as one of the great colonial success stories of the region. Revisionist historians on the other hand see Singapore's history in the manner of Fernand Braudel's (1972, 1973) *longue durée*, as spanning 700 years (Kwa, Heng, and Tan 2009). Choosing a date for the genesis of Singapore history and its civilisational influences, cultural trends, and key personalities is thus no easy task. It reflects a dilemma which historians face, or what Craig Reynolds (2008) has termed "the myth of a fresh start", versus "the myth of continuity". Did Singapore have a continuous 700-year history or a new historical beginning in 1819 with Raffles' founding?

In each of the three phases of Singapore's history, the port-city made a notable statement. The thalassic kingdom Tumasik, 'sea town' in old Javanese, created a key regional footprint in the *Alam Melayu* (the Malay World), becoming a pivotal entity which would be difficult to ignore in the historical narratives of the region. Yet, Tumasik was never the centre of the *Alam Melayu*. Its importance lies in having been a historical link between the two great centres of the golden age of Malay power — the Sri Vijayan mandala kingdom and the Malacca sultanate. Raffles mentioned that without a knowledge of Malay history he would have never discovered Singapore. Regional histories recorded Tumasik's existence but the port-kingdom never attained the same grand significance that the regional hegemons of Sri Vijaya, Majapahit, and Malacca had of their own accord.

The narratives of Tumasik and Singapura, concerning their origins, history and regional influence are complex because they are evidence of several cultural undercurrents, historical processes, and geopolitical crossroads, and are often subject to varied interpretations. Tumasik was geographically located in the Riau Archipelago (Long 2013); culturally, it formed part of the *Alam Melayu*, especially the Malay linguistic realm (Benjamin 2002); historically, it was linked to the Indianised state of Sri Vijaya (Wolters 1999). According to the *Sejarah Melayu* or *Malay Annals*, it was economically a precursor to the great emporium and sultanate of Malacca; and in legend and mythology, it remains central to regional Malay folklore (Kwa 2010). Despite its connections, however, Tumasik is not always recognised in the Malay historical process. Unlike the *Sejarah Melayu* which links Singapore to Sri Vijaya and Malacca, the famed colonial scholar Richard Winstedt (1953), who wrote his classic overview *The Malays: A Cultural History*, never mentioned Tumasik or Singapore as part of Malay cultural history.

Hence, the historical unlocking of Tumasik's past has not been a satisfactory process. Its opaqueness has remained a matter of curiosity and interest for European historians. The birth of 13th-century Tumasik gradually began to have implications for the region's geopolitical machinations, and this lent a historic aura to the Lion City. The audacity of Tumasik's rise amidst regional hegemons was no doubt short-lived, but it filled an important void between the end of the Sri Vijaya empire and the flowering of the great global port of Malacca. In a cultural sense, one might view Tumasik as the continuation of the great Malay empire of Sri Vijaya; the surrogate kingdom that kept alive the importance of the *Alam Melayu*. Generally, as far as European accounts of Tumasik are concerned, the legendary image of this port remained undiminished, despite the sacking by the Majapahit empire and the Siamese that finally led to its downfall in the 14th century. Like for many ports of the region, Singapore's diminished role was best explained by economic factors. Malacca's rise overshadowed Singapura's economic importance, and merchants gravitated to the new emporium of Malacca.

Since Singapore attained its independence in 1965, its various place names or toponyms (topo = place; nymic = name) have gained more interest. Many countries have names derived from historical events, dates, personalities, or geographical features. The modern name of Singapore comes from a mix of history and myth. Singapore's former name of *Tumasik* dates from before the 13th century. It is difficult to ascertain its meaning and what it referred to specifically, about which there is much speculation and educated guessing. However, given that the *orang laut*, or 'sea gypsies' (Sopher 1965) populated the area, the island or part of the island must have derived its name from them. Many of the early names in the area came from wandering *orang laut* who often identified prominent coastal features as their reference points in navigation. Around Singapore, the Orang Suku Laut (literally, 'People of the Sea') remained the main *orang laut* group which inhabited both the northern and southern gateways to the Straits of Malacca.

In the southern gateway, the *orang laut* roamed around the island of Batam and the wider Riau Lingga Archipelago (Chou 2013, 43). It is difficult to determine whether they used either *Tumasik* or *Singapura* as terms of reference to define Singapore Island, or whether their references were purely to geographical features as signposts around the island in their navigation of the area. Space is an abstract concept but the *orang laut* perceived the seas through their mental maps as "life- and living spaces not hampered by state-defined borders and boundaries" (Chou 2013, 50). Interpretations of the precise and perhaps variant meanings of the terms *Temasek* (Malay), *Tumasik* (Javanese), or the Chinese transliteration of *T'am-a-siak* are supposedly broadly derived from the term *tasikor* meaning 'the sea', which might be the name the *orang laut* gave to the island we also now identify as *Tumasik*. The *orang laut* also had names for parts of coastal Singapore such as *Pasir Panjang* or 'long sands', and *Tanah Merah* or 'red land', a reference to the red lateritic soils. The rock outcrop in the sea east of Singapore was also well identified by *orang laut* as *batu puteh* (white rocks) well before the Portuguese navigators translated it to their language as *pedra branca*.

The *orang laut* derived their place names based on two different types of reference to their areas of operation: (1) *tempat saya* refers to 'my place' or 'my area'; and (2) *tanah saya* refers to 'my territory' or 'my region'. *Tempat* (area or place) refers to moorage and settlement zones whereas the network of these areas constitutes a *tanah* (territory or region) (Chou 2013, 58). By the time Raffles landed in Singapore in 1819, the island was the *tempat* to many *orang laut* groups: Orang Geylang, Orang Kallang, and Orang Seletar. The *orang laut* comprised the majority of the estimated population of 1,000 to 1,700 (Hooi 1985, 11).

It is also difficult to say whether *Tumasik* referred to the island of Singapore or just the trading kingdom at the southern tip of Singapore. Contemporary regional chronicles and historians appear to have used the name in association with its thalassic form, in reference to the 14th-century port-kingdom which was ruled by a princely ruler or raja. On the other hand, Western cartographers, historians, and travellers used the term

Singapura to define the port-city in a manner more descriptive of its urban function. Certainly, when Western cartographers from the 15th to 18th centuries were locating Singapura, they did not know it was an island. The Western cartographic references to Singapore have a variety of spellings: *Cingapura, Singapoera, Sincapure, Simcalura, Cingapolo, Sirapura,* and *Singapura*. They place the port-kingdom on the southern end of Johore, in various locations that ranged from its east to west. Singapore was a place name imprinted on numerous maps of the region but its history, lifespan, and native rulers remained a subject of myth, historical speculation, and legend. The early references to Singapore as *Ujong Tanah* (farthest land) reveal the contemporary ambiguity of the kingdom's geography. As an island off the southern end of the Malay Peninsula, Singapore was never the extreme southern tip of the Asian continent. That appellation should rightly go to what is now called the modern Malaysian state of Johor.

II. What's in a Name: The Mythological Toponym

Unlike the history of the region since the 16th century which reflects a rich Western documentation through books, letters, maps, charts, artefacts, and paintings, the pre-16th century recorded perception of the region is generally sparse. Insights into the history of Tumasik and Singapura come from varied local historical records, Chinese dynastic records, and accounts of travellers from the Middle East and China. There are written testimonies of Singapura's existence by the Chinese traveller Wang Dayuan, and several other Chinese references to *Tan-Ma-Hsi* (Tumasik), *Lung Ya Men* (Dragon's Teeth Gate), and *P'u Luo Chung* state (Pulau Ujong or Ujong Tanah) (Hsü 1982). There is the Majapahit 14th-century poem *Nagarakretagama* (written in 1365), also called *Desawarnana*, meaning 'a description of villages', as well as the records known as the *Pararaton* and the *Tantu Panggelaran*. Later publications like the *Sejarah Melayu* (called the *Malay Annals*, but more correctly translated as *The Dynasty of Melayu*) (Lach 1965, 505), provide interesting insights into the origins of Tumasik. All the early Chinese references to *Lung Ya Men* describe it as a pirate-infested area, where the crews of ships were butchered, and merchandise looted (Hsü 1982, 2).

Despite numerous regional references to Tumasik and Singapura, there were hardly any on-the-spot accounts of these port-kingdoms. The only eyewitness account of the Tumasik town comes ironically from an unknown Chinese traveller Wang Ta-yuan (Wang Dayuan), in his text entitled *Tao-I Chih-lioh* (*Tao Yi Tchih Lueh* or *Daoyi Zhilue*). The other

Chinese sources do not refer to Singapore and the modern Chinese scholar Hsü Yün-Ts'iao (1982, 9) has stated that *Pulau Ujong* is the oldest name of Singapore. Wang, however, noted that the port-kingdom of Tumasik had Chinese residents and that they dressed like the native population (Hsü 1982, 2). This seems to have been a feature of the overseas Chinese population in Malacca, Batavia, Burma, and Siam. The soils in the kingdom were said by Wang to have been "infertile" and hence yielded "little rice". Trade appears to have been the main economic activity though the residents in the port were apparently accustomed to pillage (Hsü 1982, 2).

Historical verification is mixed with mythology in discussing the birth of Singapore, and this has been particularly accentuated by local perceptions of how it received its name. The most authoritative Malay history text, the *Sejarah Melayu*, according to John Miksic and Cheryl-Ann Low (2004, 15), "stands as a mythicized history, rather than a mythical history". The Portuguese historian João de Barros gave a whimsical etymology of Singapore's name. He wrote, "anciently, the most celebrated city which existed in the land of Malacca was called Cingapura, which, in the language of the country, signifies 'false delay' (*false demora*)" (Dennys 1894, 347). Nicholas Dennys (1894, 347), however, gave his own interpretation for Singapura's name, stating that it derived from *Singahor*, a place of call, and *pura*, a city. The Chicago historian Donald Lach (1965, 507) partly endorsed Dennys' view when he stated that both Barros and Alfonso de Alburquerque believed *Singapura* to have meant "treacherous delay" in the local language. For the Australian historian Anthony Reid (2009), the chronicle of the Malacca-Johore dynasty explained "the cataclysmic loss of the dynasty's great capital to the Portuguese". Thus 16th-century Portuguese interpretations of the name *Singapura* differ greatly from that of the *Sejarah Melayu*, the supposed authoritative source of the historical processes, personalities, power plays, and political events that led to the rise of the Malacca sultanate.

Working through the various preceding European versions of the *Sejarah Melayu*, the linguist John Leyden (2009) wrote its first English translation which was printed by Raffles in 1821 after Leyden's death (Bastin 2019, 82). The *Sejarah Melayu* is often used as the most important source dealing with the transfer of royal power from Sri Vijaya to Malacca via Singapore. While there are two major variants of the text, the most commonly cited version is the *Raffles MS No. 18* publication, which was copied by Raffles in 1812 and published by Winstedt in 1938

(Wake 1983, 129). The *Sejarah Melayu* records that a Sumatran prince, Sri Tri Buana, who fled from Palembang (the centre of the former Sri Vijayan thalassic empire), landed in Tumasik in 1299. It identifies more personnel surrounding the 'discovery' of Singapore Island than subsequent Western historians, administrators, and travellers have dealt with.

In his version, Leyden (2009, 36) noted that the Sumatran high official Demang Lebar Daun had a grandson called Sang Nila Utama, who married a princess. He later became the raja of Bentan, and also the character central to Singapore's discovery. It was Sang Nila Utama who landed ashore around the mouth of the river "Tamasak" (Leyden 2009, 43–44). A vivid description of what transpired is narrated:

> There they saw an animal extremely swift and beautiful, its body of a red colour, its head black and its breast white, extremely agile, and of great strength, and its size a little larger than a he-goat. When it saw a great many people, it went towards the inland and disappeared. Sang Nila Utama enquired what animal was this, but none could tell him, till he enquired of Damang Lebar Dawn,[2] who informed him that in the histories of ancient time, the singha or lion was described in the same manner as this animal appeared.
>
> ... and thus Sang Nila Utama settled in the country of Tamasak, named it Singhapura, and reigned over it, and was panegyrized by Bat'h, who gave him the name of Sri Tri-buana. He reigned long over Singhapura, and had two sons, both of them very handsome ... (Leyden 2009).

In his translation of the *Sejarah Melayu*, C. C. Brown (1982, 39) had a slightly different interpretation of the events surrounding Singapore's discovery and naming. He noted that while in Tumasik, the prince (Sri Tri Buana) saw a mammal in the bushes at Kuala Tumasik. Not knowing what it was, he asked his prime minister for its identity, whereupon he was told it was a lion. Brown himself (1952, 30–31) had earlier translated from the *Sejarah Melayu* the passage of Tumasik's name change:

> And they all beheld a strange animal. It seemed to move with great speed; it had a red body and a black head; its breast was white; it was strong and active in build, and in size was rather bigger than a he-goat.

---

[2] An alternative spelling of *Demang Lebar Daun*.

When it saw the party it moved away and then disappeared. And Sri Tri Buana inquired of all those with him, "What beast is that?" But no one knew. Then said Demang Lebar Daun, "Your highness, I have heard it said that in ancient times it was a lion that had that appearance. I think that what we saw must have been a lion." ... Sri Tri Buana said to Indra Bopal, "we propose to establish a city here at Temasek" ... Sri Tri Buana then established a city at Temasek, giving it the name of Singapura.

The prince, pleased with the sighting, called his island-kingdom *Singapura*, the Lion City. Leyden's (2009) translation would appear to suggest the Sumatran royalty's familiarity with Indianised culture and perhaps the idea of other cities in the region being named after lions. Leyden, however, did not make as pointed an identification of a lion as would Brown's translation. The latter's statement of Demang Lebar Daun's belief in the sighting of a lion should call attention to the incongruous fact that this was not an animal found in the Southeast Asian ecosystem. However, lions are found on the Indian subcontinent. The long history of trade and religious pilgrimages between India and Southeast Asia must have led to the diffusion of Indian symbolism and lion myths to Southeast Asia. As Sheldon Pollock (2006) has shown, the Sanskritisation process which began in India came to include Southeast Asia in one cultural-geopolitical entity without distinction.

The general Western view is that the name *Singapura* is derived from the Indian language to mean the 'city of the lion'. As Oliver Wolters has suggested, one cannot take the *Sejarah Melayu* at face value. The historian believed that the author of the *Sejarah Melayu* was trying to interpret history in a changing geopolitical sense rather than provide an authentic record based on real events and documentations (Wolters 1970). Anecdotal evidence from modern Singapore might indicate just how problematic taking the *Sejarah Melayu*'s account at face value could be. Malays have been brought up with the knowledge that *Singapura* refers to *singha* = lion and *pura pura* = pretending, which is supposed to mean either an animal 'pretending' to be a lion or the early discoverers mistaking it for a lion. Were the *Malay Annals* a fictionalised attempt to celebrate the rise of Islamic Malacca and subtly but ultimately put down the Buddhist-Hindu kingdoms of Sri Vijaya-Palembang and Singapura?

If one uses the literal translation of *Singapura* based on Sanskrit, then the meaning of 'Lion City' is more evident after comparisons with regional towns with similar names. The Sanskrit reference to lion cities is found in several other places — Singaraja in Bali, Singasari in Java, and Singapura in Champa, Vietnam. The town of Amaravati (now Tra Kieu) was under the Chams called *Singapura*. In the Kra isthmus area, the small state of Singora, near Songkhla, was named as an abbreviation of *Singapura* in Sanskrit. The historical geographer Paul Wheatley (2008, 255) noted that the Chinese sent a mission to *Simhapura* (the Lion City), the capital of the Red Earth Country, which he believed was located around Pattani. *Singapura* became an auspicious name in the region, but none of these lion cities were sustainable thalassic states. The 14th-century Tumasik-Singapura trading port too was short-lived, although it revived in 1819 after Raffles founded his British entrepôt.

While earlier Western references were cartographically represented as mere dots in southern Johore, one of the earliest clear representations of Singapura (Singapore) would be in the 1548 map by Giacomo Gastaldi with its enlarged version of "*cincapula*". The mathematician Emanuel Godinho de Erédia was the first 'Westerner' (actually a Portuguese Eurasian) to provide an outline of Singapore Island in 1604. In his report on the Golden Chersonese, produced between 1597 and 1600, Erédia (1997, 228) mentioned that at the end of the promontory (meaning the Malay Peninsula) was "*Sincapura*, or *Ujontana*". The Malays referred to Singapore Island or Johore as *Ujong Tanah*.

Unlike other Westerners, the Portuguese mathematician did not say much about the origins of Tumasik or Singapura. Erédia (1997), using Ptolemy's earlier cartographic demarcations, had divided the 'Indian region and island world' into three areas: (1) India within the Ganges (*India Intra Gangem*); (2) India beyond the Ganges (*India Extra Gangem*); and (3) Meridional India or Southern India. The Portuguese were interested in finding cartographic representations from various earlier travels in the region, such as Marco Polo's (1871). Given their quest for gold and other treasures, they were keen to discover Ptolemy's "beach" and "veach" (a misspelling of "beach" which made its way onto maps) or "the land of gold" (what might be identified with the Australian continent) (Erédia 1997, 67–68).

The journalist Dick Wilson attributed the 'Lion City' (*Singapura*) name to the Majapahit empire. He noted that a sect of Bhairava Buddhism was dominant in Majapahit in the 14th century. According to the British journalist, esoteric priests might have adopted the "soubriquet 'lion' to symbolise the character of their demoniacal orgies", and as Singapore passed from Sri Vijayan to Majapahit hegemony it acquired its name for "religious reasons" (Wilson 1975, 33).

Despite the supposed name change by its ruler, the regional and Chinese empires referred to Singapura as *Temasek* or *Tumasik*. In its century (1299–1398) as a thriving trading port, Tumasik was a magnet for Southeast Asian and other traders from China, India, and the Middle East. In the Majapahit records, Tumasik and Singapura are referred to as dependencies of the Javanese empire in the mid-14th century, although Slametmuljana (1976, 194) noted that they probably were "not identical" places. The 14th-century literary work *Desawarnana* (*Nagarakretagama*) by the Majapahit court official Mpu Prapañca (1995, 34) details travels in East Java in 1365. The *Kakawin* (form of verse or poem) mentions many kingdoms, regional ports, and Malay lands including Tumasik. Wang referred to the new port as *Longya men* (Dragon Teeth Strait) because of the prominent rocks on either side of the entry into Singapore. By 1340, the Malays were referring to Singapore as *Tumasik*. The area was viewed as dangerous because it was infested with pirates.

Wang Dayuan, one of the first known Chinese visitors in the region, whose voyage lasted four years, wrote the *Daoyi Zhilue* (*Description of the Barbarians of the Isles*), where he mentioned 99 places in his travels (Bowring 2019, 105–106). Wang visited Singapore twice during the Yuan era; the first time he referred to the place as *Longya men*, and upon the second as *Tumasik* (Bowring 2019, 106). In 1349, he noted that people in Tumasik lived around what the British would later call Fort Canning Hill. The Chinese traveller also recorded that the town had city walls, which served defensive purposes. Wang gave the first eyewitness account of the people in Tumasik. He observed that they wore short hair, and had patterned satin turbans and red cloths (*sarongs*) around their bodies (Bowring 2019, 106). This being the only known eyewitness account of the port during its heyday, historians have had to hinge their views of 14th-century Singapura society and trade on every word of it. By the time the great voyages of Zheng He (Cheng Ho) were made into the region from 1405 onwards, the port of Tumasik was being passed over and the new port of Malacca had become the mecca for both regional as well as East-West trade.

III. The Thalassic Kingdom Remembered

Historians view the period between the 15th to 18th centuries as the 'black hole' of Singapore's history. In Dennys' (1894, 349) *A Descriptive*

Dictionary of British Malaya, one is reminded of Singapore's absent history: "... for a period of about five centuries and a half. There is no record of Singapore having been occupied, and it was only the occasional resort of pirates". While nothing significant was documented during this time, the myths surrounding Singapore's past took root more deeply through the *Alam Melayu.*

Ironically, while the port of Singapura lay dormant for several centuries, Western historians, travellers, explorers, merchants, and bureaucrats were reviving its name, image, and importance in the narratives of the region. Singapore's fame would grow over time. Part of this lay in the myths and legends in Malay folklore surrounding its origins and demise. European scholar-administrators, who were deeply interested in the history of the region, fed the European public imagination and kept alive the memory of Singapore as a fabled thalassic kingdom. Despite the fact that there were no European eyewitness accounts of the thriving 14th-century port, Singapore's name in association with that period became ever more legendary.

Though no Westerner was known to have yet visited Tumasik, Western historians of the time paid tribute to it. Barros referred to "the celebrated city of Cingapura, to which resorted all the navigators of the western seas of India, and of the eastern of Siam, China, Champa, and Camboja, as well as of the thousands of islands to the eastward" (Danvers 1888, 109). John Crawfurd would prove sceptical about Barros' high praise of Cingapura as he himself found no real evidence of permanent building materials on site: "Earth, brick, unknown sandstone, and wood, seem to have been the only materials made use of, and there is not a vestige of granite which abounds in the neighbourhood and is now so largely employed" (Crawfurd 1856, 402). What Crawfurd was implying was that there were no permanent structures and buildings to testify to Singapura's past greatness.

Tumasik was modelled after the Indianised cities in Indonesia which had a long period of gestation based on Hindu-Buddhist cosmic symbolism (Nas and Boender 2002). Tumasik was a kingdom, and hence the port-town revolved around the *kraton* or palace. The town was marked by a moat and rampart covering 54,000 square metres (Kwa, Heng, and Tan 2009, 44). The native quarters for merchants, traders, and others were located below the *kraton*, around the Singapore River. The *kraton* was located on the hill of today's Fort Canning, thus overlooking the town.

Like all thalassic (sea port) kingdoms in the region, Tumasik represented the morphing of the religious-ceremonial and secular-commercial roles. For Western sojourners of the 16th century, Tumasik's significance was in trade, while historians of the region gave tribute to its legendary ritual function. Unfortunately, the commercial importance of Tumasik was short-lived and had already been overtaken by the dazzling flowering of Malacca in the 15th century. But its ceremonial stature persisted in the region's myths, legends, and folk tales.

Paradoxically, the historical myths and fables of the 14th-century Tumasik-Singapura grew deeper and wider in the Western consciousness after the Portuguese conquered the prized Malacca in 1511. While contemporary regional and Chinese records use the term *Tumasik*, European documentation refers overwhelmingly to *Singapura*. Portuguese, Spanish, Dutch, and English historians and bureaucrats (Barros, Tomé Pires, Duarte Barbosa, António Bocarro, Diogo do Couto, Erédia, and later Raffles, Crawfurd, and Winstedt) over the centuries all gave their own versions of the birth of Singapura and upgraded its importance in the *Alam Melayu* through their writings. The British lawyer Roland Braddell (1935, 164) turned the spotlight on Singapore's misty past by noting that the Sri Vijayan empire had planted a colony in "Tamsak or Tamasak" and founded a settlement called in Sanskrit, *Singapura*, the City of the Lion, which recalled an earlier Sri Vijayan inscription that titled one of its kings 'Royal Lion'. Based on varied spellings of earlier Western travellers such as Johan Nieuhoff, Jan Huygen van Linschoten, and Pires, which emphasised the 'k' sound in *Sinkapura* or *Symgapura*, Miksic (1985, 28) has, however, hypothesised that an earlier place name of *Singapura* derived from Singki Point (Batu Belayer) and Singkir Straits (between Sentosa and Berani Islands) was a more likely possibility than a reference to the mythological lion city fable.

For Roland Braddell (1935), Singapura was founded sometime in 1250 and conquered by Majapahit by 1365. Yet, the British administrator found it strange that, despite its "considerable importance", neither the name *Singapura* nor its phonetic equivalent appeared in any records until the earliest Portuguese books on the region in the 16th century. Braddell (1921a, 1:18) also called the founder of Malacca, Iskandar Shah, 'The King of Singapore'. Miksic (1985, 19) has interpreted the *Sejarah Melayu* to mean that earlier on, Demang Lebar Daun (district chief of the 'Palembang' area; 'Lebar Daun' refers to the broadleaf vegetation around

Palembang) had surrendered power to Sri Tri Buana who became the first king of the Malays in AD 1179. It was Sri Tri Buana ('Lord of the Three Worlds') who founded Singapura (referred to as *Ujung Tanah* or Land's End) and lived there till 1226 (Miksic 1985, 19). Both Sri Tri Buana and Demang Lebar Daun were buried on "the hill of Singapura" (Miksic 1985, 20). Western historical interpretations of Singapore's mythical history, according to Kwa (2010, 140), have been based on the Western bias towards *logos* or rational argument, and are dismissive of *mythos* or fable and folklore. The place of Singapore is baffling because while so little seems to be known about it, it appears to have been a central piece in the jigsaw of geopolitics of three historical narratives: those of the Majapahit empire, Sri Vijaya, and the Malacca sultanate. The narratives also underscore Indian religious and cultural scaffoldings which colonial and present day historians still debate. Furthermore, there are the inconsistencies in the translations of the *Sejarah Melayu* by various Westerners (Miksic 1985, 19–20).

Currently archaeologists use the huge number of artefacts and trade items from their digs as testimony to the thriving 14th-century port, thus underscoring the Malay narrative of Singapore's golden age (Miksic and Low 2004). Like the other native thalassic kingdoms of the *Alam Melayu* (Sri Vijaya, Malacca), Singapura is bereft of monumental structures to glorify its greatness. Unlike the agricultural kingdoms of Angkor Thom and Java with their significant ruins, Singapore has nothing similar to show for its purported golden era. One might ask whether this is common with all port-kingdoms, where perhaps the evidence lies in their trading produce and artefacts? Or did the greatness of the Singapura kingdom lie more in its utility as a concept or idea formulated by historians to demonstrate the struggles for hegemony between great regional powers, which they recalled in terms of the 'historical' events of Singapore's founding and existence?

IV. Geopolitical Tussle by Regional Hegemons

The names of the port-kingdoms of Tumasik or Singapura reflect the intense geopolitical competition in the 14th century, between the dwindling Sri Vijayan empire in Sumatra, an ascendant Majapahit empire in Java, and the dominant Siamese kingdom. In reading the *Sejarah Melayu*, one might conclude that Tumasik was the creation of the ailing Sri Vijaya.

Given that Tumasik-Singapura was the intermediate polity from the fall of Sri Vijaya to the rise of Malacca, it is opportune to view the Singapura connection between these two towering thalassic kingdoms. The major studies of these kingdoms are Wolters' (1967, 1970) *"Origins"* and *"Fall"* of Sri Vijaya, and Kernial Sandhu and Paul Wheatley's (1983a) two-volume tome on the "transformation" of Malacca (1400–1980). Each provides some insights into the links of these great international emporia with Singapore. Wolters' is one of the most important case studies of the creation and "fall" of Sri Vijaya which underpinned the birth of Tumasik-Singapura.

Basing his work heavily on the *Sejarah Melayu*, Wolters (1970, 49–127) attempted to make historical sense of the events that led to the birth and demise of Singapore and the creation of the famed Malacca sultanate. The trigger of this historical sequence was the fall of Sri Vijaya, which caused a political vacuum in the Straits of Malacca that spawned Tumasik-Singapura, a surrogate port of the famed Sumatran thalassic kingdom. Singapura was, according to the *Sejarah Melayu*, an extension of the dying Sri Vijaya-Palembang kingdom. As Wolters (1970, 78) has noted, the ambitious Palembang prince Sri Tri Buana tried to "recoup his fortunes" by fleeing Palembang, appealing to the Malays of Bentan for support, and making Singapore his "permanent capital".

In their historical overview of Malacca, the historical geographers Sandhu and Wheatley hardly mentioned Singapore's role in the rise of Malacca in the 15th century. They were more concerned with the origins of Malacca as a precolonial thalassic kingdom within the context of the region's historical developments of ports and Indianised cosmic cities (Sandhu and Wheatley 1983b). It would seem that they were more interested in demonstrating Malacca's independent rise as a thriving Malay emporium on the one hand, and its links to the Sri Vijayan empire on the other. Singapore's role in Malacca's birth is insignificant in their analysis, indeed omitted, even though the historical reality points otherwise (Wolters 1970; Wake 1983).

Thus, Singapore's heyday as a "great city, to which foreigners resorted in great numbers" was rather short-lived. As fate would have it, the Singapore emporium became the unfortunate geopolitical victim of two spheres of rivalry between maritime and mainland Southeast Asia: the Javanese Majapahit empire and the Siamese kingdom. The city-state was first attacked from the south by Majapahit and then from the north by Siam, the Siamese attacks occurring twice in the 14th century.

Reading sources from Majapahit, the birth of Singapura becomes a creation of the Javanese empire. The powerful Majapahit had defined its State in the *Nagarakretagama* in three spheres: (1) administration for the whole of Java (*Javabhumi*); (2) sovereignty over "other islands" (*nusantara/dvipantara*); and (3) authority recognised by all "other countries" (*desantara*) (K. Hall 2011, 279). From this edict, Tumasik was thus part of Majapahit's *nusantara*. The golden age of the Majapahit empire (1334–1364) was when Gajah Mada became the *patihamangkubhumi* (the chief minister of administration). According to the *Pararaton* records, when Gajah Mada became the highest-ranking minister, he announced his ambitious geopolitical programme, referred to as the *sumpahnusantara*, in which he expressly set out to conquer all the kingdoms in the *Alam Melayu*, including Tumasik, before he retired (Slametmuljana 1976, 59). This ambitious plan caused consternation amongst courtiers in Majapahit, which was then a very small kingdom. Under its second king, Paduka Sri Pikrama Wira, Tumasik-Singapura was attacked by Majapahit because its king failed to pay proper homage and respect to the empire (Miksic and Low 2004, 37). Tumasik was under Siamese patronage when Majapahit successfully conquered it in the mid-14th century, whereupon it became Majapahit's "dependency" (Slametmuljana 1976, 139).

Singapura's fifth and last ruler Parameswara was supposedly a usurper, who fled the kingdom via Seletar because the Siamese were unhappy that he had overthrown the Singapore ruler whom they recognised. Lach (1965, 506–508) has provided a more detailed account of Singapore's fall and the birth of Malacca. According to Malay tradition, the ruler of the "great mart" of Singapore was called a *sangesinga* or the 'lord of Singapore', who was a vassal of Siam (Lach 1965, 507).

During the 14th century, there was a revolt in one of the Javanese kingdoms, and one of the rebels came to Singapore for refuge. The Javanese émigré called Paramiosa (Paramesvara or 'the supreme lord') was graciously received by Singapore's *sangesinga*, but Paramesvara repaid his host by treacherously killing him (Lach 1965, 507). He took over the kingdom and ruled Singapore for five years with the aid of Javanese rebels. The Siamese king, on hearing that his Singapore vassal and son-in-law had been killed by Paramesvara, attacked the city by land and sea. Paramesvara fled the city with his followers, the Cellates (people of the straits, who lived on fishing and piracy) and founded a new city, near the Muar River (Lach 1965, 507). When Paramesvara died, his son,

Xaquem Darxa (Sikandar Shah) took over and called the city Malacca in memory of his father. According to Lach (1965, 508), *Malacca* means 'exile' in the Malay language. Hence, Malacca's founder was an exile from the Singapore kingdom or his earlier birthplace of Java.

The names of Singapura's ruler and the founder of the Malacca kingdom tend to lead to historical confusion. The *Sejarah Melayu* refers to the last ruler of Singapura as Sultan Iskandar Shah, a Muslim. Yet history tells us that the last king of Singapura who fled the city when attacked by the Siamese still bore a Hindu name, Parameswara. It begs the question of whether Sultan Iskandar Shah and Parameswara were the same person. In piecing together this puzzle, historians believe that the position of the last king of Singapura, Sultan Iskandar Shah, was usurped by a renegade Sumatran prince Parameswara, who had been expelled from Palembang and spent six years in Singapura (from 1391 or 1392, to 1397 or 1398) before being driven out by the Siamese. *Parameswara* was a high title that was used in India, Java, and Bali, rather than the name of a person. Hence, the reference to Singapura's Parameswara was likely a reverent one by *orang laut* to the chief of Singapura. However, the *Nagarakretagama* notes that Parameswara converted to Islam in 1413 when he was 72 years old and adopted a new name: Megat Iskandar Shah (Slametmuljana 1976, 146). The *keramat*[3] at today's Fort Canning is said to be the grave of Singapura's last king Iskandar Shah; certainly, it is the belief amongst Singapore Malays that it holds the remains of a royal personage. The Muslim name of Iskandar Shah creates another puzzle as to when Singapura's rulers might have converted to Islam. Is the Keramat Iskandar Shah the grave of the Muslim convert Parameswara whose body was brought back to Singapura from Malacca for reburial?

Until the Portuguese conquered Malacca in 1511, the port city thrived and became one of the most important trading centres in the world. The resident apothecary Pires showed that Malacca controlled the trade in Europe. The rise of Malacca also cast an economic shadow on other regional ports and kingdoms. Jambi and Palembang became quiet, and the ports of Surabaya, Gresik, and Tuban lost their merchant visitors from China, India, Persia, and the Arab lands because they preferred Malacca (Slametmuljana 1976, 191). Historians speculate as to why Malacca

---

[3] A *keramat* in the *Alam Melayu* is a sacred or holy site (grave of a Muslim holy person) which is a product of religious syncretism between the earlier native animistic beliefs and Islam.

thrived without regional military interference, unlike Tumasik, which had been attacked by regional hegemons. Seen in its historical context, however, the flourishing kingdom of Singapore did not end with the Siamese sacking of the port. Singapore's demise as a regional port had more to do with the rapid rise of Malacca. As Lach (1965, 508) has contended, Malacca soon rivalled Singapore, and "merchants began to emigrate from Singapore to the new mart at Melaka".[4]

Likely aware of a continuing threat posed by regional hegemons which had attacked Tumasik, Parameswara knew that he needed Chinese patronage to stave off similar attempts on Malacca. After fleeing Singapura, he founded the famed Malacca port-kingdom around 1400 and sought almost immediately Chinese imperial recognition in 1405 (Miksic and Low 2004, 17). According to the notable historian Felipe Fernández-Armesto (1995, 128), the voyages of Zheng He were designed to "show the flag" and to demonstrate China's "launching-bay of a seaborne empire". The visit of the Chinese Muslim eunuch admiral to Malacca underscored the Chinese protection of the city-kingdom. He gave Parameswara "a silver seal, a cap, and official robes and declared him king", upon which he also remarked that "Malacca ceased to be a dependency of Siam" (Purcell 1965, 236). From then on, Malacca would fall effectively within the Chinese geopolitical sphere and its sultans would give tribute to the Chinese emperor. The journalist Philip Bowring (2019, 139) observed that Malacca had not been previously viewed as a real country, but that Zheng He raised its status to that of a state so that "Siam dare not disturb it". This significant political intervention by Zheng He demonstrates that, contrary to what many historians say, his Indian Ocean voyages were far from pacific explorations. Malacca's political allegiance to the Chinese emperor was an important historical event for the region.

V. The Tumasik Legacy

Despite the economic significance of Malacca and the overshadowing of Singapura, the 14th-century port-kingdom remains important in the history of the *Alam Melayu* for three reasons. Firstly, Tumasik-Singapura was the key historical link between the Sri Vijayan empire and the rise of

---

[4] The historical name for Malacca is spelt variously as *Melaka*.

Malacca. Without Singapura's role, the historical narrative of the *Alam Melayu* would be incomplete. Singapura was founded by a Sri Vijayan prince, and the 'last king' of Singapura, the rebel Parameswara, founded the Malacca sultanate. The significance of Singapura is in having filled a large part of the *Sejarah Melayu*, especially as a precursor to the Malacca sultanate. While Javanese historical sources proudly praise the Javanese empires of Singasari and Majapahit, the *Sejarah Melayu* clearly places Singapura as a central strand in the history of the Malay World. Indeed, all the references (*Tumasik, Singapura, Pancur, Ujong Tanah*) to the 14th-century trading prodigy were derived from Malay. As Chinese traveller Wang noted, the port-kingdom was governed by "natives".

As much as it has an Indianised history, Singapore was also an important historical touchstone in Malay history. So much has been written recently about the origins, identity, diffusion, and impact of Malay culture (Benjamin and Chou 2002; Long 2013; Kozok 2015), that one should not forget that its heart lies in the Straits of Malacca. The regional and international recognition of Malay culture was developed in the thriving emporium of Sri Vijaya-Palembang (Wolters 1967, 1970). Trade created a functional *Alam Melayu* where Malay became the common language of its commercial networks. Every Westerner in the region from the 15th century onwards realised the importance of Malay and many spoke a smattering of it. Is it any wonder that Indonesia on gaining independence, chose a minority language within its own borders (a variant of Malay, otherwise known there as Bahasa Indonesia) as its national language? After Malacca's glorious history, the seat of Malay culture shifted to the Malay Peninsula, which would be named *Tanah Melayu* or Malay land. Wolters (1967, 1970) has demonstrated how the pivot of Malay culture shifted from Sri Vijaya-Palembang to Malacca via Singapore in the 14th and early 15th centuries. Till this day, the tussle for the origins of the Malay cultural hearth seems to be between Indonesia and Malaysia, both continually dominating headlines with regard to which place was the origin of different aspects of Malay culture, be it dance, music, or food.

John Bowen has argued that the link between Sri Vijaya-Palembang and Malacca was cemented through genealogy. There was a major shift in the "politically salient Malay model of kinship", from an "alliance model" to a "descent model" (Bowen 1983, 162). With the coming of a Sri Vijayan prince to Tumasik, a foreign historical intervention would change regional history. Western historians, geographers, and anthropologists have essentially chosen two ways to link Sri Vijaya to Malacca: (1) genealogically via their royal families; and (2) symbolically through royal-spiritual signatures. The Chinese Ming historian T'ai-tsu had also reconstructed the Malay historical lineage using the Palembang royal family rather than basing it upon the spatial capital of Palembang (Wolters 1970). This meant a migration of the Malay royal lineage from Palembang to Singapore and finally Malacca. As Wolters has argued, "Palembang could once again have become the Malay *negara*. Singapore could also have been that *negara*". However, with Iskandar's expulsion from Singapore and his flight, "Malacca therefore became the new capital" (Wolters 1970, 173). A *negara* is a Malay polity or state. Wolters meant that with the rise of Islamic Malacca, both Palembang and Singapore lost out on the future chance to be the Malay state par excellence. It is unsurprising that he titled his book *The Fall of Srivijaya in Malay History*, thus alluding to the monumental nature of the end of the long raja-dominated history of the Malay World over 1,200 years.

Singapore's brief involvement in Malay history was clearly significant because it was the go-between for Sri Vijaya-Palembang and the Malacca sultanate. The baton of Malay culture, carried by royal personages, was passed from Sri Vijaya-Palembang to Singapore, to Malacca, and finally to the Johore kingdom based at Johor Lama (Wolters 1970). C. H. Wake has observed that local chroniclers shifted the links between Sri Vijaya and Malacca from those of alliances to genealogy; hence the meaning of the *Sejarah Melayu* being 'The Descent of Kings'. In fact, the 1638 Aceh edition provides a genealogy of the Malacca kings (Wake 1983, 129). Wolters (1970) on the other hand has contended that the purpose of the *Sejarah Melayu* was fictional, in order to legitimise Malacca's claim to the overlordship of the Malay World. What we see in the shifting of the Malay cultural centre reinforces what the Berkeley historian Frederick Teggart (1962, 217) has argued, that in history, one sees a "continual shifting of culture centers" where a single geographical area is outstripped by another.

Secondly, despite its declining importance between the 15th to 18th centuries, Singapura remained a key symbolic licence for sanctifying kingdoms in the region. Kwa Chong Guan (2010) has put Singapore in a central place in Malay history and identity. In reviewing the historical evidence, however, Kwa (2010, 150) debunks the argument that Singapore was "a strategic or geographical centre for the Malay world". He believes rather that Singapore held an "important central place in

Malay myths and social memory". Ironically, the Western travellers, bureaucrats, and traders turned the Malay oral mythical tradition into a more substantive written documentation.

The early Portuguese historians and administrators (Pires, Barros, Couto, Erédia, Barbosa, and Gaspar Corrêa) who wrote on Malacca and its Singapore connection based their writings on an "oral tradition" rather than the "aristocratic" written tradition of the *Sejarah Melayu* (Wake 1983, 134). Going by the oral tradition, there are varied interpretations of the significance of the transfer of power from Sri Vijaya to Singapura. The reference to Sri Vijaya-Palembang could have alluded to a hero-chief or a temple rather than a lion. One might deduce whether the *singha* in the name *Singapura* was a corruption of the Sanskrit word *simha*, denoting temples based on Indian architecture (*vastushastra*). The word *singha* does not only mean a lion but also a 'chief'. In Bali, the word *singaraja* refers to a hero-chief rather than a lion-king. However, the *Sejarah Melayu* disregards the colloquial meanings of these terms and superimposes its own interpretation of the rise of Malacca. As such the whole 'historical account' of the origins of Malacca has been clouded in myth, varied versions, and different interpretations (Wake 1983, 134–140). The writings of various Western visitors and sojourners in the 19th century like Capt. Peter Begbie (1834, 355–360), Thomas Newbold (1839, 1:272–278), and John Thomson (1849a, 618) recount and elaborate on Singapore's mythicised history in a similarly ambiguous manner.

Three of these mythical stories relating to Singapore and the region deal with magical stones. They were probably taken from the *Sejarah Melayu* (C. Brown 1952; Leyden 2009). The association with magical stones comes from a long tradition of animistic beliefs in the region. The Malays believed in *batu hidup*, meaning living stones, often venerated as *keramats*. Singapore's three myths with regard to stones are: (1) the death of Tun Jana Khateb who was executed by the raja of Singapore, whereby his blood turned into stone but his body was buried in Langkawi; (2) the invasion of Singapore by the Majapahit empire through the treachery of Sang Ranjuna Tapa, who was put to death by the raja, whereupon his body turned into stone; and (3) the lifting and throwing of huge stones far away, by a man of remarkable strength named Badang, during the reign of Sri Rajah Vicrama. One of them landed at the mouth of the Singapore River and another in India (Begbie 1834, 355–358). Narrations like these from Singapore's legendary past intoxicated Western travellers with the romance of the Orient. Yet, after its brief historical sparkle the Lion City fell into what Thomson (1849a, 618) called "obscurest insignificance". If Kwa's perspective is correct, these stories demonstrate that Singapore played a myth-making role for the Malays in the *Alam Melayu*, which would have given the Lion City its binding relevance to Malay social history.

In the *Alam Melayu*, the sacred power of the kings emanated from the sacred mountain of Bukit Seguntang Mahameru in Sri Vijaya. The mythology of the sacred mountain goes back in time to a Tamil text referring to an "ancient Malaiur, a stronghold situated on a high hill", which also reminds us of Marco Polo's (1871, 223) reference to a "fine and noble city" called Malaiur in Sumatra which Polo himself had never visited. For Roland Braddell (1935), *Malaiur* was the Tamil version of Melayu, the Sumatran origins of the Malay.

The sacred hill in Sumatra is significant because Malay sultans traced their ancestry to Alexander the Great through an Indian prince who married a mermaid, the daughter of the kings of the sea. The prince revealed himself on the hill of Seguntang, around Palembang (R. Braddell 1935, 167). This was the mountain at which was the divinely ordained centre of the cosmos, used by Southeast Asian kingdoms to legitimise their kingship traditions based on the cult of mountain worship. Mountains in the region were symbols of dynasties and sacred power. In central Java, the dynasty of the Sailendras was based on the imperial title 'King of the Mountains', and was responsible for the Buddhist stupa of Borobudur which was modelled after a mountain. In the ninth century, a prince from Java ascended the throne in Sri Vijaya with that same title of 'King of the Mountains' (Le May 1956, 77). According to Reginald Le May (1956, 84), E. J. Thomas, the great authority on Buddhism, had informed him of *Sailendra* being the name for the Himalayan mountains, and of the Ganges as being the 'daughter of the Sailendra'. Le May (1956, 83) asked therefore whether the Mahayanist Sailendras, who spread their art and culture in the region, had originated from India. Mountains were viewed as the abode of ancestral spirits, as well as of Hindu-Buddhist deities from whence rulers derived their supernatural and magical powers. The Sri Vijayan kings, for 600 years, took as their title 'Great Maharaja, King of the Mountain', the adoption of a royal mountain-cult having "played a tremendous part in the creation of the Malay civilisation which we know today" (R. Braddell 1935, 168).

When the Sumatran prince established his kingdom in Singapura, he brought with him the magical power of the Sumatran sacred mountain to his residence on Fort Canning Hill, otherwise known to the Malays as *Bukit Larangan* or 'forbidden hill'. In Singapore, unlike Sri Vijaya, however, the kings lived on the hilltop. The use of the term *forbidden* has two possible origins. One is that the hill was forbidden to people in reverence of its sacred and royal aura, because the first king of Singapura and his chief minister, Demang Lebar Daun, were said to be buried there. Hence, from the time of Singapura, all sultans and rajas in the Riau Archipelago needed to derive their transference of spiritual power from Fort Canning Hill. The other is that the hill was forbidden because Malays believed it to be the haunt of ghosts and evil spirits. Raffles debunked the latter, believing the sacred royal hill to be in need of respect.

Given that the mountain symbolism from whence the *devaraja* or god-king received his spiritual powers was so prevalent in the region's Indianised kingdoms, Fort Canning became a sacred hill or Mount Meru. In the Malay World, the sacred hill, amongst other paraphernalia, legitimises *daulat*, which is a kind of "mandate from heaven", thereby imbuing the ruler with semi-supernatural powers (Miksic 2004, 46). According to local beliefs in the region, it was through the mountain symbolism that Tumasik would have been linked to the Sri Vijayan empire. Fort Canning functioned as the symbolic hill where the royal power of Sri Vijaya's Bukit Seguntang Mahameru, its 'Mount Meru', was transferred to Tumasik's first king, Seri Teri Buana or Sri Tri Buana (Kwa, Heng, and Tan 2009, 41). Fort Canning Hill became the centre or Mount Meru of Tumasik's *vanua* or empire.

Singapura remained an important icon and symbol of Malay royal *daulat*. The *daulat* of the king is well captured in the *Sejarah Melayu*. It relates how the conquest of Tumasik by the Majapahit army was due to a conspiracy by the Tumasik high official Sang Ranjuna Tapa. Subsequently, the king uttered a curse against him whereby he turned into stone by the Singapore River, while his house collapsed and his rice turned into soil (Slametmuljana 1976, 135). One could say that Raffles, who read Malay and was steeped in Malay history, built his house on Fort Canning Hill, seemingly in the belief that he was a Malay raja with all the attributes of one. In his words:

> The tombs of the Malay kings are ... close at hand; and I have settled that if it is my fate to die here, I shall take my place amongst them (S. Raffles 1830, 535).

Seen within the broader historical context, Singapore was probably one of the last kingdoms in the region to underscore important mythical narratives. Using the mountain symbolism, Singapore's 13th- to 14th-century historical flourishing gave Southeast Asia's historians and court chroniclers a way of linking it to the many surrounding thalassic and agricultural kingdoms. The mountain symbolism used to define kingdoms, empires, and native dynasties was a pivotal link that gave legitimacy to kingdoms and kingship. It is one of the most pervasive Indian motifs in the region, designating the association with royalty and the city as cosmos (Wheatley 2008, 248–257).

The mountain symbolism was also significant to the region in other ways. It fused the indigenous cult of mountain spirits with the Indian conceptions of monarchy (Wheatley 2008, 256). Hence the mountain symbolism provided 'historical' continuity in the region despite the arrival of the foreign Indianising culture. Also, the mountain symbolism linked the royalty and cosmic cities of mainland Southeast Asia with the region's island kingdoms. There was a common recognised royal symbolism across political entities in the region. Furthermore, the mountain symbolism allowed for an indigenous, mass awareness and recognition of royalty, order, and social hierarchy. The adoption of mountain symbols took various forms. In indigenous cities, the designated cosmic mountains were located outside the city. With Indianisation, the royal temple-palace was located on top of a hill or mountain like in Singapura. In most post-Angkorian Indianised kingdoms, the sacred temple (Wheatley's 'ceremonial centre') or palace had architecture symbolising a mountain; one sees this in the tiered *chandis* in Bali, the Khmer Angkor Vat, and Buddhist Borobudur in Java.

The third reason for which Singapura remains important to the *Alam Melayu* is that its founding gave historical insight into the importance of the Straits of Malacca as a maritime conduit of trade, and for the diffusion of religion, goods, people, and ideas. It demonstrates that location plays a key role if percipient leaders can capitalise on it. Since Ptolemaic times, thalassic kingdoms have developed along the Straits of Malacca (from Kataha or Kadaram, these being ancient names of Kedah, down to current-day Singapore). The lucrative funnel of trade has been the stage of not only thalassic kingdoms, but also the mobile *orang laut* and pirates. Roland Braddell (1935, 156) put the importance of the straits in a wider geopolitical context when he observed that the tide of trade shifted from India and Ceylon in the seventh century with the rise of Sri Vijaya, "and as the Straits of Malacca form the essential passage for that tide, the power which commands those Straits obtains a position of paramountcy".

VI. Summing Up: Tumasik's Historical Watershed

In a way, Singapore signalled the end of Indianisation in island Southeast Asia as the rise of the Malacca sultanate in the 15th century did not associate itself with mountain symbolism. The rebel Parameswara broke Indianised cultural ties with the region's kingdoms when he wished that Malacca be "treated as a subject state of the Middle Kingdom in order to excel and be distinguished from the barbarian domains" (Levathes 1994, 109). As Craig Lockard (2009, 67) argues, Parameswara had probably political and commercial as well as spiritual intentions. After his supposed conversion to Islam and change of name to Sultan Megat Iskandar Shah, Malacca became the *Dar al-Islam* (House of Islam) in the region. The emporium's powerful trading links were important conduits for the religion's spread in Southeast Asia.

The religious conversion of Malacca's ruling house diluted the Indian cultural influence and modified its symbolism with the adoption of Chinese imperial yellow as the badge of Malay royalty as reflected in its laws (the *Undang-undang Melaka*), which were culturally borrowed from China after Zheng He's visit. Under Zheng He, Malacca was elevated to the status of a vassal of the Chinese empire, and the West mountain of the city-state was no more a symbol of the Hindu Mount Meru, but viewed as the "Guardian Peak of the Kingdom" (Levathes 1994, 109). After converting to Islam, the sultans then drew comparisons of Malacca with the Middle East and not South Asia. The last ruler of Malacca Sultan Mahmud Syah (1488–1528) wanted his state to be of equal importance to Mecca (Andaya and Andaya 2015, 103).

In ancient Southeast Asia, both the mountain symbolism and the idea of the *devaraja* taken from Cambodian kingship, among other religio-cultural trappings, provided links to Indianisation. The Singapore raja represented both Indian symbolic attributes. The Sanskrit name of the Lion City also supports Pollock's (2006) thesis that Sanskrit was a lingua franca that linked the Indian subcontinent to Southeast Asia. The Sanskritisation process covered a vast area, which transcended kingdoms in South and Southeast Asia, bringing them into cultural unity. Singapura was a product of Indianisation and in that vein, very much an expression of the then identity in Southeast Asia.

Miksic's 2013 archaeological excavations testify to 14th-century Singapore's strong Indianised religio-cultural influences. Subsequently overshadowed by the rise of Malacca, its economic and political importance would fade into oblivion. Hence the thalassic kingdom never became a major centre of Islamic diffusion in the region once the tide began to turn in favour of that religion. It would be Raffles who much later reinvented Singapore's importance, capitalising on its locational advantages, and cementing the British strategic stake in Asia.

Did Sang Nila Utama stumble on Tumasik by chance or was his visit to the island a deliberate intervention? Whatever his intentions, the Lion City which he established became the envy of regional hegemons. Singapura's rise as a trading centre was a threat, whether imagined or real, to neighbouring ports. As an emporium it was a great success story. Had it grown unimpeded, the region's history might have been different. Would Zheng He have stopped in the Lion City and not Malacca, or the Dutch have initiated the region's colonial process in Singapore?

Ironically, the colonial era interpretations of the genealogical and symbolic links between Sri Vijaya and Malacca via Singapore are somewhat confusing, complex, fictional, and tenuous. The connections between Sri Vijaya and Singapore are stronger than the hazy ones between Singapore and Malacca. Nor can there be a direct genealogical relationship between the rulers of Sri Vijaya and Malacca when counterarguments show that Parameswara, the fugitive from Singapore and founder of the Malacca sultanate, was a renegade from Java, a "subject to Majapahit" (Wolters 1970, 108) rather than a prince from Palembang-Sumatra. Wolters (1970, 128–153) has provided the most exhaustive interpretation and analysis of the genealogical links between the rulers of Singapore and the early rulers of Malacca. Contending that the rulers and events in the Singapore story cannot be taken at face value, he has argued that Sri Tri Buana (first ruler of Singapura) and Iskandar Shah (last raja of Singapura) provided a "substitute" in Palembang history. Furthermore, elements of the story have been "deliberately modelled on Malacca history" (Wolters 1970, 144) in the sense that they have been scripted to legitimise the narrative of Malacca's rise. Whatever the truth of the matter, it appears that Singapore's role in the Malay historical narrative from Sri Vijaya to Malacca cannot be taken lightly. It seems to have been an integral component in the golden years of Malay power, when the Malay maritime focus was a controlling pivot in world trade.

The symbolic (royal-spiritual) relationships between Sri Vijaya and Malacca are also weak compared to the Sri Vijayan-Singapore connection. As we have seen, the regional maritime community viewed the transfer of spiritual power and symbolism as being from Palembang's sacred hill of Bukit Seguntang Mahameru, to Singapore via Sri Tri Buana, the "supernatural" founder of Tumasik-Singapura (Wolters 1970, 128–135). The Buddhist-Hindu spiritual connection between Sri Vijaya and Singapore was severed, however, when Parameswara converted to Islam and became Megat Iskandar Shah. Buddhist-Hindu spiritual hegemony in the *Alam Melayu* died with the birth of Malacca and the diffusion of Islam throughout the island world of Aceh to the Sulu Archipelago. According to Wake (1983, 150), the first five reigns of the Malacca sultanate provided "a dynamic model of the processes of Islamisation in a *passisir* state". Singapore's rulers represented the tail end of the Hindu-Buddhist influence in the thalassic kingdoms of the Malay Archipelago, and Malacca the new religious influence of Islam in the region.

Singapura's short blip in the historical narrative belies its importance in the regional myths and legends surrounding its existence. Singapura was a precursor to Raffles' great 19th-century foundation of the British East India Company factory. What today's Lion City continues to represent is the ability of an extraordinary location to stand the test of time. The importance of Singapore's location has unfolded in the manner by which each of its historical polities (Indianised kingdom, colonial city, independent city-state) would over time discover and capitalise on its own relevance, its pivot, and its centrality in the changing geopolitical environment.

4

One Man's Vision: Raffles' Singapore 'Child'

Chapter 4

ONE MAN'S VISION: RAFFLES' SINGAPORE 'CHILD'

I. Singapore: The Raffles Gamble

> Raffles was high-strung, clever, articulate, impetuous, charming, small in stature and physically fragile. He had unusual resources of energy, curiosity and resilience. He had a loving heart. He was loyal, supporting and promoting his friends to an extent that was injurious even in a time of accepted patronage and nepotism (Glendinning 2012, xiii).

Western perceptions of Singapore must begin with an understanding of how its colonial creator, Sir Thomas Stamford Raffles, thought of Singapore and altered the trajectory of its historical narrative. The founding of Singapore is a crowning achievement in the annals of British history, but these have surprisingly little documentation of Raffles' choice and administrative decision to make Singapore an East India Company (EIC) factory. There was not much discussion with his superiors over Singapore; Raffles simply acted on his own. The establishment of British interests in Singapore was thus unprecedented in colonial history. Raffles' own written promulgation of this great achievement first appeared in the *Calcutta Times* (Moore and Moore 1969; Flower 1984, 29). The article was reprinted in *The Times* of London, and beamed forth optimism about his own feat for a home audience:

> We believe and earnestly hope that the establishment of a settlement under such favourable circumstances, and at a moment when we have

every reason to fear that the efforts of the Dutch had been successful in excluding us altogether from the Eastern Archipelago, will receive all the support which is necessary to its progress and that by its rapid advance in wealth, industry and population ... it will attest hereafter the wisdom and foresight of the present administration, and its attention to the commercial and political interests of our country (Flower 1984, 29).

In trying to understand Raffles' choice of Singapore, one needs to uncover his political-philosophical thinking, as contained in sources such as his book *The History of Java* (T. Raffles 1817), or his letters compiled by his wife Sophia. In an unequivocal sense, the choice of Singapore as the location for a trading settlement between India and China was a product of one man's percipience. Despite the fact that by the 19th century Europe had overtaken the East in economic terms (Pomeranz 2000), European fascination for the Orient had not dimmed. China still remained an objective in many colonial ambitions. For the British, the prospect of securing China would have promised to fulfil its Oriental equation of bringing two Asian economic giants under its direct influence.

Against all odds, Raffles was determined to make Singapore the lasting legacy of his Oriental administrative sojourn. His locational choice and far-sighted vision of Singapore's potential still reverberate in the present circumstances of Southeast Asia. Colonial Singapore would become the linchpin of the India-China maritime trade route, and Singapore's port would be the ideal location for a regional emporium. From the point of view of understanding the importance of the geopolitical environment, Raffles' selection of Singapore remains an interesting case study in cognition. Based on his earlier accounts of the region, one deduces that he chose Singapore for three reasons distilled through his comprehension of Western narratives at the time: (1) as a geopolitical trump card against Dutch influence; (2) to destroy and dilute the powers of neighbouring polities; and (3) to make Singapore the regional centre of trade. In short, Singapore was to become the catalyst of Southeast Asian commerce.

Reading the contemporary Western travel literature, one might wonder whether Singapore had been totally beneath the Western cartographic radar at the time, as Raffles appears to have made it out to be. It seems that Capt. Alexander Hamilton (1727), in *A New Account of the East Indies*, had recorded his own meeting in 1703 with the prince of

Jehore (Johore), who offered him the island of Singapore as a present. Hamilton turned down the offer, reasoning it to be of no use to a private individual. Singapore was thus already 'on offer' a full century before Raffles 'founded' it. Did Raffles first chance upon the possibility of Singapore's importance through the account of Hamilton's 35 years (1688–1723) of wide-ranging travels and trade in the region, and did this lead him to his choice of Singapore? John Crawfurd's (1830, 2:401) own later reference to the Johore prince's offer to Hamilton was meant to prove that Singapore's commercial importance was not only a product of Raffles' 19th-century vision. As Crawfurd (1830, 2:401) wryly stated, "the island of Singapore was well known to be a suitable place for a commercial emporium, above a century before we occupied it as such". Rather than having read Hamilton's episode of the offer, however, it is likely that Raffles discovered the importance of Singapore's history and location in reading the *Sejarah Melayu*. From studying the location of thalassic kingdoms over several centuries, he must have realised that the Straits of Malacca was the heart of maritime Asia, and that Singapore provided an enviable location.

Subsequent travellers often cited Singapore as being well known to discoverers, merchant captains, and navigators well before Raffles (I. Anderson 1934, 169; Crawfurd 1856, 403; Dennys 1894, 349; Robequain 1958, 136). Raffles himself had toyed with other locations such as Riau, Carimon Island, and the Johore River before he settled on Singapore (Dennys 1894, 349; Crawfurd 1856, 403; Buckley 1965). On this point, Crawfurd (1856, 403) tried once again to diminish Raffles' importance in securing Singapore. While Raffles had obtained a small patch of the island for the EIC, the second British Resident of Singapore asserted, the "sovereignty of the whole island, with its adjacent islets to the Malay princes, were quickly experienced, and obviated by a treaty which I drew up in 1824 under the direction of the Earl of Amherst, then governor-general".

Despite attempts to discredit Raffles' 'discovery' of Singapore, there is no evidence that any of his contemporaries had thought of Singapore as a base for the EIC. The company had had a rather interesting history. It had been in existence for over 200 years before Singapore's founding by the British. By the 18th century, the two European East India Companies, the Dutch (*Vereenigde Oost-Indische Compagnie*; VOC) and the English (EIC), were competing vigorously in the region for territory, produce, and trade. Both were chartered joint-stock companies, independent organisations to which certain "extra-territorial rights" had been allotted (Barendse 2002, 424). As the British colonised India, the EIC set up three Presidencies (Bengal, Madras, and Bombay) to look after its interests, and factories (for example, Singapore) established under these Presidencies had considerable autonomy (Barendse 2002, 430). The EIC within England was purely a trading company, but outside the country it operated like a state, taking on political, economic, and defence roles (Barendse 2002, 429).

When Raffles sealed a deal with the sultan and *temenggong* for Singapore, it was a major cause of geopolitical friction between the VOC and EIC. At that time, there was little public awareness of the friction. The major knowledge of Anglo-Dutch rivalry comes from an 1824 letter by the Dutch Col. Nahuijs, who asserted his "strict neutrality" on the matter and went on to give a glowing account of Singapore under British governance (Miller 1941, 192). Steering away from the bitter rivalry, Nahuijs averred that he spoke not as a "citizen of Holland, but as a World citizen" (Miller 1941, 192). He was all praise for the EIC taking Singapore out of the hands of "pirates and murderers" and bringing it under the "possession of civilized Christians", and regretted as a Hollander that they had not themselves wrested Singapore from the pirates (Miller 1941, 192). To cool Dutch anger over the British takeover of Singapore from right under their noses, Nahuijs stressed that the "free port of Singapore [would] not be so detrimental" to Dutch interests (Miller 1941, 198), but would prove an asset to exports from both Holland and Java (Miller 1941, 199). The spheres of territorial jurisdiction between the Dutch and English were finally settled in 1824 and remained so till the time that both their colonies attained independence. Albeit, the Dutch would, during the colonial era, continue to smart with the EIC's possession of Singapore and so set up their own free port in Macassar to compete with it.

If there is any lesson that independent Singapore has learnt from the legacy of British colonialism and the EIC, it has to be the importance of maintaining global linkages and macroeconomic optics, so as to tap into the vitality of the global economy. Before the institutionalisation of the nation-state, trade in the region was based on port-cities like Tumasik. With colonialism changing the geopolitics of trade, Singapore's free port status allowed it to operate like a free political entity. As such, for a long time international trade would be based at a pre-national level, or what Barendse (2002, 5) calls the "ecumenical age".

Raffles was a beneficiary of the Malay history and culture of which he was a student. He also had a hands-on appreciation of geography and ecology; a geopolitical understanding of the Indo-Chinese region that gave him an edge over his peers in advocating the locational advantage of Singapore in free trade. For him, Singapore's contemporary attraction did not lie in buried treasure, fabled romances, or hidden mysteries. In fact, the early allure of the place had been short-lived, dramatic, and almost defeatist. But it taught the lesson that sustainable success has to be defended and managed well. Raffles was a product of his time. He was an Englishman caught up in the nationalistic competitions that were unfolding in Europe and being translated to Southeast Asia. The Dutch were a revered mercantilist power, whose dominance in the spice trade gave them a certain superiority over the British. The British contempt for Dutch ascendancy in the region was reflected in much of Raffles' thinking. He was also an agent of imperial ideology and served loyally in British empire-building. Like many of his contemporaries in the 19th century, he believed in the superiority of Western intellectual thought and governance, and hence took a patrimonial stance to colonial policy.

With his landing on the island in January 1819, Raffles initiated a game change in colonialism with the establishment of modern Singapore. This was the year Singapore became a factory of the EIC, beginning nearly 145 years of its colonial rule. It would become the main beachhead of the British colonial process in the Malay Peninsula, and its primate city: the political nerve centre, its economic gateway, and cultural capital. As Singapore grew and flourished, so did Raffles' name become synonymous with the colony's success. Yet, it is ironic that despite this single-handed establishment of the EIC's settlement with which he is credited historically, Raffles might be better known as a naturalist, a scholar, the discoverer of Borobudur, and an Indonesian expert. Certainly, the British Museum's exhibition (held from December 1998 to April 1999) of the Raffles Collection acquired in 1859 is said to have been of the oldest systematic collection of Indonesian material in Europe, overshadowing Raffles' fame vis-à-vis Singapore (Barley 1999). The exhibition threw light on his interests in nature, *batik*, *wayang kulit* puppets, magic coins, the *gamelan*, and Tengger Buddhism, but nothing on Singapore. In many ways, the exhibition mirrored Raffles' eclectic abilities, his diverse curiosities, and fascination with regional native culture. As a long-time resident in Singapore, Noel Barber (1978, 16) astutely observed:

his greatest asset was his lack of single-mindedness; he was master of so many pursuits that from the very first discussions when he landed on Singapore, the people greeted him as friend, above suspicion; they were delighted (and astonished) to hear him speak their language fluently, astounded that he knew their manners and customs.

Singapore, it seems, was Raffles' idea, dream, and vision that was 'becoming'. He rode on a mystical past and envisioned a virtual future for his 'child'. There are few examples in history where one man's stoic belief and vision becomes a successful idea of a colony and city. It is difficult to imagine the gamble that Raffles took on his Singapore proposition. In his 1819 letter to William Marsden, he considered the risk of his failure to realise success in Singapore should his superiors not support him: "This will probably be my last attempt. If I am deserted now, I must fain return to Bencoolen[1] and become a philosopher" (Coupland 1934, 101).

Many other writers and scholars have paid Raffles prodigious compliments for this achievement (Barber 1978, 15–51; Coupland 1934; Earl 1837, 352; Buckley 1902; Cross 1921). Charles Burton Buckley (1902, 1:1–61) dedicated several chapters of his anecdotal history of Singapore to Raffles and the circumstances surrounding the EIC acquisition. He affirmed that Munshi Abdullah, a contemporary of Raffles, was impressed with the way Raffles had treated and conversed with the native chiefs in Singapore. Abdullah's *Hikayat Abdullah* in a way confirms Raffles' credentials in the *Alam Melayu* as a British administrator who was well versed with the Malay language and culture. His knowledge of Malay was an asset few Western administrators of his time had acquired. Over the decades, the *Hikayat Abdullah* has been translated by many Western residents in Singapore (D. C. Boulger, John Thomson, Roland Braddell, and in James R. Logan's *Journal*) both in part and in full, becoming for Westerners a holy grail of Malay perception of Singapore's founding, and establishing a benign view of Raffles.

In short, Raffles, despite his superior knowledge of science and history, demonstrated respect for the natives and Malay culture that won support for his proposal from the *temenggong*'s people. He did not appear to have exhibited Western contempt of native culture in negotiating a British factory in Singapore. Buckley (1902, 1:35) has shown that constructing a treaty with the *temenggong* and sultan was a

---

[1] Named variously as *Bengkulu*.

delicate and tricky exercise. Separate compensations had to be given to each of them. Given that neither the *temenggong* nor *sultan* could write, Raffles ensured that the treaties were fair and transparent. The Malay leaders thus viewed him as trustworthy and as a friend. Abdullah, according to Thomson's translation, wrote that Raffles hated the Dutch who lived in Malacca, and who had the habit of "running down the Malays. But Mr. Raffles loved always to be on good terms with the Malays, the poorest could speak to him" (Buckley 1902, 1:47).

As Buckley (1902) reflected, Singapore was secured by Raffles at a time when competition amongst the Dutch, French, and Americans for a share of the China trade was developing intensely. As the English hydrographer James Horsburgh argued, "If we retain the settlement of Singapore, great security will be afforded to our China trade in the event of war" (Buckley 1902, 1:61). Raffles had seized upon Singapore at the right time, against the conventional wisdom of the many directors of his company. Historically speaking, the rise of Singapore from nowhere was like a freak occurrence; as if one morning, the EIC had awoken and inherited a great entrepôt. In some parallel sense, the Dutch historian R. J. Barendse has tried to enunciate the sudden rise of Britain as a global power. But historians are "uncomfortable" with explaining historical milestones as flukes (Barendse 2002, 492). Hence, the following detailing of Western narratives of Singapore's rise hopes to fill a more reasoned account of its success.

Revisionist historians of Raffles such as Syed Hussein Alatas, Victoria Glendinning, and Nadia Wright have tried to take away some of Raffles' historical shine and the many roles ascribed to him. Alatas (1971, 51) has provided a damning correction of the "persistent historical canonization of Raffles". Glendinning (2012, xiv) wants to "demythologise him without diminishing him". For her, Raffles was a visionary with a stroke of genius. On the other hand, Wright (2017) feels that the person really behind Singapore's early development was William Farquhar. Yet, his role has been downplayed and almost forgotten in history. According to Wright's treatise, Farquhar was instrumental in keeping Singapore in British hands, away from the Dutch at a critical phase of its history. For what he did, Farquhar received no gratitude but was humiliated by Raffles. Accusing Farquhar of not following his commands, Raffles dismissed him from his post as First Resident, a term used in the early years to define what was essentially a governor's position. In response, Farquhar would swear that he was not one to contravene Raffles' commands. Wright has come to the historical defence of Farquhar's contributions and there is no need to rehearse them here. However, while Raffles' name is emblazoned on many streets, place names, institutions, and businesses, Farquhar's name does not appear at all — 380 streets in Singapore are named after Britons, but none after him.

Unfortunately, Farquhar was in Raffles' eyes the upstart, the spoiler of his plans for Singapore. The tragic irony is that it was Crawfurd, not Farquhar, who had been jealous of Raffles occupying the limelight and tried subtly in his writings to rob him of credit for Singapore. While few would doubt the singularity of Raffles' idea of Singapore, it would in hindsight be difficult to deny Farquhar's important contribution in defence of the factory at the critical phase immediately after its foundation. After all, Raffles was not a continuous resident in Singapore during this time, when Farquhar had to uphold British possession of the factory without any real support from the colonial authorities in India. He displayed independent thinking, and a sharp understanding of the geopolitical ramifications of the British taking of Singapore from under the noses of the Dutch. Nevertheless unlike Raffles, Farquhar had fewer supporters and friends in high office, and his dismissal by Raffles was accepted unproblematically. Such is the fate of accurate accounting for facts.

With regard to the historical interpretations of Raffles' contributions, it seems always easier from hindsight to denounce, criticise, and demolish the efforts and impacts of past personalities. One of the few 'Orientals' to have reviewed Raffles' role in Singapore's history is Alatas, former head of Malay Studies at the National University of Singapore. Adopting a sociological approach, the professor was critical of historians using "unhistorical" approaches and "ethnic biases" to the extent that Western biographies of Raffles look like a "conspiracy". Alatas (1971) levelled trenchant criticisms at Raffles, stating his role in Singapore's history as having been "exaggerated". He further stated that Raffles' political philosophy was an "ideology of imperialism" that was prejudicial, politically manipulative, and "contradictory". He felt that Raffles' reforms of native society were based on "imperialist ideology", that he had been a "parochial nationalist", and far from a "humanitarian reformer", or an "enlightened despot or autocrat".

While Alatas was right in stating that one should evaluate Raffles' contributions "in the light of changing circumstances" (Alatas 1971, 2) and the "entire historical configuration" (Alatas 1971, 41), he missed the point that Raffles was a product of his time, and not one acting from the hindsight of postcolonialism. Raffles' actions reflected in many ways his political philosophy, nor did he claim consistency in executing them in varied administrative duties. To criticise Raffles for being a "parochial nationalist" is to identify something that was not peculiar to his generation. Since the Western creation of the nation-state, nationalism had been a motivating force in colonialism. In the 21st century, nationalistic politics still remain the order of the day in geopolitics. Presidents Trump, Putin, and Xi are not global humanists. Furthermore, Raffles was a relatively small player in the wheels of a large bureaucracy in the EIC. At the end of the day, we have to credit him, and not later colonial administrators and their subsequent management, with the idea of Singapore, his lasting legacy.

As Francis Fukuyama (2018) argues, 'identity politics' will remain an important ingredient in nationalism because human societies are always searching for recognition. Raffles was an astute administrator and he capitalised on Malay culture as a means of galvanising local support. Right in the heart of Singapore's European Town he planted the *padang* or town square, a feature common to most Indonesian indigenous towns. Richard A. O'Connor (1983, 80) has contended that the British administrator "manipulated indigenous symbols" as a way to rule. Likewise, one could say that Raffles' location of his house on Fort Canning Hill was a symbolic attempt to demonstrate to native observers his status as a divine ruler.

Yet, for all his lauded achievements in establishing Singapore, Raffles spent hardly more than 10 months there. He only visited three times: (1) for nine days in 1819; (2) another four weeks in May-June of the same year; and (3) eight months between 1822 and 1823. He was an absentee dreamer, schemer, and planner of Singapore, and got credit for it. It might seem to be splitting hairs to describe Raffles as the chief executive of Singapore, and Farquhar and Crawfurd the executors of his policies. From a broader perspective, however, Raffles was the visionary and thinker, and Farquhar the practical implementor of his dreams. As Nadia Wright (2017, 218) argues, "Raffles raised the British flag, but Farquhar ensured it stayed flying". It took two to clap and bring Singapore to fruition. Despite the brunt of Raffles' criticism landing on Farquhar, the second Raffles appointee, Crawfurd, was certainly more shrewd, manipulative, self-centred, and materialistic than Farquhar had been. Notwithstanding, Crawfurd escaped without blemish to his image in his administration of Singapore.

Raffles gained wide publicity for his Singapore vision. Given the slow pace of communication in those days, he exercised audacity in securing Singapore for the EIC. He had already recently gained public credence with his writings, especially his *History of Java* (T. Raffles 1817), a monumental effort that demonstrated local knowledge and understanding of indigenous history. Raffles brought to Western colonial bureaucracy a new type of official, the scholar-administrator, who was adept with local culture, language, traditions, and the tropical nature. Like Julius Caesar, argues German historian Jürgen Osterhammel (2018, 138), Raffles was the model of "the conqueror as historian and ethnographer". More importantly, Raffles had his wife to thank for creating a benign image of him in the region's history. Sophia's (S. Raffles 1830) publication of his letters distributed to various administrators revealed his most private thoughts and exposed his percipient thinking on Singapore, as he envisioned its future and expressed faith in its development.

Without Raffles' vision for Singapore, its history and success might never have been. The Raffles name has been synonymous with Singapore's development as an extraordinary trading centre, international port, and British military bastion, and has resounded through the decades with the many Western biographies of the man. Oxford University historian R. Coupland (1934) was one of the earliest academics to frame Raffles' vision and selection of a winning location within a wider regional context of the *Alam Melayu*. His biography sets Raffles' importance against the background of his experience in Bencoolen, Malacca, Penang, and Java before his proposal and defence of the takeover of Singapore as the EIC's factory, entrepôt, and settlement. To view Raffles' founding of Singapore in geographical context, one needs to know the historically changing emphasis of the company's motives. Raffles was so steeped in Asian history that he saw himself in various Oriental power roles: as the great Mogul, just as Queen Victoria was the Empress of India (Glendinning 2012, 256), as the Solon of Java (Osterhammel 2018, 337), and as Raja in Singapore (T. Raffles 1817). Raffles threw his political weight and commanding influence in India House and the Foreign Office behind his choice of Singapore and it paid dividends for the EIC from 1819 onwards. He acted against the odds in a sense, for at the time, the Dutch and some of Raffles' own colleagues saw him as a "pirate and a poacher" who did not observe the conventional rules of the game (Coupland 1934, 94). As Coupland (1934, 128) has argued, Singapore has been "Raffles' true memorial". His statue on the island still watches over his political child:

"There, if anywhere on earth, his spirit lingers, at peace, his dream fulfilled" (Coupland 1934, 129).

A century after Singapore's founding the Raffles legacy continued to be apparent to travellers visiting the colony. The naturalist Charles Hose (1927, 37), of his one-week stopover in Singapore, said mainly that he had visited the Raffles Museum for reasons of sentiment: "for it is some consolation that the memory of the man who was so badly treated by his own generation should pervade a great city which he founded". He observed that the Raffles statue at the Esplanade and the landmarks of Raffles Square, Raffles College, and Raffles Hotel perpetuated the notion that "his spirit dominates the whole place" (Hose 1927, 37).

II. The Raffles Vision

Raffles was a one-man visionary of Singapore. The celebrated historian of Singapore C. M. Turnbull (1989, 30) has asserted that it has been his only successful project. If indeed Singapore is Raffles' only achievement, then it has been a massive, incredible, and worthy legacy. The EIC had been looking for a strategic place to establish a trading base for its activities between India and China; Labuan (James Brooke), Balambangan (Alexander Dalrymple), and Carimon Island (Crawfurd) were other suggestions, but Raffles went ahead with his own proposal of Singapore. In reading Crawfurd's (1820) history of the British colonial extensions in the region since the 16th century, it seems evident that Singapore had never before surfaced as a place of geo-economic or geopolitical importance to them. The British over the century prior to Singapore's founding had first concentrated their efforts on making Bencoolen in Sumatra a spice garden as a competitor to the Dutch (Bastin 2019), and later they focused their administrative efforts in securing Penang (Prince of Wales Island) as their prized factory (J. Anderson 1824). There was no reference to Singapore in any of the administrative correspondence at this time. Singapore was clearly Raffles' invention.

In the history of colonisation in the region, few Westerners have single-handedly made an impact in terms of starting the ball rolling. Two come to mind: James Brooke in Sarawak and Stamford Raffles in Singapore. They candidly revealed their colonial schemes through their personal letters. Raffles was a bold individual who was clear about his decision. While languishing in Bencoolen, he studied the region and hatched his plans on Singapore. Once he had made up his mind, he defended them tenaciously. Critics believe that Raffles should not have the high credit which he has often been given for the founding of Singapore; yet, there was no one else in his time who had thought of the island as the ideal site for a British entrepôt. As the Rev. William Cross (1921, 32) later prophetically noted: "Raffles planted a seed of a city, and the city was destined to become a nerve-centre of the whole world".

Colonialism was a turnkey endeavour. Whites were supreme in the social and intellectual hierarchy, dabbling in everything in their colonies, and Singapore was a ripe laboratory for their entrepreneurship. Raffles acknowledged that Singapore's success would be a product of the "energies of her sons" (Buckley 1902, 2:789). He noted that colonialism was not a blind conquest of territory, but saw a broader attribute to Singapore's success, where men would pause in their careers and with moderation and justice consolidate what they had gained (Buckley 1902, 2:789). His was the major task of converting a haven of piracy to a legitimate trading centre. Upon suggesting to the sultan that piracy be stopped, the latter was horrified at the suggestion and averred: "We have always been pirates. The pastime is inherited and so is no disgrace" (Hahn 1946, 469–470). The Malay ruler and his son noted that they could not trade and wondered what the Englishman took them for (Hahn 1946, 469). However, the transformation of Singapore from a den of freebooters and pirates to a market of respectable traders and merchants would be a major coup for the British administrators.

The establishment of colonial Singapore was thus different. This was not a mere imposition of draconian British rule of territory; Singapore from its 1819 founding would be an entrepreneurial experiment. It required traders and merchants of varied European and Asian communities to endorse its entrepôt trade. Singapore's colonial port has been best defined through Manuel Castells' (2010) and Giovanni Arrighi's (2010, 83) conception of a "space-of-flows", whereby a diasporic trading community could be served by the entrepôt space functioning both as a place of identity and a conduit for change. The EIC had to ensure that there were conducive economic conditions to entice entrepreneurs to set up business in Singapore. This was a delicate management strategy that British administrators would become cognisant of. Singapore was also a colonial trading prodigy because the 19th-century global geopolitics had radically changed and in some ways abetted Singapore's success story. Singapore was another important port in what Geoffrey Gunn (2011, 183) characterises as the "Eurasian Exchange", which lasted several centuries. For Anthony Reid (1988) the great period of exchange for the Southeast Asian region was between 1450 and 1680. Yet, most historians would classify the period before 1750 in the Eurasian Exchange as being dominated by India and China; after that the trading pendulum favoured the West (Pomeranz 2000; Mokyr 2017).

By then, the British had become a global power with formidable naval supremacy, while China and India were reduced to poverty-stricken political entities, with the floodgates being opened to Chinese and Indian immigrants in European colonies throughout Southeast Asia. Singapore's thriving trade would be built on the backs of migrant Asian labour.

Buoyed by his immense knowledge of Malay culture and the *Alam Melayu*, Raffles was convinced that Singapore had the perfect location as a trading centre. He had considered the Riau Islands and Carimon before settling on Singapore. In his earlier *History of Java* reflections, Raffles (1817) expressed his nascent geopolitical notions of the Malay Archipelago, and observed the ripeness of the thinly-populated territories of Sumatra, Borneo, and other archipelagic islands as potential European colonies, and receiving art and civilisation from the metropolitan power of the Indian Seas[2] (Britain). He laid down his vision that commercial intercourse, aided by friendly relations or the development of political institutions, might bind the "dispersed communities in one great insular commonwealth" (T. Raffles 1817, 1:71), with trade connecting the great empires of Japan, China, and the countries of Southeast Asia. One might perceive that when Raffles picked Singapore as the EIC factory, this vision of trade and emporium was actually being realised. The centuries of uninterrupted laissez-faire trade via Sri Vijaya, Singapura, and Malacca had cemented the *Alam Melayu* and, as historian Oliver Wolters (1970, 176) has noted, provided the Malay World with "a momentum of its own". Had Raffles not identified Singapore as the outpost for his company, one would never know how regional history might have turned out. Would the Dutch have colonised Singapore? Would Singapore have had a trajectory very different from that of a free port?

Raffles' perceptions of Singapore and his adamant belief in its ideal location were rooted in his broader views of the region. Though he never penned his reasons for the choice of Singapore, aside from that of his knowledge of Malay history, one might approach his thinking on the

---

[2] Referring to the East Indies.

region's geopolitics and administration by comparing him with two other philosopher-administrators, Marsden and Crawfurd. Although none were formally trained academicians, all three men were erudite, deep thinkers on a macro-scale of human evolution, and evinced rather interesting classifications of human development. All three had laid down their political philosophies in writing. They were ahead of their time in thinking and clearly had to struggle between prejudicial Western conceptual thought and their own beliefs developed from observations on the ground. None of them quite fitted into the prevailing East-West cultural dichotomy, nor did they view native populations through the exclusive lenses of the Orientalist prism identified by Edward Said (1979). In a relatively objective manner, they saw the path to enlightened civilisation as one which societies must follow. Hence, the low-level cultural development of societies in the region was rather an intermediate state they were witnessing, than a finite system of societal progression. For them, this state was not a reason for condemnation, for smug comparisons with Western civilisation. They saw before them various early stages in societal evolution, which reinforced their belief that development was a process. The primitive and simple forest denizens or more advanced agrarian peasants were not in a finite condition, nor were their circumstances a given. Such philosophy certainly spurred Raffles into believing that education could make a difference and uplift native peoples from their predicament.

Four important factors need to be considered about Raffles' decision on Singapore. Raffles' 'genius' can be understood by exploring the greater geopolitical and intellectual context of his thinking. Firstly, he was one of the few early British administrators who had been exposed to different administrative commands in the region. He had become well-acquainted with Sumatra at his post in Bencoolen, and before that had been the lieutenant governor of Java for over five years (1811–1816). His administrative tenure at Fort Marlborough in Bencoolen overlapped with his founding of Singapore. These prior positions prepared him for his thinking on Singapore. Unlike Sumatra and Java which were fairly well defined, populated, and developed areas, Singapore was like a blank canvas requiring administration and development from scratch. Raffles proved that he could think independently and afresh when he proposed Singapore as a British factory. Unlike Bencoolen where he strongly supported and encouraged agriculture and the growing of spices (Bastin 2019, xxxi–xl), in Singapore, his economic advocacy was strictly for trade. He was able to customise the importance of Singapore to fit its locational advantages. While Singapore was the fiefdom of the sultan of Riau, Raffles saw it as a relatively unformed cultural landscape that could be developed for British interests.

One might interject that Westerners had not been totally oblivious to Singapore; but foremost among them was Raffles who sensed its potential as a trading port. Raffles' focus on trade underscored a long history of the partnership between global urban development and commerce. Though capitalism was never defined in the context of Raffles' ideas on trade, the political, economic, and cultural foundations of Singapore were linked very much to the development of modern capitalism in the colonial city. Singapore's operationalisation of capitalism has been best summed up in Jacob Cornelius van Leur's (1955, 16) definition of capitalism as "the search for profit on the rationalized basis of money (capital) calculations". It was no coincidence that the EIC as the institution of Singapore's founding was economically motivated and interested in profit and capital accumulation for itself. Hence, Singapore from its modern genesis was modelled on economic life and political capitalism.

Secondly, Raffles, and along with him Marsden and Crawfurd, will go down as three of the early celebrated British scholar- or philosopher-administrators of the region. Each wrote an important history revealing his own knowledge of the *Alam Melayu*. Marsden (1783) wrote *The History of Sumatra*, Crawfurd (1820) penned the *History of the Indian Archipelago*, and Raffles (1817) related *The History of Java*. All three were astute observers of tropical nature and cultural landscapes. Though not academic historians, they saw developments in the region through what Fernand Braudel (1972; 1973) would later articulate as the *longue durée*. All three tried to place local history, indigenous societies, and native kingdoms within a time frame of evolutionary history as developed by Western historians. Unlike smug Western colonialists who were dismissive of native satrapies, the three philosopher-administrators, however, were reflective about native culture and history.

All three subscribed to the Enlightenment ideas that people should be scientifically classified. Unlike Raffles neither Marsden nor Crawfurd had the benefit of knowing that Java had complex historical ruins. Hence, their views of native societies were more negative as compared with his. Raffles had the edge in this matter, given his 'discovery' of the ruins of Javanese kingdoms which shaped his appraisals of the native peoples and their royalty in the archipelago. The British envoy Crawfurd (1820, 1:15), in his history of the region, extended James Brooke's environmental deterministic argument by stating that people in the Indian Archipelago had rich offerings of the animal and vegetable kingdoms but no tendency to "promote civilization". He added that one was tempted to believe that they were "prejudicial to it" since the countries most abundant in nature were among the least civilised in the archipelago (Crawfurd 1820, 1:15). Underscoring his Western bias, Crawfurd (1820, 1:15–16) argued that civilisation originated in the West and decreased in geographical ratio as one went eastwards till New Guinea. Raffles' discovery of the ruins of Borobudur and Prambanan on the other hand brought for him and Western historians of the time the surprising awareness that these societies had already reached great heights in the past. It was a black swan event that changed their hitherto negative perceptions. It is no wonder that Raffles acquired a huge collection of Javanese cultural artefacts and wrote his two-volume tome on Javanese history.

Thirdly, Raffles, as did Marsden and Crawfurd, had interesting ideas about governance within the hierarchy of political development. Unlike the administrator-intellectuals (Hugh Clifford, James Brooke, Hugh Low) of the later 19th century who were influenced by Romantic thinking; the defence of native living in line with the idea of the noble native; and the criticisms of colonial rule and capitalism, Marsden, Crawfurd, and Raffles seemed to justify colonial administration with pragmatic thinking. Their perceptions of the region, native history, local culture, and colonial administration were measured and cast within the context of Western belief in its own dominance. Reflecting on native living in Sumatra, Marsden (1811) provided a hierarchical conception of civilisation within five classes. The first class was ancient Greece and Rome and the refined nations of Europe; the second class comprised the great Asiatic empires (Persia, Turkey, Mongols); the third class were the Sumatrans and a few states of the Eastern Archipelago; the fourth class contained less civilised Sumatrans, the South Seas, and the Mexican and Peruvian empires; while to the fifth class were consigned the rudest peoples — the New Hollanders, Laplanders, and Hottentots.

Crawfurd, who succeeded Farquhar as the Second Resident of Singapore, was an erudite administrator. His Residency in Singapore benefited from his previous administrative sojourn in Java. He was one of the more successful British administrators in Southeast Asia, which led to his embassies to Siam and Cochin China in the early 1820s, and Ava in Burma in 1827. In his history of the region (1820), he saw recurring patterns. Based on his experiences and observations, the scholar-diplomat developed an evolutionary model which provided an early conceptual theme of political anthropology as reflected through five distinct forms of social union: (1) the unconstrained egalitarianism of savages; (2) elective kingship; (3) a hereditary monarchy subject to aristocratic oversight and control; (4) federation with elected head; and (5) unrestrained despotism. Despite the personal abhorrence for despotism, Crawfurd believed controversially that despotism increased when societies became more civilised. Hence, he did not subscribe to the view that despotism was particularly an Oriental manifestation. However, owing to his Javanese experiences, he did feel that the Asiatics were ignorant and unappreciative of liberty, and thus deserved oppression. Nor did he believe that advancing modernisation would check despotism. His personal perceptions make one wonder whether deep down, Crawfurd acceded to the value of colonial rule and what the French called the *mission civilisatrice*, which by his reckoning would lead to despotic rule.

Raffles formed his own opinions on native society based on his experiences in Sumatra and Java. Ahead of his time in his administrative capacity, he did not subscribe to the general Western thinking of environmental determinism, which is the belief that the environment is the major causative factor in the development of human physiognomy, culture, civilisation, and behaviour. Nor did he believe in a one-size-fits-all philosophy of governance; he showed temperance and percipience in advocating colonial administration. Unlike administrators who carried the Saidian Orientalist biases with little qualification, Raffles displayed a more even-handed judgment of native behaviour and society. He praised Javanese society and was equally laudatory of the Minangkabau in Sumatra. He anticipated the French geographic philosophy of possibilism in observing how the right management of society and land could reap benefits for society, noting that the British failure in Sumatra had been due to an error of judgement.

Raffles proposed different systems of governance for the two islands, arguing that they were needed to stimulate economic activity for prosperity and progress. In Sumatra, he proposed an authoritarian system of colonial rule since the island was made up of innumerable petty tribes with no government, which had little intercourse with one another, and where people remained sullen and inactive. There, he unabashedly supported despotism to bring people together in order to promote civilisation. In Java, an island of well-developed native governments, laws, and systems of production, he felt the need for an easing of colonial governance — giving liberty to people and protecting "the individual rights of man". Critical of Dutch authoritarianism, he recommended an opening up of colonial rule. He felt that this would ease the repressive Javanese land tenure system (*adat*) and neutralise the "most abject state of vassalage" (S. Raffles 1830, 105) to enhance economic productivity.

Due to his greater familiarity with local history and his hands-on management and interaction with native rulers, Raffles subscribed much less than Marsden and Crawfurd to an Orientalistically indulgent view of Western historical superiority over local historical societies, or what Eric Wolf (1982) has called "people without history". Raffles' discovery of the ancient ruins in Java had given him a better appreciation and respect of native society and history, which he carried through in his negotiations over Singapore, despite his not being the ideal humanitarian reformer (Alatas 1971, 51). The eyewitness account by Munshi Abdullah of Raffles' relationship with local Malays and their rulers shows that the British administrator knew Malay culture, and had a respect for Malay leaders and their customs. Unlike the romantic administrator Clifford who, for all his ideas of the noble native, had unfortunate contempt for the Malay rulers by making fun of them in the Malay public eye (Savage and Kong 1995, 409–425), Raffles understood the role and importance of Malay rulers in society, and never attempted to belittle them nor demonstrate his intellectual superiority over them.

Raffles, however, could not apply all of his lessons in colonial administration from Sumatra and Java to Singapore because the tiny island had a relatively sparse population. Residing at the Singapore River was the *temenggong* and his followers. Though the *orang laut* numbered over 1,000, they were spread over the whole island and in nooks and crannies of rivers. Raffles' interest in Singapore was quite different. Here, it was not agriculture that he was managing. He showed no interest in the island's soils, climate, minerals, resident population, nor natural resources — save one. His was a much wider perception of the island's advantage. Singapore was attractive because of its location. The administrator acknowledged that his choice and belief in Singapore would never have been possible without "my Malay studies", as he put it, and added, "I should hardly have known that such a place existed; not only the European, but the Indian world was also ignorant of it" (S. Raffles 1830, 379). For him, the external geopolitical environment was crucial to Singapore's development: the colonial city needed to ensure good trading relationships. Raffles' understanding of Singapore's locational and geopolitical potential as an entrepôt showed that he was astute in making informed decisions based on percipient strategies and trading tactics. In this regard, he demonstrated his leadership and clear ideas for Singapore's future development.

Raffles' five-year experience in running the British administration in Java taught him an important lesson that the 'School of Tyranny' should not be applied to Singapore. His new trading station would be "a deliberate blow at tyranny and monopoly and racial prejudice" (Cross 1921, 38). As the young administrator argued, the *kris* and sword would finish a colonial story leaving behind destruction and death, "whereas the prosperous effects of fair and statesmanlike dealing come to the surface every time" (Cross 1921, 38).

A fourth influence upon Raffles' perceptions of regional geopolitics and his choice of Singapore was that of his friends and contemporaries, one unelaborated upon before John Bastin's (2019) commemoration of the 200th anniversary of Singapore's founding. The Raffles scholar par excellence, Bastin has meticulously demonstrated how Raffles' friendships influenced his many interests to bring about his intellectual and administrative development as an EIC official. To take one example, he benefited immensely from his six-year friendship with Dr. John Leyden, an exceptional linguist, who had mastered some 45 languages (Bastin 2019, 27). However, it was Leyden's mastery of Malay that was probably key to Raffles' knowledge of the same language and culture. It was Leyden's translation of the *Malay Annals* which helped to give the Western world an insight into the *Alam Melayu*. He encouraged Raffles to translate the Malacca laws (*Undang-undang Melaka*), and this possibly helped the latter in understanding Malay customary law (*adat*) and its importance in developing a sensitive land tenure system.

Raffles was one of the early British colonialists to foreground the idea of the *Alam Melayu* when he published an article in *Asiatick Researches* in 1816 on the "Maláyu Nation" (T. Raffles 1816). He viewed this nation not as a nation-state but a cultural area:

> I cannot but consider the Malayu nation as one people, speaking one language, though spread over so wide a space, preserving their character and customs, in all the maritime states lying between Sulu Seas, and the Southern Seas (T. Raffles 1816, 103).

Raffles held the Malay royalty in high esteem. At the same time, he did not simply pay lip service to Malay customs and traditions. In 1823, when he fell sick in Singapore, he preferred ascending the hill (by then named Government Hill or Fort Canning) where if he died, his bones, if they remained in the East, would have the "honour of mixing with the ashes of the Malayan Kings" (Buckley 1965, 95). It would seem that Raffles believed that through a process of osmosis, he would be elevated to Malay royalty by residing where the former Malay rulers of Singapura had resided and were buried.

III. Entrepôt Singapore: Free Trade

Raffles' choice of Singapore was premised on three factors: trade, location, and a free port. Unlike his governorship in Sumatra and Java where agriculture was the mainstay of economic productivity, he viewed Singapore as purely a trading centre. He saw that Singapore could galvanise the trade links in the region and become the focus of its trade with Europe; that it could be a geo-economic pivot and an ideal centre for archipelagic commerce. He realised that the rapid rise of 14th-century Singapura had been based on trade and felt that this could be repeated under British rule. Singapore's importance as a major magnet for regional trade would be something that the British could encourage, control, and manage. As historian Anthony Milner (2003) has argued, Raffles was an 'open regionalist' who saw trade as its catalyst in three ways: (1) trade and commerce were a 'bonding element' in the region through their facilitation of "constant intercourse and circulation"; (2) commerce was a way of galvanising the "flow of ideas", with Singapore as the centre of the archipelago facilitating this flow through an educational institute (what would become the school, Raffles Institution); and further, (3) Raffles emphasised how trade and education could provide the "moral and intellectual improvement" that would foster the "general security and good order" of the region. In his 1819 letter from Singapore to his friend Col. Addenbrooke, Raffles declared:

> Our object is not territory, but trade; a great commercial emporium, and a *fulcrum*, whence we may extend our influence politically as circumstances may hereafter require (S. Raffles 1830, 379).

Given his vision of trade, Raffles realised that the most important factor for a successful trading centre was location and not good soils, water availability, but not favourable climate. Raffles (S. Raffles 1830, 379–380) believed in Singapore's location in geopolitical terms, as being the British *point d'appui* or fulcrum: "what Malta is in the West, that may

Singapore become in the East". He felt that Singapore was his idea and expressed his intimate relationship with it, affectionately calling it a "child of my own". He was bent on making the island a regional commercial prodigy and like the Malacca of old, a mecca of East-West trade. In securing Singapore as the location of the major British entrepôt in the area, Raffles had set in motion the 'Pareto efficiency' effect, whereby resources benefiting Singapore would hurt other ports and thalassic kingdoms.

Given the stranglehold of Dutch trade on the region for centuries, Raffles hoped that Singapore's rise would have an impact on Dutch ports. The Anglo-Dutch rivalry was intense. Writing in 1824, Col. Nahuijs gave a candid overview of Britain's founding of Singapore. In it, the Dutchman, though full of praise for the form that the fledgling town was taking, provided cautious assessments of its entrepôt. He stated, "all that glitters is not gold" and advised his readers, "Do not attach too much value in appearances" (Miller 1941, 197–198). Specifically, Nahuijs was rebutting a *Singapore Chronicle* article which argued that the China trade would be confined to Singapore; he noted that this was certainly not the case with Malacca and Penang (Miller 1941, 198). Nonetheless, Singapore's success over the decades would cast a negative economic shadow on other regional ports. Unlike during its earlier history, this time rival regional and European powers could not challenge Singapore because the British were a rising global power.

Indeed, in a matter of years, Raffles would boast about his political child — "it is already one of the first ports in the East" (S. Raffles 1830, 422). Singapore, he noted, was a "great and flourishing city" (S. Raffles 1830, 431), promising "to become the emporium and the pride of the East" (S. Raffles 1830, 459). It had been a fortuitous location awaiting discovery and it was Raffles who uncovered the hidden gem.

As an island it had both a strength and a weakness. It was a neat place that could be acquired without much territorial baggage. Had it been linked by land mass to other areas, complications in its lease would have arisen. As an island, and without recent prior trading connections, Singapore was also able to better develop its entrepôt trade with the region and beyond on a clean slate; it was seen as an independent port open for trade with all other ports, states, and kingdoms. Indeed, in 1822, the first record of native boats counted 139 square-rigged vessels and 1,434 native crafts (Buckley 1965, 71). On the other hand, as a small island, Singapore was vulnerable. Until the Johore causeway was built, it had to be self-reliant. The fact that the colonial port had no immediate hinterland, determined at its very founding, reliance on a wider regional hinterland for basic necessities, food, and natural resources. The causeway would give Singapore its secure water supply and open the city to a vast Malayan hinterland. It also arguably made true Singapore's historical appellation as *Ujong Tanah* — the Farthest Land. The island now became the farthest southern point of the Asian continent reachable by land.

The rise of British power nourished Singapore's development. The rest might be said to be history; the saying however was easier done than the translation. Raffles had conceived the idea of Singapore as the EIC entrepôt, but the fledgling factory had to be sustained economically. It was left to Farquhar and Crawfurd to make that happen. Throwing aside Raffles' moral objections to opium, both the Residents embraced the selling of the drug as a means of obtaining much-needed revenue to run the factory. Singapore then became the test bed of Chinese opium addiction. The British founding of Singapore led to a new geopolitical reconfiguration of the region which was further cemented by the 1824 Anglo-Dutch Treaty. With it the British retained Singapore and gave up Bencoolen which had been under them from 1712 to 1824, and all claims to Sumatra, while the Dutch gave up Malacca. The Dutch thus became an insular Southeast Asian power and tightened their control of the Indonesian Archipelago, while the British consolidated their continental Southeast Asian role and removed its barriers to the development of trade with China. Singapore in the decades ahead would become the worthy bridge of East-West trade.

The third factor that led to Singapore's promising start as a trading centre was the creation of a free port. Raffles in his very conception of Singapore, believed that in order for it to flourish, there had to be free trade. He did not think one could force trade; as Rev. Cross (1921, 35) argued, "Associations, native customs, historic memories, provided you have the natural facilities, all act as magnets for trade". Given that most of the ports and kingdoms in the region imposed tariffs and taxes on imported goods, Singapore's free port status was a major economic coup. The British ensign Thomas Newbold (1839, 1:290) felt that Singapore's free port status was a master stroke that made it outstanding: "The first port of modern times, in which the principles of free trade have been carried into practice, is Singapore". At about the same time, Joseph Balestier, the trader, plantation owner, and US consul, echoed Newbold's sentiments when he wrote in the *Singapore Free Press* that

Singapore's free port status was a great advantage compared to what prevailed elsewhere amongst the region's kingdoms and ports. The erudite ship captain, lawyer, and official George Windsor Earl (1837), voicing the ongoing British contempt for the Dutch, noted the difference in political culture between Batavia and Singapore that underscored the latter's free-port environment:

> At Singapore there exists no political bar to social intercourse; no dread that private conversations may be reported to a jealous and unforgiving government; indeed, the contrast altogether is so great, that I have often felt surprised that a British resident in Batavia who visits Singapore on commercial business, or for the recovery of his health, can ever prevail upon himself to return to that pestilential and misgoverned city (Earl 1837, 357).

IV. *Mission Civilisatrice*: The Educational Institution

Both Marsden and Raffles embodied Eurocentrism as part of Western ideology, and were influenced by the colonial ethos of making colonies in the image of the metropolitan countries. Both men, and later enlightened administrator-intellectuals, espoused the conviction of the *mission civilisatrice* by which they believed their colonial undertaking was to spread Western civilisation to enlighten the Asiatic darkness. In some ways, Raffles' founding of Singapore was an experiment in the development of the archetypal colonial city, a Western model of progress and fountainhead for educating native peoples.

Raffles was a firm believer in the power of education. He saw this as one of the twin objectives of colonialism and the complement to commerce. Contrary to criticism, in many ways Raffles showed that he was relatively enlightened in being concerned with justice and mutual advantage in the colonial enterprise. In particular, from his early foundation of Singapore he articulated the setting up of an educational institution. Buckley (1902, 1:16) underscored Raffles' belief in education, and hence the subtext of Raffles' Singapore was in having a "fit spot in which to plant a torch that would send its rays into the depths of native ignorance, idolatry and superstition". Sir William Norris endorsed Raffles' view that, "If commerce brings wealth to our shores, it is the spirit of literature and philanthropy ... and of religion and justice, ... which teaches us how to employ it for the noblest purposes" (Buckley 1902, 1:16). Raffles believed that the legacy of the British in the region would be the 'software' they left behind in creating the "characters of light", that which was to revive "slumbering seeds of mind" and call native life from the "winter of ... oppression" (Buckley 1902, 1:16). In the minutes of the founding of the 'Institution' (Raffles Institution), Raffles gave an eloquent reflection of his thinking:

> While we raise those in a scale of civilization over whom our influence is extended, we shall lay the foundations of our dominion on the firm basis of justice and mutual advantage, instead of on the uncertain and unsubstantial tenure of force and intrigue ... Commerce is the principle on which our connections with the Eastern States is formed ... Education must keep pace with commerce in order that its benefits may be ensured and its evils avoided; and in our connection with these countries it should be our care that, while with one hand we carry to their shores the capital of our merchants, the other shall be stretched forth to offer them the means of intellectual improvement (Buckley 1902, 2:789–790).

Raffles saw these achievements as the monuments of British colonialism, even if the empire were to fade. Like many of the things he initiated, Raffles' legacy was fulfilled by succeeding Western residents. The Raffles Institution got its library in 1844, with 32 of them contributing $30 each as shareholders and a further $2.50 monthly subscription (Buckley 1902, 2:419). The institution, a premier school in the Singapore of today, is a tribute to Raffles' interest in education for the Asian population. Foreshadowing the idea of progress that directed the Western colonial ethos in the later 19th century, Raffles was ahead of his time in thinking. Education has been a pillar of development that independent Singapore's political leaders have not lost sight of.

V. Colonial City Foundations: Ethnic Segregation

From its inception as the British port-city, there has been increasing debate about the role of Raffles in the early development of Singapore. Bastin has been the most overt in downplaying this role, the reckoning of which he notes is "exaggerated" and totally obscurantist of Farquhar's "solid and meritorious work" (N. Wright 2017, 24). Raffles evidently has been a controversial figure. Yet despite detractions from his role in establishing Singapore as a trading hub, the number of biographies on the man by Western historians and writers (Hahn 1946; Wurtzburg 1954; Cook 1918) clearly demonstrates the recognition of his astute perception and contribution.

Singapore was one of the first colonial cities in the region to have an urban plan. It is to Raffles that several policies have been ascribed, which laid the foundation stone of Singapore's future trajectory. He spelt out his intent in reserving the north side of the Singapore River for European merchant residences and government buildings — specifically the area from the Singapore River to the Rochor River "including the whole of the great Rochor plain, [was] to be considered as set apart exclusively for the accommodation of European and other principal settlers" (Moore and Moore 1969, 85). Following the Spanish grid cities in the New World and Manila (Reed 1978, 39–42), Raffles' instructions for his town were also based on a grid system, with streets to "run at right angles" so as to "preserve uniformity and regularity hereafter" (Moore and Moore 1969, 86).

Raffles took his town plan seriously, and distinguished space for public purposes near the Singapore River, as opposed to residential areas. He thus was very cross with Col. Farquhar when he found that under him, Europeans had been purchasing and building houses on land reserved for government offices. When his plan was contravened, Raffles replaced Farquhar with Crawfurd as the new Resident of Singapore. Disgruntled with Farquhar's administrative oversight of town planning, Raffles initiated both the Town Plan Committee and a Land Allocation Committee. This was to ensure that Farquhar did not have the final jurisdiction of land sales in the new colony. The Town Plan Committee comprised Capt. C. E. Davis (Farquhar's brother-in-law), S. G. Bonham (superintendent of lands), and A. L. Johnston (merchant), and saw to the orderly laying out of Raffles' town and to the "appropriating [of] places for the different classes of natives" (Buckley 1965, 74). Writing to the committee in November 1822, Raffles laid out his spatial idea of the town. He established three functional components: (1) a European Town; (2) Mercantile Establishments; and (3) native divisions or *kampongs*,[3]

---

[3] The word *kampong*, meaning village in the Malay language, is variously spelt as *kampung*, and even *compong* and *campong*.

(Buckley 1965, 82–86). For the native kampungs, Raffles identified major Asian groups in the factory: Chinese, Bugis, Arab, Chuliah,[4] and Malay.

The Land Allocation Committee involved Nathaniel Wallich (Danish surgeon and botanist), James Lumsdaine (medical doctor), and Capt. Francis Salmond (harbour master at Bencoolen), who considered the specific implementation of the town plan which would involve the first land tenure system for Singapore. This system allowed for all races (Chinese, Malay, Arab, Indian, European, Jew, etc.) to purchase land and hence have a stake in the development of the young colonial factory. The Land Allocation Committee could be seen as the operationalising agent of the 1822 Jackson Town Plan drafted from Raffles' idea of the town. The colonial city which developed from this process was open to trade and immigrants from everywhere. Through enlightened land tenure, first implemented in the commercial centre (later known as Raffles Place), Raffles initiated a multiracial system of land ownership without the *type* of ethnic segregation which was the norm in South Africa, Rhodesia, and the American and other colonies. In this sense, the Singapore colony from its inception was religiously and culturally tolerant.

Among his many early administrative policies, Raffles mounted a comprehensive coastal survey of the whole island, and initiated a population census. He created a port out of the Singapore River, established a botanic garden, and set up the first school for local students, what would later be named Raffles Institution. The early Western perceptions of Singapore were recorded in sketches, drawings, maps, paintings, and word descriptions of these things in books and articles from residents, sojourners, and travellers. In the later years and decades of Singapore's development, Western sojourners would have many remarks and opinions about the increasingly pronounced bifurcation in character between the areas to the north and south of the river as first established by the plan.

Using the Singapore River as a convenient demarcation line, the city was developed along a spatial apartheid system. The colonial critic Frantz Fanon (2004, 5) would have labelled Raffles' plan as a creation of a "compartmentalized world ... divided in two" and "inhabited by different species". The north side of the river was reserved for Whites, including the Armenians, and the south side of the river was meant for 'others' (Jews, Chinese, Indians, Malays, Arabs, and other Asians). That cardinal

---

[4] The Chuliah were the earliest immigrants from southern India.

distinction led roads and locations to be named accordingly: North and South Bridge Roads; North and South Boat Quays.

On the southwest side, the objective was to establish the 'Chinese Compong' as well as the 'Chuliah Campong'. This ensured that the natural features for commerce were reserved for those with commercial interests (Logan 1854a, 105–106), so that these people would be left undisturbed in their occupations. The plan also identified the Bugis quarter around 'Campong Glam' and included the sultan's residence and the Arab quarter (Logan 1854a, 107–108). According to Crawfurd's (1830, 2:403–404) account, the sultan of Johore who died in 1810 had two illegitimate sons, who were in a state of "vagrancy and poverty" and were competitors for the throne. The British and Dutch "for their own purposes" took one son each (Crawfurd 1830, 2:403). The one who would have otherwise become the subsequent sultan of Johore resided in the *istana* in Singapore's Kampong Glam.

The spatial apartheid policy has been interpreted in many ways. Was the intent of dividing the town into two distinct ethnic areas a product of Raffles or really Lt. Philip Jackson's, who drafted the town plan, supposedly according to Raffles' vision? Was this 'Raffles-Jackson' Town Plan[5] an exemplification of Raffles as a racist and schemer, as Alatas (1971) has stated? Was Singapore's Raffles Town Plan a demonstration of the British colonial system of 'divide and rule'? Was the separation of Whites from 'natives' another way of underscoring the Orientalist ethos of separating 'us' (Westerners) from 'others' (Asians)? Or was the ethnic segregation policy a pragmatic system ensuring security and defence of the minority White population? In his June 1824 visit, Col. Nahuijs, commenting on the orderliness of the planned town, grudgingly accepted that "no person with any feeling can help being impressed when setting foot in Singapore" (Miller 1941, 192).

The logic of the Raffles Town Plan was never revealed nor debated, but it was implemented. The 1822 plan governed the development of the city — its spatial demarcation (town spread between north and south of the Singapore River), land use activities (housing areas for Europeans and Asians, marine yard, markets, burial grounds, government offices, and European merchant offices), and architectural features which have prevailed for 200 years. Houses on either side of the street have

---

[5] Usually referred to as the Raffles (Town) Plan or Jackson Plan.

"verandahs as a continued and covered passage", or what is now called the covered five-foot way of shophouses for pedestrians.

The 1822 cartographic plan as drafted by Jackson, with its geometric road representations on paper, was an idealised one. According to H. F. Pearson (1982, 154) the Jackson Plan, which was later published in Crawfurd's book in 1828, was the first blueprint of Raffles' idea of how the town should be developed. It was not a plan based on any actual survey. It would only be George Coleman's 1836 Map of the Town and Environs of Singapore that provided the first actual translation of Jackson's plan into reality. The Coleman map demonstrates the unevenness of the grid pattern of the town at the time, given the undulating nature of the terrain. It also shows that the north side of the Singapore River, the European sector, was well laid out and developed, while the south side comprising the Asian sector was undeveloped, including in terms of its roads. The map reveals the north side of the river stretching across to Kampong Glam as having been four times larger than the Asian sector of the colonial town. Subsequent government efforts to develop the latter meant that by Thomson's 1843 map the Asian Town could be represented with its intricate grid pattern of roads.

The resulting morphology or form of the city, however, emanated basically from the Raffles Town Plan. Over the decades, it shaped the cultural landscape in three ways. The first was the ethnic distinction of Europeans versus Asians. The White residents to the north conversed in English whereas the Asians in the south reflected a babel of languages. The north side of the Singapore River formed the heart of the colonial city: stately, orderly, spacious, and a living environment for Westerners. Col. Nahuijs in 1824 noted the neat grid-like layout of the European Town and the palatial homes of its population:

> Singapore can already boast of about thirty tastefully built European houses. These are placed a short distance from one another and in front of them runs a carriage-way, which they all make use of in the afternoons (Miller 1941, 194).

In the mid-19th century, Thomson (1865, 201) remarked that the European Town was studded with "handsome mansions and villas of the merchants and officials".

The second was the cultural foundations and social undergirdings it encouraged. All the churches, European houses, Western cultural amenities, and government institutions were located on the north side of the river. In a small area was a crowd of churches: Armenian, Catholic, Anglican, Methodist, and Presbyterian. Right down through Queen Victoria's long reign, the north side would be marked by the British colonial imprint: the Victoria Memorial Hall, Victoria Street, and Empress Place. The south side held the sacred spaces of Hindu, Buddhist, Taoist, and Chinese ancestral temples, Muslim mosques and *keramats*; clan houses of the Chinese associations; Chinese traditional medicine shops; itinerant hawkers; and wet markets. The narrow streets were lined with shophouses and domestic life spilled into the streets.

Third, the plan led to a spatial distinction of living standards. The Europeans lived in a low-population density area in houses with gardens, while the Asians lived in crowded, unhealthy shophouses that grew into slums. While class distinctions emerged, the Westerner generally viewed the slum conditions of Chinatown as 'communal living' and as tourist attractions. The north-south spatial binary of Singapore reflected the colonial imperialism of rich versus poor, winners versus losers that David Harvey (1973) adumbrated in his book on social inequality, *Social Justice and the City*. "Winners live in central districts of collective symbolic value or leafy suburbs with green trees and clean air. And losers live in slums" (Zukin 2006, 103).

For the government surveyor Thomson, the contrasting landscapes of the European and Asian sectors lay in their graveyards. In the European sector the graveyard was a "beautiful and romantic resting-place, sloping towards the harbour on the eastern face of Government Hill" (Thomson 1865, 13). The Asian burial places were more haphazard and scattered. He observed how Malays buried their dead on *permatangs* or ridges, while the Chinese liked to use round knolls and hillsides as burial grounds. Given the rapidly increasing Chinese population, Thomson observed, "Chinese burial grounds increase so fast that Singapore seemed likely to become a vast Chinese cemetery" (Thomson 1865, 282). Like Maria Balestier's quizzical reflections on a Chinese funeral, Thomson was also puzzled by the cultural difference between Western and Chinese funerals and graveyards. He noted how the Chinese treated their graveyards as "sites for picnics and family plays", and while a widow was grieving the death of her loved one, her children, brothers and sisters, and mother were "amusing themselves eating, laughing, talking, in the midst of perfect enjoyment" (Thomson 1865, 283). While Thomson was obviously surprised by Chinese burial customs which were different from the reserved, austere Western behaviour, he accepted that it was difficult to judge another culture by one's own norms (Thomson 1865, 283–284).

Raffles received credit for many of the institutions that were set up in early Singapore although in reality, he was not greatly involved in all of them. He hatched many ideas, but was rarely able to implement them since he was an absentee administrator. Given his wide interests and circle of influential friends (Bastin 2019), Raffles was infused with many such plans and ideas. It took numerous other European administrators, friends, and settlers, however, to translate his vision. Despite his personal interests as an amateur naturalist for example, it was not he who established Singapore's first botanic garden at the foot of Fort Canning Hill. It was Dr. William Montgomerie, an avid planter with his own pepper and sugar plantations, who initiated the garden, building terraces on the hillside and planting various kinds of plants such as spice trees (Pearson 1955, 87–88). Though Raffles himself did not claim credit, over the decades, many of his realised visions would be named after him. His aura somehow became synonymous with Singapore.

There were two aberrations to the Raffles Town Plan and its bifurcation of the colony into two 'towns', the European and Asian. After Raffles set up his Land Allocation Committee, two important districts developed. On the predominantly European north side was also Kampong Glam, which was set aside for the sultan's *istana* and his followers. This became a royal, Muslim area where Arabs congregated. Farquhar had been the original owner and resident of Kampong Glam (85,800 square feet) before it changed hands to become the sultan's property. And then within what had become this Muslim-Malay dominated area, Europeans (two named Carnie and Ker, for example) began to move in (Buckley 1902, 1:216). By 1840, James Fraser and Christian Baumgarten had taken over the houses of Carnie and Ker (Buckley 1965, 216). The French doctor Yvan (1855) also recounted his experiences in the area.

Conversely, Raffles had the *Temenggong* Abdul Rahman and his followers moved out of the north side of the Singapore River into Telok Blangah. Several of the Temenggongs were later buried in the area. Strangely, both communities (the sultan's and *temenggong*'s) developed within their own spatial enceintes on the island with little evidence of them relating to each other. Essentially, both the Malay communities were symbolic custodians of Singapore and very much left unmolested. Unlike in other colonies, the British colonialists never felt seriously threatened by Singapore's former Malay rulers, whose spatial and social presence remained as the colony developed. Western residents like Roland Braddell viewed them as reminders of Singapore's role in the *Alam Melayu*. The irony was that at some point a *temenggong* was elevated and made sultan of Johore by the British, while the real sultan at Kampong Glam and his entourage faded into historical oblivion. Having lost his legitimate historic title to Johore and Riau when the Dutch recognised another sultan over Riau in what was now their sphere of influence, the sultan at the Istana Kampong Glam could only be seen as a 'sultan of Singapore'; a position of no real merit in the Malay World.

VI. Land Tenure: Colonisation and Capitalisation of Land

One of the pervasive effects of colonialism in the region was the introduction of the Western-based land tenure system. Given that Singapore was a relatively virgin area with an originally small resident population in place, this notion of land tenure was a new concept for the local population but a requisite for the incoming Western residents. The native Malay population (the *temenggong* and his followers) had no sense of 'permanent' property ownership; they only had ideas of traditional usufruct rights (i.e., if I use the land, I am the owner) and no formal legal system. The Malay community had for centuries governed their land according to *adat* or customary rights. Ultimately, for the Malays, the owner of all land was God. The predominant *orang laut* were a sea-based community and hence for them land tenure had never been a legal or cultural issue. Raffles was aware of the traditional land tenure system given his administrative sojourns in Bencoolen and Java. Fortunately for the British, the Malay residents (sultan and *temenggong*) had no agricultural activities in Singapore, and so Raffles had a free hand in implementing a Western land tenure system with leases of 99 or 999 years.

When one reads through the early documents, newspaper articles, and settler debates of Singapore, the land tenure system surfaces as a fairly central issue. This was a new colony trying to establish universal land tenure for all its residents. For Raffles and the early administrators, the establishment of such a system provided four important factors in the British colonisation of the island. Firstly, a formal land tenure system sowed the seeds of the British claim over territory and their exclusive ownership of the island. A formal tenure system under British law prevented other counter claims to the island's land area. This was especially crucial in the early years of Singapore's founding when the Dutch felt that a prized area of their geopolitical jurisdicôt had been snatched from right under their noses. Raffles thus issued land 'grants' (574 were issued by 1823) under his own name for the portion of the island which the EIC had leased. For Raffles, the creation of a land tenure system seemed a crucial issue in the early establishment of the EIC's factory. Certainly, the Rev. Cross (1921, 39) opined that Raffles understood its importance. While land tenure was one way of enhancing the government's income, he was also mindful that a successful tenure system was dependent on "people's prosperity". The barometer of brisk land sales indicated that Western and Asian traders and merchants had the money and were ready to invest in the young entrepôt. This was a major area of contention between him and Farquhar that led to the latter's dismissal as First Resident, when Raffles felt that Farquhar had allowed land allocations which did not respect his directives. Raffles wanted specific knowledge of hills owned by individuals (all named after Western residents), lands bought by merchants, and the spatial allocation of lands. As a result, he set up the aforementioned Town Planning Committee and Land Allocation Committee to underpin the future land tenure system.

Secondly, by cementing a land tenure system, Raffles and the early administrators were legitimising British power and rule over the island internally. Such a system could only be invoked by the presiding political power. In this case, having the system meant that the British administration had the authority, legal rights, and adjudicative powers over the sale, leasing, and ownership of lands in Singapore. Singapore's land area soon became Crown land, the property of the British empire. The colonisation process was thus complete, and the island essentially became prized real estate. When the British left Singapore, their ownership over large areas of land (military land, naval base, airports, etc.) was given over to the Singapore government, which thus inherited a great deal of valuable property.

Thirdly, the early establishment of a formal land tenure system provided security and encouraged confidence in Singapore's survival and sustainability. Raffles was keen on getting European settlers to own property, as a sign of faith in Singapore's success as an entrepôt. A century later, James Lornie (1921, 301), the Collector of Land Revenue, in reviewing the 100-year history of the land tenure system, would note that successive administrations had put in place the "best means of encouraging the permanent occupation of the land and the amount of compensation to be paid to the State for the total or partial surrender of its rights". However, it was not under Raffles' tenure that the final seal of British land jurisdiction took place, but rather during Crawfurd's Residency. With the whole island under British control, the land 'grants' system was changed to a formal land tenure system in 1826. These formal leases of land were made out for 999 years. Some 300 land leases were issued and covered both the north and south sides of the Singapore River. Land plots were auctioned and quickly seized by Chinese, Arab, and European merchants. One might speculate that these long leases of land were given to tie in Western and Asian land ownership to the fledgling colonial city, and entice long residencies in Singapore.

Lastly, the Western land tenure system led to the capitalisation of property. Land assessed in monetary terms had been a concept alien to the peoples of the Malay World, but became a source of wealth for the Europeans, Chinese, Indians, and Arabs. Until 1830, there were no records of payment between buyer and seller though the assignment of the land owner was recorded on the lease (Leong 2004, 26). Given the large available land area relative to the small population of Singapore in the 19th century, land ownership by Western residents was of fairly large plots. This ownership was divided between town and country — prime town land in Commercial Square (later known as Raffles Place) was especially sought after, while the 'country' lands were areas which Western speculators used for agricultural plantations. The biggest beneficiary of the formal land tenure system in Commercial Square was Crawfurd, who in June 1826 bought 28 properties and controlled 41.6 per cent of the land area. In fact, the legal legacy of Crawfurd's land ownership in and around Raffles Place continued up to the 1980s (Leong 2004, 39). As the historical geographer Paul Wheatley (1954, 63) has noted, Crawfurd was a "shrewd judge of land". One might say he had an unfair advantage in acquiring prime properties given his chief executive position as Resident of the colony.

Those who engaged in agriculture in the 'country' felt that the taxes the government charged for these lands were exorbitant. The high land taxes that the directors of the EIC imposed were reflected in an 1833 *Singapore Chronicle* article stating that the government officials imagined "this island [to contain] an *El Dorado*, somewhere in its unknown parts, from which they or their successors in governing [would] derive, at some future time, incalculable wealth, arising from hidden mines of gold or tin" (Bennett 1834, 199). The colonial land tenure system seemed to disfavour agricultural pursuits as the annual quit rents were viewed as uneconomical. If a planter failed to pay the quit rent for one year, the government was at liberty to take back the property without any pecuniary compensation (Earl 1837, 409). Balestier lamented that the colonial administration gave 15-year leases at exorbitant prices of two Spanish dollars per acre (Hale 2016).

Earl (1837, 408–409) observed that though commerce and trade were of paramount importance over agriculture, no British-born resident would "venture to engage in agriculture speculations, since the system of land tenures would destroy all confidence, and all hope of profit in the planter". He added also that the insecurity in the suburbs due to Chinese bandits and plunderers made agriculture unsafe for Europeans (Earl 1837, 409). In short, while the land tenure system was good in having the ability to enforce the holding and protection of land under British colonialism, the system, however, did not appropriately cover the legal rights of all cultivators. Balestier (1848, 145–146) noted that the Chinese gambier planters made their money because they did not adhere to the legalities of land tenure. These planters were known to adopt a hit-and-run swidden system. John Cameron (1965, 82–83) noted that they located their farms deep in the jungle, because of their "desire to obtain land without purchases".

Given the EIC's small administrative arm, it was unable to police the violations of the land tenure system and hence Chinese gambier farmers used land without owning it or paying rents. The lawless spread of their plantations in Singapore's interior landscape underscores an important principle of land tenure. A tenure system only functions appropriately when there is a strong government in administrative control, when laws are well framed and executed, and when there is sufficient policing in upholding laws.

VII. Summing Up: The Raffles Legacy

Raffles saw Singapore as the crowning achievement of his work in the East. He had backed the right horse in his choice of the island as the EIC factory, as well as in making it the free port of the region. Singapore's rapid development in the 19th century reflects the 'core-periphery' paradigm that evolved under colonialism. To rephrase it in Kenneth Pomeranz's (2000, 25) terms, Singapore's colonial development might be seen as an outcome of the development of the world's first 'modern' core (Britain), which spawned one of the first 'modern' peripheries (Singapore). Raffles was a fortunate son of his times.

Despite this, as Cross (1921, 63) wrote in a tribute to Singapore's 100th anniversary, the East would lose its fascination for Raffles. The loss of Raffles' first wife Olivia, and all his children and good friends (Drs. William Jack, John Leyden) during his administrative tour left him lonely, dejected, and emotionally upset. The biggest blow to Raffles' legacy was the loss of all his material work of research deriving from the region when the ship, *Fame*, carrying his precious cargo went up in smoke in 1824. Raffles' loss could not be counted in monetary terms, although it was valued at £30,000. The Raffles collection was an "accumulation of natural and literary memorials to his Eastern life". The menagerie and museum of materials included dried specimens of tapir, birds for the Zoological Gardens, 3,000 drawings and maps, including one great map of Sumatra, and plants and curios (Cross 1921, 65).

And yet, Singapore was Raffles' dream come true. No doubt the personal price he paid for the realisation of his political child seemed too much to bear. It is questionable if the Orient had been a pleasant experience for him. When he finally left Singapore and the East with his second wife Sophia in 1823, Raffles was 42 years old, tired, diminished, disillusioned, and inconsolable. As Moore and Moore (1969, 79) observed, Raffles "yearned no longer for glory, but for a modicum of peace, a modicum of good health, and England". His administrative days in Asia were over. In her *History of Singapore*, C. M. Turnbull (1977, 32) has paid the highest compliment in stating, "Raffles reflected to a remarkable degree the most advanced radical, intellectual, and humanitarian thinking of his day. The type of society that he tried to establish in Singapore was ahead of that in contemporary England or India".

Raffles made Singapore an entrepreneurial enterprise of the EIC. It was a start-up British factory which came with all its risks, uncertainties, and difficulties. He planted the idea, but Singapore's take-off was also a result of many other factors and individuals who were responsible for its success. The torch of his Singapore creation was passed on to other administrators, professionals, merchants, and naturalists. He did not seek self-glorification per se; he was more obsessed with ensuring that his factory succeeded.

It is difficult to deny that Raffles gave modern Singapore its genesis and life. He identified the most precious asset of the Lion City. Singapore had no raw materials but it had in geography the invaluable and infinite natural resource of an extraordinary location for a free port, East-West trade, and a regional emporium. He outlined his vision in bold strokes, was percipient and clear about the entrepôt's future, provided the administrative scaffoldings, set the rhythm of the economic pulse, and laid the foundations of his colonial city. He left the verdict on his achievement for others to make, comment upon, applaud, criticise, and analyse. Raffles was a product of his time, the age of British imperialism, and his achievements are best evaluated within the constraints of history. Donald Moore (1975, 45) sums up Raffles' outstanding contributions:

> Raffles was one of the prototypes of that strange and ambivalent animal, in which no one but the British have ever believed, the liberal-minded British imperialist. He believed devoutly in the God-given mission of the British people to cover the globe with their empire. It therefore followed that he took the British to be the elect of God and the Dutch, French, Spanish and Portuguese to be less blessed. Equipped with this philosophy and driven by an insatiable longing for personal fulfilment on a grandiose scale, he was the empire-builder *par excellence*, confident, tireless and obsessive.

5

Tropical Nature and the Agricultural Mania

Chapter 5

TROPICAL NATURE AND THE AGRICULTURAL MANIA

I. The Historical Background

The history of human colonisation of land has always revolved around the negative and positive use of natural resources, the alteration of landscapes, the human role in changing nature, and the degradation of the environment (Simmons 2008). These ideas of human-nature relationships have been magnified with climate change (Flannery 2005), the reduction of biodiversity and increase in endangered species (Kolbert 2014), and the recognition in the scientific world of the Age of the Anthropocene (Scientific American 2016). Never in human history has the concern with the environment become so acute, immediate, and foreboding than in the 21st century. There have been natural disasters throughout history, but the global scale and frequency of current climate change impacts are likely to be without comparison.

Tropical nature and the Oriental landscape were powerful frames that captured the Western mental pictures of Singapore — the settings within which were placed all other experiences of the place. This chapter shows how Westerners were drawn to the diverse displays of tropical nature, their aesthetic appreciation of it, how the human-nature relations embodied ideas, and how the Westerners invested in agriculture that shaped the Singapore landscape. In an age when Europeans were enthralled with the plenitude of tropical nature, the endless diversity of flora and fauna, the fertility of soils, and the heavy rainfall, the idea of an environment threatened by human activity, however, seemed farthest from Caucasian minds. After all, the East had for centuries been seen as the Garden of Eden.

In contrast with descriptions of natural bounty and endless comparisons by naturalists of their species collections, the theme of environmental degradation in the colonial narrative was rather subdued. While the fascination and use of nature has had a long history in Western thought, the European perceptions of nature have changed over time. The Westerners who resided in or passed through Singapore over the decades formed their own opinions of nature, landscape, tropical climate, and vegetation. For much of the 19th century, Europeans in Singapore lived in a space-bound society delimited by horse carriages which served as the main form of transportation. Most of their social interactions took place predominantly within the boundaries of Raffles' planned city confines. Travellers and residents had much time to reflect on what they perceived, and revealed opinions about their personal comforts and discomforts, aesthetic appreciation, human-nature ideas, and likes and dislikes of the tropical environment.

Western ideas of the tropics go back to ancient times. Both the Greek and Roman civilisations had varied notions, ideas, and theories of the tropics (Glacken 1967). The idea of hot, burning, and uninhabitable tropics came from encountering the expanse of the Sahara Desert, south of the Mediterranean. The Greeks and Romans felt that they were the fortunate recipients of the best climatic conditions — sandwiched between the frigid northern cold areas and the torrid southern tropical region. This sense was further supported by the black skin colour of Africans, which led Greek philosophers to believe that residents of the tropics were burnt in their boiling climate.

The first exposure to tropical climate and the mysterious Asia came with Alexander's exploits and conquest of empires and kingdoms east of Greece (Strabo 1917). Many of the earliest-known Oriental fables and myths came from his adventures in India. The excitement of experiencing its fabulous civilisation initially overshadowed the experience of the tropical setting in which it was placed. Despite the fact that for hundreds of years the West had traded with tropical satrapies in South and Southeast Asia before the Age of Discovery, the ancient fears of getting burnt in the tropics would persist in the West till the 14th century. Once Portuguese mariners broke that psychological barrier in their voyages along the coast of tropical West Africa, the Europeans finally paved their way to the tropical East. Portuguese adventurers 'discovered' the East and in the process expanded the Western ecumene. They conquered Goa in 1510, Malacca in 1511, and reached Macau by 1557. The 16th century began the colonial age in Asia and with it, East and West, Orient and Occident, met face to face.

II. Tropical Experience: The Singapore Experiment

As early European travellers experienced the tropics first-hand, many of them did not survive tropical fevers and diseases. While the tropical experience might not be anything to rave about today, in the 19th century, without such household conveniences as air-conditioning and pesticide, the whole White-tropical relationship was a continual series of new revelations narrated in different ways. While ideas and theories about the tropics had fed the Western imagination for millennia, it was the personal experiences in the colonial era that led to a variety of different descriptions of what it meant to be living a life in the tropics.

Nature may be defined as the non-human world and cosmos, wild, untamed, and pristine, whereas environment is humanised nature, modified and cultivated. The Oriental tropics retained in the late 19th century the aura of a distant land, where the East gleamed like an illusion, an undefined location, filled with risk, inciting of foreboding and surprise. Joseph Conrad summed it up best: "The mysterious East faced me, perfumed like a flower, silent like death, dark like a grave" (Cox 1974, xi). Rudyard Kipling identified what had for centuries been perceived as the deadliest and most dreaded of tropical intermittent fevers and miasma, that is, malaria.

The descriptions of nature emerging from the Western experiences in Singapore range widely. They began with views of coastal nature, followed by those of what it was like to live in the tropical climate, and at times the personal ideas about tropical nature. As Western residents became more familiar with the *environment*, they developed discerning perspectives on human-nature relations, as well as ideas of environmental determinism and the challenges of confronting insalubrious climates. Given that any Singapore stopovers were generally confined to the town and port, there was less interest in tropical *nature*; the bulk of landscape perceptions dating from that time were confined to cultural landscapes and the town. And since many Western travellers had already experienced tropical nature in their journey before arriving at Singapore, their views of its tropical landscapes were rather subdued.

Singapore was fortunate to have among its early administrators two avid amateur naturalists: Stamford Raffles and William Farquhar. Despite Raffles' condemnation of Farquhar's Residency in Singapore, they both shared an enthusiasm for natural science. While Raffles had developed his zoological knowledge in Bencoolen, Farquhar earned his zoological spurs in Malacca as Resident. Farquhar had the distinction of publicising first knowledge of the Malayan tapir, bearcat, several species of hornbill, and discovering the fern, *Matonia pectinata* (N. Wright 2017, 54–59). Raffles, on the other hand, was the co-discoverer of the biggest flower, the Rafflesia, and a founder of the London Zoo. Raffles surrounded himself with naturalists in Bencoolen and Singapore: Dr. Joseph Arnold (1782–1818), William Jack (1795–1822), physician and naturalist, Dr. Thomas Horsfield, French naturalists Pierre-Médard Diard and Alfred Duvaucel, and Nathaniel Wallich (1785–1854), superintendent of the Calcutta Botanic Garden from 1815 to 1846 (Bastin 2019, 91–191). This interest in botany and fauna led Raffles to develop the idea of the first botanic garden in Singapore at the foot of Fort Canning.

In Singapore, like other Western colonies in the region, interest in agriculture as an entrepreneurial exercise became a tempting proposition. Much of the island was turned into an agricultural settlement, with the Chinese growing gambier (*Uncaria gambir*) and the Europeans experimenting with a range of crops. Agriculture changed the island's landscape from pristine forest to species-poor *belukar* or secondary forest. It had been the luxuriant growth of diverse primary jungle vegetation which first gave Western 'planters' the illusion that any plant could grow in tropical Singapore. John Crawfurd and Nathaniel Wallich were early official endorsers of this view.

The mistaken belief notwithstanding, Western perceptions of nature were based on personal experiences in the tropics. These perceptions were conveyed repeatedly by each traveller and resident as 'new' experiences. Hence, despite the thousands of White travellers who had written about the tropical experience since the 16th century, from the 19th century onwards, there were always new, refreshing accounts of that experience from every subsequent sojourner who visited Singapore. At times, the descriptions bordered on hyperbole to drive home a point. Given that travellers were writing for an audience back in Europe and America, experiences were conveyed in many vivid ways — with numerous comparisons, detailed descriptions through word pictures, and the liberal use of adjectives and adverbs. The landscapes were personified as being with human emotion and feeling; the pathetic fallacy came into vogue in writing.

Writing in the post-war years, the English don Patrick Anderson was perpetually punctuating his Singapore experiential narratives with reflections on the tropics. For him, the tropical experience seemed difficult to define: "There's something literary about the tropics, something nostalgic and false. In between daydreams and dramatics a whole area of life is missed" (P. Anderson 1955, 266). The tropics were something Whites relished because there it seemed like perpetual summer, and yet they pined for their seasonal changes. For many, it was an irritating experience having to tolerate the numerous insects that appeared to pester them all day and night.

III. The Torrid Tropical Climate

One of the most defining features of the White tropical experience in Singapore was the climate. Depending on their personal experiences, sojourners had a variety of descriptions and definitions of what this climate meant to them. Besides the personal experience, perceptions of tropical climate were augmented by two other inputs: (1) classical ideas and theories of the tropics; and (2) experiences of other White travellers in the region and other tropical places. Given that European travellers, mariners, and adventurers sampled different ports and places in Southeast Asia, they were able to make comparisons and evaluate the environmental importance of places as residential abodes.

Before the advent of public hygiene, the inroads of tropical medicine, and the creation of public cultural landscapes, Westerners could only rely on what they viewed as naturally healthy tropical environments. Salubrious tropical climate became a defining feature of a suitable place for White residence. The European experience of defining tropical weather in Singapore underscored three themes. Firstly, there was a chorus of travellers who found the tropical climate to be torrid; the sweltering heat for many was unbearable. The heat of the afternoons was the time when sweat poured out and Europeans felt that their perspiration was like having a bath. One of the great modifications to the perception of tropical weather that resulted from personal experience was the realisation that the traditional Western definition of the Torrid Zone was not fully accurate.

White adventurers, bureaucrats, and tourists were now well aware that the tropics were also defined by heavy rainfall and damp weather.

Another element of Singapore's weather was the winds. Given its island geography, the colonial city was exposed to sea breezes, which helped to moderate the tropical heat. John Cameron (1965, 153) noted that the sea breezes in Singapore ensured the "coolness" of the air, which helped to "moderate the heat" of the sun's direct rays and hence made the weather "tolerable" for humans. Westerners often contrasted their temperate homes with their tropical sojourn, and such recollections led to the longing for home and its climate. The more seasoned Western traveller, however, saw the temperate-tropical contrast as a mental stimulus:

> The tropics demand their opposite, palms call forth images of ice and snow, and this not only because the modern mind enjoys a paradox and likes to see different kinds of experience wrestling together; rather because behind the difference there lies a dreaming similarity (P. Anderson 1955, 226).

Thirdly, coming from temperate climates, Caucasian residents were quick to use environmental determinism as the reason for various White and local characteristics. John Thomson's (1849b, 751) overview of 19th-century Singapore saw the climate as a distinguishing factor influencing White and Chinese labour. He noted that the Chinese were inferior to Europeans in physical strength, but cautioned that one had to consider the oppressively hot climate with regards to labour (Thomson 1849b, 751). He argued that the Chinese had an advantage over the Europeans because their constitution allowed them to labour on without injury in the tropics, whereas the European would sink in all events and become "much impaired in strength". Thomson (1865, 250–253) thus made his major thesis on environmental determinism in relation to the creation of the Eurasian population, whom he observed behaved unlike the Whites. He believed that keeping White racial purity was difficult in the tropics, especially with regard to maintaining their distinctive European physical and mental attributes. He reasoned that:

> Climate weakens their energies, and deteriorates their moral powers, which are the real foundations of their great influence. The cold, virtuous, Anglo-Saxon habits, are, by inexorable nature, too surely

replaced by self-indulgent patriarchal tendencies (Thomson 1865, 253–254).

Given the long history of Western discussion and debate about tropical environmental determinism since ancient times (Glacken 1967), one can see why Western residents in Singapore were worried about whether their long stays would make them indolent, biologically prone to tropical disease, dull-minded like the native population, and lacking in vigour and vitality because the weather was said to sap one's energy. There were enough examples to compound these fears, in which White residents, including spouses and children, were buried in Singapore due to fatal sicknesses, and long-time resident White bureaucrats were viewed as being lazy, while many White traders and merchants after a spell left for home to be rejuvenated. The most well-known example of tropical disease casualty was the family of Raffles himself, who lost four of his young children in Bencoolen. Given that the cure for malaria was only discovered at the end of the 19th century, the European fears of little-understood tropical diseases must have permeated their gossip sessions in colonial Singapore. For a small community, the death of any White resident due to sickness would have been a devastating event that sent shudders through the social network. Without a medical cure for the fatal sickness of malaria, one can imagine the endless discussions of folk prescriptions amongst the White population.

IV. Coastal Scenery

For Western sojourners in the 19th century, Singapore's introduction came via the coast, when sea travel was the major mode of transportation. Given that many travelled by ship and boat, there were numerous descriptions of the seas and coastal landscapes. The colours, shapes, forms, and variety of vegetation and landforms made coastal scenery a perpetual theme of reflection and contemplation. Isabella Bird (1831–1904) was one such traveller who was fascinated by the coastal scenery around Singapore. In an 1879 letter to her friend, she grasped at the sights and let her imagination unfold: "here too, are treasures of the heated, crystal seas — things, that one has dreamed of after reading Jules Verne's romances" (Bird 1883, 135).

The scenery of the Straits of Singapore came across to Bird as a Jules Verne landscape, but to Chinese travellers in the 14th century, this place left an indelible mark on them that reflected the importance of the iconic dragon in Chinese mythology. Given its picturesque character, the entry into the straits was labelled by them as the Dragon's Teeth Gate, and would also continue to be referred to by Western travellers over the centuries (R. Braddell 1935, 31). For the Chinese, the gate was fearsome because it housed pirates notorious for their brutal killings at sea. Singapore was a choice maritime location, but unfortunately, for centuries its scenic coast and natural harbour had been marred by pirates who inhabited and guarded their residential dens in and around the island. Hence, for a long time, Western travellers would associate Singapore and its maritime environs with piracy and freebooters.

While the scenery and landscape did not change much, European viewers were constantly re-presenting them in their personal reflections, and for each of them, the scenery was seen anew, with fresh inputs and lively descriptions. For each traveller, the experience was different; no traveller could capture or relay someone else's experience. The descriptions were often detailed and vivid because before the period of mass tourism, the travels of the 19th century were like an adventure, risky and surprising.

For the Westerner, the views were worth beholding. Roland Braddell (1935) described the approach to the Singapore harbour as "one of the most beautiful in the world". The aristocratic Bird (1883, 136) provided a more detailed perspective of the Singapore coastal pier scenery, which she observed as "a world of wonders" that "opens at every step". This was a scenery which she felt was intensely tropical, involving varying hues, shapes, sizes, and forms in the "vegetation rich, profuse, endless, rapid, smothering, in all shades of vivid green from the pea green of spring and the dark velvety green of the endless summer to the yellow-green of the plumage of the palm" (Bird 1883, 136). Not only was the island filled with tropical nature and mangrove swamps, but there was also the hand of human cultivation in coconut palms, banana groves, sago, tree ferns, mango, jackfruit, durian, lime, and pineapple orchards. Bird (1883, 136) was astounded by the varied vegetation, and lamented at the "perpetual battle between man and the jungle" — clearly a reference to the human colonisation of the landscape.

While travellers marvelled at the picturesque coastal scenery, naturalists began to take an interest in the diverse corals of Singapore's surrounding seas. One of the earliest was Cuthbert Collingwood (1868, 258–259), who noted that the islands around Singapore were "wonderfully rich and unexplored". Though limited, the marine zoologist noticed "magnificent species" of the feather-star, and novel and interesting species of crustacea, especially the genera *Alpheus* and *Galathea* (Collingwood 1868, 258). He concluded, "Singapore must be added as a locality for the interesting sea-anemone" (Collingwood 1868, 259).

Given that Singapore for centuries had been viewed from and accessed via the sea, it is no wonder that the old references to Tumasik and Singapura were often defined by the Singapore Straits (Gibson-Hill 1954). The Chinese in the 14th century referred to Tumasik as where the people of Lung-ya-men lived. The geographer Paul Wheatley (1961, 82) identified Lung-ya-men as the *"dragon-teeth strait"*. In the colonial age this was defined as the Keppel Harbour passage between the southern coast of Singapore Island and Pulau Blakang Mati (now called Sentosa Island). Western adventurers, mariners, historians, and explorers made perpetual references to the narrow water passages and straits south of Singapore. Their records of the 14th-century historical kingdom were often filled with much confusion, conjecture, and contradictory views.

As is usual in historical confusion, Henry Keppel was given the distinction of being known as the discoverer of Singapore's 'new harbour' whereas in fact, this channel between the Malacca Straits and the China Sea had been earlier 'discovered' by Farquhar in 1819, by Capt. Henry Rous who first navigated the area in 1826, and by Capt. Daniel Ross who first surveyed the area in 1827 (Gibson-Hill 1954, 210). In truth, the *orang laut* would have known the place long before any of them. Keppel who rediscovered the water channel "came to the scene rather late in the day" but his name was immortalised in the new port. Even the British defence of Singapore was viewed as sea-borne, and they viewed access to the island as being from three straits in the area, which gave Singapore a natural defence.

V. Tropical Nature's Plenitude and Diversity

For centuries, Western travellers and administrators marvelled at tropical nature's plenitude and diversity. This was perceived in nearly every area that White travellers visited in the region. Though there were relatively few reflections on this concerning Singapore given Raffles' late discovery of it in the 19th century, White travellers who stayed in Singapore did remark at its rich tropical nature. The early White perceptions of the Singapore Island defined it as a place of jungles and swamps. The trader and traveller G. F. Davidson (1846) was overwhelmed by the luxuriant vegetation of Singapore's "primeval jungles". He observed that they were so "thickly timbered and covered with underwood and large, tough creepers" that to clear it would be a "Herculean task" (Davidson 1846, 44). Based on information available to him, Davidson (1846, 44) noted that it would require $60 per acre to clear the jungle, and even this would not remove the roots and tree stumps. In his perception of the Bukit Timah vegetation, we have some early impressions of the jungle surrounding the hill, about which James Brooke (1848) also wrote, "the jungle en masse is a lovely sight", where "the richest foliage attracts admiration".

Swamps seemed to have covered much of Singapore's coastal areas and were frequently reported by Caucasian residents and sojourners (Davidson 1846, 44; Little 1848b; Bennett 1834, 204–205). As commonplace features, they did not solicit the interest even of naturalists. Alfred Russel Wallace hardly paid attention to them. Given that there were so many theories and explanations for malaria or intermittent fevers, by the 19th century many Western residents saw a correlation between swamps and malaria, and made finer distinctions between types of swamps and the dreaded illness. Davidson (1846, 44) observed that though swamps abounded in Singapore, fortunately they were salt-water swamps flooded daily by the tides that kept them refreshed, or as he put it, "sweet, so that no one suffers from residing in their neighbourhood".

The British surgeon and naturalist George Finlayson tried to explain the plenitude of nature in Singapore. He observed that high temperatures affected all life in the tropics. This was not only with vegetable life; lower orders of animal existence were also affected by its power. The vegetable world was afforded an "inexhaustible source of nourishment" (Finlayson 1826, 51). Hence, in Singapore, the earth, air, and ocean teemed with life and myriads of insects succeeded one another. Finlayson (1826, 51) noted that the ocean had a similarly organised nature and that there was "dependence which is established between animals of more perfect organization". In this regard, he was of the opinion that the coral bank provided one of the most interesting spectacles of nature.

For the occasional naturalist who stopped by Singapore and went on to other islands in the Malay Archipelago, Singapore was seldom seen as a naturalist's paradise. Those who ventured out from the Singapore town, however, were able to provide some descriptions of the island's pristine nature. Two of the early Western travellers in the 19th century who climbed Bukit Timah Hill were James Brooke and Wallace. Brooke was able to reflect on the scenery that surrounded him on the hill. He left us vivid word pictures of his sights:

> the depth of perspective, the lively green, the freshness of the morning in the dewy jungle, and the entire loneliness and solitude reigning around, struck me as enchanting (J. Brooke 1848, 1:10).

Unlike Brooke who was impressed with the scenic tropical landscapes, Wallace (2015) was more concerned with the scientific appeal of Bukit Timah. Soon after his arrival in Singapore in 1854, he made a beeline for it. He was one of the few early naturalists who climbed Bukit Timah Hill in search of natural specimens. Some of what he discovered and found paled in relation to his many amazing discoveries in his eight years elsewhere in the Malay Archipelago. As a naturalist, Wallace was more discerning than Brooke about the vegetation on Bukit Timah. He observed that the forest was very similar to that of South America, although in Singapore, the numerous palms were generally small and horribly spiny. He was not impressed as he had been in the Amazon, with its majestic species. Although, where the fauna was concerned, the British naturalist noted that Singapore was rich in beetles and hoped to have a beautiful collection before he left the island (Wallace 2015, 18).

Given that Singapore was his gateway into the region, Wallace tended to compare his finds in other areas with his natural specimens from Singapore. In his short stay there, he found a treasure trove of a variety of beetles, butterflies, and other insects. In his first foray into the region in Singapore, he observed the "assemblage of a great variety of species in a limited space" and noted how "satisfied" he was in his "first attempts to gain knowledge of the Natural History of the Malay Archipelago" (Wallace 1869, 19). In Borneo, Wallace repeatedly compared various insects found in Singapore. The *longicornes* (long-horned beetles) and the ground beetles were more abundant in Singapore than Borneo; the checkered beetles in Borneo were similar to Singapore's but not so numerous (Wallace 2015, 37). He was particularly pleased with his collection of *longicornes* in Singapore, noting that in 10 days he had collected 50 beetles and managed to collect 160 species in Malacca and Singapore, compared to 290 in Sarawak (Wallace 2015, 74). Wallace

(1869, 19) observed that in one square mile in Singapore alone, he had collected 700 species, many of them new to science. In Sarawak, he marvelled at the 1,000 beetles he had gotten in Singapore and Malacca, against 2,000 in Sarawak, noting that at least half of his Singapore specimens occurred in Sarawak (Wallace 2015, 73).

Clearly for Wallace, Singapore might have been a small area, but it was rich in the diversity of insect specimens compared with much larger areas in the region. The compactness of tropical vegetation in Singapore made it a more satisfying and rewarding fieldwork location than the more arduous environments elsewhere, where specimens were spread over wide areas. Ironically, while naturalists were enthralled by nature's diversity of bugs and beetles, most Western sojourners had incessant complaints of tropical pests — flies, mosquitoes, white ants, red fire ants, bed bugs, centipedes, bees, and sand flies that were irritating, pestilential, and at times deadly.

Unlike the variety of insect specimens in the region that many naturalists boasted about collecting, it was quite another story when it came to confronting wild animals in their travels. The American naturalist William Hornaday (1885, 298) in his stopover in Singapore obtained insights to the variety of wild animals one could buy: a tiger for $150; baby orang utans for $20 to $30; a pair of proboscis monkeys for $100; a pair of full grown tapirs for $100; *manis* and slow lemurs for $2; rhinoceros for $250; and a full-grown orang utan (*Simia satyrus*) for a ridiculous price of $65. Bird (1883, 110), however, observed that turtles were so abundant that turtle soup was anything but a luxury; turtle meat was sold ordinarily in meat shops.

One can see that the European travellers were divided among themselves about hunting and specimen collecting by naturalists. The long-term sojourner in Singapore, French doctor Yvan (1855), was troubled by the Western mania for hunting animals. While the native hunted animals for food, the European engaged in hunting for recreation, sport, and personal egoistic satisfaction. Yvan lauded the harmonious and respectful way natives and animals had interacted in Singapore and Malaya and left readers food for thought in his ideas of the 'Design Earth':

> Philosophers and *savans* [sic] have written a great deal upon the different natures of animals, and have reasoned the various ways upon the subject; but in this Eastern land, in which God originally placed the earthly Paradise, in which he fixed the first fruits of the creation, the

humblest man knows far more of this interesting subject, than all the doctors of the Sorbonne, or any other institution (Yvan 1855, 134–135).

Western naturalists, administrators, and travellers wrote a lot about the different plants in the region that the native population relied on. The common plant references were sago, bamboo, and coconut. The surgeon and naturalist Arthur Adams (1848, 381–383) in his short stopover in Singapore had much to say about the gum trees. Specifically, he noted the *gutta percha* (the name being derived from the Malay word *getah*, meaning gummy exudation), and observed that the plant's sap was not as "viscid and tenacious" as that of the *Ficus elastica* of Borneo or the *Urceola elastica* of Penang, thus having an excellent kind of *caoutchouc*. Adams (1848, 382) noted that gutta percha is a *caoutchouc* (rubber-like substance) of great tenacity that retains its solidity in the tropics but "wants elasticity". This was probably a plant which Adams identified long before rubber was known in the Western world. Decades later, Singapore would be an initiation point for the diffusion of rubber in the region through the Singapore Botanic Gardens and its curator, 'Mad Ridley'.

VI. Salubrious Singapore

Most Western sojourners who visited Singapore were not one-stop or one-venue travellers. Singapore in the 19th century was not the only place of visitation for naturalists, entrepreneurs, administrators, and missionaries. It often formed a station in the rosary of places they visited. These experiences in various ports and places made for comparative descriptions, reflections on cultural relativity, and evaluations of locations. The most common White benchmark of the worthiness of a place for visiting had to do with its healthiness. The vocabulary used in the 18th and 19th centuries to define a healthy or unhealthy port or town included 'salubrious' and 'insalubrious'. Despite the inconveniences of tropical heat, insects, and the presence of swamps, comparatively, Singapore still enjoyed a reputation for being a healthy place (Collingwood 1868, 257–258; Dennys 1894, 352).

Among Westerners, complaints about the tropical heat and its unhealthiness were legendary. However, for Maria Balestier, contending with it in Singapore was less challenging: "Many of the days it is even unusually hot for Singapore where the heat is always great; fortunately, it is very healthy and I am getting strong again" (Hale 2016, 34). Even doctors endorsed Singapore as a place for the sick to convalesce. Dr. Thomas Oxley had this advice to share in the 1840s:

> So far the Invalid can enjoy the best exercises for the recovery of health, in occasional boating, or riding and driving in the open air during the cool mornings and evenings which he can remain out with perfect safety until 7 o'clock unless on some particularly hot morning (Wise and Wise 1985).

The region with its legendary hotbed of fever, sickness, and death came to be known as the White Man's Graveyard. Travellers gossiped about the notorious 'Dilly fever' (Dili, Timor), the 'Tjilatjap fever' (Cilacap, Java), and the dangerous fevers of Dong-Phaja-Fai (Korat, Thailand) (Savage 1984). However, for centuries, the most legendary ubiquitous fatal fever in the region was that caused by breathing in 'malarious fumes'. Since the time of the Hippocratic Corpus and the work of Vitruvius (the father of architecture), 'malaria' was equated with 'bad air', a product of unwholesome and poisonous environments that had over time become the plague of tropical areas.

Given the dangers of contracting fatal 'malarious fevers' in the region, Raffles' 'founding' of a fever-free Singapore was akin to the discovery of a healthy oasis in the tropical jungles. The island was the most well-known town for rest and relaxation among White sojourners in the 19th century. Its salubrious environment was lauded and documented by Crawfurd, James Brooke, John Cameron, and Robert Little. In his 1822 stopover in Singapore, the envoy John Bull declared, "no part of Asia can perhaps be said to possess so good a degree of salubrity and such an equable, though rather high temperature" as the British factory (Moor 1837, 224). He added that in Singapore, tempests were almost unknown and oppressive heats equally rare.

Two long-term British residents in Singapore also testified to its salubrity. The surgeon Dr. Little (1848b, 494) gave a clear medical endorsement by stating that the town had been free of febrile diseases. The editor John Cameron (1965, 150–153) believed Singapore's environment had therapeutic properties. He noted that the salubrious climate was not only kind and genial to European constitutions, but observed that invalids exhausted from their journeys from India and China left the island in six to seven weeks "in health and vigour" (Cameron 1965, 150–153). Charles Burton Buckley (1965, 186) observed how Thomas Owen Crane had 14 children, 13 of whom were still alive, which spoke well of the "healthiness of the place".

The positive Western perceptions of Singapore's salubrious environment by successive travellers vindicated Raffles' choice of having the East India Company (EIC) factory in this tropical *Alam Melayu*. This was an important yet originally unforeseen factor in Singapore's development. The travellers' advertisements of the island as a place for recuperation in the tropics were a bonus for Singapore's image. At a time when malaria plagued the region, finding healthy places of residence gave confidence to the establishment of a White settlement.

VII. Miasma Fevers: The Singapore Deduction

For over 2,000 years, the cause and cure for malaria eluded Western science. The idea of malaria was based on the miasma theory in which noxious fumes from swamps corrupted the air, and when inhaled were said to cause malaria. In 1898, the British doctor Sir Ronald Ross first proved in India that malaria was transmitted by the anopheles mosquito.

Notwithstanding the fact that Singapore was not known by Western travellers to be plagued by malaria, it produced one of the early theories of the cause of its chills and fevers. Dr. Little put forward a convincing argument ahead of its time. Based on his long-time residence and medical experience on the island, Little (1848b, 1848c, 1849a) concluded that malaria or miasma finds in moisture an "excellent medium of transmission" and argued that in tropical countries where moisture was dominant, there was corresponding increase in the disease. He believed that swamps were a major cause of fevers. He contended that some malarious influence was generated in freshwater swamps which was not in those subject to tidal influence, or, if generated, that there was some counteracting agent which rendered the malaria innocuous (Little 1848b, 482). He then provided a solution that if freshwater swamps were to be drained, fevers would disappear, and when the swamps formed again, fevers would reappear (Little 1848b, 481).

Despite being unable to identify the mosquito as the cause of malaria, he had provided an environmental theory for it. Based on his local findings, Little (1848b, 1848c) drew the following conclusions: (1) that the town of Singapore was exempt from endemic fevers even though it was surrounded by swamps because they were salt water swamps subject to tidal influence; (2) that Europeans and natives located near fresh water swamps (e.g. in the Siglap area) were prone to malarious fevers; (3) that whenever a coral reef was exposed by low waters, they were the cause of fevers due to the decomposition of the reefs; (4) that mangrove swamps might provide an effective barrier to malaria; and (5) that the simplistic correlation between swamps and malaria was to be debunked, with the assertion that whenever:

> mangrove swamps occur to any extent subject to tidal influence, and the disengagement of Sulphuretted Hydrogen, in the Malay Peninsula, Borneo and other islands in the Eastern Archipelago, that provided there are no other causes of fever, these swamps will not generate malaria, and fevers will not there be endemic (Little 1848b, 494).

While the cause of malaria was only discovered in 1898 by Ross, the remedy for the dreaded fever was known to Westerners as a result of traditional medicine used in Peru. Taking a side trip to Malacca in 1854, Wallace (2015, 31) met a government doctor who gave him a huge quantity of quinine, which must have served him well in his eight years of travel in the Malay Archipelago. Thus as other Westerners died from malaria, Wallace never succumbed to it despite being sick for several months in his travels.

VIII. The Tiger Menace

Western perceptions of Singapore oscillated between those derived from experiences which were pleasant and those which were dramatic and life-threatening. Nothing captured the sense of wilderness and pristine nature more than images of wild animals. The most fearsome was the king of the jungle, the tiger. One of the remarkable aspects of Singapore's zoological history was the endless reports of human killings by tigers (Wilkes 1984, 9–10; J. Cameron 1965, 83; Davidson 1846, 51–52; Keppel 1853, 1:9–15). In a place which was hailed for its urban cultural and economic development, it seemed strange that the island could be simultaneously characterised by its wilderness and tiger menace. Singapore in the 19th century had a reputation for deadly tiger attacks just as Batavia had been labelled a White Man's Graveyard in the 18th century. The first tiger to have killed a native was reported in the *Singapore Chronicle* in September 1831 (Buckley 1965, 219). From then on, tiger killings of humans would be monthly affairs.

Thus when the colonial masters were engaged in developing their city and White residents were cultivating the land, the most menacing wild animal was making periodic appearances of utmost terror. The surprise tiger attacks and human deaths created an urban landscape of fear and brought the image of Singapore closer to that of savage wilderness than a cultivated landscape. Collingwood (1868, 254) noted how the common statement on Singapore was that the island was "infested with tigers". He quoted an old guidebook which stated that travellers from steamers could see tigers come down to the "water's edge to drink (salt water, of course)" (Collingwood 1868, 254). The fear of tigers in Singapore was less evident, however, in the resident Caucasian population, but more so among the Chinese, Malays, and Indians who lived and worked in the outlying areas.

Davidson (1846) provided an early alert to tigers preying on human beings. He noted that three of his previous informants since 1839 had been killed by the lords of the jungle. The fear of tigers had led to many of the remote gambier farms being deserted (Davidson 1846, 51). The government, recognising the tiger threat, offered a $100 reward for every tiger captured or killed but this proved unsuccessful (Davidson 1846, 51). The few who did capture the tigers got the reward and sold the meat for $40 because the Chinese believed that eating tiger's flesh gave them the "courage of the animal" (Davidson 1846, 51). Thomson (1865, 230) also noted that the government paid 100 Spanish dollars for a tiger head, and the flesh was sold for as much, as medicine. Two men were said to make their living killing tigers for monetary rewards: the French Canadian Carrol and the Eurasian Neil Martin Carnie (Buckley 1965, 221).

Capt. Keppel (1853, 1:9–15), famed for his creation of Keppel Harbour, provided a dismal account of human loss in Singapore as a result of killings by tigers. The ship captain seemed more taken up with the rampant killings than the development of Singapore's new port (Keppel 1853, 1:9–15). He stated that no less than 360 human lives were lost a year due to tigers, so much so that the government gave rewards for killing them (Keppel 1853, 1:9). By 1849, Dr. Oxley (1849, 594) estimated that 200 human beings had been eaten by tigers; but he also cited another source which stated that 300 humans were killed in one year though only seven had been reported to the police. According to Buckley's (1902, 2:407) anecdotal account, the weekly newspaper regularly reported several deaths by tigers. Quoting John Cameron, Collingwood (1868, 253) in 1868 observed that there were 365 deaths arising from tiger attacks, mainly among Chinese cultivators on gambier plantations in the interior of the island. As a result, most White residents in the town did not feel threatened or fearful of tiger attacks because they believed that the tigers only roamed the interior jungle areas. A 'Tiger Club' was formed and gave a $100 reward to the Chinese for each tiger caught. A century later, G. P. Owen (1921, 2:368), writing about the tiger infestation in Singapore, would say jocularly that Singapore's name as lion city ought to be changed to *Rimaupore*, or tiger city. The Malays call tigers *rimau*, an abbreviation of *harimau*. The *Rimaupore* name would have been more faithful to the city's 'local colouring' since no lions occurred naturally on the island.

According to John Cameron, there were about 20 tiger couples on the island while others believed that there were no more than six to eight tigers (Collingwood 1868, 253). Not accepting that the island had indigenous tigers, Collingwood (1868, 254) wondered what was inducing tigers to come over from Johore. There were only a few deer and plenty of pigs in Singapore compared to much more game in Johore. Quizzically, he reflected, "Can it be a taste for human flesh, which is more plentiful in the island?" (Collingwood 1868, 254). Clearly, one of the reasons for tiger attacks in the interior that had been missed by Western accounts was the fact that widespread Chinese gambier plantations were destroying the natural habitat of the tigers. Hence, tigers were turning to human beings instead of their natural jungle prey. Thomson (1865, 226), the government surveyor, noted that the gambier and pepper plantations in the interior were good cover for the tigers and the "naked, lusty Chinaman" provided food the animal was fond of.

While the local population was frightened by the tiger menace, White settlers saw the tigers as some form of sport, and tiger hunting was much talked of (Buckley 1965). However, Western hunters felt that hunting in India, while riding on elephants, was not as dangerous as hunting in Singapore, where the surprise element in the jungle could be fatal. Furthermore, Singapore tiger hunting was affected by local spiritual beliefs and superstitions. Owen (1921, 375) for example, noted the Malay reverence for animal *keramats* and hence the lack of motivation to shoot them for fear of the "superior cunning of the animal in evading the guns". Another Malay belief was the notion of tigers changing into humans or vice versa, as narrated by H. N. Ridley in a 1906 *Straits Times* article

(Owen 1921, 375). Europeans found the ghostly relationships with tigers difficult to swallow. Buckley (1965, 577) declared, "Europeans do not believe in evil spirits". Ridley saw such stories as another example of how myths were mixed with the "superb and mysterious" animal, and the role that they played "in the magic dreamland of the East, and in the reality of the life of the peasant" (Owen 1921, 375). The eventual end of the tiger menace, hunting, and fatalities signalled to Westerners that the island was losing its wilderness characteristics and pristine vegetation, which were being replaced by more cultural landscapes — agriculture, settlements, urban expansion, and more people. Owen (1921, 380) lamented the end of tiger hunting as "one of the most delightful pastimes" in Singapore. He regretted the "all-conquering rubber" industry, by which plantations had removed the natural vegetation and with it the wilderness experience.

IX. The Agriculture Mania

Agriculture had the greatest impact in shaping and changing Singapore's pristine landscape. This was an intermediate landscape between the jungles of the interior and the colonial town. As Bird (1883, 113) observed, the "dense, dark jungle" was broken up by pepper and gambier plantations. For the aristocratic socialite, the interiors were far less interesting than the city. For Western residents in Singapore, a move from the north side of the Singapore River to the corridor of Orchard Road brought with it changes in their relationships to the environment. Orchard Road and its immediate environs was a large area that was hilly, and Europeans liked building their houses on top of hills.

The idea of having gardens adorning their houses soon developed into dabbling in plantation crops, beginning with varied spice plants and fruits. The settlers became crop entrepreneurs and their ornamental gardens quickly turned into orchards and experimental gardens. Dr. Oxley, the resident surgeon, and Dr. Little, a private medical practitioner, led the Western agricultural interest. The European residents saw the gardens as therapeutic (cooling the surrounding environment and embalming sleep), as well as being opportunities for making money. As Little (1849b, 678) expressed, "the formation of a plantation is a profitable investment of our spare cash", as this helped to "adorn our hills, and which will ere long change this island from a jungle to a garden".

Little (1849b) provided only one side of the story of the island's landscape change. The resultant impact of decades of burning, cutting down forest, and planting of cash crops was to leave the island with small pockets of pristine nature. For the nature lover, agriculture was destructive and damaging to nature conservation. To the entrepreneur and capitalist merchant, the replacement of nature with crops was a positive function, adding value to the landscape and changing the tropical forest into a harvestable garden. Though Raffles established Singapore as a trading emporium for the EIC, the subsequent European residents seemed obsessed with making the island an agricultural enterprise. The commercial dabbling in cash crops reflected the varying external influences on the value of crops, which would shape the choices of White planters over a century of British colonial rule. Hence, through the decades, the experimentation with agriculture switched from gambier to pepper, fruit trees to pineapple and coconut, and finally ended at the turn of the 20th century with rubber. In the process, the island's lands were colonised and commercialised, and some Western residents went bankrupt with agricultural failure. Like trading, agriculture attracted both the European and Asian populations. Unlike the Chinese planters who worked on smallholdings and transient farms, however, the Europeans invested in relatively large plantations and local labour was hired for the estate work. Many of the areas which the Europeans colonised with plantations were identified with place and road names which persist till today.

a) *Why Agriculture?*

The early European attraction to agriculture in Singapore was boosted by several factors. Firstly, Singapore was the third factory of the British EIC, after Bencoolen (Sumatra) and the Prince of Wales Island or Penang, hence Western planters in early Singapore used the agricultural success stories from the Western experience in these places. The exchange of information among European merchants and residents was instrumental in the planting process between places; but the physical properties of climate and soil, as well as labour costs, were not interchangeable, and these were factors that handicapped Singapore's success in agriculture. Singapore from its early British roots seemed to have had official endorsement of the favourable environmental conditions for agriculture. In his 2 November 1822 letter to Raffles, Dr. Wallich, the superintendent of the Calcutta Botanic Garden, gave his candid verdict on Singapore's agricultural conditions:

> under circumstances the most favourable for indigenous as well as foreign vegetation and forming part of the richest archipelago in the

world — its soil yielding to none in fertility, its climate not exceeded by any in uniformity, mildness and salubrity. It abounds in an endless variety of plants equally interesting to the botanist, the agriculturalist and the gardener, with unrivalled facilities and opportunities of disseminating these treasures and exchanging them for others (Tinsley 1983, 17).

Secondly, the publications on agricultural practices by various Europeans in these places gave Singapore's European planters an important agricultural guide. In particular, Dr. James Lumsdaine's 1820 publication in the *Singapore Chronicle* on the mode of cultivating spices in Bencoolen carried weight in Singapore. Capt. James Low (1972, 28–30) reproduced Lumsdaine's essential spice guide in his book. Low (1836) was one of the earliest Europeans to write an entire book on agriculture in Penang. Summarising the earlier experiences of crop growing in the region, he gave a comprehensive account of Penang's crops: nutmeg, clove, pepper, coconut, sugar, indigo, gambier, tobacco, coffee, cotton, corn, and betel vine (*sirih*), which stimulated the European crop experiments in Singapore. In short, the earlier British factories in the region and their experiments with farming shaped the outcome of agriculture in Singapore.

Thirdly, with the Dutch agricultural successes with spices in the Moluccas since the 17th century, Western residents in Singapore were attracted to agriculture as an entrepreneurial activity. Though the island was not large, its many environmentally friendly elements for agriculture were the source of much crop experimentation in the colony. Furthermore, the Dutch had made Java a haven for tropical agriculture and nothing was more convincing for Singapore's budding planters than the sweet success in their colonies. Since colonialism in the 19th century had become synonymous with the colonisation of land, agriculture was the archetypal expression of land under colonial jurisdiction. Land was given monetary value under capitalistic assessments, converted as real estate, commodified under the colonial land tenure system, and given a lease period for ownership. Unlike elsewhere in the region where native communities had an existing *adat* based on their own land tenure system, in Singapore, without an agricultural resident local population, the British governing authorities (Raffles, Farquhar, Crawfurd) had a free hand in setting down a Western-based land tenure system.

Finally, the earliest assessment of Singapore's agricultural potential was made by apparently authoritative sources. While Raffles never considered agriculture for Singapore, the envoy Crawfurd (1830, vol. 2) gave mixed encouragement for agricultural pursuits. Crawfurd (1830, 2:354) noted the perpetual succession of flowers and fruits even though there was a lack of seasons in Singapore. Given his many travels in the region, he found Singapore to be free of storms and hurricanes, with no pests like locusts, palmer worms, and Hessian flies. Clearly not anticipating the later tiger menace, Crawfurd believed that the absence of tigers and elephants was encouragement for plant husbandry. The Resident of Singapore for three years of the early 19th century gave a rather mixed assessment of Singapore's environment with regard to agriculture. Later, he would note that Singapore soils were poor though its tropical climate was congenial to agriculture.

Gilbert Brooke (1921a, 68) remarked that Crawfurd in 1824 had been prophetic in indicating how certain crops (cotton, sugar cane, indigo, cacao, tobacco, clove, and nutmeg) would not thrive in Singapore. At the time when Europeans were not involved in agricultural activity, he observed that agriculture was "exclusively carried on by the Chinese" (Crawfurd 1830, 2:355). Unlike Crawfurd, the ship captain George Earl (1837) felt that agriculture was one way of enticing Europeans to settle down in Singapore, and hence to help boost the rather small European population. He saw that the authorities provided little encouragement in this manner, as most Whites were engaged in commerce. Following Crawfurd's agricultural assessment, the government surveyor Thomson (1849a) decades later would provide one of the most comprehensive physical geographical (geology, soils, rivers, topography, climate) overviews of the island tailored in part to agricultural needs, but he never drew any conclusions about whether the island's physical geography was suited to agriculture or specific crop growing. In most European assessments, soils were the Achilles heel of Singapore's agricultural development; they were no comparison with the rich fertile volcanic or alluvial soils elsewhere in the region.

b) *European Agricultural Enterprise*

The Western mania for cash crops led to the colonisation of Orchard Road and other adjoining areas of the city centre. In the mid-19th century, there was a lot of experimentation with crops. Earl (1837, 410) observed that merchants had small "*amateur* plantations of spice-trees" near their homes, whereas other plantations for profit were found in larger areas.

Unlike trade, which grew with each decade (Newbold 1839, vol. 1; J. Cameron 1965; Bennett 1834), agriculture elicited lots of speculative economic activity among Western residents and travellers (Davidson 1846; Thomson, 1849a, 1849b; 1850a, 1850b; Oxley 1848; Collingwood 1868; Buckley 1965, 359–362). The name *Orchard Road* underscores the fact that orchard gardens lined both sides of the road. Part of the Western interest in agriculture was facilitated by the botanic garden that was established in 1827 at the foot of Fort Canning Hill. Dr. Wallich had advised Raffles on the garden in 1822, and Dr. William Montgomerie would be the first superintendent of the so-named Botanical and Experimental Garden (Montgomerie 1855). According to Montgomerie (1855, 62), one reason for the garden was to experiment with the cultivation of spices. George Bennett (1834, 174–177) was one of the few Westerners to comment on the Fort Canning garden, and he observed in 1833 that it would soon cease to exist. He perceived, though, that it had a large number of thriving nutmeg and flourishing clove trees laden with fruit.

Collingwood (1868, 255) was one of the earliest to mention the newer botanic gardens on the outskirts of Orchard Road. He also shared his thoughts on the small private gardens along Orchard Road, "one of the prettiest outlets of Singapore". He noted, however, that the botanic gardens were more like "pleasure grounds" supported by merchants (Collingwood 1868, 255). Nonetheless, the new Singapore Botanic Gardens were a bastion of tropical research and its various directors added scientific and commercial value to tropical botany. One such man was Isaac Henry Burkill, who after retiring as director in 1925, spent the next decade working on his pet subject in a handbook of economic products derived from tropical nature. The result is his two-volume dictionary on economic products of the Malay Peninsula which was done in collaboration with other contributors writing on local vegetation or flora, and animal and mineral products used for varied purposes by native communities in Singapore and Malaya (Burkill 1935). Burkill's most visible contribution was the 'vegetable' aspect underpinning the cultural appropriations of natural resources. From these, local communities derived food, desserts, drink, alcohol, cooking condiments, sugar, medicines, scents, housing materials, poisons, kitchen utensils, hunting equipment, fishing tackle, basketry, and health supplements (Burkill 1935).

Burkill was one of many White scholar-administrators who contributed greatly to an understanding of Singapore's flora and fauna.

He did so in three ways: (1) by providing the scientific classification of species of tropical nature which had previously only local names, hence bringing about universal definitions; (2) by providing an insight into the vernacular names (from Malay, tribal groups, *orang laut*, Thai, and other regional groups) of various plants and animals which sometimes had multiple names. Hence, Burkill (1935, 1:ix) noted that the original index of the dictionary had 17,000 errors or redundancies, which were later reduced; and (3) by demonstrating that the Malays and tribal groups in Singapore and Malaya utilised a wide variety of vegetation for different cultural, spiritual, economic, and social activities.

Singapore's experimentation with commercial crops included spices (clove, pepper), coffee, nutmeg, gambier, sugar, coconut, and cotton. Numerous early White settlers experimented with agriculture: Crane, Joseph Balestier, Dr. Oxley, Jose (Joaquim) d'Almeida, Dr. Montgomerie, Charles Scott, Capt. William Scott, and Dr. Little (Thomson, 1849a, 1849b, 1850a, 1850b; Oxley 1848). Oxley is said to have had one of the finest nutmeg plantations (Davidson 1846, 40), and Charles Scott a diverse garden of local fruit (Thomson 1850a, 134–136). Montgomerie's sugar plantation of 121.4 hectares was called Kallangdale. Charles Carnie had a nutmeg plantation in Tanglin; Crane grew coconut and cotton; Francis Bernard had a coconut plantation in Katong; and d'Almeida and Thomas Dunman too had coconut plantations. Of all the crops grown in the early years, nutmeg was the most extensive and successful. Raffles had sent nutmeg seeds and clove plants in 1819 from Bencoolen, which were grown at the botanic garden in Fort Canning. Earl later brought plants from the Moluccas.

By 1848, there would be 20 European nutmeg plantations in Singapore (Buckley 1902, 1:405). Nicoll had the highest number of trees followed by C. R. Prinsep, William Scott, and Carnie. After the early success, the nutmeg trees died from disease and inadequate soils (Buckley 1902, 1:406). Despite the early interest of Western traders in agriculture as an economic enterprise, there was little official support for their experimental endeavours. This was unlike how the Dutch in Java had implemented the Culture System that forced farmers to grow cash crops, and developed the Buitenzorg Botanical Gardens that pioneered research in tropical agriculture. In Singapore, the interest in the commercial and economic aspects of crops came rather late with the Singapore Botanic Gardens, upon the arrival of Henry Murton from Ceylon in 1875 (Barnard 2016, 120).

Singapore's first Europeans lent their views about getting involved in agriculture. The aura of spices had not dissipated, and many early planters were still interested in growing them. Crawfurd (1820, 3:213) in his historical overview of the Malay Archipelago was sceptical about the Western fascination with spices in the region in the 19th century. He found this to be an "erroneous opinion" and criticised British politicians and entrepreneurs, saying that it was "strange enough" that such "chimera should continue to haunt the imaginations of the politicians of the present age, and be acted upon by one of the most polished nations in Europe, in the country which gave birth to the science of political economy". Capt. Thomas Newbold (1839, 1:270–271), who was familiar with Penang and Singapore, advised potential planters in Singapore that they had to bear in mind three essential things for the successful cultivation of spices: (1) to have sufficient capital to bear heavy expenses for seven years; (2) to be a permanent resident; and (3) to have a long lease of the soil.

Davidson (1846) had rather mixed views about agriculture in Singapore and had specific evaluations for different crops. He raised serious doubt about growing coffee because there was not sufficient depth of soil, and labour was expensive for planters to compete with Java (Davidson 1846, 41). With regard to sugar plantations, he noted that they were uneconomical given how labour in Singapore cost twice as much as in Java (Davidson 1846, 42). The main impediment to agriculture in Singapore was often put down to expensive labour. A Malay or Chinese commanded $3.50 to $4 a month whereas in Java, three rupees was considered a good wage (Collingwood 1868, 273). While quoting others that Singapore's soils were not conducive to pepper production, Bennett (1834, 183) observed, however, that the pepper gardens were doing well and stated that two to three thousand piculs of pepper were collected annually.

Balestier provided a positive assessment and argument for an agricultural plantation in mid-19th century Singapore. Writing to his friend, Henderson, in 1834, the American consul sought his views about the planting of cotton and sugar. Balestier was optimistic that Singapore had the right ingredients for sugar planting. He observed that the soil was rich with red clay, the climate refreshed by "copious showers", the country having "undulating hills and valleys" but no high mountains, and that Chinese labour was available and cheap, costing $4 per month, besides food (Hale 2016, 251–252). He noted that the Malays would have to be employed to clear the "thick masses of jungle" and this would cost

8 Spanish dollars per acre. Balestier gave a detailed breakdown of expenditure for a 500-acre estate with 300 acres planted with sugar cane and 200 acres for pasture and gardens. He was so obsessed with agriculture that in May 1836, he formed the Agricultural and Horticultural Society with the other Western enthusiasts, Drs. Montgomerie and d'Almeida.

However, Balestier's success as a trader was better than his experimentation with agriculture. Like other Westerners of his time, he made the erroneous correlation that the luxuriant tropical forest in Malaya was a sign that the soils were generally fertile, having seen "the gigantic trees and the thick underwood of which the interminable forests were composed ... along the whole coasts from Johor to Province Wellesley" — a distance of over 400 miles (Balestier 1848, 141). Later, Western administrators like Hugh Low (1968, 32) would debunk the idea that luxuriant vegetation was an indicator of fertile soils: vegetation "is not so fertile as the appearance of the forests would lead the cultivator to expect". Buckley (1965, 359) noted the clay soils of Singapore would require more agricultural labour than the friable soils of Java, thus making agriculture a less feasible proposition.

Balestier's cotton plantation was attacked by red worms, nor did his sugar plantation fare well as a commercial venture. His misfortunes were all the more painful as he lost his wife, Maria, on 22 August 1846 and buried her on Government Hill. He ended up bankrupt; his personal property and the sugar plantation were sequestered by the sheriff for debts due to several mercantile firms he owed money to, for his land, house, stores, and engines (Hale 2016, 288). Collingwood (1868, 265) felt that many English and Chinese nutmeg planters had also been "reduced to ruin" and become "absolutely penniless" because of the failure of nutmeg production arising from plant disease.

As the 19th century came to an end, Nicholas Dennys (1894, 356), in his descriptive dictionary of Singapore, gave a litany of crops (rice, sugar cane, indigo, pulses, maize, tobacco, and cotton) that could not be grown due to poor soils. Indeed, many White planters had not been successful in agriculture, proving that Raffles' vision of Singapore as a trading centre was more economically viable.

In looking back at the Western experience with agriculture in 19th-century Singapore, one can say that there were three major areas of consideration in its development: (1) the assessments of the natural environment; (2) the economic evaluation with regard to costly human labour which made agricultural exports expensive; and (3) the colonial government's high rates of land lease and tax for agriculture, which meant that land tenure for agriculture was not encouraged by the state. Buckley (1965, 359) noted in the 1840s how agricultural labour was not so exorbitant ($3.50 to $4 a month) but because of the poor clay soils, unlike the volcanic soils in Java, more labourers were required in Singapore, and that made agriculture an expensive undertaking.

In many ways, the land tenure system for agriculture transformed Singapore's human-land relations towards direct private property, and direct state control and ownership of land. Since there were few native customary controls on land in Singapore, the British colonial government was able to introduce its capitalistic system for land tenure. Unlike the locals in Java and other parts of Southeast Asia, in Singapore, the Malay native population (mainly *orang laut*) was not actively involved in agriculture, hence this economic sector would be the domain of White planters and the Chinese. In this sense, agriculture in Singapore could not rely on native expertise and thus, for new White planters it was an experiment of trial and error.

c) *Chinese Gambier*

Early Western residents were witnesses to the Chinese gambier mania that covered nearly the whole island (Bennett 1834, 183–190). Wallace (2015, 11), in a letter to his mother in 1854 from Singapore, noted that the greater part of inhabitants in Singapore were the Chinese living in villages and cultivating "pepper and gambier". Balestier (1848, 145–146) observed that they had turned the whole island into gambier plantations, which were not successful ventures. However, he lamented at the way gambier planters, not respecting land tenure requirements, were getting away with their short-term ventures. Though Western planters were not personally engaged in gambier, nearly all early 19th-century visitors and residents mentioned the Chinese engagement in it.

The Chinese gambier system was basically a transient exploitative system, somewhat like shifting agriculture elsewhere in the region. The Chinese did not continually cultivate the same plot, but rather abandoned their plantations after they harvested gambier for its leaves. These plantations were often in the outlying areas of Singapore and beyond the agricultural plantations of White settlers, or the judicial watch of the government in terms of policing an effective land tenure system. Bennett, the editor and first master of the Singapore Institution,[1] mentioned how he, John Henry Moor (1803–1843), and a Dr. Martin made an excursion into the interior of the island to observe the gambier and pepper plantations. Bennett was one of the early White sojourners to have the opportunity to observe the gambier boiling houses where the leaves were boiled and the extracts collected. Despite the lucrative Chinese manner of growing gambier, by the 1860s it was said to be fast disappearing from Singapore. Collingwood (1868, 270–271) provided an astute reason for its failure — he observed that it "rapidly exhausts the soil" and that to boil the shoots required an "inexhaustible supply" of forest wood. According to Bennett (1834, 187–190), there were 150 Chinese gambier plantations at that time in Singapore compared to 6,000 in Bintang; there were also 170 pepper plantations. He noted that 2,000 Chinese were involved in growing gambier in the interior (Bennett 1834, 207). Despite the fact that gambier plantations were the cause of much deforestation in Singapore, he had a positive perception, stating that it "rendered the island a garden instead of a jungle — productive, instead of barren" (Bennett 1834, 192).

Bennett (1834) observed the government's high quit rents (land rents) for settlers outside the town area to be a heavily debated issue. Balestier was one of those who openly bemoaned the high land rents. Bennett (1834, 193) himself felt that the taxes should be rescinded and that this would "encourage both emigration and cultivation", whereby one could have expected "to see the dense forest give place to houses and plantations, smiling with the animation such scenery would occasion, encouraging industry, and adding to the wealth of the settlement".

A shrewd observer of early Singapore, Capt. Peter Begbie (1834, 353) opined that the island should have been "looked upon more as a commercial than an agricultural settlement, and it therefore [produced] but little within itself". Collingwood (1868, 271) was likewise sceptical about agricultural plantations in Singapore as investments. He questioned why "so many different crops have one by one proved ruinous to their proprietors, what will grow remuneratively in the island? — or will anything do so?" Unlike the Dutch, the British were not great agriculturalists and the directors of the EIC were not interested in promoting agriculture. Clearly, Raffles' initial interest in Singapore as a trading mecca would prevail as the dominant economic legacy.

---

[1] The original name of Raffles Institution.

In contrast to the 'hit-and-run' gambier investments, Chinese market gardens reflected a stable long-term investment in the land. The Chinese had few skills with plantation agriculture and seemed more adept with vegetable gardening. Their market gardens developed in tandem with the town's development. The Chinese love for fresh vegetables probably made these gardens an indispensable economic activity wherever they settled in large numbers. Wallace (2015, 21) was an early observer of the Chinese market gardens in Malacca. A century later, the most famous academic description of these small vegetable gardens would be J. M. Blaut's (1953) account of the one-acre Chinese market garden.

d) *Tropical Fruit*

Since Raffles' founding of Singapore, the comments on the diversity of tropical fruit by Western residents and visitors have been never-ending. This was surely a paradise for fruit lovers. Based on various accounts of meals Westerners detailed, local fruits were consumed for breakfast, lunch, and dinner. The demand for them came from both the Asian and European homes.

Regarding the plenitude of tropical nature, the new 19th-century settlement of Singapore was given mixed reviews. Crawfurd (1830, 2:353) observed that the soils and climate in Singapore were well adapted to the production of tropical fruit. He listed a litany of them grown in Singapore — coconut, orange, mango, mangosteen, *duku*, and pineapple. Wallace (2015, 78), on the other hand, noted that Singapore's fruits were "scarce & poor" compared to Sarawak's and Malacca's. For him, the two favourite fruits in Singapore were the mangosteen and durian. Given the many reviews of the durian's pungency by Western residents and travellers, Wallace's (2015, 78) praises of the durian are surprising. With its "thick glutinous, almond-flavoured custard", the durian "far surpasses" other fruit. For the naturalist, the durian was a "wonderful" and "unique" fruit "worth coming to the Eastern Archipelago to enjoy" (Wallace 2015, 78).

While other Caucasian residents were busy growing pepper, nutmeg, and sugar, Capt. William Scott created a plantation of fruit trees, both native and exotic. Thomson (1865, 233) noted that the elderly resident had a "maze of rambutans, dukus, and durians". The land surveyor observed that Scott's fruit oasis was admired by everyone for its "variety, scientific regularity, or fertility". In particular, the "garden afforded one of the most picturesque, shady, pleasing retreats that could possibly be imagined, illuminated as it was by the old gentleman's lustrous blue eyes, his silver hair, and warm, hearty welcome" (Thomson 1865, 233). One might speculate that Scott's fruit orchard had been the catalyst for the name 'Orchard Road'.

Generally, the verdict on the growing of tropical fruits in Singapore was positive. Besides Crawfurd and Wallace, Collingwood (1868, 271–273) was one of the earliest Westerners to provide an optimistic view of it. He observed that fruit trees flourished in the Singapore soils. Besides fruit, coconut and sago were suggested (Collingwood 1868, 272–273). Dennys (1894, 357), too, noted how both soil and climate were conducive to intertropical fruits: banana, pineapple, durian, mangosteen, *rambutan*, *rambei*, and *blingbing*. The environment was also conducive to tapioca and yam. Maria Balestier and John Cameron mentioned specifically local fruits that were served at breakfast, lunch, and dinner for the Caucasians, which indicated their popularity.

e) *Enter Rubber*

By the end of the 19th century, the agricultural mania would be dominated by rubber, coconut, and pineapple plantations, as well as Chinese market gardens. As Europeans began to settle down in areas outside the town, many of them continued to dabble in agricultural pursuits. Following the footsteps of Balestier (sugar, cotton) and Dr. Montgomerie (sugar), new cash crops and estates became known from the late-1800s onwards.

Despite the fact that Singapore lacked the land area for plantation agriculture, it provided an important foothold in the diffusion of rubber plantations in the region. The patron of rubber in Singapore and Malaya was H. N. Ridley (1855–1956). Europeans called him 'Mad Ridley' or 'Rubber Ridley', and as the head of the Singapore Botanic Gardens from 1888 to 1911, he was very much the father of the rubber industry in Malaya. Ridley made such a great impact as director of the gardens in 1888 that he was second only to Raffles in Singapore's historical 'Who's Who' (Tinsley 1983, 30). Another former director Nigel Taylor (2014, 123) maintains that "Ridley must rank amongst the greatest botanists and plantsmen in history and a biography of this remarkable man is long overdue".

Though rubber estates (the equivalent of plantations) were mainly owned by the Chinese, there were seven European estates. Such was the rubber craze that Europeans grew rubber in their gardens, according to H. Price (1921, 90). As rubber grew in popularity, other estates switched to rubber. For example, the Malakoff Plantation Company (later known as the Malakoff Rubber Company Ltd.) changed ownership many times, switching from tapioca and coconut to rubber in 1906 (J. C. Jackson 1967, 20). Similarly, the Chasseriau Estate (later the Chasseriau Land and Planting Company Ltd.) switched from tapioca, coffee, and coconut to rubber, while the Trafalgar Estate under Walter Knaggs which had been growing tapioca and coconut changed hands to Guthrie & Co. and grew rubber. The Trafalgar Estate later broke into two other estates: the Bukit Sembawang Rubber Estate and the Seletar Hills Housing Estate (J. C. Jackson 1967, 23). Johore's rolling landscape was conducive for rubber growing and became the rubber cash cow for Singapore *towkays* (wealthy Chinese businessmen). Singapore's colonial economy would be anchored by rubber and tin, trade, banking, and industry, with 70 per cent of commercial investments in British hands (Drysdale 1984, 88).

X. Summing Up: Singapore's Changing Landscape

In this chapter on Western human-nature relations, it is opportune to reflect on the historical processes that led to Singapore's colonial sedimentation. The human-nature theme during the period of colonial rule was an important one, but not in the same manner of the current context of changes in climate and biodiversity, and environmental degradation. On the one hand, Westerners were enthralled by the plenitude of tropical nature and naturalists came in legions during the 19th century to claim scientific credit for discovering new species. On the other, Western merchants and administrators had, since the 16th century and beginning with the Portuguese and Spanish rivalry over the Spice Islands, viewed the region as a goldmine for natural resources. In the 17th century there was Dutch and British rivalry over monopoly of the spice trade, and finally the Dutch colonisation of Java and introduction of numerous cash crops (sugar, cinchona, tea, coffee) under their Culture System (Geertz 1971). Singapore came at the tail end of the Western obsession with cash crops and it was evident that early Western traders and merchants in the colonial city were still hoping to make it rich through plantations.

Nineteenth-century Singapore was thus for White residents an entrepreneurial tussle between trade and cash crop production. The early decades of Singapore's founding were dominated by White settlers caught up with economic nature, entrepreneurial botany, and agricultural experimentation. Private settlers were abetted, either directly or indirectly, by British administrators like Raffles, Farquhar, Crawfurd, and later William Butterworth and Hugh Low, who were interested in agriculture and the diversity of tropical nature.

Though Singapore never became a major area of plantation agriculture, it was the node that launched the rubber boom and plantation agriculture in the region. It was through the passion and enthusiasm of Ridley that the rubber boom took off in the 20th century, and created a lucrative industry for Europeans (Dunlop; Harrisons & Crosfield; Boustead) and Asians. The majority of Chinese *towkays* who formed the pillars of the Chinese banks (OCBC, UOB, OUB) made their fortunes mainly through rubber. Given that space was a constraint in Singapore, the undulating, uninterrupted rural landscape of Johore became the rubber landscape. While trade made the initial wealth of Western and Chinese merchants, by the 20th century, Singapore would develop a reputation for conservative entrepreneurs who invested mainly in plantations, property, and banking. Even as a small colony, Singapore provides interesting lessons.

Over the decades there have been various calculated guesses of the impact of development on Singapore's landscape, especially its vegetation. The biggest spatial impact under the colonial period derived from agriculture — the destructive gambier growing of the Chinese, the varied experimental plantation crops by White planters, and Chinese market gardening. The New Zealand historical geographer and biogeographer, Ron Hill (1977), did an "intuitive" survey of the state of the island's vegetation in 1973, a decade after a century-and-a-half of colonial rule. The results were rather alarming: less than 1 per cent (0.31 per cent) of the island was classified under "substantially undisturbed types" of vegetation; 23.27 per cent was under "disturbed types"; messicol vegetation (agricultural, gardens) accounted for 53.80 per cent, and the "urban desert" was 14.85 per cent (R. Hill 1977, 28). The human-nature relationship under colonialism was ultimately imbalanced and the colonial interest in preservation and conservation of flora and fauna poorly developed. The fact that tiger hunting was a celebrated White pastime in Singapore says a lot about attitudes to wilderness.

Plate 1
Animal specimens and faunistic curiosities in the Raffles Museum.

Plate 2
Children of the ubiquitous *orang laut*, or sea gypsies at play.

Plate 3
Panorama of the Padang, with Raffles' house on Government Hill, later renamed Fort Canning Hill.

Plate 4
Portrait Painting of Sir Thomas Stamford Raffles (1781–1826).

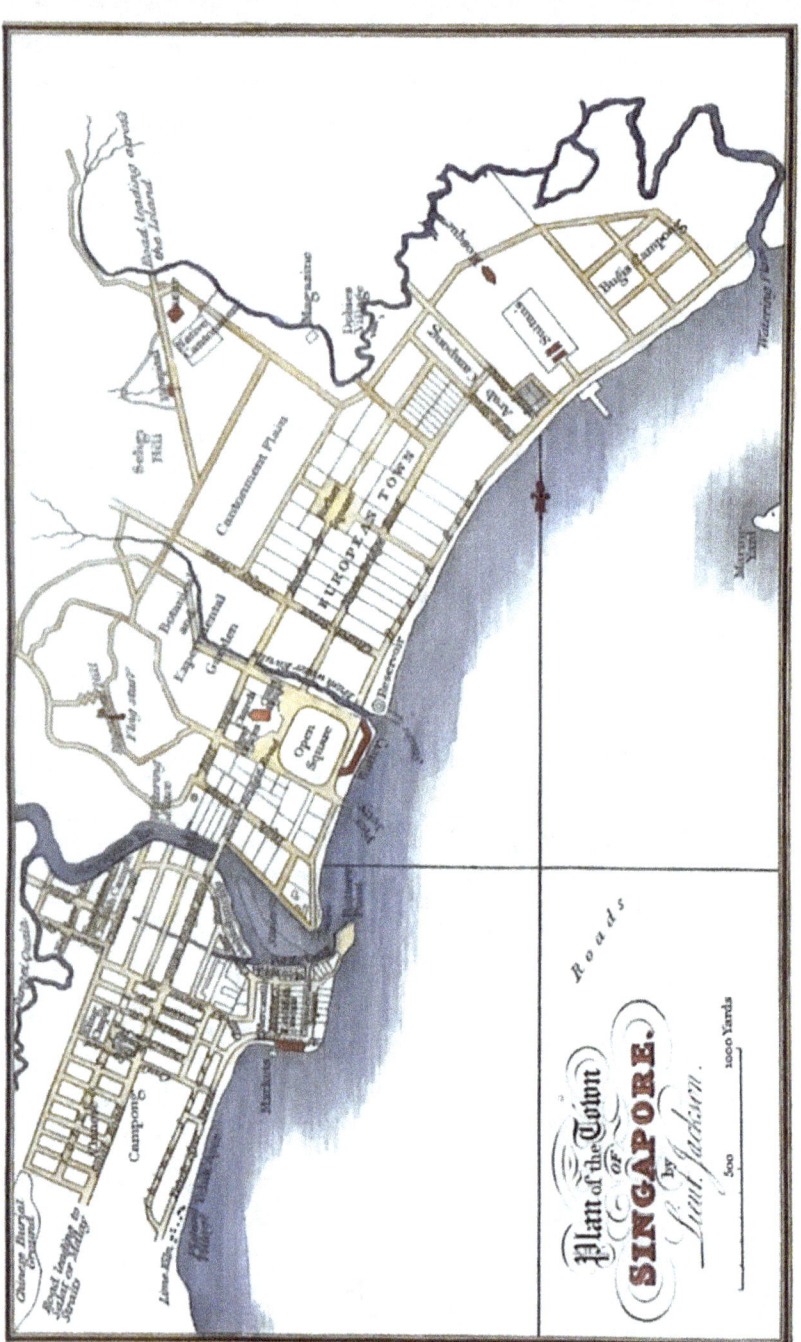

Plate 5

The 1822 Raffles Town Plan which formed the spatial outline of the colonial city, as mapped out by Lt. Philip Jackson.

Plate 6

An 1839 version of George Coleman's map of Singapore town, based on an actual field studies survey.

Plate 7
A European lady dressed unsuitably for the hot humid tropics posing before a colonial bungalow house.

Plate 8
The first Christian cemetery at Fort Canning, with the eastern part of the town in the background.

Plate 9
Istana Kampong Glam before recent refurbishment. Built by Coleman in 1840, it remains a key part of Singapore's Malay-Muslim community.

Plate 10
Fullerton Road with trolley buses and rickshaws heading toward Anderson Bridge and Fullerton Building, originally housing the General Post Office.

Plate 11
A Chinese hunter with the prize tiger, taken when tiger hunting was considered a sport.

Plate 12
A favourite spot in the Botanic Gardens off Orchard Road, with its waterlily pond which Europeans enjoyed.

Plate 13
With agriculture becoming an economic activity, both Westerners and Asians were avidly involved in plantations. Here is a pepper plantation.

Plate 14
At the turn of the 20th century, Chinese market gardens growing popular local vegetables thrived around the colonial town.

Plate 15
Gambier cultivation was a major Chinese activity that changed Singapore's landscape. This *atap-roof* shed is part of a gambier processing cottage industry.

Plate 16
After 'Mad Ridley's' promotion of rubber, Singapore would have many plantations owned by both Chinese and European companies. Lim Nee Soon is visiting his rubber estate.

Plate 17
Flanked by shophouses, early 20th-century Orchard Road was busy with motor cars and rickshaws.

Plate 18
'Koek's Bazaar' at Orchard Road was an agglomeration of itinerant multiethnic food hawkers servicing the colony's cosmopolitan population.

Plate 19
Chinese food hawkers referred to as 'travelling kitchens' catering to the huge bachelor coolie population.

Plate 20
The picturesque Singapore River with its motley bumboats and sampans was for decades Singapore's port; hence the nearby godowns that processed the import-export trade.

Plate 21
A unique engraving of Keppel Harbour which seems like a scene from the Arabian Nights, with camels ferrying goods and minarets in the background.

Plate 22
This Chinatown scene best captures the framing of the street and its pedestrian traffic by the ubiquitous shophouses with their laundry hanging from windows.

Plate 23
Singapore's multireligious society is on display in this Hindu procession of deities on a chariot pulled by bulls. The procession celebrates Queen Elizabeth II's 1953 coronation.

Plate 24
The most famous retail street 'Change Alley', in Raffles Place, was a Westerner's shopping paradise where one could tailor suits and buy small souvenirs.

Plate 25
Commercial Square, later baptised as Raffles Place, was the upmarket shopping area of White residents. Featured is the big department store of John Little which lasted 174 years.

Plate 26
Here is a transvestite who 'entertained' tourists on Bugis Street after midnight.

Plate 27
A wildly comic scene at seedy Bugis Street, a landmark of night entertainment. Here three foreign sailors try to mount a trishaw, much to the bewilderment of the trishawman.

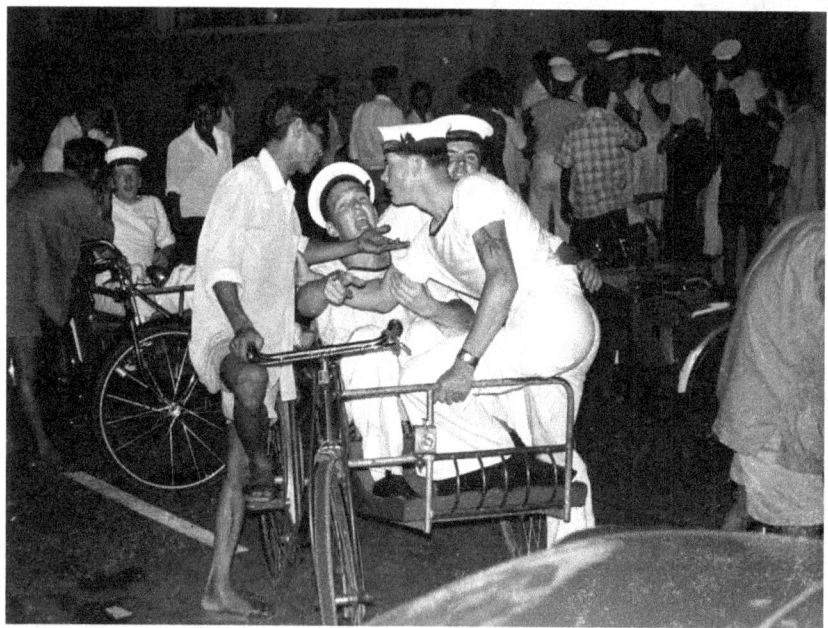

Plate 28
Mourners outside a death house. Sago Lane was perhaps the most depressing sight in Singapore for Westerners viewing sickly old Chinese on their deathbeds with their coffins awaiting them.

Plate 29
An elaborate early 20th-century Chinese funeral, complete with mourners, pallbearers, and monks.

Plate 30
As an entrepôt, Singapore had several luxury hotels, amongst them the Grand Hotel de l'Europe at the site of the current National Gallery Singapore.

Plate 31
The minority Armenians were wealthy traders in the European Town north of the river. Here they are at their landmark 1835 church. Some intermarried and became part of the Eurasian community.

Plate 32
The Singapore Cricket Club, one of the island's oldest recreational clubs, was for most of its history exclusively for Whites. The scene shows a New Year's Day outing in the 1880s.

Plate 33
Opposite the cricket club was the Eurasians' Singapore Recreation Club, whose location north of the Singapore River demonstrated that they had something in common with the White community.

Plate 34
Though Whites married locals to form the Eurasian community, the British, unlike the Spanish and Portuguese, never encouraged mixed marriages. This photo typifies late 19th-century Eurasians who dressed like Europeans.

Plate 35
Hiring ayahs or servants who looked after children was an established practice, although these Indian ladies were only found amongst wealthy European and local families.

Plate 36
Malays lived in coastal fishing villages and later, inland rural areas. A typical Malay village with its children and a hawker, all dressed in customary Malay outfits.

Plate 37
Chinese, Malay, and Indian coolies formed the backbone of Singapore's bustling port. Without machines, man was the beast of burden.

Plate 38
The Peranakans came mainly from Malacca and Penang. This photo shows gender differences in clothing: males followed European styles while women were attired in Malay outfits.

Plate 39
Hoo Ah Kay, often referred to by Whites as *Whampoa*, was an outstanding symbol of a mid-19th century Chinese *towkay*.

Plate 40
Street hawkers and onlookers showing a male-dominated multiracial gathering: Chinese, Indians, Malays and Indian Muslims.

Plate 41
After three-and-a-half years of Japanese Occupation, the British liberation in 1945 was a momentous occasion of joy for locals as seen by the attendance at this victory parade.

6

Urban Morphology: Street Life and Iconic Places

Chapter 6

URBAN MORPHOLOGY: STREET LIFE AND ICONIC PLACES

I. Defining Singapore's Urban Morphology

All cities carry with them some characteristic morphology, meaning the form, shape and spatial layout, street system, and iconic places. Despite the opaqueness of this concept, 'morphology' refers simply to the "visible form or appearance" of the landscape (Hart 1975, 13). Unfortunately, while travellers and sojourners in Singapore concentrated on the "visible" landscape, they either ignored or speculated on the invisible function and processes of the landscape morphology. However, to fully understand the city is to be able to read both the visible and invisible urban landscape. Cities are after all human expressions. As Lewis Mumford (1970, 5) in *The Culture of Cities* has astutely observed, "mind takes form in the city; and in turn, urban forms condition mind". Different cities are distinguished in peculiar ways; some by their many monumental and iconic buildings, others like American cities by their grid-like road patterns, and yet others by their picturesque images of varied buildings. This chapter hopes to capture the physical forms, urban shapes, and activities of Singapore as a city, and explain what might have been behind these manifestations.

While town planning today serves functions more in line with economic interests, the Raffles Town Plan seemed more bent on ethnic segregation, dividing the city into two parts, and a concern with maintaining White colonial security. In Singapore, it would appear to Western visitors that the city was morphologically divided into two towns: a European Town and an Asian Town. This distinctive feature of the 1822 plan was based on a 'divide-and-rule' format. Given the small White population, Raffles must have had security uppermost in his planning considerations. Edward Said (1979) would have seen the Raffles Town Plan as another indication of the colonial Orientalist ideology of distinguishing the colonial master 'we' from the colonised native population 'others'.

While the town plan was theoretically based on a geometric grid system of streets, in reality, this was not possible. The Raffles Town Plan was designed for a flat plain, but Singapore's topography was uneven. Various travellers noted this rolling topography. Alfred Russel Wallace (1869, 35) observed that the island consisted of a multitude of small hills, 300 to 400 feet high, while Horace Bleackley (1928, 123) noted that the island was "undulating", with no place more than 500 feet high. John Thomson, the government surveyor, had in the mid-1840s identified 29 hills in and around the Raffles Town Plan area (Buckley 1965, 573). Thus in his operational execution of the Raffles Town Plan, he had to adjust the layout of roads according to the many topographical features. The ensuing Thomson Plan consequently showed a lopsided town. The north side or European Town was well laid out because the area from the Singapore River to Kampong Glam was a plain with few topographical interruptions. The south side of the river, the largely Asian Town, was delimited and circumscribed by hills, swamps, and undulating terrain. Roads could not be laid out in grid form but in a winding fashion.

To add complexity, the Singapore town actually also had an unplanned third spatial component — besides the European and Asian quarters, there was a Malay part (Crawfurd 1830, 2:386), that of the sultan's palace and his followers, around Kampong Glam. Moreover George Earl (1837, 382–384), the visiting lawyer and ship captain, astutely observed that the Malay community was split largely between two chiefs and located in two different places: the sultan and his followers in Kampong Glam in the Singapore town, and the *temenggong* and his followers who resided exclusively westward of the town in an area concealed by hills. With time, the fate of the two Malay families would be reversed. By 1868, Temenggong Abu Bakar through British support was elevated and became the maharaja of Johore (Tate 1971, 127). The sultans at Kampong Glam did little to assert their royal lineage of the Riau-Lingga sultanate and thus lost their throne, and their descendants went into self-exile in Pahang and Trengganu (Tate 1971, 122–124). Kampong

Glam, nevertheless, became an attractive place for both the peoples of the *Alam Melayu* and Europeans. The Bugis had their community east of the mosque and close to the Kallang basin where their boats were moored. Kampong Glam was surrounded by communities originating from throughout the region: Malays from Bencoolen, Johore, and the Riau Archipelago, as well as Bugis, Javanese, Boyanese, Minangkabaus, and *orang laut*. Hence, the area developed a distinctively Malay-Muslim cultural manifestation, with the Sultan Mosque and the Istana Kampong Glam defining its place identity — one symbolising the Islamic area and the other advertising the Malay cultural rootedness.

Since the birth of Tumasik, commerce and trade had been the agencies which brought a variety of peoples and cultures together. Malay culture, with its congenial social system (bi-lineal, meaning the possibility of male and female descent systems), its flexible concept of 'nation' (*masuk Melayu*, meaning that there were ways by which one could become Malay), its regional lingua franca, and its ability to be adapted culturally (seen for example in the Peranakans), gave the city-states of Tumasik, Malacca, and colonial Singapore a cultural foundation which facilitated a cosmopolitan outlook. Westerners tended to depict the Malays as easygoing, friendly, simple, and pleasant, and this in a way affirmed their accommodating behaviour. Charles Wilkes (1845, 393) described the Malay as rarely engaged in "steady employment", preferring "light" jobs and having a "roving character". While trade played a role in abetting cosmopolitanism, the early mix of races, cultures, and religions remained, however, more of a matter of accommodation than the assimilation that Westerners alluded to.

Singapore's mosaic of varied cultures and ethnic groups were balkanised, whereby each group answered to its own community leader (O'Connor 1983, 79). Richard O'Connor (1983, 79), in dealing with Singapore's urbanisation under colonialism, has argued that the main challenge of the British administrators was "how to segregate the parts and so keep them in thrall to the centre"; most political commentators have called the British colonial system one of 'divide and rule'. What Singapore's plural society demonstrated, both about Whites and Asians, was their respective self-interest in making a living. Within the culture of pluralism, community, and hierarchy (the latter referring to both colonisers and colonised), the Asian community accepted the authoritarian colonial rule.

In the 20th century, Western travellers arriving from East Asia would compare Singapore to Shanghai and Hong Kong. They noted that

Singapore "appears to be a very poor effort until one has got used to the different size of the buildings" (Sidney 1926, 34). Without the term *shophouse*, early references to this type of architectural form were to 'two-storey' buildings. Except for some Chinese buildings, one visitor observed that this was a "two-story [*sic*] town" that was "perfectly innocent of style" (Hornaday 1885, 294). In the 1930s, Singapore was a city becoming modern. As the American socialite Isabel Anderson (1934) marvelled, she had never seen "so many motor cars in [her] life", nor the Ford buses called 'mosquitoes'.

By that time, the city's morphology had become more architecturally definitive due to the increasing multireligious differentiation within its landscape. This was a "city of violent and vivid contrasts", noted Ambrose Pratt (1931, 18). In it one observed splendid public buildings "replete with all the beauties of Saracenic and Hindu architecture rise like mountains from a ruck of huddled native houses" (Pratt 1931, 18). Such religious places of worship, religious festivals, and ethnic celebrations constantly reminded Western sojourners of their Oriental experiences elsewhere. Singapore was a strange morphological fusion of East and West, modern and traditional landscapes, capitalistic and religious pursuits, and secular and sacred manifestations.

Despite the boundaries set by the 1822 Raffles Town Plan, by the 20th century, Singapore's urban areas were expanding spatially, and the island was horizontally dichotomised between "town and country" (Dobby 1940). The buildings in town and its outskirts were different from each other; the houses in town were built of brick while those on the outskirts were composed of wood and thatch (Earl 1837, 348). The country consisted of outlying suburban areas, temporary dwellings, villages, market gardens and agricultural estates, and fishing villages in coastal areas. The temporary houses were seen as an expression of "local poverty, easy climate, transient population, and the youth of the whole human development here" (Dobby 1940, 103). The town itself was now being defined by motorised traffic as opposed to bullock-carts and rickshaws. Maj. Richard J. H. Sidney (1926, 25) noted that one was "bound to be amazed when first seeing Singapore at the enormous amount of motor-traffic in the city".

For decades since Raffles' founding, Singapore's town morphology had remained unchanged. Hence the town could be easily identified even if it were unnamed. Although writers like Joseph Conrad chose not to name the "Eastern port" in his many novels and short stories (Sherry

1966), they contained certain identifiable landmarks, such as the Sailors' Home, the Grand Hotel de l'Europe, the Esplanade, Singapore River, and St. Andrew's Cathedral, that frequent visitors and seamen could easily relate to. Without naming Singapore, Conrad referred to many aspects of its landscape with "remarkable fidelity" (Sherry 1966, 7). While his portrayals of tropical nature in the Malay Archipelago were flamboyant and lush, his descriptions of Singapore were "authentic" (Sherry 1966, 194). Singapore as the archetypal Eastern port appears in Conrad's *Lord Jim*, its so-called Sailors' Home in *The Shadow-Line*, and an extended description of its town in *The End of the Tether* (Sherry 1966, 173–194). Singapore was Conrad's base from 1882 to 1889, in both his roles as a deck officer and writer, and he travelled on many boats between Singapore and other regional ports such as Bangkok.

The Australian historian Anthony Reid (2010, 38) has referred to the "spirit of commerce" as the cement that bonded the diversity and encouraged the intermingling of different ethnic and religious groups which defined Singapore's 'cosmopolis'. Social scientists remain circumspect with this deduction and leave it open to debate. However, the reality of Singapore's economic activities on the ground did speak of a modicum of interethnic exchange, cooperation, and competition, and an economic commonality that in some ways transcended cultural difference. Commerce, the ingredient facilitating capitalism, became increasingly the common language of economic and cultural exchange. Though not mentioned frequently, capitalism was developing as the major economic system in Singapore by the 19th century. Singapore by most European accounts was the archetypal commercial city, a place where trade, transportation, and travellers interacted. But above all, the colonial British believed that they had created a White city for themselves. 'White' Singapore was an exceptionally beautiful city. Not only did the sea beckon at each corner, there were patches of green everywhere — sports grounds, golf courses, parks, and gardens between straight streets leading out of the city to the island's villages, where the gentle Malays lived on the edge of rubber and coconut plantations, or by the sandy beaches with their fishing traps (Barber 1988, 19).

II. European and Asian Towns

Over the unfolding decades of the 19th century, the town's morphology and spatial layout, particularly the contrasting human ambience of the

European and Asian sectors, would become a subject of attention for various European residents and visitors. Capt. Sherard Osborn (1857, 11–13) observed that the European sector had an "esplanade with bungalows standing in pleasant detached patches of ground", while the native part of the town south of the river was characterised by energy, "where everybody was in a hurry". The naturalist Cuthbert Collingwood (1868, 251–252) observed that Europeans lived in bungalows amid gardens and plantations, whereas native streets consisted of "two-storied houses" with an arcade running in front which would have been chock-full with merchandise. Unlike in the old cities elsewhere, the Singapore buildings were relatively new and the city seemed to some to lack an imposing character. As one Western visitor lamented, there was a "scarcity of tumble-down, drunk, and disreputable old buildings" which would have given integrity to a large city like Singapore (Hornaday 1885, 294).

Singapore was a tale of two towns: the European and Asian, the formal and informal, static and dynamic, and the colonial authoritative order in contrast to the native vernacular spontaneity and chaos. It would have affirmed the American landscape authority John Brinckerhoff Jackson's (1984, 148) broad definition of landscape as the "ceaseless interaction between the ephemeral, the mobile, the vernacular on the one hand, and the authority of legally established, premeditated permanent forms on the other".

Isabella Bird (1883, 117–118) in her 1879 visit observed the wide differences between the "dull and sleepy looking" European Town, which was no comparison with the "bustle and noise" and "picturesqueness" of the native town with its "huge, mingled, coloured, busy, Oriental population". The contrast between the European and Asian Towns was especially sharp because of the lively street scenes in Chinatown. Visiting Singapore in 1857, the German historian Fedor Jagor (1977, 37) noted that the streets came alive in the Asian Town between eight and 10 in the evening, while the European areas were "empty and dark". Singapore in the early decades appeared like a city with a split personality: one side European and the other Asian, with stark distinctions in spatial layout, residential living, and activity.

While no mention was made of Asian landowners, the *Notices of Singapore* document that in July 1821, there were 22 Europeans who were occupiers of land (Logan 1855, 451). By January 1824, there would be 40 Westerners who were recorded as owners of land (Logan 1855, 469).

The European Town was, according to Thomson (1865, 201), studded with "handsome mansions and villas of the merchants and officials". In contrast to the squalor and teeming population of Chinatown, it seemed like a "blessing [to] the eyes" with its "soul-reviving vision of spacious loveliness and loneliness and peace" (Pratt 1931, 20). The European Town was to Western visitors stately and orderly. In the initial years, John Crawfurd (1830, 2:387) noted that the streets of the town there formed on a "regular plan, intersecting each other at right angles"; they were laid out in a geometric grid pattern. The European Town was a "colourful city" with houses of blue, violet, white, and yellow (I. Anderson 1934, 171). The roads were avenues of gracious trees whose luxuriant foliage gave shade. Pratt (1931, 20) said the houses stood out like "palaces", with gardens that invited "the mind to dream" and brought "a sigh of envy to the lips". He found their gardens set like "emeralds in forests of a darker green, with bungalows etched in bosky purple corners".

The American naturalist William Hornaday (1885, 294) observed that architecturally "Singapore [had] little to boast of except solidity and uniformity". The town being delineated between its Old (Chinatown) and New (north of Singapore River) Towns, on the right (south) side of the river what met the eyes were "some very good European shops". One portion of the south bank of the town was inhabited by Chinese shopkeepers and artisans (Begbie 1834, 351–352). According to Crawfurd (1830, 2:386), the best warehouses were said to be in the Chinese sector.

On the south side of the Singapore River were also the rest of the Asian population, including Jews, Parsis, Indians, Arabs, some Malays, and other ethnic groups. This was a conglomerate of peoples speaking different languages, professing a variety of faiths, and engaged in a multitude of economic activities. Earl (1837, 348–349) gave a rather vivid description of the Asian quarter of the city in the early 1830s. Compared to the large homes and gardens of the Europeans, he said, "The houses which have only one upper story [sic], are fronted by wide piazzas, which screen the passengers from the rays of the sun, and shelter the goods exposed for sale by the native occupants". In contrast to the Western cultural homogeneity of the north side of the Singapore River, the south side was marked by ethnic and religious heterogeneity, a dense population, the din of noise, chaotic movement, vibrant colours, a variety of smells, and dynamic street scenes.

For the Western sojourner and traveller, the Asian Town epitomised the Oriental city: mysterious, captivating, and engaging. For the Asian population, this was the heart of the city. While the British had placed the colonial administration on the north side of the river to indicate the power and status of their rule, the Chinese 'reversed' the roles by naming Chinatown *toa poh* or 'big town' and the administrative colonial centre *sio poh* or 'small town'. For many subsequent Western visitors to Singapore, the Chinese *toa poh* would seem the right appellation to highlight the Asian Town's vitality, vibrancy, its economic importance, and seemingly endless buzz.

Singapore's contrasting dual 'towns' gave European sojourners and residents a first-hand taste of the differences between Western standardisation and Oriental diversity. While Whites might have felt safe and secure in their sterile landscapes, they did not hide their emotional curiosity and attraction to Chinatown. In many ways, Westerners were perpetually questioning their cultural and aesthetic dictates through what they appreciated and enjoyed in the Singapore experience. It was as though the "ghost" of their "own civilization still [stalked]" them (Steadman 1969, 285), and in this sense impinged upon their free evaluation and 'objective' perception.

III. The Sense Landscape

For the White visitors and sojourners, the streets in Singapore were not a purely visual treat, but rather an enticing, intoxicating concoction of sights, sounds and smells, tastes and feelings. The streetscape was the consummate sense landscape for White travellers and residents. Western perceptions of Singapore were derived from all the human senses and walking through the city's streets was a sensual experience.

Over the century since Raffles' founding, the Lion City would develop a reputation for its many smells, some noxious, and others pleasant scents to Western nostrils. No other Oriental city invoked the same olfactory power. White travellers recorded their many experiences of smell, from the indescribable durian odour to putrefying muddy swamps, from joss-sticks to aromatic woods and oils, from the stinking Singapore River to pungent spices, from filthy pig sties to fragrant foods, which gave the East its distinctive identity in contrast to Western cities. Smells defined Singapore as they did the Orient. For Westerners, the Orient was captivating because it emitted a diversity of peculiar perfumes and even undefined stenches into the air.

Unlike other travellers who captured the smells of tropical nature in the region, Western sojourners in Singapore were sensitive to the smells of the colonial city's cultural landscape. Walking with Joseph Balestier in the streets of Singapore, the French doctor Yvan (1855) noted that the shops in Arab Street and Kampong Glam were redolent with perfume. He provided one of the most vivid descriptions of the varied scents of Singapore's streets:

> the air we breathed was heavy with all the rich scents of Arabia, and the still more enervating ones of India and China — sandal wood and aloes, the precious balms distilled from the eastern trees, essences from Mecca and Delhi, and musk from Tonquin, combined to form an atmosphere so oppressive as to cause an irresistible feeling of drowsiness (Yvan 1855).

There were often depictions of smells coming from the Singapore River and Chinese market gardens. Patrick Anderson (1955, 179) noted the market gardens and squatter settlements of Braddell Road, where "coolness and heat caressed my face in a series of lulls and puffs, mingled with the scent of flowering trees, damp earth, latex and pig-sties". The intoxicating smells of Singapore gave Western residents their place bearings, their sense of security; they were a manifestation of the legibility of the town. For the journalist Noel Barber (1978, 146), the "sweet and sour stink" of the Singapore River was ironically a welcome sense experience for residents from Europe and India returning from the war as it gave "a comfortable feeling of sameness, of never really having been away".

From her short visit, Isabel Anderson (1934, 174) remembered Singapore through the "thousand smells — not all pleasant ones" for which the city was "famous". Pratt's (1931, 15) "magical" experiences in Singapore were evoked by the "queer perfume of the East, made up of a thousand smells ... a thing to which one becomes speedily accustomed and easily forgets; but when first experienced ... produces sensations that equally stimulate and suffocate". Of all the places experienced, Westerners captured especially the varied smells of Chinatown. Maj. Sidney (1926) in recollecting his sojourn in Malaya and Singapore, noted his memorable Chinese street experience which was filled with eating stalls that had a pervasive smell of *"mee"* (noodles). Hornaday had mixed reactions to the city which he candidly expressed. The entry into the city from the port was like a "back door entrance", where mud and slime of a creek greeted him through sensuous perceptions: the "creek stinks — pardon, I mean sticks — by us until we are well into the city itself" (Hornaday 1885, 293). As R. H. Bruce Lockhart (1936, 127) noted in his revisit to Singapore, the

Lion City, despite being cleaner and healthier than a quarter century ago, still retained the old "stinks". In short, the White memory of Singapore was captured not only visually but also through various odiferous sensations.

According to P. D. Smith (2012, 262) in his guidebook on the city, some 2.5 billion people eat street food daily around the world. Singapore's street food culture had its origins in the early establishment of the colonial city in 1819. In colonial Singapore, with a migrant demography, large bachelor population, and the absence of families, street dining was a common sight accompanied by varying food smells. Bleackley (1928, 133) observed food stalls everywhere with "travelling kitchens" that never lacked patrons, for the Chinese person "appears to be always hungry". Street foods developed in tandem with the vibrant itinerant hawker tradition. To the Westerner the Lion City had unfamiliar smells from street markets, dried foods, hawker meals, fresh fruits, joss sticks, spices, shark fins, roadside cooking, and even garbage piles. Before the establishment of restaurants and eating houses, the streets were turned into makeshift dining places in the evenings.

The Chinese quarter had great activity, with "big, colourful paper lanterns which also serve as signboards", and the streets had portable cookshops where people bought their evening meals to "eat ... on the spot", according to Jagor (1977, 37). For the Caucasian not used to the many Chinese gastronomical delicacies, Indian spices, and local fruits, the street smells had to be described and were difficult to define for a Western audience. To Western nostrils, the smells were either pungent or repugnant, fragrant or disgusting. The newspaperman Ronald McKie (1942, 196) detailed these contrasting smells when he noted that the city was filled with "the prevailing stench" of garlic which seemed like "perfume, subtle and pleasant, compared with the smell of the durian", while Pratt (1931, 15) observed the thousand smells which he sampled to be "some evil, some delectable".

In Singapore, the streets were alive with all sorts of noise. If Westerners heard the incessant voices of insects and birds in the forests, the city seemed to have an endless conversation of pedestrian voices, radio music, and traffic rhythms. The roads swarmed with rickshaws and bullock carts, and innumerable Ford motor-buses with black and yellow men "packed like sardines" (Bleackley 1928, 133). Many Westerners captured the road scenes in terms of sound. Robert Foran (1985, 227–229) described his auditory experiences in 1934 as those of "indescribable noise, a cacophony of sound, an impromptu symphony of the motor-driver's orchestra". The streets were repositories of sounds from various origins: canned radio music at full blast, strident voices in a dozen tongues, cackles of laughter, shrill hawkers' voices, the hoarse hoots of rickshaw coolies, the high-pitched rattle of mahjong tiles, the tick-tock tapping of noodle sellers advertising their presence, and the clip-clop of thousands of pedestrians' wooden clogs beating the cement in musical rhythms (Sidney 1926, 29; McKie 1942, 87; Moore 1955, 235).

Part of the audibility of sound resulted from the population congestion in Chinatown, the spillover of living into the streets, and the jostling competition of passageway pedestrians, itinerant hawkers, rickshaw pullers, and motorised vehicles. More than any other White visitor, Maj. Sidney demonstrated the greatest receptivity to the varied sounds of Singapore. He listened to the undefinable music, the vibrations and hum of the city, the "multitudinous noises of small animals", the "shrill cries" of food-sellers, "rhythmic movement" and chants by gangs of coolies moving heavy loads, and itinerant vendors using "rattles and other toys" to attract customers (Sidney 1926, 28–29). As he opined, one would certainly have needed "a Controller of Street Cries had he lived in Singapore!" (Sidney 1926, 29).

These chaotic street scenes and the din that they caused were part of the essence of what Westerners found memorable. What the streetscapes captured was the buzz that defined colonial Singapore's economic pulse in the eyes of European visitors. This never-ending business and hive-like activity was an important barometer of Singapore's thriving economy, as well as cultural vitality and social activity. Those Westerners who travelled between Singapore and Malayan towns found the contrast in activity very noticeable. The 19th-century aristocratic traveller Bird (1883, 125) contrasted in 1879 the "veritable Sleepy Hollow" of Malacca with the ceaseless vibrancy of Singapore. The first governor of the Straits Settlements Presidency of Penang, Malacca, and Singapore, Robert Fullerton, had envisaged making Malacca its capital because of its settled population, location, and healthy climate (Turnbull 1983, 248). However, Singapore quickly established its ascendency and became the capital. Singapore had a characteristic economic dynamism which Westerners could not overlook. In the end, British officials accepted that Singapore's strength lay in commercial activity, while Malacca's economic future would be in agriculture (Turnbull 1983, 249–253). Singapore also had a distinct advantage over Malacca and Penang, in that it was an attractive place for Europeans and British settlers.

As C. M. Turnbull (1983, 271) has noted, the British officials found Malacca "un-English". Moreover its Dutch pre-eminence had faded, and it would only have 113 European residents by 1891. Yet unlike in colonial cities such as Batavia, Saigon, and Manila where Westerners felt at home with their respective Dutch, French, and Spanish ambiences and architecture, European visitors and residents rarely felt that Singapore's cultural landscape reminded them of home. There was hardly a British reference to Singapore that was reminiscent of London or England. Singapore's urban ambience seemed unique. It had a characteristic Asian cultural feel, but with an economic energy that was universal of major cities in the West, and was therefore somewhere in which Whites never felt social discomfort or out of place.

IV. The Roadside Narratives

Jane Jacobs (1961, 29) in her study of American cities concluded that the life of cities is represented in the life of streets: if streets are lively, the city is interesting, if streets are dull, the city looks dull. Given his short time in various places in the region, the secretary of the British Admiralty John Barrow (1806, vi) observed that a person would have a more "correct notion of a city or town from walking the length of one of its principal streets, than from the most detailed description".

Cities are defined by streets just as the rural countryside is characterised by agricultural plots, crops, and farms. Streets contain the lifeblood of cities, are the veins of human circulation, and the theatre of the living. In Singapore the city spoke to Westerners in public displays, sensual exhibitions, and various cultural enticements, all of which were manifested in its streets. Legions of Western travellers, residents, and sojourners had impressed upon them indelible images of street scenes. Before shopping malls, recreational grounds, and exhibition sites became the norm in modern cities, streets were the display cases of goods and commodities, and the places of communication, social connection, and the crossroads for meetings. Singapore streets functioned as the laboratory of interacting Asian cultures, the stage for overt manifestation of ceremonies, rites of passage, and public airings of family life; and the place of business for hawkers, street bazaars, wet markets, and no-frills commercial dining. In reviewing Western perceptions of Singapore over the decades, nothing appears to have captured the perennial Western fascination with the city better than the bustle and cultural effervescence of Singapore's street life.

These qualities that characterised Singapore for Westerners were found in the Asian sector of the city. This was the urban sector in which life, work, and recreation spilled out of their designated quarters into the streets. The street life, to a large part, defined Singapore's imageability or distinctiveness of character. The Western optics captured the busyness, the crowded congestion and throngs of people, the never-ending sizzle of activities, and the effervescence of bustling life which made the streets a living diorama of unending interest for the European. Singapore streets were where business and family fused, where the children's playground was mixed with food stalls and dining areas, where shophouse goods competed with itinerant hawker wares. Above all, the Asian quarter was the quintessence of economic activity. The British naval officer Osborn captured its street scene in 1838 vividly:

> The one was purely commercial, with its bazaar and market-places, its native town, its overflowing stores, a perfect commercial Babel, where, if a confusion of tongues would induce men to cease building temples to the goddess of wealth, they would have taken ship and fled the spot (Osborn 1987, 11).

Singapore's street scenes as captured in word descriptions, paintings, photographs, and scenic postcards were mementoes of these iconic landscapes. Singapore streets were the most dominant expressions of the city's morphology and became in themselves a tourist attraction for Westerners. Used to their residential privacy, White sojourners were puzzled about whether the Chinese had a penchant for community congregation and public living. For the Western observers, the Chinese seemed to enjoy living their lives in the streets with no concerns about privacy. Maj. Sidney (1926, 31) observed how workers in a shophouse would break for a meal, setting up a table outside the shop "on the pavement". But this active street life was not just a cultural phenomenon, it also represented the crammed living conditions in Chinatown. As Sidney (1926, 31) noted about entering a shophouse, "we may begin to appreciate what the word 'overcrowding' really means". The streets and back lanes were used as extensions of the living space of the shophouse.

One often finds great variety in the accounts of street scenes by various sojourners. The American explorer Wilkes (1845) was in Singapore in 1842 during his global expedition, and was fortunate to witness several cultural events and ceremonies during his transient stay. He was obviously fascinated by the colourful procession at Chinese New Year in February, with its accompanying music of loud gongs and cymbals. He watched a Chinese *wayang* or opera in front of a 'joss-house' (temple), recorded several small processions supposedly celebrating marriages, and also noted the occasional Chinese funeral as well as a religious procession of the "Hindoo Mahomedans" (Wilkes 1845, 384–388). In the 1920s, Bleackley (1928, 133) was amazed at how Tamil and Chinese women acted "as beasts of burden" carrying heavy firewood and water on poles across their shoulders like "a pair of scales".

J. B. Jackson (1984, 148) would have found Singapore's internally varied colonial landscape to be an expressive "language", "the field of perpetual conflict and compromise between what is established by authority and what the vernacular insists upon preferring". This was a city representing a "gigantic compound of wealth and poverty" (Moore 1953, 987), encompassing the dull and sleepy European Town and the vibrant Eastern Town (Bird 1883, 119); the monotonous rubber estates and the "variety and colour of streets" (C. Cameron 1924, 14). The Singapore experience was complex, as one visitor of 1911–1912 remarked, "You'll like it, or you'll hate it, but if you go there you'll never forget it" (Redfern 1985, 170). That unforgettable experience in many ways defined Singapore's imageability for the Westerner. This was a mysterious Oriental city that mirrored the European image of the inscrutable East: difficult to define, pushing the boundaries of Western comprehension, always evoking hidden meanings for reflection, criticism, and comment.

For Western visitors, Singapore had no elaborate edifices to boast about, no historical ruins to study, no antique monuments for exceptional praise. Instead, discerning sojourners like Donald Moore (1953, 221–222) distinguished between the city's central slums and the outer areas of squatter dwellings, marked by "tawdry houses, unkempt, overcrowded, unhealthy", in places like Kallang and Rochor. Squatter dwellers he observed did "not like ... new land" and were "obstinate" in crowding in the same old areas; "whatever you give them they will overcrowd it" (Moore 1953, 221). The colonial authorities were thus resigned to the squatter propensity for squalid living: "Let them stew, they are quite happy and will only become unhappy if you persuade them that more congenial living conditions will make them more happy. They are interested only in themselves, so leave them alone" (Moore 1953, 221).

At another level, Singapore was a merchant's city, organised according to trades and wholesale wares. This was a frenzied hive of busy people in a hurry to get things done. To many sojourners, it was seemingly characterised by a perpetual buzz right into the wee hours of morning. Unlike more grandiose civilisational attractions for the tourist elsewhere in Southeast Asia, in Singapore the main interest was its streets and alleyways. This was where Westerners ferreted out native stories, formed interesting perceptions, and surveyed quotidian lifescapes in which daily activities were played out in the landscape of the streets.

V. The Singapore River and Keppel Harbour

In Singapore, despite the many colonial buildings which the British built (Hancock and Gibson-Hill 1954), the main perceptions of the city seemed to be focused on places, streets, and the iconic Singapore River. The river was one of the earliest 'landscapes' that caught the eyes of European travellers. It was the only waterway that served as a transportation 'street' for goods and people. While the river was a dividing line between the White and local settlements of the colony under the Raffles Town Plan, it was also a picturesque site and drew many Westerners to comment upon it. One of the earliest commentaries was by Capt. Peter Begbie (1834) who noted the differences between its north and south banks. The view from the river gave the whole town "an appearance of great bustle and activity, which [inspired] the spectator with an idea that he [was] gazing upon a settlement that [was] rapidly rising into importance under the united influences of English capital and industry with advantageous locality" (Begbie 1834, 352). The left side of the north riverbank contained private or gardened houses of the merchants. On the top of Government Hill (otherwise known as Fort Canning) were "neat wooden bungalows with venetians and *atap* roofs" (Begbie 1834, 352).

References to the Singapore River would grow over the decades and Western perspectives of it also elicited increasingly colourful descriptions. The river, from Raffles' early days, formed an important highway of the city and was also its natural port. Begbie's (1834, 351) relatively early description, however, was a terse depiction of physical geography, dry and lacking in colour. The river served three important functions as the colonial city developed: (1) as a dividing line, physically segregating two ethnic spheres of the town; (2) as the first port of the island and first location of the shipbuilding industry; and (3) as a waterway that would become the site of nine bridges conjoining the bifurcated town. Over the century of colonial development, the river remained a hive of economic activity.

The Singapore River grew in importance after Raffles decided to make it the line of demarcation between the north and south of the city. Osborn (1987, 10–11) described the "little creek or river" of Singapore in 1838 as separating the town "into distinct parts"; it "[split] the good town in two". In the decades ahead, this type of ethnic partition would become a defining characteristic of the evolving urban landscape. Singapore was the first colonial city in the region with internal ethnic segregation between the White and Asian populations who otherwise lived close to each other. As objectionable as that might seem to many today, it was actually an advance from the earlier fort-cities in which Whites had lived, whose vestiges still remain as reminders of the Western fear of being attacked by the native population. The new British factory of Singapore was one of the earliest colonies in the region where the White population was not fortified within walls.

At the time of Raffles' 1819 visit, there was said to be a native wooden bridge, later called the Presentment Bridge. This first wooden bridge, now replaced by the Elgin Bridge, would be the only direct land link between the European and Asian Towns for several decades. In that time, Europeans by and large stayed within the confines of the north side of the Singapore River. The only reason for Whites moving to the south side was to access Commercial Square or Raffles Place, which was the Central Business District (CBD) and heart of the Western retail sector. While other colonial cities were defined by their old and new towns (Jakarta), or directly contiguous White and native sectors in the form of districts (Hanoi), colonial Singapore was unique because the European Town and the Asian Town of the same city were clearly demarcated and separated, with the cultural distinctions continuing throughout the history of the British colony.

Given the small-sized ships and regional boats, the Singapore River area developed to undertake many port activities. Despite the port being relocated to Keppel Harbour in the 1840s, the river would remain a locus of many entrepôt activities and services up to the late 1970s. Keppel Harbour for its part would serve as Singapore's major port for over a century, and was the conduit of trade, transshipment, and all sorts of exotic cargo. One 1861 image by A. van Otterloo[1] was perhaps inspired

---

[1] See Plate 21.

by the harbour's growing fame. In it, camels appear as if to ferry goods to and from docked ships, although they are not known to have been used for that purpose in Singapore. In reality, the scene, apart from several pigtailed individuals and Chinese-looking sailing vessels, seems to be a fanciful rendering of Singapore as an Oriental port.

Much of the Keppel cargo was transferred to godowns along the Singapore River where it was reprocessed or repackaged for export. Early visitors talked frequently about the warehouses and quays along the river (Begbie 1834; Osborn 1987). Numerous private wharves lined the riverbank and numerous *sampans* were moored throughout the breadth of the river (Begbie 1834, 352). The cost of renting a warehouse ranged from 30 to 100 Spanish dollars a month (Buckley 1965, 357). Later visitors would note that the river was crowded by bumboats ferrying cargoes to and from cargo ships, wharves, and godowns. It was the unmistakable sight of bare-bodied coolie gangs shuffling goods between bumboats and godowns which Western visitors found fascinating.

VI. Chinatown

For all the impressions of Chinatown by various travellers and sojourners, there were few academic studies that documented its slum conditions that people lived in. Since its early colonial inception, the Lion City had been seen as a Chinese town because of the sheer numbers of the Chinese population. Chinese immigrants in Singapore had been steadily increasing and each census reflected the rise: 6,088 in 1827; 50,000 in 1850; 86,766 in 1881; 219,577 in 1911 (Marriott 1911, 356; Carlos 1921, 1:376). In his 1925 visit, Bleackley (1928, 133) pictured the whole southern portion of Singapore town as a Chinese city of 300,000 people and observed that there was no separate Chinatown of the type in Saigon. The Celestials had spread over the centre of the city.

Discussions of the Chinese community were focused on their organisations and economic contributions to Singapore. There were scant references to the overcrowded, unhealthy, and deteriorating living conditions. As Maj. Sidney noted, such living conditions excited no comment whatsoever. The Major said that in Chinatown, one's "eyes [had] really [to] work" to see things which in the "ordinary way [were] invisible" to those who passed them daily (Sidney 1926, 30–31). For him, the most impressive sight was the washing hanging out from balconies. A certain Ashe marvelled, "whole streets appear to be bristling with the washing of the inhabitants! This is truly an economic clothes-line and a very efficacious one" (Sidney 1926, 31).

The crowded conditions of life in Chinatown and the Asian sector (*toa poh*) might be hard for many of today's Singaporeans to imagine. Bleackley (1928, 133) opined that the Chinaman could not help making his home like a "pigsty, abominable both as regards odour and dirt". The tragedy is that Westerners believed that these living conditions reflected Chinese culture and their social system. Chinatown captured the Western imagination in the mid-1950s. This was a place that epitomised crowded streets and frenzied activity. At ground level, one found the mysterious Orient encapsulated in Chinese medicine shops and the weird gastronomical delights of the race — snakes, monkeys, tortoises, eels, frogs, all being sold as food.

Many of the Western perceptions of 'overcrowding' were impressionistic rather than studied. Maj. Sidney (1926, 31) noted that he knew of one small house which contained "no more than three rooms on the ground floor and two smaller floors above to accommodate 30 people". He went on to elaborate on the poor shophouse quarters he had observed, noting that a room could be used as "a shop, a diningroom [*sic*] and a living-room, and at night, with narrow wooden planks laid down, it [became] a sleeping-apartment" (Sidney 1926, 32). The marine biologist F. D. Ommanney (1960, 37) gave his own impressionistic observations: Chinatown was "appallingly overcrowded, with twelve or fifteen people living in one small room". Despite the new flats which had been built by the government, the residents appeared to prefer "their lousy, insanitary, horizontal" housing compared to the "hygienic, vertical", but "characterless" apartments which would nonetheless also end up being considered slums for their persistent unanticipated overcrowding. Ommanney (1960, 37) provided vivid descriptions of Chinatown's street scene: "the crowded, noisy alleyways", "vertical signboards", "intimate laundry", "shouting, swarming life", "food stalls", and the Chinese eating in the street — "thin men in striped pyjama trousers and singlets", "perched on stools like hungry emaciated birds". Given the activity, and the noise and smells in the streets, Ommanney (1960, 36) came to the conclusion that "the Chinese [had] an extraordinary power of concentration" due to their being used to the "overcrowding and din" they lived with. In geographical terms, this overcrowding would be interpreted as the power of place (de Blij 2009), with ethnic groups congregated in areas because of their 'sense of place'.

The most famous academic work about the crowded living conditions in Chinatown was *Upper Nankin Street Singapore*, by Barrington Kaye (1960). This thorough study documented the living conditions when the stirrings of independence were making political waves. Kaye (1960, 5) condemned living conditions in Chinatown as "among the most primitive in the urban areas in the world". Before Kaye's study, most official references to Chinatown's overcrowding were estimates and impressionistic assessments. The British sociologist chose its overcrowded, unfavourable conditions not to shed light on poverty or poor public health per se, but to question the "presence or absence of community identification" on a society-wide basis by residents (Kaye 1960, 31). For him, the fact that they did not identify with public activities was not in keeping with a society seeking independence.

As the population grew, the shophouses became places of residential involution as spaces were subdivided. Shophouses were inadequate for residential living, especially when parts of each shophouse were used for retail space, wholesale storage, coffee shop, and cottage manufacturing. Rooms were subdivided into several cubicles and sometimes families were crammed in these cubicles. The shophouse would be the main type of residential space that housed 60 per cent of Singapore's population until the early 1970s. Having a large bachelor working population, however, meant that shophouses were not used predominantly as family residences but as rented places for labourers. *Upper Nankin Street Singapore* provides a vivid picture of the living conditions of these workers. The shophouse was like an expanding and contracting accordion with regards to its resident population. Each shophouse was divided into cubicles and the number of cubicles per floor in the shophouse varied from six to 24. Over time the mean cubicle population per shophouse dropped from 14 to eight and the mean shophouse population from 36 to 30 (Kaye 1960, 45). There were three to four double-decked bunks in one cubicle which were rented out. Workers did not rent the cubicle but the bed on which they slept. Night shift workers rented beds in the day and day shift workers rented beds at night. Kaye (1960, 91) found it difficult to identify households as there were residents sleeping in bunk space outside the household cubicle or in the corridor; these lodgers were subtenants. The decrease in cubicles led to more people being crammed into a cubicle (Kaye 1960, 52).

These living conditions gave rise to slum development in Chinatown. Given the shortage of living places, the poor wages of workers, and their central location, Chinatown shophouses were popular places of residence.

The Chinese residents were mainly singles. Of the 1,608 households, 54 per cent were unmarried. Of the men, 75 per cent were bachelors compared to the women who comprised spinsters (45 per cent) and widows (25 per cent) (Kaye 1960, 188). Considering the abundance of singles, one could expect that much of their lives were spent outside their cubicles in dining, recreation, and meeting friends. Unfortunately, most Western perceptions of the crowded conditions were based on poor background knowledge of the residential population. Thus, many concluded that these awful living conditions were preferred by residents. Since many immigrants were single, there was indeed a propensity for them to live in ethnically familiar neighbourhoods like the predominantly Chinese Upper Nankin Street.

Kaye specifically chose Upper Nankin Street to demonstrate the overcrowding in Chinatown, focusing on cubicle density of the shophouses. In his 1955 survey, the street had 1,840 resident persons (Kaye 1960, 27). His breakdown of population showed 70 per cent of residents being of single-generation households (Kaye 1960, 33). His study indicated that 18 per cent of residents on the street lived in households with unrelated occupants, while 82 per cent lived in related households (Kaye 1960, 43). Sanitary conditions were generally poor. Inhabitants were obliged to share kitchens, and bathing and toilet facilities with other households (Kaye 1960, 83). Seventeen per cent of floors had no toilets and hence 40 or more adults were obliged to use one toilet. All the toilets were open bucket style and 36 per cent were emptied daily (Kaye 1960, 84). Despite the overcrowded living conditions, residents in these slums showed a high degree of local neighbourliness. Kaye noted that residents had many friends living in the same street; 16 per cent of respondents noted their relatives on the same street, 35 per cent had relatives in Chinatown, and 32 per cent had relatives in Singapore (Kaye 1960, 276).

Street after street was "crowded with these active and energetic Celestials", observed Collingwood (1868, 250). One can point to several possible reasons why Chinatown was crowded. Firstly, perhaps there was an element of truth in Western sojourners' observations that the Chinese had a "spirit of centralisation and co-operation" (Collingwood 1868, 250). They seemed to prefer to live their lives in public spaces more than private homes. Up to the 1960s, Singapore's Asian population would be more comfortable with community living over private residential confinement. The streets had become the venues of family socialisation, neighbourhood bonding, the children's playground, and the workplaces of family cottage industries. Pratt (1931, 19) noted that the native quarter was "inexpressively humble, homely and mysterious", and its streets "[twisted] and [turned] like wounded serpents". There, naked children were "ceaselessly at play, spilling from the darkness of the interior into the garish sunlight".

Secondly, the streets were filled with populace because by the turn of the 20th century, there was a housing shortage, especially in the central city. With increasing population growth, the bulk of new migrants stayed in the city as parts of extended families, clan groups, and diasporas of villages back home.

Thirdly, the covered five-foot ways of the two-storey houses had become arcades of merchandise. Hornaday (1885, 294) shared such perceptions of the Asian quarter of the town, noting that the streets were wide, and the shops "trim and orderly" and "overflowing with their respective wares". This was a "two-story [sic] town throughout, solidly built of brick, plastered over, and painted".

The White visitor in Chinatown saw economic specialisation: one street of blacksmiths, another of carpenters, and yet another of stonemasons. Each artisan specialised in his own craft with one objective, to return to China to cease work and live comfortably with their family (Collingwood 1868, 250). However, such crammed, congested places were also the breeding grounds of disease. A rampant one was tuberculosis.

All the perceptions of an overcrowded Chinatown had statistical validity. In the 1947 census, Chinatown had 135,000 persons and its average population density was 200,000 persons per square mile, all living in two- or three-storey shophouses. On average, every cubicle in the shophouse which was "dark, confined, insanitary and without comfort" had a household of seven or more persons (Kaye 1960, 2). In 1907, the British government recognised these problems of congestion and unhealthy living conditions. Governor Sir John Anderson engaged a public health expert, Dr. W. J. Simpson of King's College London, to assess the overcrowding and sanitary conditions (Kaye 1960, 2). Unfortunately, his report was also impressionistic. Although it led to major changes in trying to relieve the population of Chinatown and the unsanitary conditions of shophouses, the overcrowding would remain a tourist spectacle in Western eyes decades after the *Simpson Report*.

VII. Change Alley

In Singapore town, the roads, streets, and lanes were essentially the shopping areas for locals. Shophouse occupants maximised the covered walkways to contain their goods. In the process, riots broke out between pedestrians and shopkeepers in the 19th century because the covered five-foot ways had ceased to be accessible to pedestrians. By the 20th century, shopkeepers would take an even bolder stand on these shady alleys, as they were also called, using them to display all sorts of goods and merchandise (Bleackley 1928; Moore 1955) rather than simply storing or holding things there as they had previously done.

Singapore streets were not only defined by the static displays in shops and walkways. The streets were dynamic because they were festooned with itinerant hawkers, food peddlers, medicine men, pugilistic displays, and local buskers trying to sell all sorts of wares and traditional medicines. There were also roadside services provided by fortune tellers, letter writers or penny-a-liners, storytellers, seamstresses mending torn clothes, itinerant restaurants, and cobblers (J. Cameron 1965, 65–66). The street fed into the 'bazaar economy' that characterised colonial cities. The significant trait of the *pasar*[2] economy was bargaining. McKie (1942, 184–185) concluded that "haggling" was the "language of trade" in the East and the means by which the spoken word was kept alive. McKie (1942) saw the virtue of bargaining as opposed to the monotony of the fixed price, the sterile atmosphere of the Western shop, and the "unimaginative attitude" of its assistant. Given that over 80 per cent of the population was illiterate or with little formal education, much of Singapore during its colonial history operated according to an oral tradition, and bargaining was also a means of communication, gossip, and obtaining news.

Thus, the famed and convivial Change Alley in the heart of the CBD at Raffles Place became popular as an area where Western tourists and visitors could engage in haggling. The short alley linking Raffles Place to Collyer Quay was a shopping paradise that catered to White tourists. Change Alley was a microcosm of where the bazaar economy met the firm-centred economy, where the local joined the global, and where cultural diversity seemed meshed into a materialistic harmonious whole of yearnings for commodity. It was a strip that catered to every age group;

---

[2] The Malay term for *bazaar*.

from a toys galore to providing 24-hour tailored suits, perfumes to providing handbags, Oriental curios to antiques, and everything in between for the demanding housewife.

In many ways, Change Alley was a one-stop shopping arcade. As Barber (1978, 78–79) recalled, it was a place where Chinese, Arabs, Indians, and Oriental Jews vied with one another "to sell shoes and watches, torches and cutlery and the gimcrack hardware and junk of the world". Westerners found the alley a lively and entertaining shopping experience. This was the Eastern bazaar where varied Oriental salesmen shouted, appealed, whined, cringed, and fluttered in the "invigorating and faintly exciting" bartering and bantering (Walling 1985, 223). And no matter where tourists, sailors, and merchants came from, there were numerous Indian money changers to convert every foreign currency to local, while keeping up their vocal advertisements of 'money-change, money-change'.

VIII. Commercial Square: Raffles Place

Tumasik had been based on the Indianised spatial order in which the centre of the cosmic city was the sacred royal residence where the raja resided on Bukit Larangan. The colonial city would develop under different secular agencies through the Raffles Town Plan. The plan, underscoring colonial thinking, had in fact two secular centres: (1) the White residential and administrative centre north of the Singapore River; and (2) the commercial centre known as Commercial Square and later Raffles Place, south of the river. The spatial development of Commercial Square replaced the earlier idea of cosmic sacred space with a secular, profane space where monetary land and economic values dictated centrality and importance.

The location of a commercially viable centre, however, was not a given. An argument between Raffles and William Farquhar regarding this ensued. Farquhar had considered Kampong Glam to be the business quarter while Raffles thought that the business quarter should be at the location where it has remained till today, and which is also presently named after him. Raffles rejected Farquhar's idea saying sarcastically that "if *Kampong Gelam*[3] were to become a business area, this side of the River would remain unimproved for as long as 100 years" (A. Hill 1982, 109).

---

[3] An alternate spelling of *Kampong Glam*.

Yet Farquhar was still confident of his idea and told Munshi Abdullah, the major Muslim personality of the time and eventual close associate of Raffles, to "get yourself a piece of land in *Kampong Gelam*, for a business area will grow up later there" (A. Hill 1982, 109).

Raffles' idea of the business centre prevailed and he had oversight of its development. The original plan had been to develop Commercial Square to the north of Boat Quay; eventually the square would be located on the south side of the Singapore River. The area on the south side was a swamp that was reclaimed. The first 'grants' of land were under Raffles' name, and the grantee's name, property area, and address were accepted as registration of land 'tenure'. Raffles noted that before he left Singapore in 1824, he had issued 574 such land 'grants' (Wheatley 1954, 63).

One of the spatial icons of Raffles' urban planning legacy was the fusion of commerce with the multiethnic population that was institutionalised in Commercial Square. Hence, while the Raffles Town Plan created spatial apartheid in White and Asian living quarters, what would later be renamed Raffles Place provided for the integration of European and Asian merchants and traders to mingle and do business together. The mixed land ownership by Europeans and Asians in Commercial Square set the foundations for a cosmopolitan trading ecosystem. Business through capitalism was the lubricant for interracial interaction and coexistence.

Hornaday (1885, 294) noted that the square was packed closely with shipping offices, warehouses, and shops of European merchants. Propelled by Singapore's own economic momentum, Raffles Place would become the commercial hub of the colonial city. Over the decades, it formed the Central Business District (CBD) of Singapore. Here, European and Asian businessmen, entrepreneurs, wholesalers and retailers, money changers and bankers interacted in trade and commerce. This meeting place of East and West was also where one witnessed the 'dual economy' operating side by side. It was what the anthropologist Clifford Geertz (1963) has referred to as the firm-centred economy, mixed with the bazaar or *pasar* system; or what Brazilian social scientist Milton Santos (1979) called the upper and lower circuits of the economy.

The bazaar native economy (Change Alley) existed in Raffles Place itself, through the "shared space" of the two economic circuits (Santos 1979). The upper circuit was based on the predominantly White, colonial economic activities operated by banks and financial institutions, European business houses, trading companies, and transport agencies. The lower circuit was the native economic sector (also exemplified by the nearby Chinatown) dominated by local processing firms, cottage industry, and native financial activity. In the Market Street shophouses, the famous Tamil money lenders or *chettiars*, as they were popularly called, remained a visible sight till the late 1960s.

Western travellers, especially in the post-World War II period, would remark at the distinctions between the native and European economic systems in Raffles Place — itinerant money changers and moneylenders operating next to Western commercial banks; hawkers and small retail shops versus the large Western-type department stores; the local system of haggling for goods as opposed to the fixed prices in Western stores; and small, local processing outlets and artisanal enterprises as against big, Western international processing and manufacturing companies.

By the later part of the 19th century, the Asian sector on the southern bank of the Singapore River had already begun to be increasingly colonised by Europeans, with Raffles Place becoming the heart of the colonial city. By the end of the century, Raffles Place was developing into a firm-centred financial centre with Singapore's then only three banks being located there: Hongkong and Shanghai Banking Corporation; the Chartered Bank of India, Australia and China; and the Mercantile Bank of India (Dennys 1894, 362–363). For a century or so since then, Raffles Place remained Singapore's CBD despite attempts to move it in the direction of Shenton Way and currently, the Marina Bay reclaimed area.

While the Raffles Town Plan had designated the north side of the city as the territorial preserve of the White population, Raffles Place on the south side would also grow as the prestigious retail area for White clientele. By the 1890s, it had upmarket department stores like John Little & Company, Robinson & Company, the Katz Brothers, and Sayle & Company (Dennys 1894, 364–365). Impressed, Maj. Sidney (1926, 30) noted, "Raffles Square contains shops which would not be a disgrace in London, and here one can buy almost anything one needs". Bleackley (1928, 153) identified the two main retail areas as High Street and Raffles Place. The three big retailers in Raffles Place were John Little, Robinsons, and Whiteaway Laidlaw, which were modelled after Harrods as "universal providers" (Bleackley 1928, 154). The shops charged a little more for the same goods sold in London. John Little advertised itself as the "finest store East of Suez". Raffles Place was the White man's retail preserve. Barber (1978, 78) reserved the greatest compliments about shopping in Robinsons, which would sell you an aspirin or a motor launch, and deliver it 400 miles up north. For him there was "no place like Robinsons" (Barber 1978, 78).

IX. Iconic Landscapes that Surprised and Disturbed

The varied shapes, forms, colours, and images left Westerners defining streetscapes as the aesthetic invocation of the picturesque. These were not scenes of symmetrical beauty, but rather the asymmetrical juxtaposition of old and new, Oriental and Occidental, sex and economy, conjoined in a "piecemeal affair of hints, contrasts, sparks" sticking out as the "wheels of commerce and vulgarity [ground] together" (P. Anderson 1955, 153). From the morphology of the city to its legibility (or identifiable definite detail), this was a city of dual landscapes, differing images, and diversified cultural meanings. Western visitors were exposed to the streets of vice and illegal activity as they were to sacred landscapes of churches, temples, and religious rituals. The surgeon Robert Little (1848a) was amazed at the amounts of money which Chinese addicts spent on smoking opium in Singapore's opium dens. Likewise, Maria Balestier was surprised at how the Chinese *towkays* could spend enormous sums of money on elaborate and ostentatious funerals (Hale 2016).

a) Bugis Street: Bewildering Nights of Passage

Singapore never failed to surprise the White resident and sojourner. For the passing traveller, the city was a pastiche of moving scenes that intoxicated and saturated the mind. Some held the Western imagination, others were discarded from memory. However, for the Western resident of the city, some places were uncovered not by chance but deliberate intervention. Singapore was a city described by roadside narratives displaying cultural manifestations, from the "hybrid street" (part Asian, part European) of Orchard Road (P. Anderson 1955) to the "ever-shifting pattern of life" in Bugis Street (Ommanney 1960, 38–39). The streets revealed a richness and diversity which frequently elicited bewildered White sentiments of admiration, disgust, curiosity, and contempt (P. Anderson 1955; Bird 1883; Pratt 1931; Moore 1953). Street narratives were an overt display of the sacred and sinful, the lawful and illegal, and the joyous and melancholic. The streets were like an open book of native life, its *genre de vie*, and its rites of passage.

Bugis Street fascinated the itinerant White traveller, the bored British serviceman, and the inquisitive sojourner. Speaking for many other White visitors, Ommanney (1960, 46) said he would sit there and "let time slide past like a dark river, flowing out of nowhere into nowhere, bearing to your feet upon its flood driftwood and frail blossoms". After midnight, they were all entertained. Here, Patrick Anderson (1955, 280) confessed, "I would think of capturing someone amongst the wildest Chinese, as a series of young boys with shaggy hair, stalwart bodies and expressions far more ferocious and attractive than those of the normal European-trained servant, bowed in front of me". A few years later, Ommanney (1960) visiting Bugis Street in its heyday had a more graphic description of the Chinese and Malay 'girls' he met — Rosie, Julia, Patsy, Maisie, and Lily, but never once mentioned that they were transvestites or what the Thais call 'ladyboys'. There appears to have been a recurrent Western taboo against the mention of anyone being a transvestite. All he stated cryptically was that in Bugis Street, "everything [was] possible, and after midnight male egos in their hundreds [drifted] there" (Ommanney 1960, 46).

Bugis Street was the underside of the Singapore experience that Europeans beheld. Unsuspectingly, Anderson found it to be beyond his imagination. Yet throughout his description of the place and its doll-like prostitutes, the Canadian too shied away from mentioning that he was being flirted with by transvestites:

> The whole thing was a crazy idea in a crazy world of flaring lamps, far too much beer, and children whose business was to flirt with Europeans for money: little girls tarted up till they were part dolls, part whores, and singing 'Kelantan, Kelantan!' to zither-like instruments while the bedraggled harpy figures of their mothers watched them from the shadows; little boys whose racket was certainly not sexual but whose jeering laughing eyes caught one's own across the forests of bottles, Siglet! Siglet! (P. Anderson 1955).

b) *Red-Light Areas*

In the 19th century Shanghai had the reputation of being the whorehouse of the Orient. At the end of the same century, Singapore too gained an unsavoury image for prostitution, of which the above-mentioned Bugis Street was but one part. Prostitution was a well-organised, thriving industry in Singapore for four reasons: (1) the colonial authorities did not make it illegal, to ensure that the industry could be controlled and not forced to go underground; (2) the disproportionate resident population of bachelor males over females; (3) the bustling free port, with its transient population of short stayers, and endless sailors and shiphands who needed an outlet to release themselves upon when they came ashore; and (4) in a commercial city, prostitution was an entertainment business that was popular among traders, businessmen, and itinerant entrepreneurs. The town was also complimented liberally for its hospitality and generosity to visitors. During their heyday, the prostitute dens attracted sex workers not only from the immediate region, but also Russia, England, France, Germany, China, and Japan. Before 1914, Singapore counted 236 Chinese, 48 Japanese, and 10 European brothels (Shennan 2015, 99).

Writing in the 1980s Raymond Flower (1984, 247), a regular visitor of the Raffles Hotel, noted that 30 years before, Singapore had been "more permissive, its people more promiscuous". This sordid environment was not a reflection of the allure of transatlantic manners, the Coca-Cola culture, nor the erosion of Asian values. He argued that it had been the post-war economic boom effect, the rubber boom, and the Korean War which led to the springing up of semi-private night clubs, with a mushrooming of mistresses (Flower 1984, 247). Mahjong parlours became the hunting ground of affluent playboys seeking out wives, mistresses, and the daughters of rich men (Flower 1984, 247).

Over the decades, different roads and back lanes would become part of a red-light district. After the war, Lavender Street was a magnet for European servicemen. Flower (1984, 247) advocated that Whites gave Desker Road a miss. He described it as a "stinking back alley" where "women lined up like cattle and could be had for the price of three beers". Sago Lane was equally "notorious" and well known as "the $5.60 area" because of its fixed going rate (Flower 1984, 247).

According to John van Cuylenburg (1982, 58), "Japanese hotels in old Singapore were notorious as prostitutes' dens, and before the outbreak of the Pacific War they numbered many hundreds". The underground vice business revolved around massage parlours, prostitute dens, brothels, and sex hotels. It flourished after the official closure of the brothels around the turn of the 20th century, with "the Japanese [starting] an orgy of Japanese hotels in the late 1920s", which were more or less disguised brothels (van Cuylenburg 1982, 59). The Japanese population in Singapore had risen steadily in the second half of the 19th century. In 1889, there were 2,690 Japanese in Singapore. Japanese prostitutes (*Karayuki-san*) were a visible force in Middle Road where their entertainment sector was located.

By the 20th century, Singapore was developing an unsavoury reputation internationally for vices of all sorts, abetted no doubt by corruption. Visitors repeatedly described the city's addiction to opium smoking, gambling, and prostitution. These developments were a total reversal of Raffles' 'first principles' of governance for the colony. The Rev. William Cross (1921, 59), reviewing Singapore's 100th anniversary, was optimistic when he wrote about those principles:

> The Malays were compelled to lay aside the kris; gambling and cock-fighting were made illegal because they induced quarrels and robbery; slavery was prohibited; the use of opium and spirituous liquors was strictly regulated in order to suppress intoxication; the far-reaching principle was laid down if a woman debased herself by prostitution, no one save herself was to be allowed to trade upon her sin — a brothel was to be an impossibility in Singapore!

Unfortunately, the good pastor was blind to the thriving sex trade. The most well-known part of the red-light district centred around Malay and Malabar Streets, known to seamen and travellers the world over (McKie 1942, 100–104; Firmstone 1905, 106–107; van Cuylenburg 1982, 59). Lockhart (1936, 122–123) provided a vivid account of Malay and Malabar Streets, where the "white wrecks of European womanhood and young Japanese girls, silent, immobile and passionless traded their bodies for the silver dollars of Malaya". He observed that Singapore was the first city where he had seen first-hand the "sale and purchase of vice" (Lockhart 1936, 122). The English diplomat and secret agent noted that "ship's officers of every nationality, and globe-trotters, travellers, miners, and planters from up-country wasted their money on an orgy to which drink and noise and occasionally brawling supplied a discordant orchestra" (Lockhart 1936, 123).

Returning to Malay Street two decades later, he observed that it had changed, the Europeans and Japanese vanished, and the Chinese like an "army of ants had taken possession of the place" (Lockhart 1936, 125). Walking through, Lockhart (1936, 125) noted that there was no more interest in the place: "I was merely one of these mad-dog tourists who poked about in the humdrum quarters of hard-working Chinese". The streets having been expunged, the area would later resurface as the Bugis Junction shopping complex.

c) *Sago Lane Death Houses*

Another place where several Western residents were left with indelible impressions was the row of 'death houses' in Sago Lane. Those who witnessed the area formed unpalatable images of it, and developed unpleasant sense descriptions and critical reflections on what they deemed unfathomable. The shocking landscape of Sago Lane, with its "dying houses", was like a time machine bringing the British entrepreneur Moore (1955, 66–72) through a journey into a past better left alone. The erudite lecturer Patrick Anderson (1955) was emotionally disturbed that such a place existed in a seemingly modern city like Singapore. The same man who had apparently enjoyed his time at Bugis Street, reflecting upon his disgust, stated:

> What could be more atrocious to the eyes of western personality than these places, facing each other across the cramped street, in which the dying lay on their beds on the first floor, knowing that beneath them their companions of yesterday were stretched out in the morgue, under paper sheets inscribed with prayers, and hearing and smelling the business of death continually carried on in the street outside — the brass bands, the groups of professional mourners, the great wheels of frangipani? (P. Anderson 1955, 276).

Visiting these "sick receiving houses" in September 1954, Moore (1955, 67) penned a vivid description of the dying:

> Here you can look on death and listen to the beat of the wings of the Angel of death; here, also you can look on decay, the slow, emaciating decay of the human organism, and decay in something still living is infinitely more distressing than the decay which comes after death.

Anderson (1955, 276) too described the morbid sight of the people on their deathbeds:

> I remembered the cadaverous torso of a Chinese, all dull stringy varnish, outlined against the small window as he sat on his bed — and another Chinese who lay on his side as he occasionally dabbed an enormous growth on his neck with a damp towel.

Moore was fascinated by his visit to places where people "[retired] to die". He noted that the Westerner does not accept death at all, not even when he is dying, but the inmates in Singapore's dying houses did so (Moore 1955, 68). For him, it was this attitude that made the business of dying a "much easier process than we in the West find it" (Moore 1955, 68).

Curious to know why families sent their dying to these houses instead of keeping them at home, Moore (1955, 69) asked the proprietor of one such house for the reason. To his surprise the man gave a litany of them, or as the White resident said, "a hundred reasons". These ranged from the practical to the superstitious: "Perhaps their homes are too crowded; perhaps they live in conditions so bad that there is no room for anyone to die; perhaps their relatives don't want them; perhaps their relatives think it bad joss for anyone to die in their house, or in their room, or in their cubicle, or their space, or whatever it is they live in".

The lesson for Moore (1955) was the difference between Western and Eastern views of health and hospital. He interviewed a young person whose brother had been suffering from probably a "burst appendix" and lain in a death house for five days because his family refused to send him to hospital (Moore 1955, 70–71). By sheer "majestic ignorance", the Chinese ironically placed less faith in hospital care than death houses. A habit of sending people to hospital only when they were near death meant that their entry to hospital effectively became a pre-announcement of their death. This sequence of events was then misinterpreted by families as meaning that the hospital was a place that killed a person.

The idea of the death house might have been revolting for Whites because the funeral took place at the same venue. However, the death house was little different from what we have in the name of hospices. There, the terminally ill were left to die as is the case today. In a way, death houses were the local colonial era version of hospices.

For Moore, it was a positive sign that the Chinese were ultimately changing their views with regard to sending their sick to hospital, hence the winning of the battle over ignorance. "People more and more are going to hospital for treatment, instead of retiring to a dying-house to die" (Moore 1955, 71). The visit to Sago Lane opened Moore's (1955, 71–72) eyes to the whole "paraphernalia of the traditional Chinese funeral" — paper motor cars and houses to be taken to the next world, joss sticks, candles, paper money, wreaths, heavily carved coffins, and the funeral procession that was organised like a military operation. The pragmatic businessman felt that the extravagance in sending off the dead should rather have been spent on welcoming a newborn safely into the world (Moore 1955, 72).

X. Summing Up: A Planned City of Contrasts

In summing up Singapore's morphological landscape, it is evident that by instituting the 1822 Raffles Town Plan, Raffles provided a blueprint of the city which would endure for much of its colonial history. The plan can be interpreted in two ways. It reflected colonial concerns about security and safety of White residents by separating the White and Asian populations into distinct areas. Given, however, that the White population was no more enclosed within a fortress as had commonly been done elsewhere in the region since the 16th century, the new colonial city was based on an open urban plan. This plan provided spatial separation and encouraged cultural interaction.

The other way of viewing the Raffles Town Plan is to accept that it underscored a policy of segregating Whites from the Asian population by creating spatial apartheid. The fact that the Whites maintained the Tanglin Club and Singapore Cricket Club as exclusive preserves till the 1960s and seldom invited Asians to their homes is evidence that European racism prevailed in colonial Singapore. Western reports about 'society' in Singapore were exclusively about Whites and clearly elitist, excluding even those deemed to be lower echelons within the White population.

Singapore's infrastructure was evident to many White sojourners. The Asians lived in the ubiquitous, crammed two-storey shophouses that defined their sector, while the Whites dwelt in bungalow homes. Yet, both 'towns' were attractive to European sojourners in their own ways. Being generally devoid of crowds, the White Town was lauded for its serenity, peace, and order, and manicured house-and-garden landscapes. The shades of green were regularly punctuated by the colours of houses. The Asian Town on the other hand was chaotically picturesque and full of riotous colour and life. While the shophouses were nothing to look at, the streets were filled with people and all sorts of activity. Those Western sojourners who dared venture into Chinatown were treated to a kaleidoscope of amazing 'Oriental' delights and curiosities, bazaars, operas, roving hawkers, religious rites, fortune tellers, and children playing in an ambient cacophony of noise. Unlike the staid Western Town, the Asian Town was powerfully sensuous, a feast of colour, sound, smell, and taste.

Like icing on a cake, there were place highlights that Westerners were drawn to. By and large, Singapore had no historical monuments and major architectural features to boast about. But it had its own unique attractions. In the compact city, there was a diversity of places that stood out and were repeatedly mentioned by Western sojourners: the Singapore River, Chinatown, Change Alley, Robinsons, Sago Lane, Bugis Street, Malay-Kandahar Streets, and Desker Road, as well as street foods, shopping delights, rickshaws, and the babel of languages. The Lion City's attractions covered a gamut of the pleasant and seedy. Colonial Singapore was a functional landscape, people-orientated, and a multifaceted cosmopolitan place. It was a blend of East and West, a fusion of tradition and modernity, and where cultures could be openly sampled in its unique street culture. In short, the Singapore experience was not defined by a major cultural tradition nor style of civilisation; it was rather a mélange of cultures and civilising influences.

The seeds of the image of a modernising city were planted in the heads of Western observers in the 20th century. The trappings of motorised transportation, upmarket retailing, the growing materialism, the plural society, cosmopolitan outlook, and wealthy *towkays* captured the Western mind. Within this colonised social hierarchy, accommodation between different racial and religious groups developed. The acceptance of social hierarchies, ethnic pluralism, formal education, urban living, cosmopolitan optics, and capitalistic transactions laid the foundations of modernity in Singapore. Singapore was ahead of other regional urban centres in the culture of modernisation but it would not be alone in this regard; the British colonial city was moving in tandem with other such cities.

In the early 20th century, Singapore was becoming a White tourist attraction; it was a comfortable city which delighted. The businessman

Bleackley (1928, 119) even made a bold suggestion to the authorities to get rid of the squalor in Orchard Road and turn it into a "great boulevard" which could be worthy of "one of the proudest and richest cities in the East". He was referring to the *kampongs* and cemeteries which beset it after the Europeans had begun moving out of the area. Later in the 1950s, however, Orchard Road would again be perceived as a Western street, and referred to by locals as the 'Tuan's street' (Moore 1955). Certainly, if Bleackley and Moore were to have seen an even later Orchard Road, they would have been astonished by its modernised major architectural facelift.

7

Singapore's Imageability

Chapter 7

SINGAPORE'S IMAGEABILITY

I. Formulating Urban Impressions

Over the nearly one-and-a-half centuries of Singapore's colonial rule, the Western perceptions of the city were generally positive and favourable, with a few notable exceptions. Unlike the other regional locations where Westerners wrote about their views of tropical nature and pristine landscapes, the Singapore experience was basically focused on cultural landscapes and concomitantly, the perceived driving forces which shaped the sense of place. These perceptions therefore form the basis of this chapter. Singapore was a colony of modified landscapes, whether in agricultural plantations, urban areas, or local villages. Westerners who resided in Singapore were essentially traders, merchants, and professionals such as doctors, lawyers, engineers, and some missionaries, and many dabbled both in agriculture and trade. Many naturalists also used Singapore as their port of entry into the region. Apart from Alfred Russel Wallace, however, few of the naturalists explored Singapore's natural landscapes. For them, the rest of the Malay Archipelago was a pristine Eden waiting to be discovered and documented. Nonetheless right down to the 20th century, the Lion City would still charm Western sojourners; it was a mix of the Orient and tropical differences with Europe, the exhilaration of sampling a new environment, and the personal discovery of undefined cultural landscapes. Paul Theroux (1973, 93) captured the Westerner's personal excitement through Jack Flowers, the American protagonist in his novel *Saint Jack*, as he relishes his working appointment in Singapore:

> At that period in my life, my first years in Singapore, I enjoyed a rare kind of happiness, like the accidental discovery of renewal singing in the heart and feet, that comes with infatuation. It was true power, mercy and boldness. I felt brave, I didn't belittle it or try to justify it, and I never wondered about its queer origin. I was converted to buoyancy, and, rising, understood survival: the surprise of the marooned man who had built his first fire.

The mixed insights and perceptions of both the transient visitors and residents provide us with a composite overview of Singapore through the 145 years of British rule. The commonality of themes tells us something of what attractions and distractions shaped Western views in their Lion City experiences. No attempt is made here to state that such perceptions were exclusive to Whites, nor that the insights were exclusively culturally Western. However, given that these impressions of Singapore were formed during an important phase in history, the long 19th century, one might hazard speculation that historical forces, especially those in Europe, were of particular significance in these Western images.

The perceptions of Singapore varied somewhat between the transient visitor and White resident. The short-staying sojourners provided more impressionistic snap shots of the city, concentrating on sense perceptions formed during urban wanderings. The colonial city in the brief sojourner's narrative was thus a continual series of ever-changing visual scenes, with fairly little cultural or historical depth in the descriptions. The long-staying sojourners or White residents were clearly more familiar with local culture and tended to give more measured accounts of what they experienced. Familiar with different ethnic groups, they provided thumbnail cultural descriptions, albeit stereotypical, of the Asian communities. Most of the long-term residents like John Crawfurd, Joseph and Maria Balestier, Robert Little, John Cameron, Thomas Oxley, James Richardson Logan, Charles Buckley, and Roland Braddell were well-versed at shedding light on Singapore's history, economic activities, and social life. They left insights into the culture and existential activities of expatriates and the local population, which are uncommon in depictions of many other colonies.

II. Imageable Singapore

The urban planner Kevin Lynch (1972) used two interesting concepts to define the image of a city: imageability and legibility. An imageable city is one with a distinctive character. According to Lynch (1972, 9), imageability refers to the "quality in a physical object which gives it a high probability of evoking a strong image in any given observer". An imageable city has a holistic image based on colours, shapes, rhythms, arrangements, buildings, environment, ambience, and people. Through these varied qualities, the city becomes expressive, evokes sensuous delight, and provides stimulus and choice (Lynch 1972) to those who encounter and can explore it.

One measure of imageability is the city streets. A city that exudes a holistic identifiable image is likely to make an impression on a visitor or resident. This is the image a visitor might receive after encountering a foreign city. Are Venice, San Francisco, London, New York, and Vancouver imageable cities? Western visitors, sojourners, and tourists provided the best proof of what 'imageability' one could speak of in Singapore, based on impressionistic, quick overviews of the city they experienced over a short span of time. The resident White population on the other hand provided the detailed samples of a 'legible' Singapore, meaning one which was both identifiable and navigable in its definite details, by ferreting out, for example, its alleys, street peculiarities, unhackneyed pathways, and favourite haunts and places.

Singapore's expatriate residents had views of the colonial city which best rendered its sense of legibility. For long-term resident Roland Braddell (1921b, 2:465), "Singapore is for the Singaporean; to him only it has its attraction". Part of Singapore's attraction were the "little things" which do not matter to the historian. Using the analogy of the spicy relish which complemented local food, he said, for "what town is more dependent than Singapore upon tittle-tattle for the sambal to its daily curry" (R. Braddell 1921b, 2:465). Singapore seemed to appeal because it was a liveable place when one got to know it. The city's charms were based on places Westerners engaged with. There were legendary outfits like the Grand Hotel de l'Europe and Raffles Hotel, department stores such as Robinsons, Whiteaway Laidlaw, and John Little, and impressionistic places like the Singapore River, Change Alley, Raffles Place, and Chinatown. Overall, it would seem that the colonial city, rather than being predominantly one with a holistically impressive and imageable landscape, was rather fragmented by individual iconic places. There was nothing collectively vintage about its buildings, it had no imposing monuments to boast about, nor was the city a coherent symbol of modernism.

To many travellers, Singapore was an undefined city, a city that Rudyard Kipling damned. The average visitor left the island "cursing the heat, the hotels and the expense", observed Braddell (1921b, 2:465). For Joseph Conrad, Singapore in the 1880s was his base in regional travels and in his writings. This was his great "Eastern port", a crossroads of intercultural mixing at a time when great technological change was underway, as steamship replaced sailing ship (Sherry 1966; de Souza 1994). If there was indeed an imageable Singapore to speak of, it was not focused so much on its built environment, but in the lively energy which characterised the city. What grabbed the Western visitors' attention was Singapore's economic vitality, its dynamic scene, a functional hub, people in motion, and an indescribable busyness that gave spirit to the urban landscape.

Travel writers like Kipling, W. Somerset Maugham, Noël Coward, and Conrad made Singapore a stopover in their regional travels and left impressionistic vignettes of their hotel stays. Singapore was full of itinerant travellers and sojourners whose stories of the region became their characters and plots. Maugham (1993, 44), noting the "gay, multitudinous streets of the city", concluded that Singapore was "the meeting place of many races". Despite its "dark and smelly" bedrooms, he observed how the "quaintness" of the Van Dorth Hotel (later the Van Dyke) attracted "masters of tramps", mining engineers, globe-trotters, and planters (Maugham 2000, 43–51).

Maugham's interlude of Singapore visits was between March 1921 and 1959, the latter being when he reached 85 years of age. In Singapore the famed author spent time writing and editing his stories, and most of all picking up other stories. As he stated in his 1959 stopover, "I would love to hear some Singapore tales" (Flower 1984, 163). Coward became friendly with Arshak, one of the ethnic Armenian Sarkies brothers who owned the Raffles Hotel, which then became the setting for *Pretty Polly Barlow*, a story made into a BBC TV film (Flower 1984, 165). For Conrad and Kipling, Singapore's Oriental and exotic allure was the backdrop of their fictions. However, it was essentially the city's nature as a colonial commercial hub which allowed these writers to create works that lived off the ebb and flow of its population.

The meeting of interesting characters, the flotsam and jetsam of White travellers, seem to occur at a few Singapore hotels: Raffles, Hotel de l'Europe, Van Dorth, and the Sailors' Home. Travellers like Maugham, Kipling, Conrad, Theroux, Isabella Bird, and Ambrose Pratt made the Singapore stopover an observation and listening post, and a hub of information gathering. It was the depictions of life in these tropical Asian settings by the professional writers which helped to foster in the eyes of the Western public the myth of the Oriental mystique. Their stories were infused with the contrasts between East and West; the Westerner in the 19th century was fascinated by everything Asian, Oriental, and native, from mode of dress to working habits, eating to cultural traditions, customs to racial features. Singapore was the Westerner's one-stop node for imbibing various facets of the Asian vernacular landscape. It was the scene of a "vernacular culture" that implied "a way of life ruled by tradition and custom, entirely remote from the larger world of politics and law; a way of life where identity derived not from permanent possession of land but from membership in a group or super-family" (J. B. Jackson 1984, 149).

Singapore seemed like an aberration to Western cultural norms. It had assumed different personae over the decades. Malcolm MacDonald, who had held both the posts of British governor-general of the Malayan Union and commissioner-general for Southeast Asia, once referred to the colonial city as a "cultural desert" which he hoped would blossom as a garden through art, literature, and music (Moore 1953, 7). Donald Moore, the British entrepreneur, made the most negative references to Singapore: he called it a "police state" under the British in their combat against the communist insurgency (Moore 1953, 172); a "prosperous" but "hopeless city" because of the slums and squatters (Moore 1953, 221); and an "abscess" at the appendix of Asia extending from a "Malayan Frankenstein" (Moore 1955, 98).

a) *Singapore Lights*

One of the persistent Western themes in describing Singapore's changing landscape was the reference to its lights, which came from both nature and culture. Light was used to signify diverse objects, places, and aspects of nature. Varied lights seemed to cast evocative landscape scenes and inspire differing perceptions of the developing city. Roland Braddell (1935) entitled his book *The Lights of Singapore*, which he found to be a fascinating motif identifiable with the colonial city. The 'lights' were metaphors for the many fascinating delights that Braddell found there. Singapore's 'lights', both natural and man-made, appealed to different sojourners in various ways.

The British naturalist Frederick Burbidge (1880, 26) noted the tropical nights that brought out nature's lights. He observed "the moonlight ... bright enough to read by, [streaming] down like a gloriously brilliant bridal veil over sweet-scented blossoms wet with dew, and the most elegant of palm-trees, over the gorgeous floral treasures of eastern gardens, and over the homes of thousands of dusky brides". For other Westerners the lights of Singapore were in the sunrises and sunsets that coloured the landscape. Braddell (1935, 1) was fascinated by the setting sun of Singapore which he was leaving behind:

> a whirl of pink opal where the clouds jostled each other against the west. To the east the sky was topaz, lemon, and turquoise, while the sea took on myriad impossible tints and the trees and slopes opposite to the rock on which we stood showed rifle-green.

For yet other travellers, nature's lights were seen in the insects of the night. The French doctor Yvan (1855, 66) observed that around the American plantation owner Joseph Balestier's home were numerous luminous insects which appeared to him like "precious stones gifted with the power of motion and animation". Entertained by Balestier, Yvan (1855, 65) was delighted to be in one of the "fairy palaces of the East: the dazzling lights, the Asiatic luxury of everything around, the soft perfumed atmosphere". Yvan's (1855) movements and explorations in the Muslim-Arabic area of Kampong Glam also provided him with enchanting images of a fabled Orient.

As the city developed, electricity lit up the cultural landscape, and Westerners took more notice of electric lights. Just as European cities competed with one another as 'Cities of Light' (Osterhammel 2014, 311), Singapore in the 20th century provided the electric sparkle of city lights. As well as nature's lights, Singapore was well known for its city lights. Like other technological innovations, electric lighting was another symbol of progress and modernisation.

Singapore was also for Whites and Asians alike a metaphoric symbol of a new dawn, a place that ushered in hope for entrepreneurs and wealth-seekers. Hence, while Stamford Raffles had founded Singapore with bright and promising ideas, the Japanese in conquering Singapore in 1942 also wanted it to be their icon in the tropical world; hence the name *Lion City* was changed to *Syonan-to* or *Light of the South*. It was their way of stamping out any aura of Western colonial influence and replacing it with an Asian statement, more specifically, a declaration of Japanese hegemonic political culture. The British historian C. M. Turnbull (1977, 201) gave the reason why the Japanese believed that they had a superior culture: "since the Japanese claimed descent from gods and the Europeans from monkeys, in any war between gods and monkeys the gods must win".

Raffles had a different expression of lights. Writing in 1823 in Singapore, he was thinking ahead to what Britain would leave behind in its colony. For the British administrator, "characters of light" were the "monuments" that would endure after the "empire" had passed away (S. Raffles 1830, Appendices, 38). Despite this, throughout much of its colonial history, Western sojourners seldom gave praise to Singapore's imperial monuments, buildings, or architecture. Many did nonetheless find its mixed, lively, urban landscape an unforgettable experience. After the Second World War, enlightened observers would find inspiration in Singapore's distinctive colonial-built traditions, 'Eurasian' architecture (this being the East-West mixture), Oriental religious buildings, stately bungalows, and even the ubiquitous shophouse.

Marjorie Doggett (1957), a long-time resident of Singapore together with her husband Victor, a major contributor to its music scene, paid tribute to Singapore's buildings and architecture. In the aptly titled book *Characters of Light*, Marjorie described Singapore as having developed beyond "Raffles' wildest dreams" as a "great port and fine city" (Doggett 1957, ix). It was a city of contrasts, from the "sordid night life" to "dying houses", and the riot of colours at sunset to the shimmering glisten of the moon. Doggett's 1957 photographic inventory of 45 "characters of light" included government buildings, schools, distinctive places, streets, shophouses, markets, churches, temples, mosques, the museum, library, university, prison, court, and the Assembly House that defined her Singapore experience. Yet, despite her thumbnail sketches of each individual building, street, monument, and place of worship, Doggett (1957, vi) was less interested in the buildings themselves than in the *lives* of these buildings and places where people "lived and worked", and the "scenes of happiness and sorrow enacted within ... walls" that would evoke nostalgia of the "life and times of old Singapore" (Doggett 1957, vi). Without knowing it, she was extolling her love for Singapore's vernacular landscapes (J. B. Jackson,

1984) — the existential, utilitarian, and functional aspects and places, rather than the monumental, historical, or ornate buildings and ceremonial places of pomp and pageantry. It was through the sum of these landscape expressions that Doggett (1957, ix) and other Westerners knew how "Singapore [had] taken a part of [their] hearts for her own".

b) *The Beehive of Activity*

Singapore seemed to grab visitors' attention because it was a hive of activity, a city busy and full of life. Wallace (2015, 63), during his second stay in Singapore in 1856, was convinced that "no one can appreciate a new country in a short visit". However, after spending some months in Singapore, he began to "marvel at the life & bustle, the varied occupations, & strange population" that had replaced in such a short time "an uninhabited jungle" (Wallace 2015, 63). The cultural and economic diversity was so rich in Singapore that a volume could have been written on the colonial city "without exhausting its singularities" (Wallace 2015, 63). Andrew Carnegie, an American philanthropist, was struck not only by the mixture of races but the never-ending, tireless work. He concluded, "Work, work, work! They never play, never smile, but plod away, from early morning until late at night" (Wise and Wise 1985, 112). For travellers like William Hornaday (1885) and Cuthbert Collingwood (1868), the Chinese shops overflowing with merchandise and wares made a lasting impression. These were "queer streets", noted Hornaday (1885, 294).

Singapore might not have been an industrial city, but by all accounts, its labour force comprised skilled artisans producing all sorts of finished products. Singapore was the best example of a city of cottage industry. The American explorer Charles Wilkes (1845, 374) observed the trade of Singapore in 1842 to be as was usual in the East, that is, carried out in the streets by artisans and tradesmen: carpenters, blacksmiths, tinners, butchers, bakers, tailors, barbers, crockery and opium sellers, and coffin-makers. A century later, Moore (1955, 111) would be listing a litany of cottage manufacturing: mosquito nets, mattresses, cushions, wooden ladders, ironing boards, camp beds, canvas beds, canvas shades, wooden desks and chairs, and barber chairs.

Singapore over the decades of Western circumspection was certainly not dull, plain, nor insipid. Through its chaotic activity, it was a city of cultural differences, one that evoked its own strong identity that travellers remembered. Once in the city, the assault of varied cultural activities was an affront to their Occidental culture: "How odd everything looks"

(Hornaday 1885, 203). Cultural differences aside, the naturalist Hornaday (1885, 294) noted that Singapore was the "hardiest city I ever saw, as well planned and carefully executed as though built entirely by one man. It is like a big desk, full of drawers and pigeon-holes, where everything has its place, and can always be found in it". Hornaday (1885, 294) was impressed with what urban geographers would call streets of specialised trades and services: "Owing to this peculiar grouping of different trades, one can do more business in less time in Singapore than in any other town in the world".

Amongst Horace Bleackley's (1928, 119) travels in southern Asia, Singapore stood out because of his comfortable stay at the Grand Hotel de l'Europe, the abundant hospitality he received, and the bungalows that reminded him of England (against the general view of Britishers that nothing in Singapore reminded them of home). All this made him a "devoted lover of Singapore". He lavished praise on the British colony, its "grandeur" in everything on a large scale (such as its population and beauty), its "opulent" business town that was "conspicuous", its "imposing city", the boulevard of Orchard Road that was "worthy of one of the proudest and richest cities in the East", and its great seaport, the "foremost in Asia, if not the world" (Bleackley 1928, 117–119). Singapore was for him "the great junction between Europe and the Far East" (Bleackley 1928, 119).

Maugham and Kipling reserved their compliments for the famous Raffles Hotel. Maugham found his stay there to be an experience of "all the fables of the exotic East" (Flower 1984, 162), while Kipling (1900, 251) had more pragmatic observations that the Raffles had "excellent" food but rooms which were "bad". His advice was to "[feed] at Raffles and sleep at the Hotel de l'Europe" (Kipling 1900, 251). Yet for the avid traveller, the riches of the stately city were not in imposing buildings, but the docks, workshops, factories, offices, warehouses, shops, and stores that suggested a trade equal to that of any port in the Mediterranean, be it in wealth or the volume of commerce.

The quick pace of activity was especially evident with the dominant Chinese population. For Westerners, their frenzied energy was always a noticeable contrast with the relaxed, slow-paced, and self-contented Malays, the comparison being between the urban Chinese and rural Malays (R. Braddell 1935). At the cusp of independence, D. J. Enright found the concern with fast-paced solutions and instant changes to still be part of the new indigenous leadership. In his poem *The Board of Selection*, the Englishman provided an ironic and amusing insight into the local mentality: a dialogue between the Dean of the Faculty and himself was one between an economist and a poet, highlighting the economist's dismissal of poetry as too time-consuming. The last stanza of the poem is revealing:

> The board make hasty calculations …
> Which means that poetry is a false economy,
> More haste, less speed.
> The chairman remembers he has to build a nation
> By the end of the month
>
>   (de Souza 1994, 268).

c) *The Amorphous City*

Despite being a colony with a British imprint, travellers and residents found Singapore a difficult city to identify and characterise. Unlike other colonial cities in the region (Batavia, Saigon, or Manila) that reminded Westerners of their home countries architecturally, Singapore was largely unique. White residents found difficulty in deriving a stereotypical image from it. No two Westerners could agree on what Singapore represented. Perhaps, the spatial bifurcation of the city under the 1822 Raffles Plan had denied the town a holistic image. Singapore was neither a Western nor an Eastern city. It was a mélange of cultures and religions, of varying contrasts. One telling characterisation was from the perceptive resident Patrick Anderson (1955, 153–154): "Singapore is a city where nobody really belongs, where no culture is indigenous, no memory authoritative, no attitude other than immature". This conclusion came in spite of the city's overwhelming Chinese population.

Yet, the organised chaos and heterogeneity of this urban scene beckoned in its own way to visitors and residents, to experience its cultures, sample its ethnic diversity, and engage its religious plurality. Life with fellow Whites was dull, but life with natives, as Anderson (1955, 156) put it cryptically, was "too mysterious and flattering to be quite secure". Despite the White cultural emphasis on individuality, in Singapore, Western residents felt "individual-minus, a representative of something no longer very clear or very confident" (P. Anderson 1955, 156). What Anderson was attempting to express was that the Westerner lost his individuality because the multicultural profusion made one insecure as their identity was diffused in the cultural plurality.

Kipling (1900) echoed the British discomfort with their colonies, whether in India, Malaya, or Singapore. In India, where the English could not breed successfully, the "lazy, languid Englishmen" who talked about "going home in indecently short intervals", had to continue to be. In Singapore, the renowned writer never quite felt safe, despite the British having a "set of complete forts" with which to defend it. He wrote, "There is something very pathetic in the trustful, clinging attitude of the Colonies, who ought to have been soured and mistrustful long ago" (Kipling 1900, 252).

Aesthetically, Singapore was still attractive to Western visitors. The city charms tugged at one in two ways: "beauty and unreality", according to Anderson (1955, 153). For a short-stayer at least, the cultural landscape came across in a disorganised fashion, what Lynch (1972) might have referred to as a very illegible city; one that was mystifying, that hid its secrets so that they were not easily discovered. This was a city of snakes and ladders, with narrow lanes and mysterious places enticing the curious and beckoning the adventurous. The inquisitive Western explorer delighted in uncovering the illegible city of landscape mysteries that tantalised the imagination.

d) *Shifting Cultural Landscapes*

For Western residents, Singapore was perpetually undergoing change and remaking. This was a colonial enterprise in whose development many White residents were engaged, along with thousands more locals underwriting the Lion City's transformation. Singapore in the first 50 years of its colonial existence was not a given; it had to be planned, constructed, and developed. Certain names stood out repeatedly in the physical development of the city: Lt. Philip Jackson, Charles Faber, George Coleman, and John Thomson. Those who made significant landscape changes did not write about their experiences. Coleman, the first architect of Singapore, was one such person whose legacy rather was in the many buildings he constructed before the 1840s, some of which remain as historical monuments till this day. The transformation was visible in the move from *atap* and wooden buildings to brick-and-mortar edifices. This was an experimental colonial city in the making and the resident White population was actively engaged in its every facet. A look at all the committees identified by Buckley (1902), which were formed by the East India Company (EIC) and staffed by White residents to manage the city's varied activities, is instructive. Given its origins as an EIC enterprise, the whole exercise of managing Singapore was generally openly published, and had involved an endlessly negotiating system from the time that Raffles acquired the factory for the company. There were no prior urban models and templates to consult, so the foundations of the factory were constructed incrementally, with Raffles himself setting the broad parameters of his trading port.

Buckley (1902) gives us a detailed year-by-year insight into Singapore's development in the crucial first four decades. Western residents and EIC administrators had no precedents for developing Singapore as an entrepôt as there were many cases of British traders, travellers, and tourists who were downright critical of the way the Dutch and Spanish ran their colonies in the region. The use of draconian administrative methods on European traders and merchants in the neighbouring colonies was constantly viewed with abhorrence, as being against the laissez-faire free port idea and economic environment that Raffles had in mind. The very attraction of Singapore as a trading mecca was its free port status and any reversal of this position would have been seen as killing the goose that laid the golden egg. Singapore was a different type of colony, and there was a chorus of approval by traders and merchants who believed in its maintenance of free port status.

This status was for Western and Asian merchants and traders an underpinning of the economic — if not political — democracy of being able to do business freely with one another and having their views heard by the administration. Very importantly, the liberal immigration policies also allowed Asians to flock to Singapore and try their luck in making their fortunes. Singapore was a sojourner's paradise and the colonial administration encouraged the influx of foreigners. Whether Western or Asian, every sojourner was in Singapore to make money and return home. In the 19th century, no sojourner — and everyone except the native Malays then considered themselves sojourners — had any intention of making Singapore their home or permanent residence, except those buried in its many graveyards.

However, Singapore would over the decades develop its own distinctive identity and character, and become generally pleasant to Western living. Already an early sketch of the town from the sea by Lt. Jackson reveals a horizontal morphology of wooden structures, against the hill of Fort Canning which dominates the scenery from the background (Pearson 1982, 135–154). James Brooke during his 1839 stopover in Singapore, wrote to his friend John Templer and stated that Singapore was a pleasant little place (Keppel 1853, 1:54). For Brooke, nature and culture seemed to have conspired into a harmonious whole, where nature nonetheless played second fiddle:

> The country is diversified; the state of native society extraordinary; the commercial importance of the place considerable; the neighbourhood unknown; in natural history confined — snakes, insects, and fish, abundant — birds few, and animals fewer" (Keppel 1853, 1:54).

A century later, Pratt (1931, 13), referring to Singapore, would note that the British had added to their "diadem a new jewel, destined one day to outshine the rest". Singapore was a port city of British colonial rule that had grown more important not only because of trade but also as a stopover for many travellers engaging the region, moving en route from Europe to Australia, or from the West to the East. In the 19th century for example, legions of naturalists (including Wallace, Hornaday, Collingwood, and John Whitehead) transited on the way to various parts of the region for their scientific field studies. In the early 20th century, global travellers and tourists would find Singapore a convenient place to catch their breath and refresh themselves during their tropical journeys.

While the spatial limits of the city remained fairly constant, change was taking place with regard to mobility within the city. The early 19th century was a scene of horse carriages called *gharries*, and bullock carts. By the turn of the 20th century, the Lion City would be alive with rickshaws and motorised vehicles — motorcycles and motor cars (Sidney 1926, 25). Maj. R. J. H. Sidney (1926, 26) found the Singapore rickshaws most interesting as they differed from those of Bangkok, Hong Kong, and Kuala Lumpur. Sidney's descriptions brought to life what Manuel Castells (2010) has asserted — that cities are made by people. Despite their being the underclass of Singapore's society, the travelling major found the rickshaw pullers fascinating to observe, running around as they did with bare feet, heads covered by basket hats, and wearing blue or black shorts and short coats (Sidney 1926, 26). Indeed, for most Westerners in the early 20th century, the ubiquitous rickshaw defined the Oriental city. On seeing rickshaw pullers working hard in the hot tropical weather, some Western sojourners penned their views of the inhuman means of transport.

Rupert Emerson, the American student of colonial politics, leaves us one such impression of Singapore:

> Equally it is all too possible for Europeans and Americans to visit or even live in these cities and see little more of the oriental world than the sweating, but no doubt picturesque, back of the Chinese rickshaw 'boy' who pulls them around at a dog trot under the blazing sun from the hotel to the department store or office and back to the bar again (Warren 2003, 159).

Yet few colonial era White sojourners, besides making passing statements, were consciously interested in the underbelly of Singapore society. The 21st-century Australian historian James Warren (2003) has made it his academic preserve to deal with 'history from below', a history of rickshaw pullers, coolies, prostitutes, opium smokers, and hawkers. Ironically, the Western colonial narrative of Singapore society would be defined repeatedly by these 'small people's' histories. Wilkes (1845, 374–392) in 1845 was one of the first Westerners to leave us vivid word pictures of the pedestrian "moving panorama", the busy "streets" of varied trades, the "idea of Babel" of spoken languages, and the people as "industrious as bees". Life in the EIC factory was in its cosmopolitan peoples darting to and fro, and always busy. This was a landscape of hundreds of nameless persons who filled the streets and added colour to places, but remained faceless and forgotten in the Western psyche. For revisionist historians, the little people have become the fodder for a subaltern historical narrative.

III. The Great Entrepôt

> ... East and West must seek my aid
> Ere the spent hull may dare the ports afar
> The second doorway of the wide world's trade
> Is mine to lose or bar
> (Kipling 1934)

Since Raffles' promulgation of his 'child' as the ideal location for trade, subsequent Western entrepreneurs, traders, and businessmen would over the decades give their positive verdict on Singapore. Singapore's success has been said to be due to the "Magic of Free Trade" (Buckley 1902,

2:788). It was a business city, an economic thoroughfare throughout its colonial history. In its early years, British Resident Crawfurd (1830, 2:356) validated the Raffles vision by stating that Singapore's chief importance as a "commercial emporium" had met its "most sanguine expectations". This was a city of shopkeepers, merchants, itinerant traders, money-lenders, and money-changers. In the 1890s, Nicholas Dennys (1894, 366) underscored Singapore's entrepôt trading activity by recording 13 brokers, 22 commission agents, 120 insurance agencies, and 34 steamship company agents.

The economic fervour was one of the enduring imageable features of Singapore. It was to become for some an economic prodigy, a very materialistic society, a place defined by trade and monetary transaction. Singapore, as Moore (1953, 21) called it, was a city of "a million money searchers". This was the hub of wheeler-dealers, and companies making profit by selling: "If there is no selling there is no profit, therefore go out and sell" (Moore 1953, 22). Singapore was a colony populated by what the geographer Harm de Blij (2009, 6) has called "mobals" — migrants who are "risk takers", willing to leave their families to venture a "chance on new and different surroundings".

In an economically driven city, White and Asian traders, businessmen, and entrepreneurs shared similar goals. They were in Singapore to make money, create profit, and do business. So long as Singapore was an attractive place for all this, the economic imageability of the entrepôt remained visible to them. They were less concerned with moral pontification, cross-cultural assessments, and urban comparisons. It took instead White administrators, academics, and journalists to evaluate Singapore's wider developmental criteria from time to time. It was Singapore's very economic character which was viewed by Moore and MacDonald as a "cultural desert" (Moore 1953). Decades later, Joseph Tamney (1996), the American sociologist at the University of Singapore, would be critical about the new state as a wealthy city lacking culture and soul.

The British administrator J. S. Furnivall (1948, 1) gave an apt definition of colonialism that captured the spirit of the British legacy in Singapore. He saw that the colonisation of the tropics was done with "capital rather than with men", and how most tropical countries under foreign rule were "dependencies rather than colonies". In Singapore, the capital outlay came from enterprising Western merchants, sales of land titles, and taxes from illegal activity (opium dens, spirits). The Lion City was to a large extent a self-supporting factory of the EIC.

a) *Singapore's Port: Product Diversity*

Western travellers and residents in the 19th century had laudatory comments to make about Singapore's great trading port, maintaining that there were "no Asiatic and few European ports of which the trade is so diversified as that of Singapore". In just about every 19th-century review of the colonial port, there was an endless litany of trade statistics and trading products that were listed (Crawfurd 1830, 2:356–378; J. Cameron 1965; Davidson 1846; Newbold 1839, vol. 1; Begbie 1834, 362–363; Earl 1837, 399–415). Richard Winstedt (1962, 60) underscored the Western obsession with trade figures in the early 19th century when he opined that the history of Singapore was written mainly in statistics.

Jacob van Leur (1955, 276) was an early Western observer to argue that the 17th and 18th centuries' economic momentum belonged to Asia, when he questioned prevailing Western views of an "impoverished, enfeebled Oriental world" that was "economically undermined, politically second-rate". The Dutch administrator might have overstated his case about the trading prowess of Indonesian ports, though he admitted that he could not ascertain whether the influence of these ports was political, maritime, or economic (van Leur 1955, 276). However, by Singapore's establishment in 1819, the global economic ecosystem had changed radically in favour of the West. Singapore's robust trade was measured in different ways by Westerners. Crawfurd (1830, 2:358) used data from the trading ships plying between England (London and Liverpool), Europe (Stockholm, Hamburg, and Bordeaux), and Singapore from 1822 to 1826 — four ships (1822), nine ships (1823), 12 ships (1824), 15 ships (1825), and 14 ships (1826). George Earl (1837, 415), the visiting ship captain, measured Singapore's trading prowess from the 20 European mercantile houses (17 British, one Portuguese, one German, and one American) operating in the early 1830s.

For the former US consul and plantation owner Joseph Balestier, Singapore's prodigious trade was the prime reason for marketing it to the US government. Writing to the Secretary of State in 1849 to request a salary as US Consul again were he to return to Singapore, Balestier argued that Singapore was near India, Ceylon, Java, Siam, and China. It had a fine harbour which was easily accessible and free from typhoons and gales and was fitted as a resort for ships (Hale 2016, 292). He began his letter with positive impressions of Singapore and reasons why the US needed to get involved in its trade:

> Singapore, though a commercial place of great importance being a free port situated between India & China, has hitherto had little American trade in part owing to the duties which are levied on tea & coffee, imported from places not that of growth and production, which articles, being largely imported into Singapore in Chinese junks & Malay prows directly from their respective countries, form a considerable part of the trade of that place and from which we shut ourselves out ... (Hale 2016, 290)

During the 1830s, Balestier and his wife Maria often mentioned the trade between Cochin China (now south Vietnam) and Singapore. In 1833, the *Singapore Chronicle* reported the fourth American ship, the *Cashmere*, to have arrived in Singapore from Boston. The cargo it took away is indicative of Singapore's regional role as a trans-shipment port for varied merchandise: 3,300 piculs of pepper, 850 piculs of sugar, 60 piculs of coffee, 585 piculs of tin, 123 piculs of rattan, and 300 boxes of Chinese camphor (Hale 2016, 18). There would be countless references to Singapore's regional trade over the century, and to the varied commodities that it dealt in.

While Balestier provided a more geo-economic overview of Singapore trade, the British ensign Thomas Newbold (1839, 1:291–335) gave a detailed inventoried listing of the imports in 1836: antimony ore, armaments, *bêche de mer*, benjamin, beeswax, beer, birds' feathers, bird's nest, betel nut, brassware, cigars, camphor, canvas, cassia, chinaware, coffee, copperware, copper, cordage, cotton, dholl, dragon's blood, earthenware, ebony, ghee, gambier, gold dust, glassware, gold thread, grain, gunnies, gunpowder, hides, ivory, indigo, iron, lead, mother-of-pearl shells, nankeens, oils, opium, paddy, paints, pepper, provisions, piece goods, rattans, raw silk, rice, sago, salt, saltpetre, seaweed, spices, spirits; and European, American, Chinese, Indian, Javanese, Straits, and Eastern sundries.

This led the French historian George Coedès (1968) to compare the region's busy intra-regional trade to that of the 14th-century Mediterranean that Fernand Braudel (1972, 1973) would subsequently encapsulate in his landmark historical study, *The Mediterranean and the*

Mediterranean World in the Age of Philip II. According to Coedès (1968, 3), maritime Southeast Asia during the colonial era was "a veritable Mediterranean formed by the South China Sea, the Gulf of Siam, and the Java Sea". Using Braudel's historical model, New Zealand-born historian Anthony Reid (1988) has similarly tried to capture the golden age of Southeast Asian trade in the 17th century, as well as its economic, social, and cultural imprints and impacts.

To understand Singapore's pivotal role as a trading hub in the region from the 19th century onwards is to realise that trade had already been the lifeblood of the region for centuries. Numerous ports and trading hubs have risen and faded over time. Their past glories were captured in contemporary regional and foreign historical chronicles. Singapore's fame as the EIC's entrepôt, a British Crown Colony, a Malaysian state, and an independent city-state over the last 200 years is, nonetheless, unique in that its economic success has continued till the present day. The story of Singapore's economic history needs to be told, in the manner that van Leur (1955) did with Indonesia. Is there a central theme that runs through Singapore's economic history as van Leur (1955, 38–43) postulated about Indonesia in his "social-economic law"? The Dutch administrator wondered whether the whole gamut of socio-economic relationships (structural, cultural, demand and supply, proportional, causal) provided a "certain regularity" for the development of a civilisation.

b) *Explaining Singapore's Entrepôt Success*

What made Singapore such a successful entrepôt? At various stages of its development, Western sojourners have had mixed views of the colonial port. Crawfurd (1830, 2:385) viewed the success of Singapore's trading city by its profit margin; native or Asian traders earned two to five per cent per annum on interest, while European merchants secured 10 to 12 per cent per annum. One of the first critical reviews of the fledgling port came from the trader G. F. Davidson, who had been visiting Singapore off and on between 1826 and 1846. From his last 1846 visit, Davidson (1846, 69–70) left a sobering perspective of Singapore's future:

> I repeat, therefore, that I think the trade of Singapore has reached its maximum; and that the town has attained to its highest point of importance and prosperity. Indeed, it is at this moment rather over-built. A beautiful and healthy town, however, it is; and that it may not suffer

materially or permanently from the causes above mentioned, but continue to prosper as formerly ...

Davidson's (1846, 67–68) pessimism about Singapore's future was ironically based on the British opening of Hong Kong. The editor John Cameron (1965, 178) felt likewise. He argued that if Singapore were to lose its free port status (by taxing imports and exports), this would lead to its doom: in "that moment the ebb of its commercial greatness begins". Cameron (1965, 178), though, unlike Davidson in his pessimism, noted that "Singapore [had] grown too great to fear any rivalry on equal terms". Southeast Asia had been China's border region for centuries, in which Chinese mercantilism thrived (Wade 2000). The British opening of Singapore to Chinese immigration provided a natural extension of the free flow of trade and migrants. While colonialism is often seen as the closing of regional frontiers and borders (Butcher 2004), in the case of Singapore, Western travellers saw the reverse trend. Singapore's demographic rise was a product of a success story that attracted immigrants through liberal colonial policies which allowed people to settle and depart easily. The White residents were quietly receptive to these immigration policies so long as they remained the dominant political and economic force.

Singapore was the envy of the Dutch in Indonesia who realised that its free port status was the goose that laid the golden egg. Hence, in 1847, they made Macassar a free port to compete with Singapore. This was the economic centre of the thriving Bugis traders and merchants who plied between the Dutch Indies and Singapore. However, the Dutch also pursued a "Java-centric" policy and naturally still wanted Java to control their trade in the Malay Archipelago. The result was that Macassar did not live up to expectations; in 1873, Macassar's exports peaked at 11.8 million guilders, while Singapore's exports were worth 89.9 million guilders (Booth 1998, 28–29). By 1908, Singapore's exports had soared to 253.5 million guilders, and Macassar was down at 10.9 million guilders (Booth 1998, 29). The momentum of trade took on a life of its own in Singapore and left other ports in the region in the shade.

Singapore's importance grew because it served as a distributing and processing centre for much of the region's natural produce. Even though it did not cultivate sago, the colonial city became the centre of sago manufacturing in the region in the 19th century. Crawfurd (1830, 2:355–356) was one of the early Westerners to reflect on sago manufacturing in Singapore. Pearl or white sago was imported from Sumatra and processed in Singapore. This processing was first practised in Malacca and introduced in 1824 to Singapore which had by this time become the "principal seat of manufactory" (Crawfurd 1830, 2:356). Echoing Crawfurd, George Bennett (1834, 210) expounded that "Singapore is the principal, if not the only place in the East, where the refining or manufacturing of the pearl sago is carried on; the process is said to be a recent one, and the invention of the Chinese".

By the end of the 19th century, the importance of the city's trade would once again be given a thumbs up. Dennys (1894) asserted that "every branch of industry is subsidiary to trade", and that Singapore was a "great commercial emporium" where lay the warehouses for the "future distribution" of the "staple products of Europe, Asia, and America". The administrator also gave broader reasons for Singapore's success. He noted that the emporium's success was due to "freedom, and its highly convenient position, with security for life and property" more like that of an American than an Asiatic settlement (Dennys 1894, 359). Unlike the Dutch who were heavy-handed in many of their colonial policies (e.g., the *cultuurstelsel* or Culture System in Javanese agriculture), the British administration in Singapore was generally light-handed. Travellers perpetually compared the two administrations and often criticised Dutch colonialism.

c) *The 20th-Century Trade*

Singapore's trade boom was fuelled by the trade in Malayan tin and rubber. The rubber and tin boom in the early 20th century provided new catalysts to Singapore's importance as an entrepôt. Western assessments endorsed Singapore as the regional distributing centre for a variety of new products. The geographer E. H. G. Dobby (1940, 106), in one of the first regional geography perspectives on Singapore, described the close trading relationship the colony had with Malaya — as he states, Singapore handled two-thirds of the whole Malayan foreign trade. With its free port status, in contrast to the restrictions of world trade movements and the regional norm of levying customs duties and taxing imports and exports, the colonial city, as "the most powerful consuming unit of Malaya", turned to Malaya for more and more of its trade (Dobby 1940, 106).

A century after Singapore's founding, Walter Makepeace (1921b, 166–234) gave a detailed record of all the European firms that contributed to its "machinery of commerce". The long tenure of European companies operating in the colonial city was testament to the stability and prosperity of the free port. As the British historian D. G. E. Hall (1968, 510) observed later, Raffles' policy of free trade was laid down with "almost religious fervour", essentially to enhance Singapore's commercial importance.

Using its central regional location, Singapore served in every possible role as a trading intermediary. The French geographer Charles Robequain (1958, 142–143), surveying the regional geography of the *Alam Melayu*, observed that the colonial port was the "principal collecting centre" for native-grown rubber from Malaya and Indonesia, and that Singapore's "essential function" by the 1930s was in distributing varied kinds of goods imported and exported against the competition of other regional ports. With the tightening of protection in many countries, Singapore's advantage was its "free trade and the absence of customs duties" (Robequain 1958, 143). Singapore would not be seen as adding value were it to go into manufacturing, as its major function was "handling, forwarding, shipping, reshipping, breaking bulk, distribution, collecting" (Dobby 1940, 106). In short, it was the go-between and middleman whose profit was based on commission rather than value added by work. Increasingly dependent on Malaya for its tin, rubber, timber, and other resources for export in the first half of the 20th century, Iain Buchanan (1972, 36) called Singapore "parasitic" as its role was more "exploitative" than "constructive".

Others might see Singapore as having taken advantage of the geographic cards it was dealt with. At different times, it processed sago, tin, and rubber, and traded them internationally. It was the hub of several cottage industries, from shoemaking to food processing, from furniture manufacturing to printing. It was a lower-end manufacturing city which traded its processed goods. Westerners time and again saw the industriousness of its population and were captivated by its economic activity. Singapore developed into a commercial-industrial entrepôt reminiscent of the Renaissance city-state of Venice, according to Giovanni Arrighi (2010, 79). Like Hong Kong which was later to develop, it became a colonial capitalist city.

As an island-city, Singapore's land was finite, hence its landscape was of prime economic value. Crawfurd believed this and bought large land parcels in Raffles Place. Farquhar, thinking Kampong Glam would be the Central Business District, likewise purchased land around the sultan's domain. Moore (1953) noted in the post-war years how Singapore's skyline kept expanding, underscoring the value of land. His percipient advice to entrepreneurs was clear: "No one in Singapore has ever lost money in land — not if he had the sense to hang on to it — since every year it becomes a scarcer commodity" (Moore 1953, 21).

d) *Capitalism Operationalised*

Before capitalism was defined and became the topic of intense debate and academic enquiry (van Leur 1955; Wallerstein 1983; Wood 2002), Singapore like many ports in the region was already playing out the processes of capitalistic exchange. Yet, throughout the 19th century, the term *capitalism* was seldom used by Western traders and merchants in Singapore. European traders did not conceptualise capitalism; they operationalised it. Westerners formed independent or collaborative companies, and some became conglomerates with household names like Boustead and Guthrie. Western merchants and businessmen knew their end goal was profit and capital accumulation, though the mechanics of getting rich were left undefined and held as closely guarded secrets. Nor was capitalism in Singapore culturally constrained, as Europeans, Chinese, Arabs, Jews, Indians, and Armenians all became wealthy and thrived in the local economic system. Capitalism transcended religious and ethnic distinctions.

In the early 20th century, White travellers like Maj. Sidney (1926, 31) were surprised by the "amazing industry" of the Chinese population who seemed to toil endlessly "at all times of the day", and at times past midnight. While Singapore had few factories, the Major observed that each shop was a "small manufactory" where one could view all processes from the streets (Sidney 1926, 31). Work was only interrupted for a meal. There was wonder about whether such endless strenuous work "over a period of many months [could] really be economically justified" (Sidney 1926, 31).

Singapore was the last Western outpost to be formed by a series of colonialist geopolitical dramas in the region. It had begun in the 16th century, with the Portuguese and Spanish carving out the world between them into spheres of trading territories, a dispute which was eventually settled in the Treaty of Tordesillas and later sanctioned by the Pope. Europe had been riven by political rivalry amongst its states and kingdoms for 500 years, and these changes in political power centres reverberated throughout the colonies. One can imagine the bitter conflict that engulfed Europe before it settled down to its current 'nation-state' configuration (Lieberman 2003; 2009). Over the centuries,

Southeast Asia had also been witness to Dutch and English rivalry in the Malay Archipelago, as well as the French and English territorial competition in Indo-China. Raffles' gamble and the Singapore entrepôt's future success would be a blow to Dutch monopoly in the archipelago, and Singapore "would break the spell" of the Dutch monopoly (D. Hall 1968, 507). It was indeed timely when Raffles founded the EIC trading post of Singapore, which coincided with the rise of Britain as the global power.

Britain's position as a global power provided Singapore with the necessary defence umbrella to thrive in peace and security for over a century. Moreover, from its very founding, Singapore would be involved in the trade of weapons and armaments. This free trade in firearms had been unknown in the region till the establishment of Singapore (Crawfurd 1830, 2:372). As Newbold (1839, 1:391) proudly asserted, in the event of a war, "Singapore would prove an excellent naval station to protect our commerce in the China seas". The importance of Singapore's strategic location thus grew over time, alongside the development of Singapore's entrepôt trade in the 19th century.

Basing itself on William Farquhar's 1820 accounts, van Leur's (1955, 284) sociological account of Indonesian trade argued that the main catalyst of Singapore's booming trade was the regional rather than East-West trade. Ships from China, Cochin China, and Siam formed the bulk of the new port's thriving trade; in Farquhar's words, "this settlement bids fair to become the emporium of Eastern trade" (van Leur 1955, 284). Van Leur argued that Raffles had understood the importance of the regional connections and trade by undermining Franco-Dutch rule in Java, and connecting with regional ports (van Leur 1955, 277).

As the China trade developed between Singapore, the region, and other parts of Asia and the West, Joseph Balestier, writing in *The Singapore Free Press* in 1845, expressed the concerns of Western entrepreneurs in Singapore: the danger of Singapore being bypassed in the China-West trade; that Singapore would be overlooked in the 'junk' trade which would go into the hands of "shrewd Malacca Chinese"; that Singapore should give new life to native trade; and the worry that regional trade would be diminished given the thinly populated countries which consumed moderately (Hale 2016, 187–189). Balestier was lamenting how the high expectations and future growth which Raffles had envisaged for his child might face drawbacks, this notwithstanding that the colony had held its own as an "important commercial mart gradually increasing in population, resources and wealth" (Hale 2016, 189). After returning to the US, with trade — including the brisk India-China one — high on his mind, Balestier wrote to the US Secretary of State in 1849, arguing for an office and 'naval depot' in Singapore to be set up to promote American trade, and offering his services once again as a paid American Consul.

IV. Singapore's White 'Society'

Western residents tried to demonstrate through their experiences of living in Singapore the makings of its 'society'. However, their references to society were quite different from the other European invention of 'society' in the 18th century, that had been based on a "single and common framework" (Osterhammel 2018, 384–390). The colonial references to Singapore society did not include the Asian population. For White residents, 'society' was a reference to the exclusive White population. Crawfurd (1830, vol. 2) was clearly full of praise for the small but indispensable British population during his term as Resident of Singapore. In the 19th century, even Whites had to be of a certain high rank in the EIC to be admitted into society and accepted by other officers. Singapore society in this sense was thus an exclusive club that perpetuated a White racial caste system. This exclusive society would carry on for nearly a century in the two White clubs: the Singapore Cricket Club and the Tanglin Club, which symbolised the colony's deep racial cleavage.

John Cameron (1965, 280–303) dedicated a whole chapter in his book *Tropical Possessions in Malayan India* to Singapore's "society — its divisions — style of life", but prefaced his discussion by commenting on the sensitivity of the subject. Ahead of his time in this regard, he was the first to point out the exclusivity of society and was himself uncomfortable with it. He described the White society as a "very small one" comprising about 40 families (J. Cameron 1965, 286). Specifically, the editor identified Singapore society as "said to be composed of the chief Government officials, the merchants and bankers with their assistants and clerks — the lawyers, the doctors, and the military — at least, any of these positions, *prima facie* give the necessary social status" (J. Cameron 1965, 287). Away from the mother country, White society in Singapore tried to ape the élan of British society in its royal distinctions and tapestry of class, the intellectual pretensions, and the pompous behaviour above Asians. Despite the "luxuries of life" they enjoyed in Singapore, however, Wilkes (1845, 391) noted that Europeans he met did not look upon the East as a home, but a temporary sojourn. He observed that Europeans constantly remarked about their temporary stays, and concluded that these people were "devoid of happiness and contentment" (Wilkes 1845, 391). It would seem that the British administrators and residents engaged in social distancing to remind themselves of their elite social status, so that they never mixed with Asians and thus never felt entirely at home in Singapore. This was an alien, Oriental abode, treated more like a hotel. The White population in colonial Singapore suffered from what Francis Fukuyama (2018, xiii) has defined as *megalothymia* or "the desire to be recognized as superior".

While the Portuguese and Spanish encouraged mixed marriages in their colonies, the British maintained racial purity, and looked down in contempt at Eurasians. The Eurasians were only grudgingly accepted by the British because they served as convenient intermediaries between the Whites and Asians in colonial administration. The British after their long colonial tenure in India had adapted the Hindu caste system to define their status; they made themselves the highest caste. Eurasians were patronised by the British but never treated as equals. Noel Barber (1978, 79) captured the Eurasian predicament. He observed that Singapore society too was based on a caste system, with the Whites as the highest caste. The Eurasians were derogatorily known as a "stengah or half"-caste (Barber 1978, 79). There was a racial ambiguity to them. They were given the Singapore Recreation Club opposite the exclusive White Singapore Cricket Club, both being on the north side of the Singapore River, thereby indicating that the colonial administration accepted them as being above the Asian population.

Cameron (1965) did not see all Whites as being part of the society he identified; the term represented those considered (by society itself) to be the elites, defined as educated, refined, and decent. He mentioned that the term *society* in "its restrictive signification in Singapore [was] not unfrequently the subject of remark and sometimes of animadversion" (J. Cameron 1965, 285–286). He also admitted of an "intermediate class of European society" that might have been difficult to distinguish, which held appointments requiring skill rather than education (J. Cameron 1965, 285). At least as far as the White population was concerned, Cameron (1965, 286) did not think a member of society should be measured by wealth: "The man of narrow means has often the doors thrown wide open to him, while his wealthy neighbour is left to grope about in utter darkness".

The Whites maintained the 'elite' class distinction in nearly everything they did — the sports and recreational activities they engaged in, the food they ate, the way they carried themselves, the houses they lived in, the clothes they wore. The White elitist society was institutionalised spatially, socially, economically, and culturally. White colonialists believed that they had exclusive rights in culture, intelligence, and behaviour. The geography of colonial takeover was abetted by imperialistic culture, as Edward Said (1994) has argued. According to him, Conrad, a frequent visitor of Singapore and the region, was among those who ideologically endorsed imperialism in his numerous novels and stories (Said 1994, 33–34).

This imperialist culture was so ingrained in Singapore's White society that when the Governor-General MacDonald practised "unconventional behaviour", resident Whites felt uneasy because "it questioned the validity of some of their cherished beliefs" (Drysdale 1984, 54). One letter in *The Straits Times*, from a "Disgusted" person, questioned MacDonald's informal dressing when attending a concert in shirtsleeves, as showing disrespect for the artiste. The Governor-General replied to the letter-writer saying that while in the sunny Commonwealth men wore black tie, white shirt, black cummerbund, and black and white trousers, he suggested that "we might now break the tyranny of the dinner jacket, just as it was broken in India and elsewhere by fine imperial statesmen and shining aristocrats who happened also to be sensible men in the splendid days of yore" (Drysdale 1984, 54). This incident created a controversy and debate in the Singapore press that reached London. The London *Daily Mirror* congratulated MacDonald for giving European "snob" clubs in Singapore a "sartorial face slap" (Drysdale 1984, 55).

The idea of society as a White elitist community filtered into the many Western sojourners' perceptions of Singapore. Crawfurd (1830, 2:383) expressed his total reliance on the few British settlers in Singapore during his term of office: "they constitute in reality the life and spirit of the settlement; and it may safely be asserted, that without them, and without their existing in a state of independence and security, there would exist neither capital, enterprise, activity, confidence or order". Maria Balestier certainly witnessed these notions of elitism in the many social events she attended and in her experiences of communicating with the officials of the EIC (Hale 2016). As Singapore's importance as trading centre and port rose in the 19th century, defence became uppermost in many Western discussions. We also get a sense of Western thinking about security for trade from the letters of her husband and then-American Consul, Joseph. By Maria's account, conditions were such that civil and military officers from different ends of the British possessions were known to one another (Hale 2016, 129). Clearly the EIC or 'John's Company', as it was nicknamed, was able to merge economic interests with both security and defence. The company's officers had ranks as in the military, but according to Maria were educated in the affairs of trade and state (Hale 2016, 129).

Somewhat oblivious to the machinations of the high society that engaged her, the aristocratic Bird was party to elitist receptions she was given on her visit to Singapore. Emily Innes (Savage 1984, 260–261), the wife of a junior official in Malaya, became Bird's ardent critic in exposing how her glowing perceptions of travels in Singapore and Malaya were a product of Bird's own high status and the warm receptions it was deemed to deserve from European elites. The first 50 years since Raffles' foundation saw a small, influential White community which socialised within itself and generated written reflections that seemed like an endless exercise in European name-dropping.

Singapore over the decades would become a British colony and part of the Straits Settlements, and later the apex of the entire colonial system of British Malaya. The White society in Singapore thus represented the very elite of the British administration in the peninsula. The privileged colonial position the Lion City held meant that its governors and civil servants were the pick of the crop, people who had proven track records, were distinguished in service, and experienced in various Crown duties. Many of Singapore's governors were high-ranking diplomats who served on ambassadorial missions in the region, excelled themselves in colonial service in Malaya, or had been knighted by royalty and hence held positions of status within the elite administrative system: Crawfurd, Sir Frank Swettenham, Sir Hugh Clifford, Sir Hugh Low, Sir William Butterworth, Sir Roland Braddell, and Sir William Black.

Aping British society back home, the White society in Singapore was highly stratified and hierarchical. Given that royalty was embedded in British society, rank and status mattered to British administration. Over the decades, references to royalty would be used in place names, as constant reminders of Singapore's status as a Crown Colony. Empress Place and the Victoria Memorial Hall marked Queen Victoria's diamond jubilee and her title as Empress of India. The ascension of Queen Elizabeth II to the throne in 1952 gave reason for the Singapore Improvement Trust, the colonial public housing institution, to name a new satellite town as *Queenstown* in commemoration of her coronation. Many of its roads were named after her family: Queensway, Prince Philip Avenue, Prince Charles Crescent, Margaret Drive, and the no-longer extant Princess Anne Close. Even persons or places in Britain associated with the royal family had their names inscribed in Queenstown (Dawson Road, Strathmore Avenue, Forfar House, Clarence Lane). British royalty made a noticeable mark on Singapore's colonial landscape.

Governor Butterworth, as Thomson (1865) observed, was a stickler for observing status amongst the White administrators. This strict observance of status and authority ensured that British colonial administrators always had the upper hand in decision-making. It also became a manner of maintaining social distance between the White elites and the Asian population; Said's (1979) distinction between ruler and the Oriental ruled was not simply hypothetical but an administrative reality.

The White community dominated everything in the fledgling six decades of Singapore's development, and every firm and company established was named after its owners, some of them remaining household names till today. Given that ownership of firms changed frequently, so did the names of companies. Buckley (1902) provided the most detailed chronological documentation of the changing European ownership of companies. The same long-time resident Europeans kept appearing in different commercial configurations as well as committees. Ironically, while the Chinese were well known for their strong family ties, few Chinese businesses lasted beyond two generations. Chinese *towkays* of the past (Whampoa, Seah Eu Chin, Tan Kim Seng, Lim Nee Soon) are generally remembered in place names in Singapore and not existing businesses; Aw Boon Haw is a notable exception. It was the European family names that would prevail for decades through business firms (Boustead; Behn, Meyer & Co.; O'Connor; Drew & Napier; Donaldson & Burkinshaw; and Guthrie). This demonstrated that the British entrepôt had a vibrant commercial system kept alive by the constant movement and involvement of European traders and merchants seeking opportunities to make money.

The writings of Maria Balestier, John Cameron, and Walter Makepeace offer precious insights into the daily living of Westerners in the 19th century. Cameron provided a detailed account of European life, beginning with breakfast (9:00 a.m.), 'tiffin' (lunch), and dinner to end the day (6:30 p.m. or 7:00 p.m.) Work began around 10:00 a.m. or 10:30 a.m. and ended in the mercantile houses by 4:30 p.m. to 5:00 p.m. At 2:00 p.m., there was an "exchange hour" where leading men in business would meet at a place for an "interchange of ideas" (J. Cameron 1965, 297). The land surveyor Thomson (1865, 202) noted another venue where news of the town was gathered and exchanged daily — Scandal Point, where the White community would meet at 6:00 p.m.

Both the Balestiers gave good accounts of what was eaten at different meals. Other Westerners also recorded what they consumed. The foods were a mix of Western and Asian fare; many substitutions were made to replace the fruit, meat, vegetables, milk, and cheese which Westerners were used to. The missionary Ira Tracy, writing to his mother-in-law in 1836, noted what he had at meals: "We ate in the morning rice and egg & salt upon it & a piece of bread & if we choose a piece of fish and sweet potato or yam, but I take no meat. Our drink is hot water with sugar and milk or pea coffee. At dinner, we have rice & curry (made of ginger & pepper & fish or meat or vegetables & water) & fish or fowl or pork (no beef or mutton, goose, turkey or other meat) with sweet potatoes or yams & rarely common potatoes ... We drink water. At night we have hot or cold water & bread and usually fruit instead of butter (or) cheese" (Hale 2016, 38–39).

The White population in Singapore certainly lived in luxury when they could afford it. Singapore throughout its colonial period was known to Western travellers and residents to be an expensive city. Without slaves and many domestic female servants, the White households lived mostly on the relatively highly paid services of male servants, drivers, cleaners, cooks, and caregivers. The hiring of servants was a "heavy item" (Buckley 1965, 357). Earlier on in 1824, the Dutch militiaman Nahuijs had noted that workmen's and servants' wages were "excessive" (Miller 1941, 194). A family of above-average means hired something like 15 people as household servants and helpers in the 1840s. Buckley (1965, 357) calculated that the combined monthly wage for the servants, helpers, and cooks was not less than 66 to 70 Spanish dollars. This worked out to hiring per month: a butler ($7 to $8); two under-servants ($5 each); maid (*ayah*) or nurse ($5 to $6); tailor ($7 to $8); cook ($7 to $8); an assistant cook ($5); washerman ($5 to $6); two grooms ($5 each); grass-cutter ($2); lamp-lighter and sweeper ($4); scavenger ($1); and water-man ($4) (Buckley 1965, 357).

The other high expenditure in the colony was house rents. A two-storey house with six bedrooms rented for $35 to $60 per month, depending on the site. Building an ordinary house cost $3,000 to $5,000, while a large house cost $10,000 (Buckley 1965, 357). The conclusion was that Singapore was an "expensive place to reside at, everything, with the exception of English supplies" being more expensive than in India (Buckley 1965, 357). In his 1824 stopover in Singapore, Col. Nahuijs noted that the cost of living in Singapore was high because the island "[produced] little or nothing" (Miller 1941, 194).

Given its commercial orientation by which entertaining was a norm for merchants, Singapore society developed a good reputation among visitors for its warm hospitality. Bennett (1834, 2:218) in his two visits in 1833 noted how Singapore society was "extremely agreeable to a visitor", greeted as he was with "unbounded hospitality". John Cameron (1965, 288) observed that merchants provided a "very pleasant style of hospitality" though "very expensive". He went on to elaborate, "Their dinners are affairs of every week: they possess the charm of being at once magnificent and unrestrained, and they do so much to maintain a spirit of emulation in household luxuriance" (J. Cameron 1965, 288). The Australian, privy to much social experience, noted that "the ordinary style of living in Singapore may be set down as luxurious" (J. Cameron 1965, 289). The tables of the wealthiest were distinguished from the poorest, not by the "greater abundance or variety of dishes" but by the "lavish supply of European preserves and condiments — and of course, by a draft from a choicer and more extensive cellar" (J. Cameron 1965, 289).

In short, White society before the Second World War was a paragon of security, peace, and easy living. The Caucasian was "cocooned in a myth of utter security", observed Barber (1988, 21), one based on the belief that nothing could disturb the British "arsenal of democracy". The British view was hollow because in actual fact colonialism had no place for democracy. Nonetheless, most inhabitants of Singapore believed that they were living on the "edge of paradise", hence when Japan unleashed its war machine on Southeast Asia in December 1941, Whites and Asians had "blinkered eyes" and did not realise the city was on the brink of war (Barber 1988, 23).

V. Landscapes of Vice: Opium, Gambling, and Prostitution

The port city with its flood of Asian migrants was also a place where vice became noticeable to Western eyes. Four vices — gambling, opium smoking, liquor consumption, and prostitution — caught the attention of White residents and sojourners. The 19th-century Chinese imperial government defined such vices as 'yellow culture', which they despised and denounced. From Singapore's early establishment, the EIC officials recognised the dangers of unchecked vice among the local population. The colonial government issued *'Notices'* periodically on various laws and other matters of the colony pertaining to these vices, which were based on the opinions of a few EIC officials predicated on English law, Christian belief, and the prevailing European morals of the time. Several *Notices* and the correspondence of government officials (Raffles, Crawfurd, George Bonham, and an individual named Hull) from 1823, dealing with gambling (gaming houses), opium licenses, and the retail of "spirituous liquor", were reproduced in the *Journal of the Indian Archipelago and Eastern Asia* (Logan 1854b, 329–348). It was evident that the government was trying to curb these activities by issuing licenses, imposing regulations, and meting out fines and punishments for any contravention of the laws. Moreover, such fines and licenses were a means by which the colonial authorities could obtain revenue. Colonial Singapore was an imperfect world, harbouring both vice and the adulterous government toleration of it for the official coffers.

These laws and restrictions, however, were not welcomed by the "principal natives and Chinese", who "repeatedly requested the suspension of the regulation", according to Resident Crawfurd (Logan 1854b, 348). Writing to Holt Mackenzie, the Secretary to the government at Fort William in India in September 1823, Crawfurd questioned the wisdom of allowing what had been reported on, that "many of the lower classes had quitted the Settlement on account of being deprived of a customary amusement" (Logan 1854b, 348). In May 1823, Raffles had signed a regulation prohibiting gaming houses and cock-pits (arenas of cockfighting) because they were "highly destructive to the morals and happiness of the people". In his overview of Singapore, Crawfurd noted that in trying to root out gambling in 1823, 1,000 Chinese were driven out (Crawfurd 1830, 2:399). In defence of the continuation of this activity, Crawfurd (1830, 2:399) stated that what was hopeless to root out, it would be "prudent to tolerate and regulate" — thus under him gaming would be "permitted" and placed under police surveillance. He disagreed with Raffles by reasoning that the Chinese had a different view of gambling from Westerners; they did not see it as "a vice of the same character which Europeans [were] accustomed to contemplate it" (Logan 1854b, 337). Crawfurd further argued that the prohibition of gambling would lead to its clandestine pursuit and a "large revenue [would] be very unnecessarily sacrificed for an imaginary benefit" (Logan 1854b, 337).

In his account on Singapore as its Resident, Crawfurd (1830, 2:394–398) did not moralise on the varied habits of "intoxication" (opium smoking, wine, beer, liquor). Rather, he highlighted the revenues collected from them and the laws involved in checking them. He had nonetheless a personal disdain for opium smokers and noted that "those who use the drug in excess, are as much shunned, and considered as despicable as habitual drunkards of any other description" (Crawfurd 1830, 2:398). In defence of the colony's permitting of such activities, he maintained, "the affair is one which the moralist or the legislator has no pretence for interference" (Crawfurd 1830, 2:399). In an earlier letter to the Secretary of the Government in July 1823, Crawfurd in producing the revenue returns of the colony clearly noted the economic reasons for permitting opium farms to exist: the sale of opium accounted for more than 50 per cent of all sales — 2,900 of 5,194 Spanish dollars (Logan 1854b, 335).

Opium smoking was perhaps the most deplorable vice in 19th-century Singapore because of its physical effects on the smokers, its impact on their economic productivity, its uncontrollable addiction, and dangerous social ramifications in leading addicts to steal or kill. Given its newness to the trade in Singapore, as well as its unforeseen health and social consequences, there were many commentaries about it by White residents in the 19th century. The most authoritative discussion of opium smoking would come from physicians. The resident surgeon Robert Little (1848a) gave one of the most comprehensive overviews in his article titled "On the Habitual Use of Opium in Singapore", which ran to 79 pages. In it, he also included the written interventions by Drs. Thomas Oxley and William Traill.

Dr. Little (1848a) was not supportive of the colonial government's legalisation of opium selling. He compared opium smoking to liquor consumption and left his readers to draw their own conclusions: "Drunkenness has its limits and fashion; opium-smoking is without a limit and acknowledges no fashion, once it is introduced it is omnipotent in its power, and universal in its application". He noted that the revenues obtained from opium farms in Singapore, from 1822 to 1847, would have been considerable, based on his estimate of 15,000 opium smokers in 1845 (Little 1848a, 60–65). The physician reasoned that the $417,884 spent on opium annually could have been better spent on clothes, food, and improved housing. He argued that if the government found gambling and cockfighting (a Malay passion) immoral and put a stop to such practices, then why not stop the sale of opium? (Little 1848a, 73) For while gambling and cockfighting were "serious offences", they could not be compared to the "evils" of opium smoking and thus required "serious attention to the legislation" (Little 1848a, 73).

Thomson noted that the 15 days of Chinese New Year were the worst time for gambling and opium smoking. "The town resounded with merriment and strife alternately. The nights were consumed in debauchery, the days in sleep" (Thomson 1865, 204). He observed that these illegal activities continued moreover after the New Year because the government earned revenue and the police turned a blind eye to them (Thomson 1865). Also, merchants and traders in the highest circles were involved in gambling and 'fashionable vices' (Thomson 1865, 203).

The opium addiction was particularly acute among the Chinese; with an estimated population of 40,000 in 1845, there were roughly 15,000 opium smokers. Using the Singapore ratio of 1:3, Dr. Little (1848a, 66) then referred to the case of China were it to follow Singapore's addiction. Using purely moral and health arguments, the Singapore doctor observed that the contemporary number of opium smokers (three million) in China, to China's population (400 million), gave a ratio of 1:133, but were it to follow the Singapore ratio (1:3) there would be 92 million opium smokers in China. From hindsight, Little's 1848 treatise on Singapore opium smoking might well have been a precursor to the impact of British opium trading in China. The bleak Chinese experience with opium in Singapore would prove a microcosm of the larger opium problem in China. Unfortunately, the good physician did not anticipate the British economic strategy in the Chinese opium trade.

Some Western observers, citing Christian virtue, human values, and Western civilisational views, were critical of the way the British handled their colonies in the region. Among its critics were Wallace and Logan. Logan was a ringside observer of British policies in Singapore and also the region. He left a stinging rebuke to them, which was in some ways an advance endorsement of the French *mission civilisatrice*. In its words, he noted that British policies should best have enhanced the true character of peoples in the Malay Archipelago:

> speedily free the slave from his bonds; suppress the trade in men and its associate piracy; mitigate and eventually abolish the heavy monopolies

and restraints which depress industry, and nourish oppression, fraud and corruption; and having thus given to the people freedom in person, property and mind, lead them, through her sympathy and pity and their docility and gratitude, to a willing reception of the humanizing and elevating knowledge of christendom (Logan 1847a, 21).

Decades later, similar references to vice would be made by short-term visitors (Collingwood 1868, 279–286; Ommanney 1960, 35). Collingwood (1868, 279) observed that the Chinese were addicted to gambling, and that it held a "prominent place" during festivals. After reaping revenues from legalised gambling houses, the government finally banned the activity in 1829, whereupon it became a public offence.

Fast forward to the 20th century, the colonial city would still maintain a reputation for vice, illegal activity, and gangsterism. As the marine biologist F. D. Ommanney (1960, 35) opined, "in this modern city the gangster, the secret society and the kidnapper are all part of life, among the Chinese at any rate". This dangerous social ecosystem did not affect the Europeans, but for some of the local Asian population in "this jungle city survival [was] to the fittest" (Ommanney 1960, 35).

Singapore between 1900 and 1945 was a city of thriving illicit activity; it would seem that the island's economic propensity, bustling trade, and entrepôt conspired with gambling, prostitution, opium smoking, and liquor consumption. The image of Singapore as city of vice is memorialised by Theroux's (1973) novel *Saint Jack*. Its main character Jack Flowers works as a water-clerk in a Chinese company, but his part-time job is as a pimp soliciting women for tourists, sailors, residents, US soldiers, and expatriates. Theroux was well versed with the brothels (Joo Chiat, Serene House) in 1960s Singapore and painted a wild lively scene. The White experiences in the bars of the 1950s and 1960s were revealed in his writings and Patrick Anderson's *Snake Wine* (1955). The flavour of low life, in brothels and prostitute dens, as frequented by White bachelors, was vividly captured by Theroux's (1973) bedroom scene:

> The completely Chinese flavor of vice in Singapore made it attractive to a curious outsider, at the same time releasing him from guilt and doubt, for its queer differences (Joyce Li-ho had the tattoo of a panther leaping up her inner thigh) made it a respectable diversion, like the erotic art anthropologists solemnly photograph, maharani and maharajah depicted as fellatrix and bugger on the Indian temple. The sequence of activities

in a Chinese brothel parodied oriental hospitality: the warm welcome — the host bowing from the waist — the smoke, the chat, the cold towel, then the girl — usually the feller chose from one in a parade: money changed hands in the bedroom when the feller was naked and excited; then the stunt itself ...

VI. Urban and Cultural Change

Western travellers who reflected on Singapore's changing landscapes usually derived their perceptions from their personal visits to the colony over a span of a couple of decades. Others saw the city's change by comparing it to other colonial cities in the region. The British diplomat Bruce Lockhart (1936) revisited Malaya and Singapore and penned his perceptions of a progressive and modernising colony. Compared to the "sleepy hollow" of Malacca, Singapore was dynamic. Yet despite or because of its growing development and modernisation, Singapore in the 1930s still remained a city without buildings old enough to be historical. While Enright (1969, 119) observed that Singapore had "no traditions", Lockhart (1936, 140) noted how:

> Singapore is still colourful, but it lacks all the hall-marks of historical antiquity. It is an international Liverpool with a Chinese Manchester and Birmingham tagged on to it. Its finest buildings are modern; it has no ancient monuments and, apart from the Raffles statue, very few monuments to the past.

Way before the city got its current name as a clean garden city, Westerners in the 1930s were labelling it as unhygienic and filthy. Singapore was "semi-puritanised" but it still had a problem. His praise of Singapore notwithstanding, Lockhart (1936, 126) did wonder how far progress could be represented by a supposedly "puritanised Singapore" in which vice was in reality still permitted, if controlled.

Singapore was viewed in Western eyes as a Chinese city. However, the westernisation of the East had removed the local colour and old glamour (Lockhart 1936, 115). The Chinese *towkays* had replaced their pigtails and picturesque robes with European dress. It had become for Lockhart (1936, 116) a city with a large middle class. As he noted, "It is the product of a city which is exceptionally rich in educational institutions and which possesses its own university, its technical colleges, and its medical school". Singapore was changing with the times. As the locals became more westernised, the foreigners felt its 'Oriental' charms fade. Across 145 years of colonialism, Western sojourners would witness cultural change in the Asian community, especially as the 20th century progressed. Raffles' educational 'institution' was working.

Singapore was a contradiction in urban development. It was peopled by risk-taking 'mobals', migrants who had left their homes in search of fortune. The mobals were often seen as agents of change and entrepreneurship (de Blij 2009). Yet, on the ground in Singapore, migrants congregated in slums and as squatters. They stubbornly clung on to the decrepit imported baggage of places — unhealthy environments, the breeding grounds of vice, and a democracy of poverty, but also to mother tongues, common traditions, and the cultural familiarity that they would need for survival. Slums and squatters were the very impediments to urban progress and White sojourners often wondered whether the Chinese relished remaining in poverty. After the *Simpson Report*, however, the colonial government made a breakthrough in public housing with the first satellite town of Tiong Bahru.

By the 20th century, it would seem obvious to some Westerners that Singapore was shedding its 'fabled' Oriental mystique. Osterhammel's (2018) thesis of the "unfabled East" was certainly playing itself out in Singapore. The inroads of Western colonialism were eroding some Asian traditions. The common language of capitalism bridged Asian and Western definitions of prosperity; the wealthy *towkay* was a symbol of status accepted in high Western society; and the Orient and Occident appeared to share common ground in viewing economics as a lever of development. Unlike earlier Western travellers' perceptions of myths, legends, and fables in the region, the Singapore images from the 19th century onwards were endorsements of wealth, development, and progress. With the Scientific Enlightenment, the Industrial Revolution, and Charles Darwin's evolutionary theory, the century seemed to capture the 'idea of progress' (Bury 1955; Mokyr 2017, 247–266).

VII. Summing Up: The Making of Cosmopolitan Identity

The archaeologist Monica Smith (2019, 12) has provided a broad definition of a city: "a place that has some or all of the following characteristics: a dense population, multiple ethnicities, and a diverse economy with goods found in an abundance and variety beyond what is available in the surrounding rural spaces". Colonial Singapore had indeed all these features. It was rather unique to the region — the only colony which did not have historical and demographic baggage weighty enough to impede colonial efforts. Rather, the earlier myths of Singapura served simply to add romance to the developing colony. The fact that the island was not part of a larger kingdom or politically organised ethnic conglomeration which had to remain inviolate allowed the British to develop the city independently without having to deal with the marked indigenous complexities that beset other regional colonies.

While Singapore had become part of the Straits Settlements and the wider Malay Peninsula, these linkages remained politically tenuous because they had only come about under colonialism. In some ways, European visitors commented on the colonial city as an entity by itself and not part of a wider geographical state. From Raffles onwards, British administrators would develop Singapore from a blank slate and hence were relatively free to act in a more or less autonomous manner. This relatively independent development of the city provided the foundations for the later development of Singapore as a city-state.

Singapore's first 50 years as the EIC factory were generally provided with a transparent and public system of development, in the sense that early White settlers and some prominent Asian merchants were actively involved in committees and decision-making processes of the colony. With so many Westerners engaged in different areas of development, one can see why their perceptions of Singapore and the region mattered in the early growth of the colonial city.

What attracted Western eyes were the economic barometers of riches, the hard work of Asian society, a thriving economic system, and the frenzied hurry of activity. All this was evident in the effervescence of street life, a pulsating movement of peoples and goods, and the general sense of the hospitality of merchants. Singapore was a paragon of the White good life. The expenses were equal to those of London, because of extravagance and opulence. Singapore's success was in its material culture, luxury hotels, operational capitalism, and business buzz. This was a city whose spirit, for better or worse, left an impression on visitors.

Wealth was not found in elaborate architecture but in the business of daily activity, expensive labour, and the high prices of goods (Bleackley 1928). Compared to colonial India, Indonesia, and Burma, Singapore had developed a reputation amongst White travellers as an expensive place. The colonial economy was controlled by the British, and the worry of

White traders and merchants was whether the decolonisation process, the left wing, socialist politics, the rise of local trade unions, and the potential nationalisation of foreign assets would cause it to deconstruct after political independence (Drysdale 1984, 88).

The legacy of British colonialism was its instrumentation in giving Singapore its independent identity, yet within a global strategic framework. The independence was defined by Singapore's geography as an island colony, its status as a British strategic outpost in East-West relations, its laissez-faire emporium of free trade, and its city of immigrants. Singapore for 145 years of colonial rule lived to survive on its own mettle, wits, and entrepreneurship within an environment of constant change. The European political scientist Philippe Regnier (1992) has argued that Singapore's early exposure to political and economic change provided the sediment for its survival. For him, colonial Singapore was gestating as a 'world city' and riding the wave whereby city-states would become the new dynamos of a globalising economic system (Regnier 1992, 14–23).

8

Asia's Navel:
Cultural Pluralism

Chapter 8

ASIA'S NAVEL: CULTURAL PLURALISM

I. The Makings of Pluralism

One characteristic of colonialism has been the creation of polyglot societies in the colonies. Whether by adopting liberal immigration policies or pursuing forced labour migration edicts such as through the slave trade or indentured labour, European colonialists provided the conditions for allowing a diversity of migrants into their colonies. Given that in earlier times nationalism was not yet an issue in the colonial territories now forming part of the US, Canada, Australia, Malaysia, and South Africa, colonialists encouraged a wide range of labour migrants to feed their developmental needs. It seems ironic that while Europe was developing into a series of more or less homogenous nation-states (Lieberman 2003, 2009), its overseas colonies were expanding as highly diversified cultural-religious societies. Colonies thus never could become nation-states, at least along the original European model, and ended up, as Benedict Anderson (1991) has called them, as 'imagined communities'. The sad result is that after World War II, when colonialism was disintegrating, colonies would become the hotbeds of irredentist uprising, interethnic feuding, multiracial riots, and genocidal bloodbaths. Colonialism left a bitter aftertaste in most former colonies. It bequeathed colossal political baggage for incumbent independent governments to tackle, a challenge that remains till today.

Before the advent of nationalism and the quest for spawning cohesive societies under an independent state, colonial governments were satisfied with keeping ethnic groups distinct but harmonious with one another. What is quite surprising is that in the culturally mixed Singapore which the British created, society was able to live quite peacefully. Singapore, a 19th-century East India Company (EIC) colonial prodigy, was a prime target of British efforts towards a liberal migration policy. In the matter of a decade, the Lion City changed from a predominantly Malay community to a Chinese town. Indentured labour of certain Indians would also bring in many, but much smaller numbers than those of the Chinese, to form part of colonial Singapore's Indian population. Thus, from its early establishment, the city developed its dual cultural identity; being both a plural society and a Chinese city. Despite the fact that Singapore was overwhelmingly Chinese by demography, Westerners seemed frequently to characterise it as cosmopolitan.

The cultural diversity in Singapore was visible in the early years after Raffles' founding. The reasons were evident. The Lion City had begun with no substantial resident population aside from the ruling *temenggong*'s followers and the scattered *orang laut*, and Singapore's smallness as an island had circumscribed its demographic growth spatially. However, this allowed Raffles and subsequent colonial administrators to encourage migrants from Asia and Europe to boost its development, and the Singapore town planned by Raffles provided for the concentration of the colony's population, which for 145 years would encompass diverse Asian communities.

Despite its brief but significant fame as a regional emporium in the 14th century, the island had no monuments to show for its past glory. Singapore's emporium in the 19th century was thus a colonial re-creation, sustained by its free port status, new immigration policies, and an expanding British hegemonic power. Singapore's rapid 19th-century development was predicated on an open-door policy of attracting labour, traders, entrepreneurs, professionals, and settlers to ensure that the fledgling EIC factory would be a success. Hence, from its 1819 inception, the cast of Singapore's cosmopolitan identity had been established. Given that most European sojourners in the 19th century stayed within the town, they were easily exposed to Singapore's multiethnic population, and for them it would become an enduring feature of the colonial city.

Throughout the 19th century, Westerners never portrayed Singapore as an ethnically homogenous place — this was not a Chinese, Malay, Indian, Thai, Burmese, Japanese, nor Indonesian city. Before J. S. Furnivall (1948) popularised the concept of "plural societies" in the region's colonies, 19th-century Singapore was already formulating the idea. Furnivall's concept of a plural society, where people "mix but do not combine", approximates the mosaic of ethnic diversity in colonial Singapore: "There is a plural society, with different sections of the community living side by side, but separately, within the same political unit. Even in the economic sphere there is a division of labour along racial lines. Natives, Chinese, Indians and Europeans all have different functions, and within each major group subsections have particular occupations" (Furnivall 1948, 304).

Benedict Anderson (1991) had a different portrayal of the colonial plural society. Reflecting on the Western development of the nation-state, and with it, national identity and consciousness, for him the colonial state was an agglomeration of diverse nations. It was an amorphous society of many communities, without an identity but tied to the colonial state. Colonial Singapore was indeed an amalgamation of many nations; Chinese, Arabs, Indians, Javanese, and Bugis were residents in Singapore but their loyalties lay elsewhere. This was the idea behind Western references to Singapore's 'cosmopolitan' population. Westerners indicated the "coexistence" of different ethnic groups, or their "living together" as an association (Appiah 2006, xix). Over the decades, other concepts such as 'polyglot', 'plural society', 'multicultural', and 'ethnic diversity' would be used. Even though Western travellers marvelled at Singapore's 'cosmopolitan' population, few of them embraced the meaning of cosmopolitanism in the way that Kwame Appiah (2006) has defined it, as *multiculturalism*. With colonial era Whites tending to maintain their racial and cultural distinctions and superiority, they only paid lip service to the idea of cultural mixing and ethnic coexistence.

The objective of colonial census-makers was to identify all the ethnic groups. There was no room for blurred identity, and when that manifested itself, they invented the category of 'others' — to ensure that everyone had an "extremely clear place. No fractions ..." (B. Anderson 1991, 166). In Singapore, the group that bore the ambiguous ethnic label of 'others' were the Eurasians. They were never considered fully part of White society, yet were grudgingly placed on the 'European' north side of the Singapore River, through their symbolic ethnic centre, the Singapore Recreational Club (or Eurasian Club, as it was called colloquially) at the Padang. Over the decades, while Europeans moved west along the Orchard Road valley and its surrounding areas, the Eurasians and Straits Chinese would move east into the Katong-Joo Chiat-Siglap area.

II. Polyglot Society

Many Westerners were pleasantly surprised by the cultural diversity, religious plurality, and ethnic heterogeneity of Singapore. In his visits to Singapore from 1826 onwards, the trader G. F. Davidson (1846) noted that it would require a full volume to describe the inhabitants of Singapore as they represented so many countries. Here, one could find varied costumes of different countries "forming motley groups that can nowhere be surpassed" (Davidson 1846, 45). The land surveyor John Thomson (1865, 201) was overwhelmed by Singapore's ethnic diversity, and in his hyperbolic description stated that the town "consisted of nearly every nation on earth; at least one or two of every civilized nation were to be found there". Half a century later, Singapore's ethnic diversity would still be a topic of curiosity. Hayes Marriott (1911, 341), the acting Colonial Secretary, noted that the 1911 census recorded no less than 54 different languages spoken by 48 different races, with all separate Chinese and Indian tongues being counted as just one language respectively for each of these two races. George Fitch (1913) referred to Singapore as the most "cosmopolitan" city in the Orient, while Marriott (1911, 341) declared it to be one of the "most cosmopolitan cities in the world".

Throughout its colonial history, Singapore would appeal to White travellers as an encyclopaedic landscape of heterogeneous ethnic groups, varied foods, diverse festivals, and a plurality of religious places of worship and sacred enceintes. Different travellers tried to capture the great cultural heterogeneity in various ways: William Hornaday (1885, 295) called it an *"omnium gatherum"*, while Malcolm MacDonald, Commissioner-General for the UK in Southeast Asia and prior to that Governor-General of the Malayan Union, said that Singapore represented not a "national culture, but an international culture" (Moore 1953, 7). Singapore's multiple ethnic groups lived in a juxtaposed relationship in urban space. In response, every Western sojourner wrote his or her own geography of the place.

The Lion City seemed to be the meeting place of East and West. Singapore was where Rudyard Kipling's (1899b) great poetic dictum was constantly being put to the test: "East is East and West is West, and never the twain shall meet". The East-West relationship is a macro-geographical issue that has persisted through the centuries (Lewis and Wigen 1997). While trade and economic affairs in the colony would bring about the physical meeting of Westerners and Asians as Raffles had conceptualised and Joseph Balestier would later express support for, Singapore's East-West relationships did not necessarily reflect a deeper and more sympathetic cosmopolitan cultural integration. After 500 years of colonial dominance in Asia, the West continued to have the upper hand in these relationships. Thus, the twain had indeed met in the 19th century, albeit on unequal terms. Colonial residents and bureaucrats wanted the best of both worlds — economic ties between Asians and Whites, while maintaining a cultural distance and deliberate distinction of Western superiority.

There was a fundamental difference between Singapore's ethnic plurality and the other colonies of the region. While elsewhere in the region, colonial powers defined and established territorial borders by capturing multiethnic communities within colonial states, Singapore's ethnic plurality was not a given, it was manufactured through immigration policies. The British did not set out to create a cosmopolitan society, but because labour was a necessity in the newly-created factory, they opened the floodgates to Asian migrants. Asian and European peoples who would make up the Lion City's diverse society came to it mainly by free will, some by coercion. It was often portrayed as a microcosm of the Orient, difficult to define, yet an obviously Asian landscape setting.

One person of European descent but using an emic approach (meaning a perspective from within) conveyed the mixed cultural chemistry that the colonial city conjured. The Singapore-born Dutch burgher John van Cuylenburg (1982, 259) recalled that pre-war Singapore had been affectionately referred to as a model city: "Pre-war Singapore provided the world with an example of how a city, teeming with people of various races, colours, creeds, and ways of life, could live together harmoniously". He added, "We were a marvel — yes, a pattern of excellence — to the world". There had been a diversity of Klings,[1] Chinese, Tibetans, Arabs, Singhalese, Japanese, Armenians, Oriental Jews, Persians, Annamites, Siamese, Burmese, Gurkhas, and other Asiatic races.

The observant ship captain George Earl (1837, 360), remarking on Singapore, described it as "an epitome of the population of the whole [Malay] Archipelago" in which "each people [formed] a separate community, and [retained their] customs as completely as if it had never been transplanted". For Patrick Anderson (1955, 154), Singapore was a

---

[1] A term often used to refer to Indians.

product of four distinct cultures: Chinese, Malay, Indian, and Eurasian. Despite the diversity of races, Roland Braddell (1935) noted that there was "little assimilation or mixture of blood". To him, only the Eurasians of mixed European and Asiatic descent, and the Indian Muslims of mixed Malay and Indian descent, were examples of the intermingling of races.

Westerners were enthralled by the diversity of cultural and religious festivals that were displayed publicly. Yet, despite the "bewildering richness of native life", they found it frustrating because they could not understand the languages, cultural beliefs, and symbolisms. There was an "exasperating lack of information", noted Anderson (1955, 154), coupled with "considerable apathy on the part of those appealed to". Given that the British were now the rulers of Singapore, few colonial administrators felt compelled to learn any Asian languages; the onus was on Asians to learn English.

III. Sexual Inequality: Domestic 'Boys'

Commenting on Singapore's 1931 census, Braddell noted that there were two demographic challenges in the colonial city. The first was that the future of Singapore was one dependent on a largely immigrant society. He observed how immigrants were bent on making their fortunes and returning home. The legal professional found that only the Europeans and educated Asiatics were willing to adopt citizenship, as in a French saying, "a man has two countries, his own and Singapore" (R. Braddell 1935, 50). Singapore was a place of transient residents, opportunistic workers, and touristic entrepreneurs. As the city grew though, its immigrant population would eventually settle down and its population expand.

The other problem that Braddell observed was the marked proportion of males over females, which led to the burgeoning of prostitution in the colony. In the 1830s, Earl (1837, 367) had observed the disproportionate sex ratio in Chinese migrants: 5,000 to 8,000 immigrants, and only 40 to 50 women amongst them. Charles Wilkes (1845, 404), the American explorer, estimated that in 1842, of the total population of 60,000 only one-tenth were females. In 1857, the German historian and ethnologist Fedor Jagor (1977, 37) confirmed the imbalanced sex ratio when he said that what was striking about the street scene in Singapore was "the almost total absence of women". He noted that the ratio of women to men was one to eight (Jagor 1977, 37). The administrator Nicholas Dennys (1894, 359) placed the number of women to men among the Chinese as one-fifth of the population or one woman to five men. He opined that this sexual imbalance was the source of much "immorality and disorder" and wondered how it could "be remedied" (Dennys 1894, 359).

The sex ratio was the reason why 'boys', as male Chinese servants were termed, were employed as domestic helpers within many White households. White residents remembered their 'boys' vividly: 'Ah Hing' for John Whitehead (1893, 6), and 'Ah Ting' for Patrick Anderson (1955). Isabella Bird (1883, 115), in her 1879 stopover in Singapore, noted that of the 15,368 domestic servants, only 844 were women. References to the male Chinese domestics were found in the numerous letters of Maria Balestier (Hale 2016). Maria wrote to her niece Helen to explain how busy she was in managing her servants who were "all males" (Hale 2016, 34). In an 1846 letter to her friend Harriett, she made an early reference to Chinese male servants as 'Chinese boys', as opposed to female servants or '*ayahs*' (Hale 2016, 213). Maria had her Chinese boy when he was 10 years old, noting that he was still "attentive and affectionate as a child" (Hale 2016, 213).

The shortage of females was evident in other activities. Wilkes (1845, 386) in his 1842 sojourn in Singapore was one of the earliest Westerners to record his impression of a street Chinese opera or *wayang*. The observant American noted that the females in the opera were represented by young men and boys (Wilkes 1845, 386). The shortage of females meant that women in the colony were at a 'premium'; rich *towkays* could afford them as wives and concubines but the poor had to solicit them as prostitutes in brothels and massage parlours.

Jagor (1977, 37) expressed that the sexual imbalance reflected the Chinese and the Klings' intentions of returning home after making a small fortune, hence they did not bring their womenfolk to Singapore. Thus ironically, the immigrant nature of the colony's Asian society, which on the one hand had brought about its diversity, led on the other to its almost uniformly male demography. The French doctor Yvan (1855) tried to explain the Chinese male dominance. Of the Chinese in Singapore, he said,

> [They] live in a state of celibacy, and it seems as though, when they arrive in this country, they made a sort of vow to renounce all the pleasures, for which they generally manifest a considerable inclination. Their laborious lives are consequently uninterrupted by any thing which might distract their attention from the one sole object which they always

appear to have in view — that of acquiring a fortune sufficient to enable them to go and live quietly in Malacca, or some part of the celestial empire (Yvan 1855, 130).

A century later, university lecturer Patrick Anderson (1955, 75–88) would dedicate a whole chapter of his book to his funny and exasperating experiences with his boy Ah Ting in 1951. As it was to many Whites, the behaviour of their boys was unfathomable. "So scrupulous was Ah Ting's routine, so deep-seated his desire to protect me and my belongings that he had locked himself out" (P. Anderson 1955, 88).

IV. Colours of Culture

Singapore's birth as the EIC's factory formed a new chapter in Western colonialism in the region. As a contrast to the earlier centuries of pinprick colonial adventurism, the Europeans would now begin a new entrepreneurship of colonising entire lands, extending territory, and investing in places. The birth of modern Singapore coincided to a large extent with Westerners seeking new frontiers to explore and experience. However, Singapore in the 19th century was also a new settlement compared to other places in the same wave of colonialism which had already been well developed. Alfred Russel Wallace (2015, 77), in discussing Singapore in relation to Brazil, complained that the "provisions & labour are dear & travelling both tedious & expensive". The naturalist noted further, the "servants' wages are high and the customs of the country do not permit you to live in the free & easy style of Brazil" (Wallace 2015, 77). Yet, Singapore was attractive because White travellers found this Oriental location to be a greenfield site compared to other Asian settings.

In capturing the ethnic diversity of Singapore, 19th-century travellers were most enthralled by the variety of colours of textiles and costumes that different ethnic groups wore. One must remember that for many Westerners, viewing a multitude of ethnicities dressed in their traditional costumes was an uncommon sight. In his stopover in Singapore, the British ornithologist and naturalist Whitehead (1893, 5) was fascinated by the ethnic mix, "where different types of the human race ... collected together", and which exhibited itself "with a variety of colour and style of costume [adding] life and beauty to the scene". He contrasted this to colder climates where people peeped out through "dark coloured garments, making our cities appear in perpetual mourning". Bird (1883,

144) likewise noted that the city was "ablaze with colour and motley with costume". Bird (1883, 148–149) contrasted the European and Asian sectors of the town; the Oriental life in the Asiatic Town was full of motion and colour, whereas the European part of Singapore was "dull and sleepy looking". By the 20th century, the British colony would be a place where the noises of tropical nature, vehicles, and people were "continuous and varied, both by night and day" (Sidney 1926, 28).

The contrast between Singapore and other towns in the region in the 19th century is best captured in descriptions of Singapore and Malayan towns, the quality of life in the latter having the most disparity with the vitality and diversity of Singapore. The differing experiences of the aristocratic traveller Bird in Singapore, and those of the wife of a junior bureaucrat, Emily Innes, in the small town of Langat in Selangor, underscored the inequality brought about by status and class under colonialism. Entertained by the governor and elites in Singapore society, Bird's encounters in the colonial city were delightful and left positive impressions. Tropical Singapore was exciting, stimulating, colourful, eventful, and enchanting for Bird. If Singapore was an urban society typified by cultural pluralism and energy, Langat was, however, a small town governed by monotonous homogeneity.

Having read Bird's glowing descriptions of her experiences with high society in Singapore and Malaya, Innes (1885, 2:242) comes across as resentful, envious, and critical, though she was quick to accept that both Bird's account and her own account of Malaya were "true" but made under "totally different circumstances". Taking a shot at Bird's book, Innes' own book was entitled *The Chersonese with the Gilding Off*. For Innes (1885, 1:36), her sojourn at Langat was defined by "heat, ennui, and mosquitoes". She complained about how her life in Malaya was dull and gloomy, and that she "vegetated" in Langat (Innes 1885, 2:195).

While 19th-century Western distinctions of race, class, and caste were often taken as givens, by the 20th century after the Second World War, Western sojourners would be more candid about the ills of racial prejudice and class distinction. To some of them who were promoters of democracy and with it, equality, the colonial ethos of White superiority seemed an abominable contradiction. From time to time, there were outspoken criticisms of racial prejudice and the colonial superiority complex over natives by the likes of such as Wallace, and even members of the colonial establishment like Thomson and MacDonald. MacDonald, in his Foreword to Donald Moore's (1953) book *Far Eastern Agent*, summed it up best when he proposed for a new Malaya (and Singapore) based on a "true understanding, friendship and partnership between all types of men" (Moore 1953, 9). MacDonald was an enlightened long-time resident in Singapore who was well versed with the cultures. He realised that all the great traditions (European, Chinese, Indian) had a history of "strange prejudices" which prevented an "egalitarian comradeship" amongst them (Moore 1953, 9). Ironically, he noted that all the major groups were racists. He observed how Europeans felt themselves superior to Asians, that the Chinese secretly nursed their ancestors' beliefs that all other races were 'barbarians', and that Indians had imbibed the caste system which prevented them from accepting the equality of men (Moore 1953, 9).

V. Ethnic Characteristics

Westerners over the decades would tend to perceive Singapore as a mysterious and mythical Oriental city. This flavour comes through in the titles of Patrick Anderson's (1955) book *Snake Wine*, and Moore's (1975) *The Magic Dragon*, the latter concerning Singapore's unparalleled economic progress. For Westerners, the city was perhaps defined more by its multiethnic population with its sacred beliefs than by its diverse physical landscapes.

Unlike the manner in which the British in India had systematically developed a body of local knowledge (Cohn 1996), in Singapore, colonial knowledge was derived from a wider field of 'knowledge' gathering from the region or *Alam Melayu*. In this vein the British scholar-administrators (Thomas Raffles, Roland Braddell, William Marsden, Richard Winstedt, Hugh Clifford, and Hugh Low) would over the decades provide a relatively more accurate distillation of colonial knowledge. However, in other ways, knowledge of local peoples and native communities would be formulated by short-term travellers in a rather impressionistic, stereotypical, and ad hoc manner. Rightly or wrongly, these latter popular impressions were more used by Whites in their working relationships with the Asians.

Of all the ethnic groups in Singapore, Westerners generally had the most definite characterisations of the Chinese and the Malays. The Malays were often viewed through romantic lenses. Yet, each Westerner typified the various ethnic groups in different ways. The British writer Noel Barber (1971, 13) summed up his stereotypical views as such: the "gentle Malays", the "industrious Chinese", the "listless Indians", and the "perspiring

British". Somerset Maugham (1993, 44) was more discerning in his racial depictions. He observed the Malays to "dwell uneasily in towns", the Chinese as being "supple, alert and industrious", the dark-skinned Tamils to be "as though they were but brief sojourners in a strange land", while the Bengalis were "sleek and prosperous, ... easy in their surroundings, and self-assured", the Japanese "sly and obsequious" and busy in secret affairs, while the English wore "a nonchalant and careless air".

John Thomson (1849b, 747–748) gave an early assessment of the Asian population with regards to their work. For example, he classified the Javanese and Boyanese as being characterised by "soberness, slowness and honesty united to dullness, patience and endurance". They were valuable labourers in nutmeg and coconut plantations. With regard to the Klings, he noted that they were useful for agriculture, and could be assigned as syces (drivers), cattle drivers, grass cutters, and nutmeg gatherers (Thomson 1849b, 748). He described them as being good workers if they chose to exert themselves, but were most wretched servants who delighted in chicanery of all sorts. The Chinese labourers were hard manual workers in sugar estates, and also needed a watchful eye to keep them honest (Thomson 1849b, 748). Thomson (1849b, 748) divided the Malays into two groups: those from Malacca, and the original inhabitants of the island and the Malay Archipelago. The Malays provided partial assistance to agriculturists and were employed for cutting firewood and searching for various forest products such as dammer (yellow resin used in varnishes) and rattan (Thomson 1849b, 748).

Generally, despite commenting on the agglomeration of various ethnic and religious groups, Westerners never felt physically threatened by them. By and large the colonial city was peaceful, safe, and harmonious throughout the 19th century. One of the earliest Westerners to remark at the peaceful heterogeneity of peoples in Singapore was Wilkes (1845), in 1842. He was "very much struck with the order and good behaviour existing among such an incongruous mass of human beings" (Wilkes 1845, 388). Despite various games he observed to be going on between them, there seemed to be no quarrels taking place. The American offered an explanation for the peaceful coexistence:

> I understood that the rarity of quarrels between the different races and religions is more owing to the consideration of the place being neutral ground, where all ought to abstain from hostility, than to any effect produced by the police (Wilkes 1845, 388).

Over the decades, White residents would treat their Asian workers as culturally distant, and could never understand these members of the population. The cultural opaqueness of Asians was partly due to Whites maintaining their insular, superior dispositions. Without much social interaction, it was no wonder that the Europeans found the Asian population difficult to fathom. Perhaps the most distinctive feature of the Asian population was their belief in superstition and the supernatural. After spending 20 years in Singapore, Mrs. E. F. Howell gave numerous examples of superstitious beliefs held by the Chinese, Malays, and Indians, or Buddhists, Taoists, Hindus, and Muslims (Wise and Wise 1985, 203–207).

These closely adhered-to beliefs created an impenetrable cultural wall which the White population could not breach. The Asian does not comment about his life, observed Patrick Anderson (1955, 155), "he lives it". Anderson himself found it hard to understand Asians because they represented the "difficult relation between art and life", and posited that one loved and understood them "intuitively, since they are beautiful", without necessarily being like them or being able "to appreciate their problems intellectually" (P. Anderson 1955, 155–156).

Moreover, one of the perennial themes of the Westerner was the economic competition he faced in different Asian societies. In the 16th and 17th centuries, it had been the 'Moors' or Muslims whom they dreaded. By the 19th century the East-West rivalry involved the Chinese because of the perceived danger of their imperial hegemony, and by the 1930s the fear would be focused on the Japanese. The Yellow Peril had shifted, but unlike the ubiquitous Chinese, the Japanese were a relatively unknown cultural entity to the Europeans. The British diplomat Bruce Lockhart (1936) captured the European anxiety in Singapore between the two World Wars as they viewed Japan's expanding military might and its economic prowess. Yet, Singapore's Europeans were not total strangers to the Japanese presence as there was a small but relatively significant community in Singapore.

The Japanese controlled the massage parlour business, were involved in specific retail businesses, and they were residents in the Middle Road area (Lockhart 1936; van Cuylenburg 1982). Japanese prostitutes were well known in Malay Street, the notorious red-light area. The more or less favourable view towards the Japanese population turned outright acidic, however, with the Second World War. In fact, the resident Japanese population practically evaporated immediately after the war. For a long time, what they left behind were only the many Japanese graves.

a) *The 'Malays' in the* Alam Melayu

Roland Braddell (1935, 45) called Singapore the "navel of the Malay countries". He was not referring to Singapore's historical links to the Sri Vijayan and Malacca empires, nor the central location of Singapore in the *Alam Melayu*. Instead, he found Singapore to be an incredible locus of the Malay population from the region, which he listed as including 'real' Malays, Javanese, Boyanese, Achinese, Bataks, Banjarese, Bugis, Dyaks, and people from Minangkabau, Korinchi, Jambi, Palembang and elsewhere in Sumatra, from Dutch North Borneo, and others of the Netherlands Indies (R. Braddell 1935, 43–44).

One of the early Western armchair anthropologists, the German Friedrich Ratzel (1898, vol. 1), not only defined the study of ethnography but also wrote a long academic chapter on the Malays (Ratzel 1898, 1:391–486). Summarising the many depictions of Malay behaviour, Ratzel (1898, 1:398) drew his own conclusions about the "fundamental traits" of "Malay character". He noted the Mongol (of whom one may presume he considered the Malay to be) as "gentle, peaceable, quiet and civil, submissive to authorities, and rarely disposed towards crime" (Ratzel 1898, 1:398). He went on to state that the Malay "taciturnity" was manifest in their "quietness in assemblies" and "formality in intercourse" (Ratzel 1898, 1:398). Unlike the more recent academic distinctions and debates about Malay identity and defining the Malay (Barnard 2004), Western sojourners in the past used a looser classification of the Malay diaspora, based on physical features, and bounded within a spatially defined contiguous archipelagic region (Ratzel 1898). Braddell's (1935) definition of the Malay population in Singapore, which included ethnic groups from Sumatra, Sulawesi, Borneo, Java, and the Riau Archipelago, was typical of the general Western colonial thinking about the *Alam Melayu*.

Marsden, the British administrator in Sumatra, confirmed the Western perspective when he observed that the term "Malay" was "bestowed by Europeans upon all who resembled them in features and complexion" (Milner 2004, 248). Many short-term European visitors were unable to make ethnic distinctions within the diverse 'native' population; hence, all 'natives' were classified loosely as Malays as distinct from the Chinese, Indians, Arabs, Parsees, and Japanese. Though Western residents in Singapore could distinguish between different *Alam Melayu* ethnicities, by and large, they too over time would integrate many groups under the 'native Malay', a reflection of blurred ethnic boundaries, overlapping cultural identities, and the permeable and flexible Malay cultural ethos which related to the idea of *masuk Melayu*, or becoming Malay by adopting Malay cultural attributes.

Since Singapore was closely geographically and culturally anchored to the Riau-Lingga Archipelago which formed a subset of the *Alam Melayu*, for 19th-century Western commentators, the early Singapore Malays were part of the large amorphous *orang laut*, or as David Sopher (1965) has called them, "sea nomads". Several Western residents such as James Logan, W. W. Skeat, H. N. Ridley, C. A. Gibson-Hill, and Thomas Newbold paid attention to the varied sea tribes in and around Singapore (Ridley 1904). The general Western perception was that the early Singapore Malays were less historically linked to Malaya (or *Tanah Melayu*, the Malay Peninsula) as they were more products of the Riau Archipelago and the Johore-Singapore coastal areas. In this archipelago, the native population was further divided into two groups: (1) *orang darat* or people of the land or inland (non-Muslim fishermen); and (2) *orang laut* or maritime Malays (Sopher 1965, 92–93). The inland Malays were said to be more civilised than the nomadic *orang laut*, because they settled ashore earlier. Through the process of extensive intermarriage, both these groups of what had originally been sea nomads eventually settled in Singapore, became Muslim, and were Malayanised. For Westerners, the maritime Malays would be legendary for their maritime skills, navigation, seaman abilities, fearlessness, and dexterity (Skeat and Ridley 1900, 248). They also earned the controversial distinction of having been the region's pirates for centuries.

The centrality of the Malays in Singapore and the region allowed various ethnic groups to communicate with one another through 'bastard Malay'; the lingua franca by which people generally made themselves understood (R. Braddell 1935, 46). Earlier, Dennys (1894, 359) had remarked about how "liquid, easily learned Malay" was the "medium of intercommunication" that united "all classes of inhabitants" who speak a "Babel" of languages in Singapore. As the Malay language was widely used in the region, Westerners used 'Malay' as a general term for its varied cultural groupings. The magistrate Braddell noted how easily Malay expresses things: *mata* means 'eye', *hari* means 'day', thus *matahari* literally translates to 'the eye of the day', but the compound word actually means 'the sun'. In the same vein, *mata-mata* means 'a policeman' and 'the eye of the government', and *mata-mata glab*[2] means 'secret eyes', referring to a detective (R. Braddell 1935, 46).

As with their views of other ethnic communities in Singapore, there were rather mixed perceptions of the Malay population among the Westerners. Their depictions of the Malays arose apparently from experiences in Singapore, but also other areas of the *Alam Melayu*. James Brooke (1848, 1:11) seems to have been influenced by environmental determinism in his statements about the Malay population from his 1839 stopover in Singapore. He tried to explain the Malay disposition by the rich abundant environment they lived in. In his words, the Malays were "denizens of a beneficent clime, which furnishes sufficient for a man's simple wants, without the necessity of toil and allows him to yield to the dictates of nature or of passion, without care or apparent responsibility" (J. Brooke 1948, 1:11).

Familiar with the 'Malays' in various parts of the region, Raffles, writing to Marsden in January 1815, remarked that the Malay, "living in a country where nature grants (almost without labour) all his wants, is so indolent, and when he has rice, nothing will induce him to work" (S. Raffles 1830, 236). The British administrator felt that civilised life made the Malay feel an obligation to "conform", whereas in the woods "he feels he is free" (S. Raffles 1830, 236). Western residents, travellers, and sojourners in Singapore repeated the stereotype that the Malays were lazy, adverse to continuous labour, and listless (Collingwood 1868, 243; Logan 1847a, 14). Cuthbert Collingwood (1868, 242) accepted that the Malays were the "real indigenous sons of the soil", but lamented that they had not contributed much to the general effect.

In the 18th century, the missionary and botanical explorer Pierre Poivre (1769, 70) commented hyperbolically that the Malays of Sumatra, Java, Borneo, Celebes, Malacca, and the Malay Peninsula were "restless, fond of navigation, war, plunder, emigrations, colonies, desperate enterprises, adventures and gallantry". He declared that while the Malays talked of honour and bravery, they were "the most treacherous, ferocious people on the face of the globe" (Poivre 1769, 71). The French priest felt that the Malay race was restless and hence lived in a "perpetual round of agitation and tumult" (Poivre 1769, 70).

---

[2] The word *glab* in today's Malay is spelt as *gelap*.

Over a century later, Bird (1883) would provide an accurate overview of the 'Malays' in the *Alam Melayu*. She did not think the Malays of the peninsula were its aborigines, and stated that they were "colonists rather than its conquerors" (Bird 1883, 27). She believed the original seat of the Malays to be Sumatra, and that the 'colonial' Malay kingdoms in the peninsula, those of Johore and Malacca, which were recorded at the time of the Portuguese, were recent. Bird was clearly well informed about the aborigines, listing them as *orang benua* or 'men of the country', who were divided into two classes, the Semangs and the Negritoes, also frequently called Jakuns and Sakei (Bird 1883, 28).

Those Westerners familiar with Malay history generally had enlightened views of the ethnic group. The historian Oliver Wolters (1967, 1970) was clearly enamoured by the economic prowess of Sri Vijaya, the fountainhead of regional trade from the seventh to the 13th centuries. He argued that the long-exposed geographical locations at Palembang, Singapore, and Malacca showed that the Malays were "always ready to innovate" (Wolters 1970, 175). Despite their elaborate court culture, they were not an "inflexible" civilisation (Wolters 1970, 177). Hence, they were able to adapt to changing foreign cultural influences: Hindu-Buddhist to Muslim religion, and integrating Indian, Chinese, and Western civilisational inputs. No serious Western observer could be blind to the pivotal trading achievements of Sri Vijaya-Palembang and Malacca before Western administrators and traders began wrestling the economic purse strings away from the Malay rajas. More recent studies of the Malays by historians, geographers, and anthropologists have shown that the Malays throughout the region differed from one another in significant ways. The Javanese themselves used the term *Melayu* to denote "a fugitive" or "an exile" (Sandhu and Wheatley 1983b, 1:viii). Given the wandering and seafaring activities of many of the region's Malay groups, the Malays as an extended whole tended to be viewed by early Westerners as a people who lacked permanent residence. However, when the city of Malacca was established, 16th-century Europeans like Tomé Pires, João de Barros, and Diogo do Couto also provided an etymological relationship between Malacca and the Malays (Sandhu and Wheatley 1983b, 1:viii–ix).

In Singapore, the regional 'Malay' groups (Bugis, Bawean, Javanese, Batak, Sundanese, *orang laut*, Minangkabau, Riau) had been identified separately in the 19th century in Western reports, but would gradually be subsumed under the local version of the ethnic group over the decades of colonial rule. Despite their internal cultural diversity, the 'Malays' were always distinguished as being separate from the Chinese, Indians, and Arabs in Singapore. In Singapore's first census of 1824, the island was still very much a Malay town. Of the population of 10,000, Malays accounted for 4,580 persons or 45 per cent of the population, with the Chinese as the second biggest segment of 3,317. If we include the Bugis population (1,925) under the Malay category, 'Malay' in 1824 would have accounted for nearly 50 per cent of the fledgling town's population.

Many Westerners realised that the Malays, including the *orang laut*, were uncomfortable with Singapore's urban life. Wilkes (1845, 393) noted that in 1842 the Malays were mainly located in the "suburbs" in "Malay villages". Horace Bleackley (1928, 135) opined that the Malay had no love for city life. According to the traveller, the Malay despised the "heathen Chinese" and "barbarous Hindu", and believed that foreigners should do the "arduous tasks" while the Malay as "lord of the land should benefit by their labour" (Bleackley 1928, 135).

In contrast to Wolter's views that the Malays were not an "inflexible" civilisation, some other observers saw the Malays as detesting change. As Clifford (1983, 227) reminded his British audience in 1899, the proverbial Malay saying was that of "Let our children die rather than our customs". Yet, despite being tradition-bound, Malay culture for many Westerners remained flexible, accommodating, and relaxed. Reflecting the 19th-century Western romantic vogue and the belief in simple native lives as being 'noble' and 'good', the British administrator Frank Swettenham (1895) had a glowing appraisal of the Malays. For him, the Malay hated labour and contributed little to taxation, but he accepted them as the rightful heirs to Malaya: "the land is Malaya and he is the Malay" (Swettenham 1895, 37). Swettenham came close to the idea of the Malay Peninsula as *Tanah Melayu* (land of the Malays) and in his writing, shifted the home of the Malays, hitherto thought of as Sumatra, to Malaya. Clearly portraying his partiality towards the Malays, Swettenham (1895, 37) declared that the "infidel Chinese" and "evil-smelling Hindu" would share profit but they were "strangers and unbelievers", while the Malay was willing to "tolerate" them and be "amused rather than angered".

Thomson (1984, 296–297), however, portrayed Malay behaviour in a contrasting way. While he observed that the Malay might deceptively appear to Europeans as "careless of life" and lacking "effervescent energy", he could become "mad with internal passion" and most villainous and diabolical (Thomson 1984, 297) when insulted. Those who knew his temper and nature and "judiciously [comported] themselves" would find the Malay "pliant, obedient, faithful, if not affectionate" (Thomson 1984, 297). More so than with the Chinese, Westerners were comfortable with the Malays: "Every Malay is a gentleman, even those of the lower orders. But he has no great love of work", nor did he see in "his city life a proper existence". Despite accolades for the Malay, Westerners also associated them with a fondness of "running amok", and provided many theories for this strange behaviour (Bleackley 1928, 125).

Debunking the general perceptions of the Malays as "lazy", Earl (1837, 376) concluded from his experiences with Sumatran Minangkabaus that the Malays "are naturally an industrious people". The well-travelled Earl (1837, 378) noted that the Malays improved themselves when in the company of Europeans, for whom they had great respect. To him, they had more regard for European morality and knowledge than they did for their Arab teachers, "a point of no small importance in the progress of civilisation".

The perceptions of the Malays from administrators like Thomson, Swettenham, and Clifford came not only from their Singapore experiences but also earlier administrative work in the Malay Peninsula. Their close association with the Malay population gave them a more balanced assessment of the local people, and in some ways even an emotional attachment. All three men wrote interesting books, with glowing tributes to the Malays. Thomson's (1984) *Glimpses into Life in Malayan Lands*, Swettenham's (1895) *Malay Sketches*, and Clifford's (1916) *The Further Side of Silence* carried many anecdotes, stories, experiences, and incidents that exemplified the Malay character. Numerous 19th-century Western residents in Singapore shared rather favourable impressions of the Malays that might be viewed through James de Vere Allen's concept of "Malayophilia" or the pro-Malay phenomenon (Reynolds 2008, 23).

From the pens of these long-term residents, one gets an insight into the peculiar beliefs, behaviour, and practices of the Malays: were-tigers, *hantus* (ghosts), *latah* (state of mind), *amok* (sudden homicidal mania), *ber-hantu* (black magic), *kinduri*[3] (feast), and *joget* (Malay dance) (Swettenham 1895; Clifford 1897; Thomson 1984). Unlike in Malaya,

---

[3] Usually spelt as *kenduri* in today's Malay.

where the Malay *kampong* culture had been kept alive, the village chief or *penghulu* had command of his *rakyat* (public, or masses), and the peasant Malays were tied to customs and traditions. In Singapore, the resident Malays were tied to a higher state order of raja and *temenggong* — yet in a sense there was no Malay *rakyat* to talk about. Upon Raffles' founding, the originally small resident Malay population would soon be diluted with the influx of other communities from the *Alam Melayu*: groups from Bencoolen, Malacca, and Penang, as well as the Boyanese, Javanese, Bugis, Minangkabau, Sundanese, and *orang laut*.

The *orang laut*, or "sea folk" (Sopher 1965, 47) and the varied other Western names by which they were known, such as sea gypsies, sea nomads, corsairs, maritime Malays, and Selates (*selat* in Malay meaning 'strait'; hence 'dwellers of the strait'), had a legendary reputation for centuries as fearsome pirates in the waters around Singapore (Andaya 2019; Sopher 1965; Skeat and Ridley 1900). Associated with Singapore Island, the *orang laut* were divided into various *sukus* or clans such as Orang Seletar (or Orang Utan Seletar), Orang Kallang (or Orang Biduanda Kallang), and Orang Gelam (those around the mouth of the Singapore River) (Sopher 1965, 104–108). According to the cultural geographer Sopher (1965, 48), the *orang laut* were skilled boat builders, good fishermen, resourceful maritime travellers, who possessed knowledgeable navigational skills, and had an intimate understanding of the sea. However, with the steady development of colonial Singapore, many of them would become sedentary fishermen in the coastal areas and islets of Singapore. Colonialism created fixed state boundaries, and the stateless *orang laut* in their 'watery Zomia' soon became not only legitimate colonial subjects but would in Singapore be classified as Malays.

Swettenham (1895, 1–11) began his book with a candid portrayal of the Malay personality which he felt he had the credentials to comprehend. He wrote, "To begin to understand the Malay you must live in his country, speak his language, respect his faith, be interested in his interests, humour his prejudices, sympathise with and help him in trouble, and share his pleasures and possibly his risks" (Swettenham 1895, 1). One of the Malay virtues that endeared them to Westerners was their warm hospitality. As Swettenham (1895, 4) noted: "As with other Eastern people, hospitality is to the Malay a sacred duty fulfilled by high and low, rich and poor alike".

Following on from the earlier favourable 19th-century British colonial impressions of Clifford and Swettenham, Canadian Patrick Anderson (1955, 203) would reaffirm the liking of the Malays:

> some of them are very beautiful (the visual sense); they have a distinctive vivacity within an encompassing, seemingly amoral, laziness and grace (this appeals to one's own physical make-up); they are supposed to be 'primitive' and 'childlike' (which is consistent with one's symbolism).

The English don continued to describe the Malays as "obvious, amenable, in technicolour, almost anyone's suburban dream". Over the decades, Westerners would try repeatedly to explain why the local Malays did not seem as industrious as the Chinese and Europeans (Savage 1984, 121–139). In his review of the region's environment, the lawyer Logan (1847a, 14), from his base in Singapore, observed that there was a correlation between the industry of human beings and the bounty of nature. He was not the first nor would he be the last in thinking this way:

> the inhabitant of the Archipelago is as energetic and laborious as nature requires him to be; and he does not convert the world into a workshop, as the Chinese, and the Kling immigrants do, because his world is not, like theirs, darkened with the pressure of crowded population and over competition, nor his desire to accumulate wealth excited and goaded by the contrast of splendour and luxury on the one hand, and penury on the other, by the pride and assumptions of wealth and station, and the humiliations of poverty and independence (Logan 1847a, 14).

Logan went further to state that the local native population was similar to the lower rural classes of the West: "Freed from the repellent prejudices and artificial trappings of Hindu and Mahomedan civilization we see in the man of the Archipelago more that is akin than the reverse to the unpolished man of Europe" (Logan 1847a, 17).

European travellers who liked the Malays stoutly defended against the criticisms and their negative stereotypes. Lockhart (1936, 157), who had spent time in Malaya, had a high regard for the Malays and resented Europeans referring to them as "black men". He found the Malays "proud, courageous and independent, their sense of humour … keen. By nature, they are courteous and cheerful. They have a profound respect for their own '*adat*' or law of customs ..." (Lockhart 1936, 157). While Lockhart noted that 99 per cent preferred Chinese to Malays as house servants, he preferred a Malay because he would "stand by you in good times and in bad", and said, "after my first year in Malaya, I had a Malay boy" (Lockhart 1936, 157).

Later, European scholars would posit that the Malays had definite means of enculturation, and find their society to have "remarkable absorptive capacity" (Long 2013, 15). As was the case with the development of Malay-Muslim culture in Malacca (Wake 1983), several Western scholars have argued that the Malays, having been predominantly engaged in trade in ports and coastal towns, had been accustomed to "exchange, hybridisation, and adoption of different cultural styles" (Long 2013, 19). Citing other Western studies, Nicholas Long (2013, 19) has said that in the maritime realm before colonialism, the cultural identity of Malayness was manifest in *passisir* culture, that being associated with the trade-based kingdoms of the north Java coast, with its influence from foreigners and their locally-based communities. In the maritime Malay states, new arrivals were incorporated readily into the *passisir* culture. This easy integration was possible because race (*bangsa*) and ethnic subdivisions (*suku*) were not part of *passisir* culture (Long 2013, 19).

Several early Western residents did nonetheless give profiles of different ethnic groups in the region. Of all the cultural communities in the *Alam Melayu*, Western travellers and residents seemed most fascinated by the Bugis. For the trader Davidson (1846), the Chinese and Bugis were the most important traders. The Bugis would arrive in over 200 "uncouth-looking vessels", bringing large quantities of coffee, gold dust, tortoise shell, *bêche de mer* (sea cucumber), native clothes, deer sinew, and rice. They would sit and do business for hours by barter trading, and take back opium, iron, steel, cotton yarn, cotton goods, and gold thread (Davidson 1846, 56–57). Though they were a "maritime people", they were not addicted to piracy (Davidson 1846, 58). This last observation about the reputable Bugis traders who thronged Singapore's coastal trading areas appears to somewhat offset other century-long Western views of regional piracy as festering especially around Singapore (Ota 2010; Young 2005). Earl (1837, 389) reserved numerous compliments for the Bugis, who for him in their "honesty, energy of character, and general conduct" were superior to the Malays. For commercial enterprise, he opined these "modern Phoenicians" to be "unequalled in any part of the world" (Earl 1837, 389). The Bugis had an "adventurous spirit" and undertook for trade the "most arduous voyages in vessels very ill adapted to brave the perils of the ocean" (Earl 1837, 389). He witnessed the Bugis and British establishing better bonds and friendships for mutual advantage, given the inclinations of both to trade.

b) *Chinese from the Celestial Empire*

In the Western mind, the Chinese and Malays were often cast as contrasting stereotyped characters with almost opposite identities: hardworking versus lazy, calculating versus easy-going, money-minded versus non-materialistic, entrepreneurial versus simple-minded, and serious-minded versus jovial and playful. By and large, Europeans identified the Chinese by comparing them to the Malays and Indians. Alongside these comparisons of different Asian ethnicities with one another, Western residents and sojourners were also unconsciously defining Chinese behaviour and characteristics by their own personal and European cultural yardsticks. The University of Singapore lecturer Patrick Anderson (1955) provided one of the best sociocultural portrayals of Singapore in the early 1950s. He had interacted with Chinese 'boys', Malay syces, Tamil *kebuns* (gardeners), and *orang puteh* (White people). Anderson's (1955, 203) descriptions of Malays and Chinese also reflected his acute perception, his "imaginative preconceptions", and his ability to turn experiences into "symbols".

The Second Resident John Crawfurd (1830, 2:380–382) gave the earliest breakdown of the Chinese population, citing what he believed to be their varied qualities depending on where they came from. Crawfurd (1830, 2:380–381) divided the Chinese into five classes: (1) Creole or "mixed race" (i.e., the Peranakans), who to him were "intelligent" and acquainted with Malay but "inferior in industry"; (2) Chinese from Macau and the Canton River area, considered "very reputable"; (3) Chinese from Canton and seaports of Canton province; (4) Chinese from Fokien, considered "superior" in "respectability and enterprise"; and (5) Chinese fishermen from the sea-coast of Canton, denominated as *Aya*, who were the most numerous but most "disorderly". The Chinese population would grow rapidly, numbering 3,518 in 1825, and then 5,513 in 1826. Concern with Singapore's role in the region as an entrepôt and with its importance in trade, Raffles created social distinctions for the Asian population and placed merchants as "the higher and more responsible class", in contrast to their traditional social status in China where the scholars were the highest class and the merchants the fourth class (Purcell 1965, 250). Raffles' social classification of the local population would become the standard in the succeeding decades of the colony, where traders and merchants were elevated as elites of society.

Crawfurd's judgement of inferiority in industry notwithstanding, there was little doubt that in the early years of Singapore's development, the colonial emporium would ride on the backs of the Straits-born Chinese (Peranakans or *Nonya Babas*) from Malacca. Educated, English-speaking, effectively bilingual in English and Malay, culturally syncretic (with Chinese, Malay, European, and Christian borrowings) and well versed with colonial administration, the Straits Chinese straddled their economic activities between Singapore and Malacca (Turnbull 1983). Many of Singapore's key Chinese businessmen and personalities were actually Straits Chinese from Malacca. The Straits Chinese, like the Eurasians, were used by the British in Singapore's colonial administration. The preference for these two groups never went down well with the other Asians.

In commemoration of the centennial of Raffles' founding of Singapore, the Straits Chinese British Association (SCBA) paid tribute to his memory in their letter to Sir Arthur Young, the Governor of the Straits Settlements, while also noting their own contributions to making Singapore one of the "great emporiums in the world" (Song 1967, 562–563). Young's reply to the letter underscored the high regard that the British authorities had of the Straits Chinese community. As he mentioned, "I learnt to admire the Chinese for their energy and independence, and for their invariable kindness and readiness in coming to the assistance of their poorer brethren. In addition to Sir Stamford's exceptional gifts to which you refer, he was a devoted and loving son and a good brother to his three sisters: that trait in Sir Stamford's character is a trait strongly possessed by the Chinese" (Song 1967, 564). Throughout the colony's development, the Straits Chinese in Singapore would be partners in Singapore's economic progress and go-betweens for the colonial administration and the Asian population while maintaining their own unique cultural traditions. The Straits Chinese from Malacca and Singapore would also play a commanding role in the rubber boom of the early 20th century (Drabble 1983).

The wider Chinese population was so dominant even in the mid-19th century that Wallace (1869, 33) observed that Singapore looked like a "town in China". Bird (1883) mentioned that the 86,000 Chinese in

Singapore were enough to give Singapore "the air of a Chinese town with a foreign settlement". Many early Western perceptions of the Asian population would be viewed as culturally offensive today. They epitomised the shock of cross-cultural encounters for the first time. Take Maria Balestier's graphic description of the Chinese in 1830s Singapore for example. Without other ethnic comparisons to make, she likened them to monkeys:

> They do not look like human beings, but more like great monkeys, their long queues, shaved heads, narrow eyes, and the different shades of copper colored skin with the position that they use in stooping give them a striking resemblance to that mischievous animal, and when they are at work they have no other covering on them than a loose pair of breeches. You cannot say [they] are plain. Ugly is the word for all who have passed thirty and if they chew the Betel Nut they are absolutely frightful, the constant use of which makes the teeth black, while the juice of it is dark blood red (Hale 2016, 33).

Aesthetics aside, as labourers in colonial development the Chinese were valued, complimented, and viewed as indispensable assets. Chinese labour in all forms was seen as a corollary to colonial expansion. At the same time, given their business acumen, the Chinese were considered by White merchants and traders to be a commercial threat, and their business dealings were always viewed with suspicion. Unsavoury opinions of the Chinese were thus held by White businessmen who rightly or wrongly depicted them as untrustworthy, deceitful, and prone to cheating. Despite these negative views, British colonialists encouraged their migration to Singapore, Malaya, Burma, and India.

All through the decades of Western contact, the Chinese were typified as hardworking and strong (P. Anderson 1955; Crawfurd 1830, 2:384; Hale 2016; Whitehead 1893, 4). The naturalist Collingwood (1868, 249) referred to them as a "busy working population, who hive together like bees". Crawfurd (1830, 2:384) singled out the Chinese population as being skilled and intelligent; three times that of the Indian labour. The British administrator was all praise for Chinese labour and observed cynically that their low wages secured good profits. He noted that the common Chinese labourer earned $8 a month while a common artisan earned $12 (Crawfurd 1830, 2:384). The same Maria Balestier who compared them with monkeys marvelled:

The working class are all Chinese. They do the labour of all kinds and you would be astonished at the burdens they will bear, and the constant labour they undergo, but they are a very strong looking people and the contrast between them and the people from every part of the earth that are here, is very striking (Hale 2016, 33).

Western residents and travellers often saw Europeans and Chinese as enterprising people who in time would reach the most secluded parts of the region. Smug Europeans who considered themselves torch bearers for moral values and behaviour distrusted the Chinese. They perceived the Chinese as a challenge to their colonial authority in the region. Logan, a long-time resident in Singapore, opined that the Chinese would "only corrupt and debase the natives". A ringside observer to the aggressive Chinese businessmen in Singapore who lived for "gain" and "physical enjoyment", Logan (1847a, 20) warned the Europeans "that the Chinese flow into every opening which European powers effect whether by supplanting or weakening native governments". He feared the Chinese for their "mature patience, laboriousness, duplicity, craft and often fraud, which is the more dangerous from the easy, open, plain and plausible manner with which it is accompanied". He called upon Europe to safeguard native governments from the corrupt, industrious and sensual Chinese civilisation (Logan 1847a, 20–21).

Despite the fact that Westerners had a close-up relationship with the Chinese through their employment of 'boys' as domestic servants, they never quite understood Chinese behaviour and their mentality. Chinese culture seemed the opposite of Western culture. While Europeans could appreciate Malay simplicity, playfulness, and faithfulness, the Chinese came across as being opaque in their passions, revealing no emotional weakness in their behavioural armour.

In the mid-20th century, Patrick Anderson (1955, 202–203) noted the Chinese as hardworking, and that they were "primarily attractive because they [required] an effort" to appreciate. What he found less appealing, however, was "their solidarity and reserve, externalized in a kind of 'water-proofing' and sexlessness" (P. Anderson 1955, 203). For the White population, the Chinese exemplified the inscrutable East. Charles Buckley (1902, 1:216) recorded how the funeral of Tan Che Sang was attended by 15,000 people, and his boast during his lifetime that he had so much influence over the Singapore Chinese that "he could empty the place of all the Europeans". Westerners could never comprehend why the Chinese made their rites of passage public affairs when the White man preferred private family occasions.

The practical, money-minded, entrepreneurial qualities of the Chinese never failed to gain the Westerner's attention. Singapore's economic dynamo was predominantly a product of its largely Chinese population. Bleackley (1928, 134) maintained that the Chinese entered the Straits Settlements through "peaceful penetration" with a vengeance; for he was the mainstay of commerce, "being a usurer and a rigger of markets as well as the chief tradesman". The White person generally had grudging acceptance of the Chinese merchant, as he had "no political sense at present and no other aspiration but to make money" (Bleackley 1928, 134). The Chinese economic obsession, their endless energy, and hardworking persona gave Chinatown its defining characteristic for the high naval officer Sherard Osborn (1987, 11): "there was an energy, a life, a goaheadism about everything, that struck me much; everybody was in a hurry, everybody pushing with a will". As Bird (1883, 151) remarked of Singapore's Asian quarter and its Chinese influence:

> the ceaseless rush and hum of industry, and of the resistless, overpowering, astonishing Chinese element, which is gradually turning Singapore into a Chinese city!

In his 1854 letter to his mother, Wallace (2015, 12) was equally impressed with the Chinese population: "The Chinese do all the work, they are a most industrious people, & the place could hardly exist without them". Raffles, despite praising the Chinese for their hard work, often cautioned Europeans about the dangers of Chinese competition in business. He said, "In addition to these circumstances, it should be recollected that the Chinese, from their peculiar language and manners, form a kind of separate society in every place where they settle, which gives them great advantage over every competitor in arranging monopolies of trade" (S. Raffles 1830, 73). The restless preoccupations of the Chinese population had defined Singapore as a "town that never entirely sleeps", where "work itself never entirely stops" in the native quarters of the city (R. Braddell 1935, 86). The American traveller and writer Harry Foster in his 1922 sojourn in Singapore noted the importance of the Chinese, ironically because of Chinese New Year. He observed how "the entire city ceased to move. Shops were closed. Ships could not be loaded or coaled for want of stevedores" (Wise and Wise 1985, 197).

For the celebrated traveller Kipling, the diasporic Chinese upheld the "unfailing signs of commercial prosperity"; he ascertained that the dominant entrepreneurial class in Asia was found "where the Englishman cannot breed successfully". Chinatown was awake at night with theatres, coffee shops, eating houses, singing halls, hotels, and restaurants, and a maze of people jostling through crowded streets (R. Braddell 1935, 86). After his stopover in Singapore, Kipling revealed enviously the thrift and industry of the Chinese compared to the indolence of the colonial elite: "Neither at Penang, Singapur nor this place have I seen a single Chinaman asleep while daylight lasted". Sir Walter Medhurst (1983, 103), in delivering his talk in 1885 at the Royal Colonial Institute, observed astutely that the Chinese immigrants used Singapore as their educational classroom. He recounted how he had been told, "Singapore has proved a school to them, in which they learn the language of the country, the customs and peculiarities of the Malays, and the nature of the products, and, above all, become acclimatized to a Malayan climate".

In his visual imaginings, Patrick Anderson (1955, 217) saw the truth of Chinese life in Singapore and the cold stark economic realities which distinguished the race from birth. While Maria Balestier had described the Chinese as "money minded" (Hale 2016), Anderson found them to be born businessmen. In his graphic description, he observed of Chinese babies: "These babies *do* look a bit like some of the younger business men or *towkays*; they have something of the smooth tough uniformity which, like a kind of hygienic water-proofing, impersonal, cold, practical as rubber, protects the middle generation of Chinese who tend to look monotonously like errand boys or jovial monks, according to the size of their incomes" (P. Anderson 1955, 217). The Chinese migrant population which had volunteered to take the plunge overseas carried with them a readiness for risk, entrepreneurship, and a propensity for hard work. Pushed against the wall in a foreign land, every Chinese migrant knew that they had to fend for themselves to survive. In one century of colonial rule, the British had turned Singapore into a Chinese city. Thus, from a small population of 3,317 in 1824, Chinese migrants would flood the colony in the 20th century — in 1900, 200,000; 1912, 250,000, and 1927, 360,000 (Moore 1975, 176).

The Westerners tolerated the Chinese population influx because many found them "peaceable, inoffensive, intensely industrious" creatures as a general rule, and when allowed to follow their inclinations, their only vice was smoking opium. In Bleackley's (1928, 134) opinion at least, the authorities did not control opium smoking for "the Chinaman harms no one by his propensity. He smokes a pipe at home or in the opium-den and goes off to sleep, awaking none the worse for the experience".

The early description of the rich Chinese *towkay* came from Wallace (1869, 32–33) in the mid-19th century:

> He wears the same style of clothing (loose white smock, and blue or black trousers) as the meanest coolie, but of finer materials, and is always clean and neat; and his long tail tipped with red hangs down to his heels. He has a handsome warehouse or shop in town and a good house in the country. He keeps a fine horse and gig, and every evening may be seen taking a drive bareheaded to enjoy the cool breeze. He is rich, he owns several retail shops and trading schooners, he lends money at high interest and on good security, he makes hard bargains and gets fatter and richer every year.

Whitehead (1893, 4) observed in the late 19th century that rich Chinese merchants pursued a lifestyle of their own: "they drove out on an evening in the best turned-out carriages, and may be seen sitting, fat and contented, bedecked in mauve and other coloured silks, watching the — to them — idiotic Englishmen playing cricket and other games. They live in large houses surrounded by high walls, with their harems, where they eat the best of food, get fat, and rich by speculation". Over the century after Raffles' founding, the personification of Singapore's affluence would be the Chinese *towkay* who also epitomised the "modern Chinese capitalist and industrialist". Lockhart (1936, 119) described a 1930s scene that could probably be simulated for a blockbuster film like the *Crazy Rich Asians*:

> the Singapore towkay lives on a scale commensurate with his wealth. His house is a compromise between the tradition of Chinese architecture and the exigencies of modern European comfort. On occasions he likes to entertain his British friends, and the entertainment is both lavish and European, with a dancing floor specially laid down for the evening and tables on a terrace planted with orchids.

If Singapore's predominantly Chinese population gave the colonial city its drive, verve, and industry, Southeast Asia's Chinese-dominated primate cities also became arenas of ethnic unease. In 1965, the Australian academic C. P. Fitzgerald's *The Third China* drew attention to the huge Chinese diaspora in the region, interrogating their loyalties as he stated: "The Chinese in the Nanyang are therefore a people, a nationality, distinct, developed, economically powerful, numerous — about fourteen million — but without a country", and postulated that "they may constitute a kind of Third China" (Fitzgerald 1965, 84). He reasoned that colonialism did not bond the Chinese diaspora to the colonies, with the Chinese population remaining a "client" of communist China, and forewarned that "the future prospects would seem dark with clouds of misunderstanding, divergent purposes and communal ill-will" (Fitzgerald 1965, 107–108). His attention to Singapore's Chinese majority was on the cusp of the formation of Malaysia. It was underscored by the subcultural split in the Chinese population: the English-educated Chinese from whom the leaders of the People's Action Party (PAP) came, and who had acquired a "stronger English cultural background", versus the Chinese-educated Chinese who were communist sympathisers and formed the "centres of communist propaganda and organization" (Fitzgerald 1965, 70–71).

Earlier Western perceptions of the Chinese were clearly upended by the Second World War. Pre-war, the Whites had viewed the Chinese for the most part as benign, with the population being seen as something of a necessity to the sustenance of the colony's trade and economic vitality. The attitudes were different after the war. The Whites would then start to take the Chinese as a force to be reckoned with, belligerent, united, communist-inspired, and a threat to European political traditions. Neither did the colonial legacy of a predominant Chinese population in Singapore ever go down well with its large Muslim neighbours. Primordial issues of race and religion remain deep cultural cleavages between Singapore and these neighbours. It has been remarked that in Indonesia, the political elites have never let up on derogatory references to Singapore as the "parasitic Chinese enclave" (Regnier 1992, 48). Nor might it be too far amiss to claim that deep down, Malays in Malaysia are suspicious of the Singapore Chinese and their state of infidels, a largely Chinese city in a Malay sea, an Israel in the midst of a Muslim area.

The post-war era would no longer see Singapore's Chinese as a homogenous ethnic group, but bifurcated into the two cultural subgroups, with serious attendant social and political ramifications. The rule of the local Chinese in Singapore was not favoured by the British colonial authorities (Fitzgerald 1965, 32), for the reasons that Fitzgerald had alluded to — that Singapore could then form a possible fifth column.

The Western perceptions of the Chinese in Singapore had changed radically. The earlier depictions of hardworking, economically motivated, materialistic, and capitalistic *towkays* and labourers were now in large part replaced by views of an emotional, nationalistic, and dangerous group of communist-sympathisers with cultural and political allegiance to China.

At the turn of the 20th century, with the rise of Japan and China, the subsequent Japanese Occupation during the Second World War, the birth of communist China, and the Korean and Vietnam Wars, the Western perceptions of the Orient turned suspicious and fearful. These negative views reinforced the idea of the inscrutable Asian and widened the wedge in East-West ties. The inviting nature of the Singapore experience would be regarded with more caution, and the place became one of circumspection by Western residents.

As Singapore developed under its predominantly Chinese character, the Western fears of China and the Chinese population were manifest in political slogans about the Yellow Peril, and cinematic and comic depictions of the diabolical character of Fu Manchu (Clegg 1994). Ironically, at the same time that the Chinese were seen as pro-communist, the rise of successful Chinese entrepreneurship in challenging Western merchants and traders spawned more and more negative European perceptions of the Chinese as cunning, treacherous, material, money-minded, and cheating. The Chinese, as caricatured by Fu Manchu, were villains who were not bound to the "'norms' of the rational civilised West" (Clegg 1994, 5). From 1921 to 1968, 13 movies were produced on Fu Manchu (Clegg 1994, 3). These popular depictions got seared into the Western psyche and deepened negative stereotypes of the Chinese.

c) *The Indians: Klings and Kalinga*

If Westerners contrasted the Malays and Chinese in behaviour and personality, they similarly made comparisons between the Chinese and Indians in terms of their economic contributions. In the later 19th century, Whitehead (1893, 5) noted that the economic competition in Singapore was between the Chinese and Indians. He divided the Indian population into two groups: (1) the Klings, who were engaged in road-mending, tailoring, and washing; and (2) the "chitties" involved in moneylending. From the colony's early years, Westerners tended to refer to the Indians as

Klings, but the local Indian community found the name to be derogatory and petitioned to have Kling Street renamed as Chulia Street. The term *Kling* originally derived from the name of *Kalinga* in India, although it was misunderstood to represent the sound of chains worn by indentured Indian convicts brought by the British to Singapore, as they moved about on their daily labours on the island.

From an academic point of view, the reference to Kalinga goes back centuries to the creators of the Javanese Sailendra empire (Le May 1956, 79). The Indians in Southeast Asia were said to have been coming from Kalinga since the eighth century, and Reginald Le May (1956, 83) noted that the name *Kalinga* was associated with Indian migrants brought to Malaya as indentured labour to work in rubber plantations. In colonial times, the British opened the floodgates for Tamils to counterbalance the Chinese population in Malaya (Nirmala 2018, 83). Earl (1837, 392) in 1833 observed that the people from India's Coromandel Coast were synonymously called *Klings, Chuliahs,* and *Tombiahs*. Three-quarters of them were boatmen manning cargo boats. According to Murugaian Nirmala (2018, 52), the British preferred the Tamils because they were cheap to hire, "docile", "malleable", "easy to manage", and "good for repetitive tasks". White depictions of the Indians could be yet more derogatory. Endorsing these White perceptions, Earl had nothing good to say about the Indian population. In his view, they were:

> cringingly servile to their superiors, insolent when they [could] offend with impunity, totally devoid of honesty or principle, noisy, dirty, and disgusting, they [rendered] themselves universally detested (Earl 1837, 392).

Nonetheless, these people fascinated many Westerners, and the sheer differences of cultures in Singapore were an amazing sight. Indians in their varicoloured costumes gave Europeans reason for comment and vivid description. Collingwood (1868, 245–246) was particularly fascinated by the Klings from the Coromandel Coast. His descriptions of men and women are blunt but complex: "They are intensely black — not the shining black of a negro, but a dull sooty colour, from which their eyes gleam out with great expression, half savage, half intelligent". For Andrew Carnegie, the American philanthropist, his 1879 stopover left an indelible image of the Indians (Collingwood 1868, 245–246). His physical description of the Kling men leaves nothing to the imagination and undergirds his acute observation:

> They are remarkably well built men, tall, slender, clean-limbed, and graceful, and their faces are often positively handsome; the features small, and finely chiselled; nose aquiline; mouth small, and teeth white; a highly intelligent cast of countenance, which, translated into a white skin, would be considered elegant and fascinating. Their hair, which is black, straight, and glossy, is shaved off the forehead, giving them a commanding look (Collingwood 1868, 245–246).

Collingwood had a more colourful description of the Kling women, whom he found physically attractive and boundless in bodily adornment of gold jewellery:

> The Kling women are dark beauties, finely made, and dressed in flowing robes, which conceal the whole figure down to the feet, but leave the arms bare to the shoulder. Their dress sits on them gracefully, and their ornaments give them an air of barbaric splendour. Armlets of gold are worn above the elbow, and bracelets of gold upon their arms; gold rings encircle their ankles, and several finger-rings glitter on their hands; heavy ear-rings hang pendent from their ears, and one side of the nostril is pierced to give passage to a gold nose-ring, more or less chased in front (Collingwood 1868, 246).

d) *The Arabs*

Despite their importance in Singapore after Raffles' founding, the depictions of Arabs by Westerners were sparse. Unlike the other ethnic groups, Westerners had little to say about the Arabs as a community. Partly this reflected the fact that the Arabs were not congregated in one area. Westerners, except for the high officials and traders, did not come into contact with the Arab community. The Arabs themselves intermarried with Malays and that diluted their ethnic identity. On the other hand, their involvement in property, the Western hotel business (Grand Hotel de l'Europe), their perceived lavish lifestyles, and easy adaptability have led Ulrike Freitag (2002, 132) to refer to them as "fringe Westernisation". The

Arab community, however, were more defined by several outstanding traders and merchants. Prominent families were the al-Kaf (Alkaff), al-Saqqaf (Alsagoff), al-Junayd (Aljunied), and Muhammad and son, Salim ibn Talib (Bin Talib) (Freitag 2002). Most of the prominent Arabs were Hadhrami from Hadhramaut. They were wealthy and became well versed in the Malay language.

Throughout the region's history, Westerners would be wary of the Arabs. Some of this had to do with tumultuous relations between the West and the Middle East during the Crusades, the influential power of the Ottoman empire, and the rise of pan-Islamism (van Dijk 2002). Early Western references to Arabs, as with other communities in their Muslim aspect, were tongue-in-cheek derogatory allusions to the Moors.

Raffles' characterisations of the various ethnic groups were mixed and, to a large extent, reflected his own administrative dealings with them. Also strongly influenced by the historical Western views of the Arabs, he was particularly critical of them and the Chinese who were seen as competitive, dangerous, and defiant, whereas he was more accommodating to the Malays, Bugis, and Bataks. He felt that the Arabs were a corrupting influence on Malay culture and Malay chiefs. Raffles' criticisms of the Arab influence have a familiar ring today as current Malay politicians and academics point to the 'unhealthy Arabisation' of Malay culture. He obviously believed that the Islamic religion propagated by the Arabs tended to fence out other forms of understanding knowledge in the community. Detesting the Arabs because of their religious prestige and influence amongst the Malays, he remarked as follows:

> the Arabs are mere drones, useless and idle consumers of the produce of the ground, affecting to be descendants of the Prophet, and the most eminent of his followers, when in reality they are commonly nothing more than manumitted slaves; they worm themselves into the favour of the Malay chiefs, and often procure the highest offices in the Malay states. They hold like robbers the offices they obtain as sycophants, and cover all with the sanctimonious veil of religious hypocrisy. Under the pretext of instructing the Malays in the principles of the Mahomedan religion, they inculcate the most intolerant bigotry, and render them incapable of receiving any species of useful knowledge (S. Raffles 1830, 73).

VI. Cultural Distancing: 'We' and 'They'

In Edward Said's (1979, 7) *Orientalism*, his central thesis was undergirded with the argument about the Western distinction between the 'we' (Westerners) and 'they' (Orientals) creating a *"positional superiority"* where the White had a "relative upper hand". The Western theories and practices of Orientalism embraced cultural, material, and intellectual relations between Europe and the Orient, and these relationships went through innumerable phases (Said 1979, 73). Having been exposed in India to the local traditions (Cohn 1996), the British adopted the Indian caste system and believed that they were the Brahmin caste, above all the Asians. The Singapore Eurasians, as a mix of European and Asian blood, were contemptuously referred to as 'half-castes'.

Resident Westerners were often tempted to describe the ethnic characteristics of Singapore's multiethnic population as a means of showing cultural difference. Whether out of personal fear or smug Orientalist distancing, many Whites based their depictions of the local population on visual perception rather than interaction or connection. Caucasians often had direct relationships with the local population because of the various kinds of jobs they employed them in. However, few really engaged them beyond their formal working relations and in most cases, relationships were those of master-servant, white-native, and superior-inferior.

Since colonial Singapore received its administrative tall orders from the British high command in India, the administrative traditions in the Lion City reflected those of British India. The British and other Whites in Singapore, maintaining their Brahmin caste superiority, kept themselves removed from social interaction with Asians, and believed in preventing cultural pollution from the local population. Maintaining themselves in the eyes of natives as the *tuans* and *tuan besars*, Whites perpetuated Said's distinction between the 'us' and the 'others'. The Caucasians in Singapore grew accustomed to the local salutations which elevated them above the Asian population (Keppel 1853, 1:13). Bernard Cohn (1996, 16–56) has noted how the colonial language in India with respect to salutations provided the colonialists with a sense of command over, and respect by, the native population. In Singapore local salutations of White superiors provided a reordering of authority within its colonial society.

Foster in his 1922 stopover noted how the British maintained their "racial superiority" by employing only Whites as managers (Wise and

Wise 1985, 194). He had the most negative views of White society in Singapore. This was a colonial city "overflowing with human derelicts", a place "so full of the down-and-out" and "professional beachcombers" (Wise and Wise 1985, 194). He remarked, "The East is the land of 'swank'. Men and women who are nobodies at home will come out on some government position, and immediately begin to assume the airs of royalty. It is the only thing for the white man to do in the British colonies" (Wise and Wise 1985, 195). Foster was one of the few Whites who got to hear what locals candidly said of their British masters. He conversed with Kwong, an English-educated Chinese proprietor who told him, "Yes Foster, I do not like to be called 'bloody Chink'. But that is the way of the White Man. If I were to resent it, I would lose his trade. And so I let him talk to me as Master to Servant. But all of his money, Foster, is coming into my cash-drawer" (Wise and Wise 1985, 196).

This policy of colonisers and colonised, us and them, East and West, was anchored by the belief of most of the British, as with other European colonialists, that colonialism was here to stay. Basking in the ideology of Western 'exceptionalism' in the 19th century, many White colonialists believed that colonial rule was an irreversible geopolitical situation, with colonialism being seen as a form of territorial conquest. While Said enunciated the conceptual thesis of Orientalist cultural distancing under colonialism, Cohn (1996) in his own illuminating book *Colonialism and Its Forms of Knowledge* has provided a more operational framework based on 'colonial knowledge' as it was developed and utilised in British India. Using Michel Foucault's idea of knowledge as an expression of power, Cohn (1996) argued that the creation and management of colonial knowledge was what colonialism was all about. Couched in many "investigative modalities" (such as those of historiography, observation and travel, survey, enumeration, museology, and surveillance) devised by the British to obtain facts in India, Cohn (1996, 5–15) maintained that the colony was managed and controlled by documentation, legitimisation, classification, and codification of knowledge to rule and govern the native population.

In Singapore, Western characterisations of the Asian population largely began as being quite positive. Two factors could have led to these favourable perceptions. Firstly, Westerners in early 19th-century Singapore were relatively long-term residents, many staying between six to over 10 years. Maria and Joseph Balestier, for example, spent 13 years in Singapore. This gave them a better understanding of the 'natives' and over time made them less ready to make quick generalisations of the population. Secondly, given that Singapore was a polyglot city, Europeans found that different ethnic groups had varying qualities and thus it was again difficult to make a blanket generalisation. The early European residents were surrounded by varied Asian workers: Chinese 'boys', Malay syces, and Indian labourers and cooks from Madras. Maria observed that the Chinese "loves money". However, in many Western households, the Chinese 'boys' became part of the family and grew up with them. She noted that her Chinese male servants were "very kind and attentive" and singled out a servant as "one of the most gentle creatures you ever saw" (Hale 2016, 69).

The last quarter of the 19th century was a period of great change when the full weight of colonialism was translated to the region. Western attitudes towards the local population would change, and indeed Singapore was by then dominated by a well-educated White population which had control over the levers of politics, administration, security, and economics. At the same time, Europeans had become more confident of themselves. Their world view was being nourished by their extended ecumene. After the Enlightenment and the Scientific and Industrial Revolutions, the idea of a collective Western identity became an ethnic currency. The German historian Jürgen Osterhammel (2018) has argued that the West discovered its own identity through comparisons with Asian civilisations. With this identity came accompanying Eurocentrism, European superiority, and European exceptionalism, with White arrogance becoming axiomatic. Once again, the stark cultural macro-distinctions of East and West took on a new life and played themselves out in the colonies. The intellectual gap between Europe and Asia led the West to adopt its self-fulfilling project: "Asia needed to be ruled and schooled, lectured and hectored, exploited and reconnoitered. Asia was hard work" (Osterhammel 2018, 517). As an act of self-appointed martyrdom, the West undertook its *mission civilisatrice* as a White man's burden.

Colonialism has been the single most important historical phenomenon that led to cultural diffusion and economic transmission on a global scale. Unfortunately, it was also a comparable force for the indoctrination of White superiority over non-White peoples. Despite the centuries of colonial rule, Westerners have not fully ascribed oddity to their social and cultural distancing from non-Whites. When Singaporean Mayor Ong Eng Guan exhibited his anti-colonial sentiments, he was branded as displaying "self-assertive xenophobia" by ridiculing "defenceless expatriates" (Drysdale 1984, 238). Even after over 100 years of colonialism in Singapore, the Whites treated the Asian population as socially distant, culturally different, and unequal. MacDonald noted that when he invited Chinese, Malays, and Indians to his home for lunch, some Europeans objected. He was astonished to find that:

> hardly any British or other whites would invite any non-whites to their houses for lunch. Hardly any of them would pursue any recreation like playing golf with non-whites. They couldn't even join the Tanglin Club and so on, and this was one of the other things which I was determined to do everything I could to stop (Drysdale 1984, 53).

One might say that the understanding of cultural relativity has had a profound impact on the Western imagination since the 16th century, when the Age of Sail expanded the Western ecumene into the tropical world and the culturally fabled Orient. It was the first modern acknowledgement by Western travellers that cultures are different, religious rituals diverse, and ethnic expressions varied. Every Western traveller, sojourner, and resident in the East and Singapore saw the panorama of cultural displays, rituals, and traditions with fresh eyes and their interpretations were personal. In short, every on-the-spot witness wanted to write his own geography. In their attempts to capture the new, strange world, Western sojourners were prone to exaggerations of other cultures. Never mind that legions of other Western sojourners had witnessed bizarre Chinese funerals or Hindu rituals before, each Westerner had to retell his or her own experiences with individualised perception. Cultural distancing thus became a norm, and colonialism over time institutionalised a standard White behaviour in dealing with non-Whites.

Take Maria Balestier's view of Chinese culture and religion. In 1835, she saw the extravagant wake, rituals, and burial of Tan Che Sang, and commented that $3,000 had been spent "telling Singapore that now its richest and oldest merchant had gone to his rest" (Hale 2016, 60). In her own frugality, she found such ostentatious funeral rites unnecessary and boastful. Reflecting part reality and part prejudice, Maria noted that the Chinese were a "proud and haughty people whose lowest and most ignorant inhabitant thinks himself vastly superior to the most cultivated and intelligent of other countrys [sic]" (Hale 2016, 202). She astutely observed that Roman Catholic converts came mainly from the Chinese because "the ceremonies of both partys [sic] are similar" (Hale 2016, 202). As a Protestant, she believed that the Catholics deformed the purity and beauty of Christianity, but was nonetheless pleased to see the Chinese converted to Catholicism as they produced "some of the most sincere Christians in their lives and writings" (Hale 2016, 203).

Given that by the early 20th century the West had colonised 85 per cent of the world's land area, it would be hard to disagree with Said's interpretation of colonial behaviour as put forth in *Orientalism* (1979). Colonialism had reinforced the White superiority complex and brought about a situation of 'the West versus the Rest'. The colonised 'they' were variously profiled as 'natives', 'Orientals', 'Easterners', Asians, Chinamen, chinks, Klings, 'locals', 'savages', and 'aboriginals'. More often than not, such references implied derogatory associations with what was uncultured, unmannered, uncouth, lazy, filthy, greedy, and uncivilised. While Western administrators wielded their superiority complex as self-appointed custodians of better administrative ability and political power, the less enlightened among missionaries would see natives as inferior because of their pagan and animistic beliefs.

For a century since 1819, British colonialists would perpetuate social distancing between the Whites and Asians. It was a way of creating a social defence against having Asians exposed to British ignorance and incompetence, and against Asians behaving with 'insubordination' — the disagreement with Whites over matters when the former had better ideas. Governor-General MacDonald was not amused by this governmental system. He criticised its "breeding of a superiority complex in the governing races and of an inferior complex in the governed. There can be no natural, unprejudiced and true, friendly relations between the Western peoples and the Asian peoples until both complexes have been destroyed" (Drysdale 1984, 55). MacDonald was an exception to the staid, class-conscious White society. Its bastion of discrimination and exclusivity was the Tanglin Club. Founded in 1865, it prevented non-Whites from joining the club until the early 1960s.

Colonialism was justified as uplifting and educating the minds of the locals and Christianity was meant to save heathen souls from damnation. The Whites who developed views of their own superiority, however, often would not themselves have represented high society back home. Many British wives came from common backgrounds and many men were ordinary servicemen with the British navy, army, and air force. Their only superiority in local society derived from their being seen as *orang puteh*.

The renowned writer Noël Coward thus found that the Whites in Singapore had smug pretensions and poor manners. At the Tanglin Club, a woman boasted that the club was "one of the best" and asked him how he liked it. Coward replied, "After meeting your best people, now I know why there is such a shortage of servants in London" (Baker 2005, 148). Decades later, the long-time resident Moore (1955, 154–155) would have similar misgivings about the Tanglin Club as a paragon of racialism, colonial class snobbery, and utter prejudicial contempt for Asian culture. He failed to see how a club, "in the twentieth century, in Singapore of all places", could consider a new member based not on whether "he [was] decent or indecent, nor whether he [was] honest or a crook", and observed the parody, "nor whether he [was] English or foreign, but whether or not he [was] white" (Moore 1955, 154).

Western administrators and missionaries were quick to form impressions of the Asian population. Soon, Western stereotypes defined the 'natives' and stigmatised them in the colonial imagination. The most easily resorted to White perceptions of the local population were perhaps the Orientalist distinctions identified by Said. Nonetheless, some British colonial administrators in Singapore had more balanced perspectives of local populations of the region; individuals such as Raffles, Crawfurd, Clifford, and Swettenham reflected relatively enlightened and objective thinking on the virtues and defects of these peoples.

VII. Summing Up: Reflections on the Developmental Software

It seems ironic that while colonialism was carrying the torch of Western civilisation, the idea of progress, and a developmental paradigm for the tropical world, the Western literati and intelligentsia were simultaneously formulating the demise of Western civilisation in their European homelands during the same period. In *The Idea of Decline in Western History*, Arthur Herman (1997) has provided a brilliant summation of this 'decline of the West' as seen through one-and-a-half centuries of Western thought.

It would seem that two Western narratives were unfolding from the 19th century onwards. On the ground, in colonies like French Indo-China, the Netherlands Indies, and Singapore, colonial administrators, missionaries, and geographers believed that they carried on the crusade of civilising natives, modernising societies, and bringing enlightenment to ignorant savages. To them, there seemed no end in sight to the colonial enterprise. In the metropolitan capitals of Europe savants, scholars, and the literati had instead a much longer perspective of the global historical processes. They provided a more sobering analysis of Western civilisation, its flaws, and the finality of the Western march of progress, its industrial challenges and environmental limitations, and of colonialism itself (Herman 1997). The strength of Socratic reasoning gave Westerners powers of self-introspection, a willingness to question their own objectives, and what Ibn Warraq (2007) has referred to as a system of 'self-criticism' and an acceptance of learning from others.

The colonial endeavour was vexed with the question of developing colonies in the service of the metropolitan powers. The ancient view of environmental determinism impeding societies in the tropics from progressing had in the earlier colonial centuries been prevalent amongst colonial administrators and sojourners. The 19th century, however, created the civilisational turn in colonial thinking, with enlightened administrators like Raffles, Crawfurd, and Low. Even before the clarion call by the French for *mission civilisatrice* was heeded in the region, Raffles had already mooted the idea of bringing education to the local population and uplifting their standard of living. Christian missionaries were likewise concerned with enhancing the moral standards of locals and bringing them spiritual enlightenment.

It was no wonder that in both depending on and uplifting the local population, White residents in Singapore got to know the Asians better — hence their vivid descriptions, from physical appearances to behaviour, from their strengths to their weaknesses and vices, that were recorded ad infinitum. Singapore as the archetypal colonial city with its myriad of ethnic groups was a place of bewildering cultures, traditions, and religious practices. Colonial administrators tried hard to translate their administrative objectives into reality so as to trump tropical determinism and to make colonialism a possibilistic endeavour which allowed man to be the final decision maker, through education, public health, urban planning, efficient administration, scientific knowledge, and technological prowess.

Nevertheless, it would seem that after 70 years (1870–1940) of high colonialism in the region there were doubts as to whether the colonial experiment had been successful in developing the societal software. Amidst the lingering view of environmental determinism, the post-war years resonated with novel interpretations of societal backwardness in the region. With new subjects like sociology, social psychology, behavioural economics, and political science entering into the study of colonial societies, the focus turned from the tropical environment to the societal software. One major impetus in explaining differences in Western and Eastern development was the monumental project initiated by Joseph Needham (1954) on *Science and Civilisation in China*. Needham (1954, 4) was interested in finding out the "inhibiting factors in Chinese civilization which prevented a rise of modern science in Asia", despite the country's scientific developments over the centuries. He felt that in China, the adoption and stagnation of science was socially and culturally dependent, unlike in the West, where it was individually driven. Needham's monumental work is still ongoing at Cambridge University today.

Needham's questions on scientific progress and development were relevant to colonies in the region, which were shedding their colonial yoke from the 1940s to 1970s. Many social and cultural theories flooded academia in trying to explain the developing world's backwardness. Marxist social scientists like Andre Gunder Frank and Régis Debray blamed colonialism for locking colonies economically to their metropolitan states and making them dependencies. Edward Said felt that colonialism created a subservient mindset in local societies that retarded their abilities to question, create, and innovate. In his book *Culture and Imperialism*, Said (1994, xi–xii) noted how Western novels underscored the desire of the West to bring civilisation to primitive and barbaric peoples: "'they' were not like 'us', and for that reason deserved to be ruled". According to Walt Rostow's (1959) posited stages of economic growth, the developing states did not have the right economic, social, and cultural mix to 'take off'.

Differing ideas on development were rife in the region. In his celebrated book *Agricultural Involution*, the renowned anthropologist Clifford Geertz (1971, 124–154) when comparing Java and Japan noted that despite their relative similarities in agricultural development, Java had been unable to take off economically. His conclusion was that the "Indonesian malaise" was beyond "the analysis of ecological and economic processes", but rather reflected the "nation's political, social, and cultural dynamics" (Geertz 1971, 154). In dealing with Indonesia's economic history over the 19th and 20th centuries, the economist Anne Booth (1998, 327) of the London School of Economics stated that Indonesia — at least at the time of her writing — was a "study of missed opportunities". What the Dutch and independent government failed to do for Indonesia was quite the opposite of what Raffles and Lee Kuan Yew focused on for Singapore — accelerating access to education and facilitating a robust class of indigenous entrepreneurs (Booth 1998, 328–329).

Ironically, despite the endless Western depictions of Singapore as a materialistic and gambling- and money-crazed city, there were misgivings about whether its people could climb the ladder of development. For the British entrepreneur Moore (1953, 66), Singapore was a "cultural desert, a city where the population is engaged in the acquisition of money and has little time for any matter not leading directly to further financial gain". Deeper reflection, however, led Moore (1953, 66–67) to believe that the Chinese and Malays did indeed have a "cultural life"; it was the Europeans who were "culturally barren". MacDonald believed that Singapore had to "develop its body and intellect" and also "its heart" (Moore 1953, 3). For a multicultural city, he perceived that there was a need for extending humanistic sentiments of kindness, generosity, and love to inspire and unite people (Moore 1953, 8).

These very issues on development addressed by an indigenous postcolonial government would become the hallmark that made independent Singapore a poster boy for the developing world. After flirting with theories on environmental determinism (Savage 2004) for the first 20 years of its independence, Singapore's first-generation leaders banked on possibilistic ideas about education, science, technology, public health, and pragmatic political management (Savage 1997) which untangled the Gordian knot of underdevelopment. That narrative of successful Singapore has been told many times, with new theories and explanations of how it has been made possible. Singapore's rise, as recounted in the book *From Third World to First* (K.Y. Lee 2000), remains one of the great stories in the book human development, a source of endless social science analysis, an example for emulation, and a marvel to politicians in both the developed and developing worlds.

— 9 —
Colonialism Challenged: Stirrings of Independence

Chapter 9

COLONIALISM CHALLENGED: STIRRINGS OF INDEPENDENCE

Cultural predispositions and national characters are real, and societies do come to crossroads and make important choices (K. Anderson 2017, 440).

The turn of the 20th century would bring colonial Singapore into greater focus internationally. Meanwhile domestically, the British authorities were responding to many local issues such as demographic congestion, health problems, housing shortages, slum and squatter challenges, and educational concerns. Native leaders had also come of age and were growing more vocal and assertive. At the same time, external issues dominated the White conversations and writings. The East-West pendulum was now beginning to swing to the Orient, and Western residents in Singapore were ringside observers of this and would in some sense be its eventual victims. The rise of Japan after the Russo-Japanese War would be noticeable in the 1930s, and the Japanese Occupation of 1942 to 1945 brought bloodshed and mayhem in Singapore. It meant that colonialism would be reversed, with the new power hegemons being Oriental. It was the Second World War that was the main catalyst of local assertiveness. The colonial slide from grace continued with communist China's birth, whereupon a new political equation engulfed Singapore society. With the changing of the global guard in the post-war era, Singapore was once again at the centre of the East-West contestation. Through Western observers residing in Singapore at that time, one gets a glimpse of the pulsating cultural dialogue, the political tug-of-war, and the social ramifications for locals and Whites.

I. *'Orang Putehs'*: Colonialism in Doubt

In reviewing the talks held between 1874 and 1928 at the Royal Colonial Institute, the historian Paul Kratoska (1983) referred to British colonialism in Asia as having "honourable intentions". Yet, as colonial rule unfolded in the region over the 19th century, White sojourners and residents would themselves have misgivings about its intent. Around that time, European visitors and administrators had begun to be critical of their own culture, behaviour, and the whole process of colonial rule. Alfred Russel Wallace (1869) labelled Western society as being hypocritical, compared to the simple denizens of the forests in the Malay Archipelago; Hugh Clifford (1916) was upset over colonial rule in Malaya; while John Thomson (1865) was candid about his views on English society and criticised the British governors in Singapore.

Despite the overwhelming control of the White population over the Asians, Western sojourners at various points in Singapore's colonial history were surprised at how small this population was. The rise of British power had given the Whites an uncanny confidence in ruling over large 'native' populations. Indeed, John Crawfurd (1830, 2:392) boasted that to keep the peace, the military in 1825 consisted of 150 sepoys and native artillery without a "single European, except the officers". Isabella Bird (1883, 115) observed during her 1879 stopover in Singapore that there were only 1,283 Whites in the British colony, excluding soldiers. The first census in 1824 showed that there were only 74 Europeans in a population of 10,683; and of these Europeans, over 80 per cent were traders, missionaries, and professionals; few were East India Company officials.

No White sojourner at the time attempted to offer any direct explanation for this rather strange situation. Generally, the Whites, under the guise of explaining environmental determinism and possibilism (Savage 1984), felt that the tropics had left native societies with a collective intellect inferior to that of Westerners, that Whites had a superior management system under colonialism, and that civilisation could not develop in tropical climes without them. Most Whites subscribed to the notion that they were racially superior to the Asians. More erudite administrators like William Marsden, Crawfurd, and Raffles saw, however, the distinction and differences between Whites and Asians as part of a historical process of development. It is also only recently that academics and savants across a spectrum of disciplines have offered a more broadly balanced variety of explanations as to why colonialism succeeded (Said 1979; Cohn 1996; Pomeranz 2000; J. Li 2012; Mokyr 2017). Viewed within Bernard Cohn's (1996) thesis on 'colonial knowledge', colonialism had doctored the mindset of the local population, allowing a few White administrators to govern its large numbers.

The Singapore land surveyor Thomson (1865) was ahead of his time in his 'objective' assessments of peoples and cultures. He was one of the rare English administrators who, in his Singapore perceptions, did not fall prey to the 'we versus others' dichotomy described by Edward Said (1979). His criticisms of Governor William Butterworth, dubbed by James Brooke as 'Butterpot the Great', showed Thomson to be a bold individual who was unafraid of questioning poor behaviour. He found the governor to be an "eccentric" whose monopoly of power made him feel entitled to continually point out the flaws which he perceived in others (Thomson 1865, 269). Hardworking, punctilious in manners, and commanding in address, he was also class and status conscious in a peculiar way: "No private gentleman in his estimation, had any rank in society" (Thomson 1865, 274). He divided society into military orders: colonels, captains, sergeants, and privates; "Wealth, birth, or learning, had no status under his government" (Thomson 1865, 275). Yet, he was a paragon of "vanity and pomposity" and like all "pompous men of plebeian origin, was very vain" (Thomson 1865, 278–279). Thomson viewed Butterworth as egotistical, as implied by his observation of Butterworth's contempt of other Whites parading their accolades in the colony by having their pictures on walls. Thomson did not see race and ethnicity as barricades in character assessment. He was effusive with praise for the Chinaman, Whampoa, because he found his principles and virtues relatable to: "a man whose actions, motives, loves, joys, and griefs were all hinged on the same great principles as your own" (Thomson 1865, 311).

Another Singapore Governor, Clifford (1897), an incorrigible romantic, had many misgivings about colonialism and the advent of modernisation on tropical nature and native life. In his earlier administrative duties in Pahang, the British administrator had used the analogy of putting chains on nature to describe the building of a dam across a river. By damming the river, its "supreme freedom" and "overmastering" had vanished utterly. He lamented, "It was in chains, a thrall to man, and to me it seemed to bear its gyves with a subdued and chastened sadness at once bitter and heartbroken" (Clifford 1916, 386–387). Clifford was not his healthy self during his tenure as Singapore's governor, hence one might never know his true feelings about the modern city in the making, the colonial abetting of the destruction of the island's pristine nature, and its materialistic ethos. Singapore's development as the archetypal economic powerhouse of the British empire in the East must likely have been anathema to his romantic disposition and grated on his nerves.

Earlier 19th-century travellers, buoyed by the appeal of Romanticism, had started to question the hypocritical deceits of colonial rule over the native peoples whom they observed as being more unspoilt and honest. By the 20th century, the chorus of White criticisms of colonialism would grow louder with respect to human rights, due to the keener sense of the injustices and inequalities of colonial rule. If 19th-century Western residents were concerned with Singapore's viability as an entrepôt and saturated their assessments of imports and exports with facts, figures, and traded goods, the 20th-century European merchants and visitors provided more nuanced and subtle evaluations of Singapore's viability. In fact, the European unease in Singapore about the perceived change of hegemonic power in Asia would be profound.

After 500 years of colonial rule, many colonies in the tropical world were prisoners of Western power, rule, and jurisdiction. Despite all the posturing of human rights, democracy, *mission civilisatrice*, and humanitarian values, the Western governments did not generally see that colonialism undermined these noble ideas, nor that their academics, politicians, and bureaucrats sounded like hypocrites. In view of his 28 months of wartime travel in India, the American Edmond Taylor (1947) would become interested in answering the question of whether Western culture had a sufficient basis for developing a "one-world concept" and the "oneness of man". His book *Richer by Asia* was based on his experiences in South Asia, which had convinced him "that the Western mind is incapable, without outside aid, of implementing its own best ideals" (E. Taylor 1947, 8). He recounted how his eyes had been opened to the contradictions and limitations of the colonial, imperial system, in which the White *sahibs* in India were nothing more than "cultural renegades" (E. Taylor 1947, 102–103): ordinary people posturing as the elites of their societies.

Colonialism was the operationalising of the Western ideological thinking that German historian Jürgen Osterhammel (2018, 383) argues was based on the "doctrine that the European master race had a God-given mandate to rule in perpetuity over its racial inferiors". Indeed, the ideas of White racism, after over four centuries of colonial gestation, have not entirely evaporated from the Western world. Chris Hedges (2018, 58), in his polemical *America: The Farewell Tour*, with content ranging from the political to the spiritual, enunciated the true credo of the White race, that *"we have everything, and if you try to take any of it from us we will kill you*. This is the essential meaning of whiteness". Just like under colonialism, the former journalist argues, White supremacy continues to dominate other races because it controls the most "efficient killing mechanisms" — industrial weapons of subjugation and exploitation (Hedges 2018, 57–58).

II. Colonialism Questioned: The Sepoy Uprising and the Japanese Occupation

In Singapore, the first noticeable Asian challenge to White colonial authority and rule ironically emanated not from those sections of the population which by then could be considered native born — Malays, Chinese, Indians, Arabs, and Eurasians. The biggest jolt came from the still freshly-imported Indian soldiers, the sepoys, whom the British had brought in from India to manage the colony's security. Yet, two decades after the Sepoy Mutiny, the Japanese invasion of Singapore would be for many of the British a black swan moment. Over a century of colonialism had lulled them into complacency; they had grown soft with a luxuriant and opulent lifestyle (Lockhart 1936). The "frontier" spirit which Clifford talked about in the 19th century had vanished, and the quest for exploration, conquest, and discovery no more goaded colonial administrators. The same tropical determinist explanations for the causes of native lethargy, laziness, and a relaxed attitude could now ironically be used for the British administrators' behaviour. Singapore was a prized posting for Whites in the early 20th century; it was a city of convenience, a modernising landscape, and a self-supporting colony.

In February 1915, soon after the beginning of the First World War, the Singapore Mutiny unfolded in the Alexandra and Tanglin Barracks.

The ignition was religious sentiment rather than any against colonial rule per se — some of the sepoys who were Indian Muslims were protesting against the British for making them fight their brother Turks. Horace Bleackley (1928, 137–150) dedicated a whole chapter in his travel book to the uprising. Mary and Edwin Brown (2015) recorded a detailed and stirring account of their personal experiences during that episode, which would only be published a century later. It was an event recounted by many White visitors to Singapore, though few of them were eyewitnesses (Shennan 2015, 123–145). The chilling narrative from one source noted that 14 unarmed White civilians had been killed in one hour, "for the cruel Sepoys wandered through the beautiful suburbs slaughtering every European whom they could find" (Bleackley 1928, 143). This bloodshed was an important lesson for all, that primordial attachments could be explosive issues. The rebellion was put down and 40 rebels given capital punishment.

The mutiny was the first sign that the British management of security was wanting; it was a precursor to their defeat at the hands of the Japanese. The uprising by Indian soldiers once again brought about White racist reflections. Bleackley (1928, 141) noted that German naval officers in prison were surprised by the mutiny as "no German naval officer can tolerate the murder of a white man by a black, even though the white man is an enemy". Yet, despite this racist German view, Whites fought Whites in the two World Wars in Europe. Singapore was the British, and not German, symbol of colonial power, White supremacy, and Western hegemony in Asia.

Essentially colonialism created a two-tier society: Whites as rulers on the upper tier, and Asians on the lower rungs. There was, however, an intermediate tier of Eurasians, anglicised Asians, and Peranakans, who acted as a buffer between the Whites and native Asians. They were interpreters and translators of colonial policies, rules, and edicts. There was no democracy under colonial rule, and this was made worse because the British administrators believed that they had the monopoly of intelligence, wisdom, and knowledge. With this, complacency set in among them. Later, a series of external events would impinge on Singapore society: the First World War, the Great Depression, and most of all, the Second World War. The watershed of changes was the Japanese Occupation during the Second World War. For both the White and native societies, the interruption of British colonialism and its replacement by Japanese hegemons was an indelible experience. Countless books narrate the unimaginable downfall of Singapore and the austere life under Japanese administration.

Yet, the changes in Singapore, since his previous visit 28 years earlier, would cause Bruce Lockhart (1936) to make personal assessments of differences that he found to be superficial, material, and based merely on the physical landscape. Lockhart (1936, 219) was critical of colonialism and pointed to the inherent weaknesses of its administration. He was pessimistic about its future in the region. He had adverse comments about the Malayan education system and its history and geography classes. He queried as to why the local children were "taught so much about Europe and almost nothing about their own country" (Lockhart 1936, 219). He argued that the British in Malaya (including Singapore) had a standard of luxury that was:

> much higher than that of any other European race in the East or, for that matter, in Europe itself. The luxury was material and not intellectual. In all parts of the world the Englishman made a fetish of opening the pores of the body; he did less about opening the pores of the brain. Nowhere had he carried this fetish to such extravagant lengths as in the tropics (Lockhart 1936, 182).

Lockhart was clearly critical of the complacent, opulent White lifestyle. After spending time in Malaya, he left the region by departing via Singapore. He had pensive and prophetic reflections on the future of Western colonialism in the East, and was obsessed with:

> the effect on the East of the spectacle of a Europe apparently intent on self-destruction. The last war had done more to undermine the prestige of the white man in the East than a hundred years of education. Another European war within the next few years would probably mean the end not only of Europe's possessions in the East, but also of the benefits of her ordered rule to millions of people (Lockhart 1936, 417).

If there is one single factor that changed the tide of colonialism in Asia, it would certainly have been the Second World War. The biggest blow to colonialism, to British military power, to Western authority, was the capture of Singapore by the Japanese on 15 February 1942. Singapore's fall would become an unbearable symbol of Western impotence. With the island's British military bastion and majority Chinese population, the

Japanese relished their occupation, and the emperor no less anointed his prized acquisition with a Japanese name. As insult added to injury, Singapore after its capture would be called *Shonan* or the "radiant South" (Allen 1977, 14). The Japanese wanted to complement the Land of the Rising Sun with an equally illuminating tropical, southern frontier.

The war sounded the death knell of imperial Western civilisation in the Orient — this would essentially be the end of the then prevailing globalised Western consensus and colonial dominion in the developing world. Keith Lowe's (2017) thought-provoking book *The Fear and the Freedom* captures the global changes resulting from the Second World War. He was correct in stating how "the world that emerged in 1945 was entirely different from the world that had gone before the war" (Lowe 2017, 422). In Singapore, those who survived the Second World War were physically scarred, emotionally distraught, and psychologically traumatised. The conflict brought different results to different countries. In Asia, however, colonies would seek independence, with anti-colonialism coming into political vogue, and a chorus of pro-independence leaders arising from its ashes.

Endless Western commentators wrote about the Japanese victory and fall of Singapore rather ashamedly. British pride had been punctured and severely damaged with the Japanese Occupation. The myth of the invincibility of their military stronghold in Singapore was shattered. The historian of Singapore C. Mary Turnbull (1977, 162–189) could not hide the British embarrassment of the surrender of Singapore: "the Gibraltar of the East", "gateway of the Orient", and the "bastion of British might" had fallen. Donald and Joanna Moore (1969, 611) lamented that "impregnable Singapore was finally exploded", that Raffles' political child had been "finally bankrupt; it was out of business". Certainly, for some English sojourners Singapore's fall was too much to bear:

> Singapore was not a fortress; it was a defenceless piece of real estate. Far from being the Gibraltar of the East, it was nothing but an embodied lump of imperial imagination. British troops were not falling back on to an impregnable bastion, but into the most efficient trap the Japanese could have ever devised. Singapore was a hoax — on a gigantic, world-shaking scale (Moore and Moore 1969, 611).

As mould-breaking as it was, the Second World War did not create Singapore's globalisation of peoples, its world economy, its cosmopolitan features, nor its urban developments, as Lowe (2017) asserts it had. These 'virtues' had already been established in Singapore before the war, as many Western residents showed in their reports, and they would resume after the war years as was also testified to then. Besides the "fear and freedom" that the Second World War unleashed in the post-war decades (Lowe 2017), Westerners in Singapore realised that their political supremacy had been toppled for good, and the myth of White invincibility smashed. The psychological barrier that had kept Whites in high esteem of the locals was broken. The White *tuans* were no more exceptional. As university don Patrick Anderson (1955) noted, after the war nobody liked the British as a ruling class. He elaborated, "Your Asian friends will tell you 'You looked like Gods before the War — now you seem to have shrunk in size, so that we can consider you as human beings and see all your faults'" (P. Anderson 1955, 156–157).

III. The Cusp of Independence: Changing Perceptions

After the Japanese Occupation, Western residents and travellers captured the cultural effervescence that was taking place in Singapore society. The British authorities seemed willing to give up their colonial rule and were looking for options to make the transfer of power to local leaders. In the 1950s and 1960s, Singapore was in turmoil at various levels. Local politics had become a war zone, with the communists infiltrating schools and labour unions in order to wield power. This was a period that many historians have written about, and in which many political players were involved, that tumultuous era before independence (Turnbull 1977; Yeo and Lau 1991).

Professional writers of the earlier part of the colonial era who had passed through Singapore recorded their perceptions gleaned through romantic lenses. The writings of Rudyard Kipling, W. Somerset Maugham, and Joseph Conrad provided keen observations of the region and colony and their peoples. Their memorable lines have become embedded in the narratives about identifiable places. In their time, colonialism reigned and there was no reason to question or doubt it. For them, the colonies were places to live in, with virtues to exhort, or vices to be condemned. The renowned writers endorsed colonial rule, provided clear 'otherings' of native society, and their reflections of travel, though astute and imaginative, were viewed through the Orientalist prism identified by Said (Doran 2016; Clark 2017). In Maugham's (1951, 116) short story, *The Pool*, Whites were portrayed as the 'gold standard' of society in the tropics. As he noted when a "white man married a native or a half-caste", the native looked upon him "as a gold mine" (Maugham 1951).

A minority of other White writers questioned colonial administration, its impact, and whether it required a more human touch. Dutch writer Eduard Dekker's *Max Havelaar* highlighted the miseries caused by the Culture System in Java (Multatuli 1995), E. M. Forster's (1924) *Passage to India* depicted the British colonialists in a frightened mood, and George Orwell's (1935) *Burmese Days* portrayed the British in Burma in a hysterical state with the rise of Burmese nationalism. Colonialism was throwing up European voices which were apologetic in more than one sense of the word. Victor Purcell (1962, 167–177) presented his overview of colonialism in part to quell the raging anti-colonial sentiments, exploring the issue of whether colonialism was a "beneficial phase" in history.

The left-wing geographer Keith Buchanan (1967, 38) noted that the cultural impact of the West was most pronounced in the region's cities: in Western-style housing, the status symbols of modern society, and mass media such as film. The cities had imbibed the "Coca-colonisation" that scarcely permeated the rural areas (K. Buchanan 1967, 38). Buchanan (1967, 81–82) characterised colonial development as widening differentials between cities like Singapore, which benefited from the "cumulative *upward* spiral of development" while rural areas experienced a "*downward* spiral", as described in Gunnar Myrdal's (1968) theory of "cumulative causation".

After the Second World War, colonial states in the region would for the first time wake up to the possibility of realising their independence. As had happened earlier in the European metropolitan powers themselves, which took 500 years to develop their own nation-states (Lieberman 2003, 2009), longings for independence were finally being infused into the far reaches of empire. There was mixed reception by Europeans to the idea of independence for their colonies. Fortunately, the British did not resist it in Southeast Asia, but the struggle for self-rule and independence in Malaya and Singapore would still work itself out in belligerent fashion, and be cause for much reflection by resident Westerners. The term *nationalism* as applied to states in the region would become a misnomer, given that they were hardly the geopolitical entities of homogenous ethnic groups but rather plural societies. Singapore and Malaya's plurality of cultures and religions, and the problems it caused for independence, was a colonial legacy which has been best captured by Benedict Anderson's (1991) *Imagined Communities*. In Singapore, the struggle for independence was a contest between Chinese-inspired communists and various stripes of Western-influenced social democrats; between Chinese- and English-educated Chinese people; between ethnic chauvinists and Singaporean nationalists; and Asian and European cultural perspectives and idioms. An East-West confrontation was unfolding to full bloom in Singapore society.

By the post-war years, a new set of Western writers would take on the torch of engaging Singapore. The biggest global event was the birth of communist China in 1949, which invigorated scholarly interest in the country as well as in the Chinese diaspora in Southeast Asia. Influential books like Purcell's (1965) *The Chinese in Southeast Asia* and *The Revolution in Southeast Asia* (Purcell 1962), as well as C. P. Fitzgerald's (1965) *The Third China*, undergirded Western perceptions. The authority on China at that time, Purcell (1965, 565) argued that the Yellow Peril would depend on whether China had intentions to expand "deliberately or through political necessity". Decades earlier, the percipient Kipling (1900, 255) had observed that colonial policies were favouring Chinese migrants in India, the Dutch East Indies, Malaya, and Singapore. The Chinese diaspora in the region and Singapore did not enter by accident; the colonial masters had paved their way.

Singapore, like the Dutch colonies, had become a "supplementary China — another field for Chinese cheap labour" (Kipling 1900, 255). Colonial development necessitated Chinese labour; as Kipling (1900, 256) reported, "We must have China coolies as the land develops". Yet, in his obtuse writing style, he worried about the future of colonies with such liberal immigration policies. As he noted, the Chinese were a "gift" in the Straits Settlements. "It is so cheap to prophesy. They will in the near future grow into —" (Kipling 1900, 255). Indeed, several decades later, the Chinese population would become a perceived threat to the region. Malaysia was formed, according to the Malay point of view, to ensure that Malays and indigenous groups would outnumber the Chinese, thus "neutralising the threat of a radical Chinese Singapore" (K. Buchanan 1967, 128).

The winds of Cold War politics began to blow across the region, abetted by China's rise as a communist power and the contestations in

Vietnam. Keith Buchanan's (1967) *The Southeast Asian World* was partial to a socialist paradigm of development. He saw a "socialist system" making inroads into the "territory-wide modernisation and diversification of the economy", and believed that urban growth was to be "controlled" rather than left to "*laissez-faire*" influences (K. Buchanan 1967, 160–161). The Marxist concluded that there would be an "inevitable penetration of the Southeast Asian world by socialist concepts of planning and development" (K. Buchanan 1967, 161).

Up until the mid-1970s, the Western paradigm of colonial capitalistic development would still be an academic staple in university classrooms. Given that most of the local faculty had been schooled in British and Commonwealth universities, the idea that 'West is best' was seldom questioned or criticised. As it had been the tradition for decades to appoint an 'external examiner' for departments, the head of geography appointed Keith Buchanan for this position (1967–1970). Buchanan went on to write a damaging report of the department's courses, stating that the geography curriculum was "reactionary" and "colonial" (Savage 2003, 71). Since the then Vice-Chancellor Dr. Toh Chin Chye was himself an ardent socialist, Buchanan's report fell on supposedly sympathetic ears.

Karl Wittfogel (1957) crucified Asian political systems by stating in his historical analysis of hydraulic civilisations that the continent was the source of despots and despotism. At the back of the minds of Western politicians, journalists, and academics, Wittfogel's "oriental despotism" would become a convenient political label for Asia's governing regimes. It was another way of separating East from West, 'we' (Western polities) from 'others' (Asian states); and pitting the Western advocates of democracy against the perceived despotism and authoritarianism of Asian political culture. Apart from India and post-war Japan, the idea of democracy seemed alien to Asian societies, and this bolstered Western notions of Asian satrapies. The Western colonial powers and most White commentators failed to see, however, that colonialism was itself the paragon of authoritarianism.

Given Singapore's predominantly Chinese population, much focus on the Chinese diaspora centred on the colonial city. Times had changed. The writers in academic portals now had more license to pontificate. Singapore society was in turmoil and culture was being questioned. Some of the best representations of this social and cultural confusion came from academics and foreign correspondents residing in Singapore. Through the lenses of C. Northcote Parkinson, Patrick Anderson, Paul Theroux, Dennis Bloodworth, John Drysdale, and most of all, D. J. Enright, a spotlight on the changing politics of the times was cast. Each of the expatriate faculty members and journalists reflected deeply about Singapore's complex social and cultural milieu. In many ways, they found the indigenous culture which was emerging from colonial rule confusing, bifurcated, and difficult to fathom. With its largely Chinese population, Western residents now speculated about whether the concepts of the colonial 'us and them', as later identified by Said (1979), would be reversed, with Singaporeans joining the rising Chinese hegemon to look upon former colonialists as a new 'them'.

In the 1950s and for the first time, Western reporters, academics, and residents recorded their surprise that the once dormant, subservient, and passive Chinese were unleashing passionately their anti-colonial sentiments (Barber 1978; Drysdale 1984; Moore 1975). The uprising of Singapore's Chinese-educated school students as the voice box of communist demands, and their belligerent demonstrations against the colonial authorities, turned the Lion City from the relatively peaceful outpost it had been prior to the Second World War, into an insecure and politically destabilised colony. Regarding the English-educated and Mandarin-educated Chinese, the geographer Iain Buchanan (1972, 277) argued that the difference between the two groups was not just "language and culture" but those of social, economic, and political realities which he felt few colonial administrators understood. Following his father Keith, the younger Buchanan (1972, 280–283) provided a socialist interpretation of the dissent of the Mandarin-educated Chinese that he felt had festered in colonial times and was even for a while embedded in some quarters of the People's Action Party (PAP). Without a national identity, it was being demonstrated how Singapore could be fragmented by the raw power of ethnic identity, racial groups, cultures, religions, and languages. Within the wider regional context, Buchanan questioned the feasibility of the unification of Malaya and Singapore, given what he and many Westerners at the time saw as the communal rift between "a pro-communist, basically Chinese oriented government in Singapore within a region dominated by Malays" (I. Buchanan 1972, 280).

Singapore's culture and society were internally contrasting: conservative and liberal, public and private, communitarian and individualistic, ethnically closed and cosmopolitan, nationalistic and global, Eastern- and Western-centric, and materialistic and otherworldly. One must be reminded that there was no comparable time when Western civilisation had seemed to be on the wane, when the rise of Eastern powers such as Japan and China were simultaneously marked, and when a postcolonial era was disrupting old Western intellectual and political traditions and straining East-West relations. With the collision of at least two greatly differing civilisational traditions which had started with colonialism, the impact on recipient Singaporeans would be a cultural dilemma. Western dons and newsmen in Singapore would thus measure the events and advents of their new post-war native leaders according to Western values, European norms, and the colonised world of which they were products. With anti-colonial and anti-imperialist political rhetoric saturating the environment, however, Western residents in Singapore would become increasingly uneasy about their future.

IV. The Enright Affair: East-West Cultural Conflict

In his *Memoirs of a Mendicant Professor*, D. J. Enright (1969) captured his post-war experiences in Asia: Japan, Thailand, and Singapore. The most controversial tenure of his academic career was in the new internally self-governing Singapore, where his writings would become central to a war of words with the government. His inaugural university lecture, entitled "Robert Graves and the Decline of Modernism", was delivered in 1960 and challenged the Singapore government's views of culture. Enright's commentary on cultural policy had to be viewed within the literary currents of his times. As one of the foremost Movement poets in the 1950s and 1960s, his poetry represented the literary practice of engaging with the social, political, and economic events to which the writer was exposed, and often critically.

Enright made several statements that grated on government nerves. He admonished the Singapore authorities for trying to destroy 'yellow culture' and called on them to remain "culturally open", advising that because culture was "personal", people should be free to make "their own mistakes, to suffer and to discover" (Enright 1969, 125–126). The term *yellow culture* is a direct translation of the Chinese phrase *huangse wenhua*, which referred originally to decadent behaviour such as gambling, opium smoking, pornography, prostitution, corruption, and nepotism that had plagued China in the 19th century.

Enright made a distinction between the Singapore government's tirades against yellow culture and what China's government had been against originally. He noted that the Singapore definition of yellow culture had become "a large, pervasive, inclusive and ill-defined concept, which ranged from juke-boxes to Wordsworth's daffodils, from prostitution (another colonialist importation) to films with a racialist tendency, and somewhere near its centre came strip-tease, the Leftist-cum-lascivious fictions of Han Suyin and, for a time, myself" (Enright 1969, 122). Specifically, the object of the government was to sweep out yellow culture (allegedly of foreign origin) in order to make way for "local culture", which was less defined than the yellow variety (Enright 1969, 123). The local culture, as Enright (1969, 123) said mockingly of the Singapore authorities, was meant to be "immaculately hygienic, moralistic, socialized, inoffensive to Malays, to Chinese, to Indians, to Ceylonese, to Eurasians, to Moslems, to Buddhists, to Christians (Catholics, Methodists or Seventh Day Adventists), to Hindus, to Sikhs, to atheists, to vegetarians and carnivores, and to all shades of colour from the whiter-than-white Chinese to the blue-black Tamil".

The crux of Enright's speech was hard-hitting for a new indigenous Singapore leadership who believed they were torchbearers of modernisation, only to be chastised for stifling it. The English lecturer was resident at the time when the pangs of decolonisation and the assertiveness of nationalism were being felt in Singapore's political context. All over the region, the detoxification of bodies politic from things Western was taking place. As Enright (1969, 121) stated, Singapore was undergoing a "cultural spring cleaning". He felt that Singapore was bereft of a dominant culture: "Singapore had no traditions in this sense, but only a number of diverse, imported and rather faded traditions" (Enright 1969, 119). Having come from academic sojourns in Japan and Thailand, where culture was unvarnished and previously un-colonised, Enright (1969, 119) found of Singapore's culture, that "the East had been sadly diluted with the West, the Orient's native hues sicklied o'er with the pale whitewash of British hegemony". He seemed perplexed by this sanitised hybrid.

Enright's debate with Lee Kuan Yew and Singapore's political leaders is a pertinent reminder of the difficult task that new societies have to deliberate over and undertake in order to achieve national cohesion.

It would seem that the leaders, in accepting English as the official language, were trying to manage and circumscribe the negative Western influences. Hence, the debate between Enright and Lee was based on different assumptions. The self-styled Yellow Professor opined that despite their Western education, the PAP leaders were undergirding a brand of Asian authoritarianism. Prime Minister Lee believed that Enright's diatribes were constructed along "imperialist-colonialist-capitalist" lines (Enright 1969, 135), and attributed the "storm in a tea-cup" arising from the matter to bad reporting in *The Straits Times*, a then colonially owned newspaper employing expatriate newspaper men (Enright 1969, 138).

Perhaps justification for the caution of local authorities about foreign intervention in politics was surmised by Enright (1969, 130–135) himself. By his own account, his speech had already brought about three local outcomes in his favour. First, 522 university students (with only five against) voted on a resolution expressing the view that the government was trying to "strangle free discussion" (Enright 1969, 130). Second, older Chinese interpreted some of his remarks as a "quite correctly low valuation of Malay culture and thus by implication a correctly high estimation of Chinese culture", to which they made encouraging nods (Enright 1969, 133). Thirdly, David Marshall, the lawyer, requested that Enright engage him to sue the government for defamation, but was sorely disappointed when Enright declined the offer (Enright 1969, 132).

University students over the years have referred to this confrontation between the government and the academic as the Enright Affair, with the issue of national culture being subsumed under that of the erosion of academic freedom (Enright 1969, 147–150). A matter for debate was whether the affair was an attempt to muzzle university freedom per se, or if it were more broadly about the direction of nationalism and an attempt to wean Singapore society away from a patronising Western cultural ethos. The government's view seemed to imply that Singaporeans should take charge of their national culture and its societal manifestations. The Enright Affair would be the first public attempt by the PAP leaders to set 'out-of-bounds markers' for domestic politics, in which no foreign interference would be allowed. As such, the episode and the varied responses to it would form the basis of political lessons for the PAP to apply in addressing future challenges to its rule.

By the 1960s, at the tail end of colonialism, the local government's quest to maintain 'cultural purity' by wiping out yellow culture was being met with criticism from Western academics. Unlike Lockhart (1936), Enright (1969) was comfortable with the hybrid culture amongst Singaporeans, as exemplified by his attitude towards the Eurasians. Though the Eurasian community were the outcome of the European-Asian fusion, they had never been wholly acceptable to either Europeans nor Asians. Their exalted position in colonial administration distanced them from the Asian communities. Enright, though, seemed to embrace the mix of East and West. For him, an evolving 'Eurasian' culture, that of an English-Asian mix, promised a happy, beneficial, and logical outcome for Singapore. Ironically, as an educator from a Western tradition, Enright (1969) himself was confused by students' reticent and ambivalent behaviour in the University of Singapore. He was oblivious to the fact that English-educated university students were torn between two pedagogical traditions, the Western Socratic one and the Chinese Confucian system of child upbringing. Jin Li (2012, 223–275) argues that learning and childrearing in Western homes are done through the method of developing critical thinking, whereas in Chinese homes, learning is acquired through obedience to an established order.

In his poems, Enright underscored his belief in cultural hybridity by interspersing his lines with Singaporean colloquial terms. He believed that a bottom-up natural development of culture, even in its hybrid manifestations, was better than an affected borrowed cultural tradition. As the mendicant professor noted, over time, he was "even preferring a diluted Orient" as he felt that references to faded traditions and national character could be "stifling". "Better a country with all before it than one with too much dragging at its heels", he declared (Enright 1969, 119). Specifically with respect to aspects of Asian language, Enright (1969, 121) felt that he had no objections to anglicisation: "it is the pure English who worry me — a race that stews in its own juice is bound to turn rancid in the course of time". The debate still continues in the political arena and amongst academics as to whether creole English should be accepted alongside the Queen's or Standard English, with creole being academically acceptable to some of the National University of Singapore[1] English faculty who had been students of Enright.

The Enright episode demonstrated the political sensitivity of cultural and social change in postcolonial Singapore. Lee Kuan Yew's PAP had to define a new ethos that encapsulated a sense of national identity for a

---

[1] The successor institution to the University of Singapore.

city-state. The subtext of Western narratives during this period was whether Singapore was becoming more left-wing, and the fear in Western circles about the once-bastion of British power going communist. Bloodworth (1970, 1986), one of the foremost foreign correspondents at that time, noted how Westerners viewed Lee as a communist. Between his and Parkinson's (1963), Enright's (1969), and Fitzgerald's (1965) commentaries, one can see how Westerners viewed the many dimensions of decolonisation and the invention of nationalism in Singapore at the close of the colonial era.

V. The Chinese Question: The Threat of Communism

This was a period of turbulent global change, the rise of China, the spreading menace of communism, the unfolding Cold War politics, and decolonisation. On the global scale, Nixon's China pivot left world leaders, political commentators, and academics guessing as to the future outcomes and roles of the rising dragon. One such academic analysis was Andrew March's (1974) *The Idea of China*, which paid too much attention to the country's geography, demography, and civilisational history, but could not portend the impact of communism, the capitalistic economic about-turn, and the country's future global hegemonic aspirations. Across the region, other Western commentators provided a more cautious, worrying, and realistic view of China's rise.

Bloodworth (1970, 1986) portrayed the chaotic political ferment in Singapore in the 1950s and 1960s that was underpinned by China's communist threat. In his thought-provoking *The Tiger and the Trojan Horse*, Bloodworth's (1986, 13) thesis was that the communists had tried to use the PAP to penetrate "the citadel of constitutional politics in order to capture power from within — in short as a Trojan Horse". This view had already been held in the 1950s by the White resident community. The British entrepreneur Donald Moore (1955) recorded their feelings in his many conversations with European friends. A pet topic was Singapore's independence from British colonialism. As one of his guests noted, the Chinese in Singapore, because of their numbers, drive and energy, would strengthen their connections with China and in time "become a part of the Chinese Red Empire" (Moore 1955, 99). In an earlier book, Moore (1953, 20) observed from his Singapore vantage point that the "spirit of China" had revealed to him "why China can never be defeated". For him, the reasons were in its peoples: "she retains four hundred million sons and daughters who, whether they be Communist or Conservatives, all possess that dogged, immovable, unutterably stubborn will to live, and that abundant satisfaction in taking what God may offer and putting it to immediate effect" (Moore 1953, 20).

The once homogenous Chinese population in Singapore would after the Second World War become divided into two cultural strands, one inspired by Western culture and the other attracted to communist China. Bloodworth (1970, 366) observed the equation to be unbalanced; for every 10 men in Singapore, six were Chinese-educated Chinese. The diaspora had become a political force under the eye of the dragon. The British were uneasy as a new geopolitical situation arose, and they debated as to "how they could rid themselves without revolution of a turbulent left-wing menace elected to the legislative assembly called Lee Kuan Yew" (Bloodworth 1970, 383).

While Western commentators worried about the rise of China and the communist threat (Bloodworth 1986; Drysdale 1984), the university students directed their venom at the White colonial power. The Fajar Generation, as they were termed, had their voice in the University Socialist Club, which was much less concerned with aping communist China than with the removal of British imperialism (Poh, Tan, and Koh 2010). In their 1954 newsletter *Fajar*, they highlighted Western aggression in Asia, the rise of Asian communism due to Western colonialism, and the 'fact' that the "West [was] still a menace" (Poh, Tan, and Koh 2010, 313–314). The colonial government considered this "seditious" and seven students on the editorial board were arrested two weeks later (Drysdale 1984, 78). The tragedy of Singapore's domestic political situation immediately after the war was the difficulty of Western commentators and colonial authorities in distinguishing the legitimate fight for independence from the change in political orientation towards communism, both of which carried anti-colonial rhetoric.

This background of student anti-colonialism in the local university claimed its victim in a White faculty member. When the Vice-Chancellor Sir Sydney Caine resigned in 1956 to take up an appointment at the London School of Economics (C. Lim 2013, 31), the university appointed the geography professor E. H. G. Dobby as acting vice-chancellor. In the hurry, Dobby was made to give Caine's own pro-colonial speech at convocation, which did not go down well with students. Given the resulting turmoil in and outside the university,

Dobby too resigned his post, in 1957, and left Singapore post-haste. His wife Denham noted that in a letter from Seattle he wrote of the episode as "a thing that haunts me more than anything else" (Savage 2003, 68).

The Western journalists seemed highly concerned with the crumbling of "law and order, a stable colonial society, imperial power" (Drysdale 1984, 3), and the potential urban communist revolution. Westerners had rarely interrogated the racist policies of colonialism that had gone on for over a century in Singapore. By and large, as beneficiaries of colonialism, most Whites had felt it to be politically acceptable. If the Western perceptions of Singapore's history are to be deemed as objectively portrayed, then Westerners themselves must record and explain why there was a deafening silence regarding the authoritarian colonial policies. It was only with colonialism in terminal decline after World War II, that Westerners championed the rights of people and the importance of democracy because communism itself posed a challenge to these values as practised in the West.

Enright for his part was preoccupied with what the prevailing culture would be upon decolonisation. He was sure the PAP leaders would back the English language to maintain their power: "As British officials move out, so American experts move in. Nature abhors a vacuum: throw one foreigner out and ten new ones come in" (Enright 1969, 162). The change of global hegemonic power from British to American seemed like a non-event in Western eyes, unlike the 21st-century contestation between Americans and Chinese which according to Graham Allison (2017) portends a belligerent Thucydides Trap scenario.

Yet, neither Enright (1969) nor Fitzgerald (1965) had answers to the question of what a decolonised and independent Singapore would become. Said the English don, "Singapore was abnormally difficult to write about readably, because there are so many reservations to make to one's generalizations, so many bits of mere or sheer information to be conveyed, that the footnotes are likely to squeeze out the text" (Enright 1969, 162). Enright was unsure about the power of nationalism, because "nationalism is not rationalism, and its devotee will practice its rites without counting its costs" (Bloodworth 1970, 31). With the compulsive political urge for indigenous national languages throughout the region, the PAP's policy to retain the colonial language of English seemed politically suicidal. Despite Lee's rationale for keeping English, his pro-Western behaviour, however, was circumspect. Enright (1969) saw in Lee the symbol of a banana, yellow outside and white inside, while Bloodworth (1969, 31) noted how the Chinese-educated regarded their prime minister as a "beer-drinking, golf-playing barbarian despite his Chinese face". Thus, their tongue-in-cheek sarcasm about Lee notwithstanding, Western residents could also envision how Singapore would have developed differently had a Chinese-educated Singaporean donned the political mantle. The development of a Chinese extreme left-wing political entity would not have gone down well with the Western hegemonic powers.

Enright (1969, 167), summarising the then pessimistic Western consensus, noted, "the republic is not viable economically, militarily, politically". He personally had a somewhat more positive outlook, and felt that it would "survive, short of course of some cataclysmic event which [affected] the whole world hardly less drastically and not much later" (Enright 1969, 167). Astute Western residents read Chinese culture and historical changes better than politicians in Western capitals. The Chinese in their cultural DNA were adept at change and Singaporean Chinese were no different. The English professor was optimistic about the Chinese of Singapore, whom he felt were "experts in survival"; and the fact that Singaporeans were not in the "mood to go down" (Enright 1969, 167). Familiar with Chinese culture, he, Fitzgerald, and Bloodworth believed that the Chinese had what the Germans called *Geist* or 'spirit', and were quick learners.

Couching his optimism in the Chinese cultural gift of "devising compromises" and their talent as a "nation of bargainers" developed from their roles as merchants and businessmen, Fitzgerald (1965, 108) predicted that the future would be found but under severe tests. Decades later, Murray L. Weidenbaum and Samuel Hughes (1996, 239) would see the Chinese diaspora in Southeast Asia as a dominant "bamboo network", highlighting what Fitzgerald, Enright, and Bloodworth typified as resilient, cohesive, and an unbreakable economic force: "Bamboo bends; it does not break".

Like Fitzgerald (1965), Enright (1969, 168) believed the future of Singapore was in the English-educated Chinese; he perceived English education to have "greater career value" though Chinese education carried greater "cultural prestige". In his observation that as "internal emigrants", the Chinese did not have public behaviour that conformed to their private opinions (Enright 1969, 169), he was parroting the general Western view at the time, that it was difficult to read Chinese personal intentions based on their overt actions.

Though the Chinese were docile because of prudence and scepticism with regard to freedom and independence, Bloodworth (1970) warned that if pushed beyond their limits, they would bite back fiercely. These evaluations on the cusp of independence clearly showed that Westerners in the 20th century saw the Chinese in Singapore in a different light from that of the 19th century. Rather than thinking of them as pliant, hardworking 'boys', they now viewed the Chinese community as a resurgent, invigorated, and motivated force to contend with. Post-World War II, Westerners would continually refer to Singapore as a 'Chinese' city as well as a 'plural society'. The difference between Singapore and other regional colonies was that the Chinese were minorities in other colonies, whereas in Singapore they were a sizeable majority. As a minority, the Chinese tended to assimilate with the dominant indigenous culture, while in Singapore, they maintained their "cultural distinctiveness" as there was no need for "ethnic integration" (Suryadinata 2004, 3). Part of this was demonstrated by how Peranakan culture evolved as a Chinese-Malay mix in Malacca, Penang, and Jakarta, while there was a less pronounced home-grown evolution of the Singaporean Chinese subculture.

What radically changed the Chinese outlook in Singapore were political externalities, as reflected by the new communist state of China, the Chinese annexation of Tibet, the Cold War contestations in Korea and Vietnam, the turbulent Cultural Revolution (1966–1976), and the communist-instigated civil unrest in Singapore itself in the 1950s and 1960s. Colin Mackerras (1999) in his book *Western Images of China* noted that the rise of communist China created in the West the image of the country as an aggressive threat, where freedom was negated absolutely. Lucian Pye (1972), one of the Western doyens of Sinology, on the cusp of Nixon's détente with China, tried to clear the cobwebs of Western bias and prejudice on China, as well as the contrary sentimental offerings of Chinese communism in which some Westerners believed. "Subjective images have blurred objectivity" he wrote, and added that "behind its veil of mysteries is a reality" (Pye 1972, 7). For Pye (1972, 358), despite the Chinese propensity to glorify and magnify their leaders, the reality was that none of these leaders, from the Ch'ing (Qing) emperors to Mao Tse-tung, had been able to provide talented leadership to "maximize their great capacities".

While drastic political convulsions were taking place under Mao's rule, the wall of secrecy that was the bamboo curtain prevented news from leaking out. Only after his death and the economic opening of China were the full extent of the sacrifices, misery, and deaths of the peasant Chinese revealed. Frank Dikötter's (2010) *Mao's Great Famine* captures the disastrous Great Leap Forward, in which famine killed 45 million people. One survivor of Mao's rule was Weijian Shan (2019), whose book *Out of the Gobi* narrates his tribulations during the Cultural Revolution and numerous other catastrophic political campaigns. He provides a riveting narrative of pain, suffering, hunger, malnutrition, and sorrow.

In Singapore, like other areas in the region, communism was gaining converts and Mao was glorified to semi-divine status despite their failures in China. Postcolonial Singapore was racked with political instability. After the Second World War, the British lost the moral authority to rule, their troops were demoralised, and they needed to build up their home economy more than take care of overseas colonies. Communism would be an inspiration to irredentism and nationalist uprising. Chinese communism had weaponised the Chinese High School students and trade unions in Singapore, unleashing a period of belligerent chaos. With China turning to communism and the East becoming Red, Singapore's Chinese had a new clarion call in Marxism, and the British an unsettling political calibration to deal with. The Malayan Emergency, in which British forces had to quell the rise of armed communist guerrilla insurgency, spread also to Singapore (Barber 1978; Bloodworth 1986).

What was most jarring and worrying to Western residents in Singapore was the rise of a totalitarianism which was diametrically opposed to the ideas of the 'free world', democracy, and laissez-faire capitalism. Singapore was seated on a fault line of East-West contestation. On the one hand, over a century of cocooned colonial life had given it a Western outlook and on the other, its dominant Chinese population appeared to Western correspondents as an underlying threat of a pro-communist alignment. It would be left to domestic politicians to slug out between themselves the matter of whether the left or right wing of the political environment would garner the national mandate to rule. European commentators had different perspectives of Singapore's domestic political scenarios. Some were positive, others downright negative, and still others fairly neutral.

The right-left competition intensified in Singapore's last decades of colonialism and discoloured many Western perceptions of the island's future. Bloodworth (1970, 382) had a more positive outlook, believing that the young were pliable and able to adjust to global changes. A long-time resident in Singapore as a correspondent for *The Observer* from 1956 to 1977, he drew on the infamous Bugis Street scene as a metaphor to observe that the young of the region were not "cultural transvestites" borrowing one another's clothing in their parades of the "Oriental and Occidental drag". He was optimistic that they were instead the new public cultural voice, and declared that "the *yin* and *yang* of East and West are part of the universal Oneness" (Bloodworth 1970, 383). That optimism was not shared by many Westerners and anglicised Singaporeans. Europeans sensing ominous changes ahead were already lamenting the end of the good old days of colonial rule as the Lion City prepared for an uncertain, turbulent independent destiny.

National identity forged out of a cosmopolitan mix has not been an easy policy for Singapore's independent government. In the decades after Singapore's independence, the debate among politicians, academics, and public commentators has been about how to shape the appropriate identity. While under colonial rule, Western sojourners viewed the cosmopolitan mix as a tourist attraction and an exotic urban persona. In a sovereign state, every ethnic group would want its own cultural expression as a means of equal representation in the country. National identity would turn out to be shaped by the country's multiple ethnic identities and cultural differences.

The idea of nationalism grew out of colonialism. The British colonialists presented Singapore with the proto-trappings of its national identity, through the development of periodic population censuses, cartographic mapping, and its museum. Two other colonial inventions tied people to the land: firstly, the formal land tenure system which gave expression to landed property, and gave people a buy-in to the colonial state. Secondly, Raffles' pet interests in nature inspired the botanical garden ecosystems that exhibited, classified, and documented Singapore's natural vegetative wealth. The gardens in some ways signified the colonial mastery of nature, as places where the indigenous flora and the region's vegetation came under its governance. Benedict Anderson (1991, 6) has argued that the colonised "imagined communities" became nationalised through these institutional trappings; nationalism "invents nations where they do not exist".

After Singapore's attainment of full independence in 1965, a litany of concepts would become political fodder in the discussion on national identity: multiracialism, depoliticised ethnicity, cultural diversity, ethnocultural nationalism, 'essentialised' race, Singapore culture, and ethnic accommodation (E. Lee 2008, 619–625). The historian Edwin Lee (2008, 624) has noted that under the "four-race-and-more" multiracial policy, independent Singapore adopted a system of "hyphenated identity", which translated to the "hyphenated Singaporean" (Singaporean-Chinese, Singaporean-Malay, etc). In many former colonies, independence led to racial and religious conflict, civil war, and ethnic genocide. Indeed, the May 13, 1969 riots in Kuala Lumpur spilled over into Singapore and have remained a stigma in race relations between the Malays and Chinese. The volatility of 1969 seared into the minds of Lee Kuan Yew and Singapore's first-generation political leaders that if nation-building were to be realised, the racial and religious equation needed to be politically fixed. The nation as an imagined community required "deep, horizontal comradeship" (B. Anderson 1991, 7).

With its mainly Chinese population in a Malay-Muslim sea, Singapore's inaugural leaders tried to capitalise on its cosmopolitan colonial legacy. Since then, the Western anti-Chinese suspicions rooted in the creation of the People's Republic in 1949 have grown with that country's rapid development and heightened global prowess. Nothing is more candid, overt, and academically blatant than Samuel Huntington's (1996) treatise foregrounding Western fears of a rising China, reappearing as the perennial broad East-West "clash of civilizations". As with how it has traditionally regarded its colonial history, Singapore today remains circumspect in the new East-West clash, balancing on the tightrope between China and the US. Having a predominantly Chinese population, the onus will always be on the government to define the city-state as 'cosmopolitan' rather than as a Chinese enclave. Indeed, the most ringing endorsement of Singapore's cosmopolitan society, despite its Chinese predominance and Western scaffolding, has come from Huntington (1996, 319) himself when he noted the government's strenuous efforts to "define a Singaporean cultural identity which was shared by its ethnic and religious communities". For the Harvard professor, the future of a "multicivilizational world" lies in implementing the "*commonalities* rule: peoples in all civilizations should search for and attempt to expand the values, institutions, and practices they have in common with peoples of other civilizations" (Huntington 1996, 320).

VI. Summing Up: The Colonial Inheritance

As we close this penultimate chapter of our discussion on colonial Singapore, one can see that the island colony had become a landscape of turbulent politics, the playground of Cold War power relations, and a place with an uncertain future. Modern Singapore was going through a baptism of fire. It would become increasingly evident that British colonialists and few Western residents wanted a part in Singapore's undefined future. Singapore might have gained independence from British rule by joining Malaysia in 1963, but its last institutional colonial bonds were only severed in 1972 when the British finally withdrew their military forces. The West had created the idea of the nation-state and given national identity to its own citizens, but it was a different situation in its colonies. For a while at least, Singapore would be bereft of both national identity and a fully-fledged administration for the mobilisation of its people for its own good.

Western historians will continue to evaluate the pros and cons of colonialism. Nationalists could persist in condemning the legacy of the colonial past. In reading history from a more objective perspective, one may realise that painful but constructive cultural and social change can come from within as well as without. Over the centuries, Europe had developed internally as a domain of numerous ideas and much creativity, political change, religious introspection, and cultural innovation (Pomeranz 2000; Mokyr 2017). On the ground, the great divergence between East and West would seem stark. N. J. Ryan (1962) in writing *The Cultural Heritage of Malaya*, noted how the West had been "developing ingredients to explode out of Europe" while the East remained "unchanged"; the West was "dynamic" while the East, "static".

Change in Europe, however, did not come easily. Since the 1500s, for the five centuries of its expanding ecumene, Europe had been in perpetual political convulsion, revolt, bloodshed, and warfare among its initial 500 satrapies. Colonialism's window on Europe would provide Singapore's nationalist leaders with important fodder for contemplation. Conversely, through the eyes of Western residents and British officials, we have seen how Singapore's changing political and economic scenarios were evaluated and analysed. Both Europe and Singapore demonstrate that the processes of history are not linear progressions, but aberrations and diversions reflecting domestic social and cultural influences, and political externalities. Colonialism set up the administrative scaffoldings for Singapore, but over the decades, the operationalisation of development would not be a straightforward proposition.

Westerners provided two sides of the story of colonial development in the region. On the one hand, despite the many setbacks it caused, colonialism in Singapore as with other European colonies in the tropical world had been a cultural tour de force. While nationalists in the region would call westernisation a product of colonialism, in another light, one might view the colonial era as a path to modernisation. Given the exceptional 19th-century developments of the West and the British empire, the island colony of Singapore was a beneficiary of globalising modernisation. Colonialism carried the seeds of the *mission civilisatrice* and was the catalyst of modernism. As Adrian Vickers (2004, 29) has argued, Benedict Anderson's thesis built on the "idea of colonialism forming a radical break which introduced modernity to a hitherto un-modern Southeast Asia".

On the other hand, nationalists and Western Marxist academics have viewed colonialism as the embedding of a capitalistic system between the satellite colony and the metropolitan power. Keith Buchanan (1967) was explicit in arguing that colonialism tied the region's cities to Europe. Singapore was once again the prime example of the European-inspired capitalistic liaison. The colonial system, as Buchanan (1967, 79) maintained, "resulted in a steady transfer of wealth from the colony dependencies to the metropolitan country". An outspoken critic of the colonial-capitalist relationship, he concluded that "capitalist development simultaneously generated development and under-development, not as separate processes, but as *related facets of one single process*" (K. Buchanan 1967, 79).

In summing up the Western distillations of Singapore's multiethnic concoction, one is able to view Singapore's cultural transition. Singapore's present-day multicultural software has been one of the enduring features from the colonial city. This has been both its strength and its potential weakness. It seemed amazing in Western eyes that the multicultural, multilingual, and multireligious local community coexisted relatively harmoniously. The end of colonialism would expose Singapore's fragile and complex societal fabric, whereby the newly independent state had to deal with its challenges.

Did colonialism provide a political cocoon for interracial harmony? Perhaps. Colonialism was ironically the glue that held society together. There were no doubt cultural, linguistic, and religious divisions, but they had not deepened into irreparably damaging fissures in the manner of some other colonies. However, the colonial city also inherited all the White prejudices and racial stereotypes of its ethnic groups. This was not a conducive condition for creating an independent cultural ethos, nor a society in which Asians could flourish as equals with Whites, or as individuals with self-esteem and confidence.

Thus, Singaporeans who had come through colonial rule had a 'live and let live' mentality of racial and religious tolerance, although they also imbibed the colonial racial prejudices. Ironically, at the tail end of this era of inequality, Western commentators would be obsessed with democratic liberties and human rights, worrying that independent Singapore would develop 'in reverse' under authoritarian rule. Decades later with the communal and racial riots in various developed and developing states, the thinking would change. James Lovelock (2015, 112–123) in his book *A Rough Ride to the Future* has discussed among other themes, the various plusses and minuses of urban development. In his many references to Singapore's development, Lovelock (2015, 112) singles out well-planned and organised states as an antidote to communal violence, wondering whether Singapore as a city-state could "act as negative feedback on communal violence".

On the other hand, Singapore's myriad of cultural groups would now be pushed into the unknown political cauldron of nationalism and be obliged to speak with a new national identity. Singaporeans had to throw up political leaders to fend for themselves. Few had expected that the experience in creating the colonial city would serve Singapore in its future configuration as an independent city-state. At the same time, without the protection of British colonial administrators, the fledgling Singaporeans were suddenly exposed directly to the vagaries of political externalities — the Cold War contestations, the rise of China, the threat of communism, religious fundamentalism, Indonesian Confrontation, and Third World non-alignment. All these changing externalities were to become important to nation-building. What Western residents in Singapore astutely observed was the cultural chasm between the English- and Chinese-educated Chinese, a colonial legacy that would become a political tinderbox for the ruling PAP in the ensuing years.

The Western perceptions of the 1950s and 1960s were diverse. The optimists saw that the Lion City's citizens were sufficiently prepared to take on the role of responsible nationalists. Malaysia looked to be the convenient political vehicle for Singapore's independence, and the PAP leaders were advocates of Malaysia — the compulsion to be freed from colonialism seemed a greater incentive than the incongruent adversities of joining the larger body politic of Malaysia with its more ingrained inequalities, cultural baggage, and racial prejudices. In contrast, the White pessimists were self-indulgent in Caucasian superiority, in Western civilisation, and racial egotism; an independent Asian polity seemed far-fetched, a recipe for political disaster.

The colonial government's self-interested policies of making a success out of Singapore had inadvertently turned the colonial city into a Chinese city. The Chinese geo-body of Singapore remained for Westerners the main variable in the future of the colonial legacy. Three schools of thought seemed to prevail in Western conversations: (1) the Chinese majority population, with its drive, vigour, and pragmatism, would be an asset for postcolonial Singapore; (2) a dominant Chinese population with the rise of communist China would turn Singapore into its satellite where communism reigned and the English-educated Chinese would suffer; and (3) the British eagerness to palm off Singapore to the Malaysian Federation notwithstanding, Malaysia's Malay leaders were sceptical about Singapore's inclusion at its very inception in 1963 because its large Chinese population would upset the racial arithmetic of Malaysia (Moore 1975, 232).

After a brief and tumultuous marriage with Malaysia, Singapore would face another watershed in 1965 as a fully independent emergent city-state. Many of the political, economic, cultural, and social vestiges of colonialism were retained and improved upon. The Lion City remained ethnically diverse and religiously plural — a source of its national identity and strength. This cultural heterogeneity is also Singapore's Achilles heel. That is a story still unfolding and reverberating in many other narrations by political scientists, economists, geographers, and so forth. The future biography of Singapore as city-state through Western lenses will be a more complex enterprise. It is hoped that the autobiography of the city-state from the pens of Singaporeans will be a passionate and epic portrayal of what Singapore means to its own sons and daughters.

— 10 —
Reflections and Recollections

Chapter 10

REFLECTIONS AND RECOLLECTIONS

I. Something Borrowed, Something Learnt

Singapore's great achievement — so rare in the postcolonial world — was using its new sovereign power not to promote a small, and corrupt elite, but to construct one of the stunning urban success stories of the late twentieth century. Under the authoritarian leadership of Cambridge-educated Lee Kuan Yew, Singapore broke dramatically with much of its colonial past and forged a new model for Asian urbanism (Kotkin 2006, 142).

To understand the issue of freedom, take first the city of Singapore, in effect one of the world's most densely populated micro-countries. Singapore's six million people are packed into about 250 square miles — 230 times the average US population density. It's an Asian financial center, a major port on one of the world's busiest shipping straits, and a tiny piece of prime real estate wedged between two giant powerful neighbours, Indonesia and Malaysia ... So Singapore's government monitors its citizens closely, to make sure that individuals don't harm the community ... Americans may view such measures with horror, as George Orwell's novel *1984* come true. But for Singapore's citizens, it's a bargain that they have made with their government: less individual freedom in return for First World living standards, health, and security (Diamond 2019, 17–18).

These thoughtful quotes on urban contemporary development by two astute Western observers give us insights into modern independent Singapore. Both Joel Kotkin's (2006) and Jared Diamond's (2019) views reiterate the storyline that political leaders need to identify their objectives, make critical trade-offs, and translate decisions into pragmatic outcomes for their citizens. One can compare the difference between colonial and independent Singapore. Both governmental systems have been depicted as lacking freedom and being authoritarian by nature, unequal in remuneration, and socially stratified. Colonial Singapore had no end goal in development. Hence, by the end of colonial rule, 40 per cent of its population would be living in slums and squatters, with the city facing major housing shortages, and the people suffering many health problems. Yet, despite its top-down rule, Western observers never felt that their system was draconian, racialised, or unequal.

It was evident that Singapore's Western community lived in their closeted world; most were unconcerned about the local population, and unperturbed about the superior status which they themselves held. In general, Westerners in 19th-century Singapore believed that colonialism was infinite, and that the West had a commanding control over its territories and subjects. As Michigan historian Victor Lieberman (2003) has argued, there seemed to be a fitting relationship between the Western colonial powers and the regional responses. Due to the various political, technological, and other advantages which Europe had, colonialism as meted out was more or less absorbed by its subject peoples, if not for which there would have been a clash. Hence, "European exceptionalism" was complemented by the corollary of "Southeast Asian encapsulation" (Lieberman 2003, 1:460) of what was provided through the colonial system.

Many Western narratives by historians, social scientists, and journalists recount Singapore's development and rise as an important city-state in global relations. In the context of relating and existing with tropical nature and an Oriental landscape, Western impressions over time, however, remained surprisingly and relatively constant. Other Western impressions, such as those about the political maturity and activism of Singapore's people, changed due to externalities such as the war and post-war nationalism. The Western perceptions of colonial Singapore were filled with opinion, speculation, and debate. The *Notices* of official decisions and issues in early colonial Singapore themselves carried at times conjecture regarding decision-making, for if decisions had to be taken from overseas headquarters, then there would have been time lapses in execution.

These Western narratives were influenced by global issues. The sum of these varied European impressions across the British colonial era of about 145 years (1819–1963) adds to Singapore's biography as an evolving city. The narratives were by many who contributed to its development, constituting a story pieced together from subjective views, distilled from personal experiences, and based on analysis through generally biased cultural lenses. Hence, what may seem ordinary or culturally prosaic today were to Westerners in the past new sights, different experiences, and surprising revelations. The idea of Singapore was like an empty canvas for Western expressionistic painting, in that expressionism strives to depict subjective emotions and responses to experiences that arouse the artist.

This book is about narrative historical geography. It reflects the popular events in colonial Singapore, and concerns landscape descriptions and changes, spatial organisation, land tenure, urban evolution, iconic places, the populations of these spaces and places, and how nationalism was to occur in this environment which contributed to the nascent Singapore state. It does not pretend to be an authenticated history of Singapore. Rather, it highlights episodes, activities, places, and peoples that captured the Western imagination, and helped to define the making of Singapore as a colony, city, and international emporium.

Westerners loved Singapore because of its informality, spontaneity, and functionality; it was far from being a city of splendid, historic landscapes and monumental buildings. In it, they had the best of both worlds. On the one hand, they enjoyed living in an authentic local culture without pretensions, pomp, or ceremony. On the other, as Whites, they had a bird's eye view of all they surveyed, without obstacles and inhibitions of action in responding to their environment since they were masters of all they saw. This was a city one lived in, and for which one developed an attachment to its multifaceted landscapes that endeared and repelled, a node that defined the exotic Oriental experience and captured the processes of progress and modernisation. The city seemed to be on the move. It was a non-stop spectacle with its endless procession of cultural and religious festivals, its escalator streets of peoples and hawkers coming and going, and its burst of economic activity. Singapore never failed to surprise, entice the human senses, and leave a lasting impression. Part of its fascination was that it was "created ... created ... out of raw nature"; in Singapore a city rose out of "steaming jungle" (Moore 1955, 98).

Singapore was a line of wealth which "ran between East and West" (Moore 1955, 98). This was a city which attracted people from all over the world to "extract, process, transport, pack and ship" wealth from Malaya, according to Tom Fernald, a friend of Donald Moore's (Moore 1955, 98).

In dealing with the narratives of Western engagement with Singapore one might ask what we have learnt from these distillations. I would suggest five major themes that have preoccupied Westerners. Generally, the White impressions of Singapore over time can be classified as: (1) an abiding interest in the many Asian ethnic groups and cultures; the ethnic stereotypes formulated; and knowledge about Asian behaviour, work attitudes, traditions and customs, foods, and cultural habits. These concerns gave rise to racial discrimination and what Edward Said (1979) has described as 'othering' in ruler-native relations; (2) the interest in the economic operations of the colonial city, whether in trade or in agriculture. The bulk of Western residents were traders and merchants concerned with the attractions of the colonial entrepôt, the flow of resources, connectivity of the port, land tenure, labour costs, and the nature of free trade; (3) the observation of Singapore's development as a colonial city — its spatial layout, imageability, legibility, liveability, safety and security, and landscape aesthetics; (4) the accounts of new and experimental Western experiences in a tropical laboratory; and (5) the rising Western consciousness of East-West relations in the 20th century, as seen through the Japanese sacking of Singapore in the Second World War, the end of colonialism, the decline of the West, notions of Yellow Peril, and reflections on the rise of the Orient, notably Japan and China.

II. Ethnic Insights, Cultural Revelations

Colonial Singapore was a microcosm of the region's plurality. Western sojourners were continually surprised to find the cultural heterogeneity, linguistic diversity, and religious differences in the Lion City. Maria Balestier and other Western residents employed an ethnically diverse range of workers in their homes and hence, saw close up the cultural differences of the Chinese domestic 'boys', Indian gardeners or *kebuns* as they were called, and Malay drivers. They gained personal insights into different races through their working relationships. Yet, they formed stereotypes of the ethnic groups and rarely got to know their employees as individuals, nor did they foresee the looming political consequences of the liberal colonial immigration policies.

Without a dominant native Malay population, the British authorities felt little local pressure against these policies. Furthermore, given that Asian immigrants had made Singapore their adopted home, they were more willing to accept British rule and jurisdiction. Unlike the followers of the sultan and *temenggong*, they could not claim indigenous status. The absence of local Malay masses, or *rakyat*, allowed the British to make outlandish historical changes. Whites referred to the Sultan of Johore (or Maharaja of Johore) with great reverence but there was little reference to the 'Sultan of Singapore' at Kampong Glam. Sultan Ali was the last sultan at Kampong Glam, having given up his right over Singapore in 1855 (Phuah 2019, 6). The royal family thus had no title, no iconic figures, and the dispersed *tengkus* (princes) have since been without state or place affiliation. Such is the irony of the historical narrative on Singapore.

The sexual imbalance in the colony was repeatedly a subject of observation among Caucasian travellers. Nearly every Western resident noted that they employed many domestic 'boys' to do all sorts of housework because there were hardly any women around. Moreover, with a youthful working population, and the thriving itinerant marine population, it is not surprising that Singapore became notorious for vice, which, along with the red-light districts, were well-covered topics in Western travelogues.

Western travel accounts of the native landscapes were generally superficial, cursory, and incidental. They showed that the resident and transient White populations seldom mixed with Asians. Hence, the management of the local population was left to select Asian *towkays*, clan associations, religious organisations, educational institutions, and community leaders. The city was thus a curious manifestation of spatial and social segregation, and distancing between White and Asians.

For Dick Wilson (1972), the challenge of the new independent state of Singapore would be in keeping alive the "poly-cultural pillar" of nation-building where the multiracial, multicultural society remained under the umbrella of a Singaporean identity. To put it in Thongchai Winichakul's (1994) terms, colonial Singapore had not created a "geo-body", a state geography defined by values and practices, where a sense of nationhood existed. Ideally, the cosmopolitan flavour was welcomed and admired, but politically, it would remain a perennial challenge for the Singapore government. Since the time of Raffles' founding, the port-city had been the envy of neighbours, a dynamic economic hub created by liberal immigration laws. Singapore was in Western eyes a fulcrum of opportunity, a regional centre abounding with trading incentives, and a place of secure living for Whites as well as the diverse immigrant communities.

On the ground, Western residents and sojourners were perpetually fascinated and dumbfounded by cultural differences between themselves and the local population: Malays, Bugis, *orang laut*, Chinese, Indians, Arabs, and other Asians. In most cases, they used their cultural and moral barometers to assess the motley Asian population they experienced in Singapore. As the supposed dominant civilisation by the 19th century, the Whites saw themselves as the measure of nearly everything from political ideology, government, capitalism, urban planning, and education to religion, civility, and cultural practices. D. J. Enright (1969, 183) observed that the forming of a national culture in establishing Singapore's independent city-state involved the worrying issue of destroying the multicultural ethos to answer a simple political objective: "to homogenize a very mixed bunch of people, and thus make them more amenable to living together, working together and being ruled together". The university don therefore sought an ideal concept but the politician in Singapore answers a pragmatist's calling. Yet, Enright himself seemed oblivious to the way colonialism too had homogenised knowledge (Cohn 1996), administrative culture, language, a two-tier society, and White authority in Singapore.

For the historian, change seems to be governed by human 'events' such as wars or revolts (Teggart 1962, 141–151), while in the physical sciences change is a slow, continuous modification of landscapes in an eventless world (Teggart 1962, 141). In Singapore, social and cultural changes remained slow, moderated by tradition and custom whereas the political and economic changes were sudden, often fuelled by externalities. Enright (1969) was at the forefront of cultural change and could as a ringside onlooker observe how the intermingling of cultures was not always logical, coherent, nor rational. The fusion of Western and Eastern civilisational thinking did not necessarily result in a 'best of both worlds' outcome, at least in White perceptions.

To understand the British experiences in Singapore, one needs to understand the White smugness that colonialism embodied. Other historians have tried to explain the differences between East and West which became pronounced in the 19th century as a result of developments in Europe. Lieberman (2009, 2:2) has referred to the gap between the West and the Rest as a product of "European exceptionalism" arising from a long period of political consolidation in creating its urban autonomy, market competition, political democracy, industrial capitalism, and other cultural virtues.

Historian Kenneth Pomeranz (2000, 3) has explained the differences between Europeans and non-Europeans in the late 19th and early 20th centuries as a product of the "great divergence", whereby the economic developmental path of Western Europe was "unique". Europe experienced a range of major changes, including the emergence of market economies, growing industrialisation, the rise of institutionalised capitalism in the form of firms and monetised wealth, and the expansion of colonialism (Pomeranz 2000). More recently, Joel Mokyr (2017), an economic historian, has provided a more comprehensive analysis of the "culture" of economic growth in Europe that altered the relationship between East and West, related to which were the Enlightenment, British exceptionalism, the Industrial Revolution, and the "culture of progress". Changes in Europe over the centuries emerged as a result of revolutionary ideas, not as a natural continuation of ancient, medieval, and Renaissance culture but in many ways in repudiation of them (Mokyr 2017, 340).

Given the great Western influences in the 19th century, it is no wonder that the German historian Jürgen Osterhammel (2014, xvii–xx) in his tome *The Transformation of the World* has viewed it as the "European century". Yet, he notes within the context of world history, the attempt of other historians to surmount Eurocentrism by neutralising the idea of Europe being the centre of the world. In Osterhammel's book, colonial Singapore is presented as an important icon of the British empire. It surfaces 14 times: as an outpost of British society, the fulcrum in defence was keeping sea lanes open, the prototypal urbanising colonial city, the economic seedbed of capitalism in the region, a torchbearer in modernisation, and an exemplification of the 'turn' in the understanding of geographic space as represented by 19th-century colonial expansion. Singapore would also later come to symbolise the binary opposites of expanding territorial colonialism and the contraction of British colonial rule, with its humiliating conquest by the Japanese in the Second World War. The lesson in history of the Second World War is how the Japanese checkmated Western colonialism by defeating its most important global hegemon in Singapore.

A reading of the literature of East-West historical dynamics often suggests evolving contests and arguments concerning the swinging of the

East-West power pendulum that led to the rise of Europe and the fall of Asia, and vice versa. To keep a balanced view, it is best to keep in mind that Tumasik and colonial Singapore were products of an "ethnosphere" which, since Antiquity, has consisted of a "large network of cultural and technological diffusions and commercial exchanges" between China, the Middle East, India, Central Asia, Southeast Asia, East Africa, as well as West Africa and Europe (Barendse 2002, 490).

The British colonial impact on Singapore cannot be measured by only the size of the contemporary White presence or weight of its military power, but more so by its introduction of a method of knowledge acquisition different from the one customary in the Chinese mode of learning (J. Li 2012). The heyday of the colonial period saw the creation of a body of 'colonial knowledge' which ensured that colonialism thrived (Cohn 1996). English-educated Asian students were caught between the colonial and indigenous pedagogical methods; they were cowed by colonial authority and their Asian upbringing prevented them from questioning authority. Enright (1969) was the first to allude to this phenomenon among university students. The challenge mounted by Japan and China as global powers in the 20th century, however, would alter Western sojourners' thinking of the East-West equation, and empower Chinese-educated students in particular.

Depending on their working relationship with various ethnic groups, the Europeans quickly formed ethnic stereotypes. Overall, the Chinese were seen as hardworking and enterprising, hence colonialists encouraged their immigration. They were the real workhorses of the Singapore economy. By the first decade of Raffles' founding, the Malays were replaced by the Chinese as the dominant ethnic group, and a liberal colonial immigration policy opened the floodgates to a multiethnic migrant population more concerned with economic survival than political liberties. In many ways, the Asian communities self-censored their displeasure with colonial rule.

Singapore 'society', as first defined by John Cameron (1965), was exclusive to White elites, and essentially cultivated on snobbery, sarcasm, and status (Moore 1953). Given that Whites were the masters, they set the benchmark rightly or wrongly, for behaviour, acceptable practices, and the models for development. Even though the Asian population was demographically dominant, they were viewed by the Whites as a cultural, social, and political minority in the colony. Over the 19th century, of all the *towkays* with whom the Western residents and visitors socialised,

Whampoa or Hoo Ah Kay was found to be the most congenial, generous, and similar in temperament to those of the Caucasians (Thomson 1865). The Western lifestyle was emulated by anglicised Asians; "European penchants often had a trickle-down effect" (Osterhammel 2014, 383). Hence, even the European love for tiger hunting in 19th-century Singapore became a prestigious sport of the Sultan of Johore and wealthy locals (Osterhammel 2014, 383).

III. Operationalising Colonialism: People, Economy, and Society

If the world were to operate with no centre, no pivot, no national civilisation, and no superior power, then the global competition for power might be translated into cooperative, collaborative, and congenial endeavours. But that would be wishful thinking. The study of Western perceptions of Singapore during the period of colonial expansion is pertinent because it underscores important factors and influences not necessarily replicable in history. It was a period when Singapore was a colonial pawn in Britain's ascent as a superpower. The long 19th century fused the Western scientific breakthroughs and the Enlightenment with the Industrial Revolution, and created new interests in raw materials and markets (Osterhammel 2014).

While Romanticism brought about a new trend in Western relationships between humans and nature, it did not necessarily translate to White respect of 'native' culture. The romantic love of the natives was mainly confined to jungle dwellers. Singapore by contrast was seen by Westerners as a city, a place of wheeling and dealing. Among Singapore's Asian immigrants themselves, capitalism and materialism became the new measures for evaluating human success. The Arabs, Parsees, and Chinese traders symbolised wealth worthy of emulation. Singapore's ethnic plurality and its material wealth seemed like human-made concoctions. Singapore epitomised the human role in changing the face of the landscape. Scientifically on the other hand, Charles Darwin's theory of evolution was interpreted by some to seriously question the Christian 'design earth' idea of the God-made world, hence bringing humans nearer to nature. This implied a paradigm shift that brought man closer to apes than angels. At the same time the science of nature was translated into new forms of agriculture, and emboldened the human mastery of the natural world and landscape. The 19th century was when new disciplines like anthropology and sociology began to seriously study culture and social interaction.

Early European merchants, traders, and professionals were torn between the lure of quick profit in regional trade and the slower returns from agricultural pursuits. While agricultural exploits continued through the early 20th century, trade and the entrepôt business became institutionalised and gave Singapore its global fame. Singapore soon thrived on being the region's economic middleman and the East-West bridge that British colonialism encouraged and coveted. In contrast to the terrifying depictions of the equatorial jungles by Joseph Conrad (1974) in his *Heart of Darkness*, and Noel Barber's (1971, 13) primordial jungle that "none can escape", a jungle that "reaches to the back of every mind" in the region, Singapore appeared as a welcome oasis of civilisation, urban civility, cosmopolitan etiquette, and most of all, self-sustainability.

Speaking at the Royal Colonial Institute in 1884, Sir Frederick Weld (1983, 44) lavished abundant praise on Singapore, compared the "Settlement" with an "entire Colony", and stated, "Singapore is virtually the 'Straits Settlements'", in that it embodied the virtues of all three of those settlements which made up the Crown Colony. While at the same talk, Dr. N. B. Dennys lamented that Singapore was "entitled to a little more notice than it usually receives", whereupon the Member of Parliament W. E. Forster replied that this was the "greatest compliment" to Singapore that there were no parliamentary questions about it because it was "going on so well" (Weld 1983, 82–85).

In general, most Western commentaries of Singapore were made from the pulpit of superior knowledge which revealed itself in three ways, through: (1) the overriding belief that the colony had to be sustained and developed for the welfare of the British empire; (2) the perpetual use of Western models in dealing with problems in Singapore, given the White superiority complex. Allowance for public feedback was limited as the authorities were not willing to customise policies to accommodate the Asian resident population (Yeoh 1996). Only when policies threatened the welfare of the economic state did they grudgingly accept the Asian positions; (3) the viewing of a residential citizenry as being secondary to what the British rulers had in mind. Since there were no elections, the colonial masters were not pressured to serve the residential population. Planning as defined by Western bureaucrats was top-down.

The White Residents, governors, and bureaucrats had the upper hand and governance was rarely democratic.

Singapore was defined by two colonial plans deemed deterministic in their intended outcomes. The 1822 Raffles or Jackson Plan set the stage for the spatial configuration and morphology of the urban area (a mere 1.2 per cent of the island's total land area) for over a century. Later, the 1958 Master Plan at the tail end of colonial rule was meant to rationalise land use, population distribution, and development trajectories for the whole island. Not much transpired from this plan under the colonial administration. Instead, after the People's Action Party (PAP) came into power in 1959 under internal self-rule, it would use the British plans and institutions to further its own goals.

If one were to compare the two plans, one could conclude that the Raffles Plan was racially defined and in spite of all its limitations, forward-looking and bold in vision. Subsequent perceptions of Western residents and visitors would be governed by the ethnic distinctions, spatial apartheid, and how this ideological underpinning shaped the morphology of the city as it has done till today. After the implementation of the plan the colonial city's spatial configuration was more or less a given and Westerners rarely criticised the administration for its ineptitude or inefficiency. Visitors were too overwhelmed by the diversity of economic activity, the busyness of street scenes, and the commercial competence which the city evoked.

Being a door to Western science and technology, colonialism was seen by the European residents and observers in the region as a panacea to tropical ills rather than the undermining of the tropical ecology. The European quest for knowledge, applied science, and technological innovation gave colonialism its endorsement. The region contained a bountiful harvest for naturalists who collected thousands of specimens of flora and fauna and thought little of the ecological disruption. Even the renowned naturalist Alfred Russel Wallace (1869, 2015) boasted about his collection of natural specimens in Singapore as compared to Sarawak.

Yet, the competition between the natural and cultural landscape had begun to unfold since Raffles' founding, with Singapore being made ultimately into a successful economic pivot of trade, with a free port able to tap a global hinterland for its sustenance. Singapore was built on a platform of Asian entrepreneurship — Chinese, Indian, Arab, Bugis, Jewish, Parsi, and Malay. At the same time, Singapore's success as a British entrepôt was a statement that Western science and technology,

Western education, and colonial administration could make the difference to a tropical colony. While the biggest impact on its pristine landscape was agricultural expansion, this would not be a money earner for the island.

For the many Western nation-states that championed colonialism, the experience was new and experimental. Colonialism began as a system to tap natural resources, enslave peoples, and create exploited satellites for the Mother country. In Singapore, however, the paramount driver of the factory was trade. Thus from 1819 colonialism was translated less by draconian rule than moderated by a laissez-faire system of open international commerce. Without traders and merchants and produce for trading, the colony's rationale for existence would have evaporated. Raffles and early British administrators were mindful of the city's delicate economic balance. The region was awash with ports and colonies which levied high taxes and tariffs on the import and export of goods, all of which benefited Singapore's free port.

In many ways, colonial policies and management of resources were an explication of capitalism. While few Westerners mentioned capitalism by name, their constant references to land rents, labour costs, demand and supply, variable differences in the prices of commodities, and profits and losses, were all lessons in the capitalistic process. Giovanni Arrighi's (2010) cross-sectional history of the 20th century has posited that the century defined the capitalist era. Momentous changes were taking place in the global economy in the "historical transition" of the long 20th century. Colonial Singapore's economy would be bifurcated between large Western business houses — the firm-centred economy, and the native economy, governed by what is termed the *bazaar economy* (Geertz 1963). Nowhere else in the region did Westerners feel a greater threat to their economic activity than Singapore, and this was because of the dominance of the Chinese. Repeatedly, there was the expressed fear of Chinese economic competition, their materialistic culture, money-minded acumen, and aggressive economic behaviour (Logan 1847a, Moore 1953, 1955). Nonetheless, Singapore had become a draw for capitalists: not only Scottish, American, German, French, and Dutch entrepreneurs; it was also an attractive place for Jewish, Malay, Arab, Indian, Parsi, Bugis, and Chinese traders all seeking to make a fortune.

Singapore was a unique blend of an island geography and party to an externally-linked ecology of ideas, goods, and peoples. Despite its small territory and lack of other natural resources, it had one asset that the British capitalised on to fuel its 19th-century superpower status — its maritime location, which made it a strategic pivot, economic magnet, and international locus. As Professor Wang Gungwu reiterates, "The global is maritime" (K. Ooi 2015, xiv).

Singapore remained an invaluable contributor to economic globalisation throughout its tenure under British colonialism. The entrepôt story was punctuated by optimism and pessimism, boom and bust cycles, successful *towkays* and bankrupt merchants. To understand the Singapore strand of the global narrative is to accept American historian Peter Coclanis' (2006, 14) argument of "globalisation as a process — a series of actions leading or conducting toward an end", rather than a "state of being". As Coclanis (2006) noted in his Raffles Lecture, "Time's Arrow, Time's Cycle", historians are locked in conceptual debate about whether that process is linear or cyclical. His conclusion about the region's economic history of globalisation, being underpinned by more Asian views of historical cycles, suggests "a process that is not linear, not inevitable, not irreversible, not unconditional, and not complete by a long shot" (Coclanis 2006, 56–57).

IV. Biography of the City through Other Eyes

Singapore is an interesting study of how urban development is segmented into two phases. About two millennia ago, Southeast Asia had become a cultural extension of India, the operationalisation of which Sheldon Pollock (2006) has argued was best translated through the period of Sanskrit diffusion. Under Tumasik, the Lion City was a regional expression of the Indianised cultural phase which the French historian George Coedès (1968) defined as part of 'Further India' or 'Greater India'. As Tumasik, Singapore embodied Robert Heine-Geldern's (1942) thesis of the cosmic city, a product of cosmo-magical symbolism, where the raja derived supernatural power from Hindu-Buddhist deities, thereby giving him godlike attributes. In Singapore, the raja's residence on the later-named Fort Canning Hill was not just a symbolic architectural construct, but deemed to be the highest point of the cosmic city. Tumasik was one of the last kingdoms in the predominantly maritime *Alam Melayu* to reflect the Indian cultural traditions. With this phase in its history, *Singapura* would remain a name embedded in Malay mythology, legend, and folk belief. Raffles was cognisant of this and capitalised on it.

Raffles' 1819 founding of Singapore, however, marked a new global cultural and geopolitical force in the region. Singapore itself would become a product of growing secular forces. Europe had been the catalyst and symbol of modernisation in the 19th century and Singapore would be the experimental laboratory, Southeast Asia's archetypal colonial city. But it did not end there.

Raffles was a progressive thinker and education was close to his heart. In his words, "Singapore is the most eligible situation for an educational establishment" because of its centrality in the Malay states and the cultural history it had been exposed to (Cross 1921, 60). Unlike many Western administrators, he saw education not as an imposition of Western and Christian culture, but a vehicle which could include local culture, tradition, and history. Whether his vision in this regard was wholly successful remains open for discussion. The British in some ways anticipated the French *mission civilisatrice*, and implemented it in terms of administration, law, education, architecture, and laissez-faire capitalism in Singapore. Especially in education, Raffles was ahead of the French colonial objectives. Nineteenth-century Britain was a symbol of progress, and Singapore was its colonised recipient. Caucasian sojourners and travellers to Singapore were agents of Western knowledge diffusion. As knowledge was not diffused easily, comparisons made by Western travellers helped place Singapore on a global radar screen.

Despite the differences in the agency of urban development in Tumasik, colonial, and independent Singapore, three constants have remained. Firstly, geography is an indelible part of the way Westerners have perceived Singapore. Robert D. Kaplan's (2012) *The Revenge of Geography* provides an updated and balanced version of environmental determinism and why geography matters in the fate of nations. Singapore's geography is both a handicap and an asset, depending on perception and governmental management. Given its maritime location and terraqueous island geography, Singapore has been suitably geared to be a thriving trading port. In defence, Singapore's naval base was a symbol of British military prowess, unchallenged before the Second World War. Notwithstanding the numerous wars that have been fought on the Eurasian continent, the control of the maritime domain has created formidable powers throughout history: the Greeks, Phoenicians, Vikings, Portugal, Spain, the Netherlands, Britain, and the US.

Singapore's pivotal connectivity is the second of its enduring assets. Its location at the Straits of Malacca between the Indian and Pacific Oceans, and its commanding position over the South China Sea, interfacing between insular and continental Southeast Asia, is enviable. The historian

Oliver Wolters (1999, 170) referred to the Malay Archipelago as a product of a "single ocean", emphasising the importance of the region in bridging the Indian and Pacific Oceans. More recently other Western and local historians have referred to the region as being 'between two oceans', an idea that was first adumbrated by the late History Professor Wong Lin Ken.

Singapore has always gained its strength and influence not merely through its own internal merits, but through relationships with other economic and political entities. It is a relational city, port, and state. Singapore's destiny is not just in geography, but also connectivity. Its infrastructure is best depicted in Parag Khanna's (2016, 5–6) *Connectography*, conceptualised as a morphed world system of ethnic economies as global connections, of nations being nodes, and free trade transcending national boundaries across cities and ports. The 21st century turns cartography upside down, maps inside out, and questions the sanctity of national boundaries. But without an understanding of the old-world system, it is difficult to appreciate the global transformation. The colonial city laid the foundations of Singapore's grand scheme for the new age of capitalism, information, instantaneous telecommunication, rapid urbanisation, liberating technologies, and anti-border infrastructure. It is best to understand Singapore's change not as evolution or revolution, but as metamorphosis. It morphed the old and new, the traditional and modern, and the Eastern and Western cultural idioms.

Thirdly, the economic prowess of Singapore, especially as a fulcrum of international trade, has been its hallmark, and for much of its history, its sustaining system. Whether under Tumasik, the colonial city, or the independent city-state, Singapore's rulers have grasped the importance of its trading ecosystem and its international exposure. Understanding geopolitics and its operational strategies has thus been a lifeline to Singapore's success, whether the decision-maker in question be Stamford Raffles, Japanese Prime Minister Tojo Hideki, or Lee Kuan Yew.

The open economic system gave the colonial city its identity as an El Dorado to migrants and a magnet for fortune-seekers. It also corroborated the perceptions of Western sojourners of the majority Chinese population as having a risk-bearing entrepreneurial nature akin to that of a gambler. Chinese traders were seen as abetting and complementing Western merchants, but were sparingly given credit as the engine of the entrepôt's economic success. Enlightened Western observers, however, paid tribute to the industrious and enterprising Chinese population. Capitalism could neutralise ethnic and racial distinctions between the Whites and Asians in the colonial city, but it ignited new class divisions and status distinctions within and between the Asian ethnic groups.

Few ports, cities, or states in the region have begun, as Singapore has, with a relatively clean slate. In the process, the Lion City has had the good fortune of being well documented and described. It is an entrepôt that has undergone scrutiny from multitudes of Westerners who touched base with the island. The detailed listings of the various products, tonnage, values, and trading places were documented by John Crawfurd (1830, vol. 2), Thomas Newbold (1839, vol. 1), and other 19th-century visitors and residents. Over the decades, successful European merchants established companies and became icons of entrepreneurship in the region: Boustead, the Sarkies brothers, and Guthrie. Singapore was a buzzword for Asian and European immigrants seeking wealth. Like other colonial cities, Singapore's orientation was geared towards receiving the "outside world" (Osterhammel 2014, 285). Every activity for Europeans became an entrepreneurial endeavour: plantation agriculture, trade, commerce, banking, shipping, and industry. But, there were also stories of White entrepreneurial failure, Joseph Balestier and Donald Moore coming to mind. The lesson they teach is that successful entrepreneurship is based on right timing; ironically, both men were ahead of their time.

Singapore's history, whether as the thalassic kingdom of Tumasik, the colonial city, or the independent republic, has been basically urban. Cities have found identity and expression in different epochs and their names remain important symbols, transcending time and space. Under colonialism, cities had become brands. Singapore came too late in the game to claim the legendary appellation of 'Queen of the East' conferred variously upon Goa, Batavia, and Manila, or 'Pearl of the Orient', as was called Penang. Nineteenth-century Southeast Asia was, however, marked by *Pax Urbanica*, a world of notable colonial cities that overshadowed their colonial states: Rangoon, Saigon, Batavia, Manila, Penang, and Singapore.

Singapore's urban imageability lay in the character of local living that played out in public spaces. Colonial Singapore was not a historical city of monuments, but paradoxically one of continual outstanding experiences of the daily and mundane — a place of frenzied activity, a landscape defined by business. It bombarded the senses. This was a cultural landscape one lived in from bottom-up, full of surprises, alluring and disgusting when experienced from the viewpoint of the pedestrians of its varied alleys, streets, and roads. Nonetheless, for inveterate travellers like Conrad, Singapore had in the 19th century its landscape anchors: the Padang, the Singapore River, the Sailors' Home (on the site of the present Capitol Building), the Grand Hotel de l'Europe, and St. Andrew's Cathedral.

The streetscape was notoriously alive, captivating, and memorable. The red-light areas were defined and laid bare; yet the midnight transvestite shows of Bugis Street were literally and literarily unutterable for Western sensibilities of the time. Even the economic artery of the city was not a static place but the winding Singapore River. Lined by godowns, wharves, jetties, merchant houses, and thronging with endless bumboats and *sampans*, the river was captured in countless paintings, photos, and video recordings in the 1960s. Despite its depictions as "soul" and "life blood" of the colonial city (L. Berry 1982, 16), however, Westerners seemed less enamoured of this waterway which was also its port, for its stench was unforgettable.

Like Manila, Singapore was one of the first colonial cities in the region to be developed according to an urban plan where ethnic segregation became its early hallmark. The characteristics of colonial cities in the 19th century were spatial dualism, fragmented urban society, compartmentalisation along racial lines, and horizontal segregation (Osterhammel 2014, 285). Given the small European populations that governed colonies, their own security was high in the minds of colonialists. For centuries, colonial factories had been built as forts to protect the European minority. Singapore was also one of the first cities where European and Asian populations were spatially segregated without the brute imposition of fortress walls. Western visitors often remarked at the clear distinction between a staid, ordered European Town as opposed to the buzzing, boisterous, and insalubrious Asian Town.

By and large, the Chinese traders and businessmen adopted a rather low-key position with regard to displaying their wealth. For Western onlookers, there was little evidence of Chinese conspicuous consumption given the crammed living conditions, roadside dining, and death houses, with streets as playgrounds for children, and socialisation in public spaces. The idea of thrift seemed ingrained in many migrant Chinese, and saving was a virtue. This was a city where Westerners sampled an exposed culture, where privacy seemed non-existent, and one could have a ringside view of the rites of passage and family life. Every Western traveller became an amateur anthropologist, their cultural and ethnic descriptions resembled field notes, without in most cases, interpretations of what they saw. Only Westerners living in Singapore, like Maria Balestier, John Cameron, Roland Braddell, and the Moores (Donald and Joanna) were able to interpret and analyse local Asian cultural events and activities. In reviewing Western perceptions of Singapore one can conclude, like in Andrew March's (1974, 45) view of the Western cognition of Asia, that they reflect "the intellectual history of Europe; and there is no other Asia", or in this case, no other Singapore.

In reviewing the city in global history, Kotkin (2006) has argued that the sustainability of the city must fulfil three critical functions: (1) it must remain a sacred place which inspires and orders its masses of people; (2) it must provide basic security for its citizens; and (3) it must have sound economic abilities as the host of a commercial marketplace. The Western perceptions of Singapore under colonialism indicate the at-least partial fulfilment of Kotkin's attributes. Ironically, independent Singapore's foundations and scaffoldings were erected by a minority foreign White population. Paradoxically, while the colonial British encouraged the freedom and diversity of religions and sacred places, under independent Singapore, sacred places would be drastically reduced. The Canadian geographer Rodolphe de Koninck (1992) in *Singapore: An Atlas of the Revolution of Territory* hypothesised that the country's independent government eradicated many places of competing loyalty (churches, mosques, Chinese and Hindu temples, schools, clan associations) so that Singaporeans could give their undivided fealty and sense of place to the Singapore state. Despite its occasional street riots, gangster and secret society clashes, and even a mutiny, the colonial city was generally peaceful and secure. Apart from the war years, few Westerners would have feared for their security. Of all the three functions, Singapore, however, best exemplified a marketplace in Western eyes. Moreover, there were many Chinese and Indian rags-to-riches stories that kept alive the dreams of migrants.

This was a city that was functional, containing things for use rather than aesthetic appraisal. Its buildings served merchants and traders in their economic activity, but its winding streets and alleys invited curiosity and White travellers revelled in their cultural surprises. Not until the turn of the 20th century did the British administration begin a renewal of civic buildings, where the style was decidedly Palladian in keeping with the global renaissance of classical architecture. These government buildings such as the City Hall, Supreme Court, Victoria Memorial Hall, and Parliament House have become heritage sites and reminders of colonial administration.

Before the internet and digital knowledge, information was passed through face-to-face communication, and via newspapers, journals, and books. The exchange of information between various officials, merchants, militiamen, professionals, and missionaries, and their concerns, disagreements, assessments, and criticisms all became public. In the early years, nothing was more important to Western traders, residents, and visitors than the endless lists of imports and exports, the monetary values of trade, profit margins, and the potential of regional markets. The Singapore 'society' comprising the White upper class, the rich and those of status, maintained their exclusive network and defined the power elite of the colony. One can imagine the gossip and rumours that bedevilled White conversation at the city's aptly named Scandal Point and the two o'clock 'exchange hour' where traders were involved in an 'interchange of ideas' and news. Only later did the British administrators accept rich or educated Asians into their exclusive company.

In the post-war years, the British were domestically preoccupied with trying to put their house in order. Their peoples were suffering withdrawal symptoms from the end of empire and uninterested in the welfare of colonies. By the time most of the British left Singapore in 1963, the island's skyline was still unimpressive compared to those of Hong Kong and Shanghai. The tallest building viewed from the sea was the 18-storey Asia Insurance Building, which remained the tallest for a decade after its development. Singapore was then a city of hidden appeal, with its economic prowess being its principal yet less immediately visible symbol, and its ground-level street landscapes manifesting its identity instead.

If the urban geographer Terry McGee (1976) referred to independent Singapore as a product of "deliberate urbanisation", the British period witnessed the "evolutionary" development of a colonial city, with the changes being incremental according to market forces (Savage 1992). Confined to the spatial delimitation of the 1822 Raffles Plan, Singapore's town population was the epitome of urban involution that manifested itself in slum dwellings and overpopulated shophouses. Having little urban hardware to speak of, the soul of Singapore lay instead in its teeming, busy Asian population.

With colonialism at its height, the 19th century was the period when the West asserted its dominant ideology, science, and technology in the tropical world (Pomeranz 2000). Indeed, despite the Second World War, Western powers were so convinced of their intellectual and administrative superiority that local independence movements in the Philippines,

Vietnam, and Indonesia had to fight bloody battles to secure freedom from colonial rule. The first Asian independence leader was the Filipino José Rizal, an icon of Asian independence, who was executed by the Spanish in 1898. Later, following the struggles of Gandhi in India, the defeat of French forces in Vietnam, the communist Emergency in Malaya, and the armed nationalist struggle against the Dutch in Indonesia, the British colonial administrators were more than willing to relinquish their rule in Malaya and Singapore with little bloodshed. Singapore, Sarawak, and North Borneo were conveniently meshed into a Malaysian Federation, thereby absolving Britain of further colonial responsibilities.

V. The Tropical Laboratory: Western Experiences

Some notable historians have used the human-nature paradigm as the underlying theme in the history of civilisations. Arnold Toynbee was one of the first to be concerned with ecology as a framework for understanding civilisations. His 'challenge and response' historical paradigm has served as a basis to interpret their rise and fall. Identifying nature as one of the challenges that civilisations have had to confront and tame, Toynbee's (1976) last book *Mankind and Mother Earth* is a sobering reflection on civilisations and their relationship with the planet. Mankind through his "mastery over the whole of the biosphere" has been "wrecking [it] and extinguishing life" (Toynbee 1976, 20). The historian regarded the "climax" of human civilisation as requiring a contemporary chronicle of "Mankind's encounter with Mother Earth", thus opening the floodgates for succeeding historians to reflect on the impact of various civilisations on nature. Far from being an environmental or spiritual determinist, Toynbee's later writings reveal him as a French possibilist whose philosophy could inform our own views of the White management of Singapore's pristine landscapes: "As human beings we are endowed with the freedom of choice, and we cannot shuffle off our responsibility upon the shoulders of God or nature" (Toynbee 1971, 45). Singapore epitomised the 19th-century human creativity in shaping the physical and cultural landscape.

Elaborating on Toynbee, Felipe Fernández-Armesto (2001) in his study *Civilizations* has noted that the heart of the problem of civilisations has been in defining the type of relationships to the natural environment. Starting from the premise that the world is "terrified and inhibited by nature's power over Man" (Fernández-Armesto 2001, 17), the British historian perceives that civilisation transformed nature by directing "the civilising impulse, to meet human demands" (Fernández-Armesto 2001, 14). In dealing with Western perceptions of colonial Singapore, one encounters the underlying belief in how civilisation, through the colonial agency, was able to change tropical landscapes for the better. There was little observation of how gambier planting was ruining the natural ecosystem; the majority of Westerners held the view of agriculture as turning forests into harvestable landscapes. The main problem Western residents alluded to in the matter of agriculture was not the destruction of pristine vegetation per se but rather the inability of the colonial administration to uphold and police the land tenure system. Without a well-managed land tenure system, colonial bureaucrats were unable to control Chinese gambier farmers in the inland areas of the island as they rampantly destroyed forested areas.

The yeast for developing a successful political entity has not changed from colonial to present times. Under European colonial rule, the tenets of the *mission civilisatrice* provided an outward rationale for developing colonies. In Singapore, the possibilist 'can do' spirit of this mission manifested itself in many ways, through small-scale and plantation agriculture, the botanical gardens, education, urban planning, public health, and public housing. Throughout the tropics, Westerners operated a human-nature experiment in their colonial laboratories. Armed with science and technology, they believed that they could tame jungles, conquer tropical diseases, exploit natural resources, and create economically productive landscapes.

When Singapore became independent in 1965, its leaders carried on the colonial mission but under a new credo of research and development involving science, technology, and industrialisation, and with a repurposed possibilist ethos (Savage 1997). Just as Westerners had used environmentalism to explain native behaviour and civilisations, the Singapore leaders, who were still under its sway, used the idea rather astutely to win votes and elections (Savage 2004), for example by impressing upon Singaporeans early on that Singapore was a small place lacking in natural resources, and thus had to be carefully managed by having the right people in power.

To understand colonial experiences in Singapore and the region, one needs to frame the Western ideological thinking at the time, which was conditioned by a Darwinian-type notion of achieving progress by deliberately setting out to do something. The biggest challenge for colonialism was the colonisation of the land, viewed often as the taming of tropical nature, the conquest of territory, the transformation of space under land tenure, the commodification of property, and the shrinking of distances. White and Chinese agriculturalists transformed the Singapore landscape, and through the land tenure system, land became property by capitalisation. Through such changes Singapore became one of the beachheads of Western civilisation in the region, and Western residents and sojourners were content with enjoying the fruits of its creature comforts and living standards.

Just as the Dutch had their 19th-century Buitenzorg Botanical Gardens for the scientific study of tropical crops, under Raffles Singapore also established its own botanic garden between 1822 and 1829 at Fort Canning (Tinsley 1983, 14–21). Its establishment so soon after Singapore's founding reflected Raffles' personal interests in the flora and fauna of the region and his close friendships with many botanists and naturalists like Joseph Arnold and Nathaniel Wallich. Singapore was fortunate to have an avid group of European horticulturalists who re-established the garden in 1859 at a new site at Tanglin. Its popularity with Westerners was best reflected in numerous picture postcards. The most successful cash crop arising from Singapore's new botanic gardens was rubber, which spread throughout the region as the plantation crop par excellence.

British bureaucrats were nationalistic, patriotic, and Western-centric in their views. However, British perceptions were also tempered by other European perspectives, which were continually sought after. Indeed, the generally positive impressions of the colonial city by sojourners, visitors, and travellers were good advertisements for the city and conveyed its economic attractions. Travellers' assessments were particularly interesting because their comparisons to other cities, ports, and hubs in the Malay Archipelago, Asia, and the world provided the Lion City with its relative worth and benchmarking. Unlike presently, when comparisons and rankings of cities and states are made annually across an almost endless array of indices, pre-World War II assessments were very much based on anecdotal assessments.

VI. Singapore: The Meeting of East and West

More than any other place in the region, colonial Singapore was where the East-West crossroads seem to have connected and conflicted in different ways. Given the unassailable power of the West in the 19th century, Western historians during that period tended to overgeneralise history and posit Western civilisation as the dominant global ideational force and economic power for all time. The notion has since been checkmated by several other historical studies. The civil servant in the Dutch East Indies, Jacob Cornelius van Leur (1955), was one of the earliest Westerners to question the validity of the dominant Western narrative, especially in global trade, economic power, and capitalism. John Hobson (2004) too, in his big picture of global history, *The Eastern Origins of Western Civilization*, has debunked the superiority of the West, and challenged the Eurocentric view as "false". Andre Gunder Frank (1998, 108–123) has also made the case for a Sinocentric world before the 19th century.

Enter Singapore, and the symbiosis of British colonialism and global power became a new geopolitical reality. On the one hand, the Lion City would have appeared to provide for the perpetuation of White rule and the narratives asserting its supremacy. On the other, Singapore was the bridge for East-West cultural intersections, a key junction on the maritime silk route, and a place where cultural heterogeneity unfolded. It developed during momentous global change in the 19th century. Britain was the pivot of the Eurocentric world and Singapore was fortuitous in having a colonial benefactor whose own fate would ultimately seal that of colonial rule in Asia. The first sign of the East-West conflict and competition was the Second World War, when Japan deflated British egoism.

Today, the perennial East-West conflict is frothing once again, with Samuel Huntington's (1996) thesis in *The Clash of Civilizations and the Remaking of World Order* seemingly at the contending edge of global politics; the matrix of 'we and others' described in Said's (1979) *Orientalism* dividing societies; and the US and China competing for global hegemonic dominance (Allison 2017). Huntington (1996, 28) has identified rivalry between civilisations as the cornerstone of global politics, thereby foregrounding the East-West fault lines: "local politics is the politics of ethnicity; global politics is the politics of civilizations. The rivalry of the superpowers is replaced by the clash of civilizations". Unfortunately, after the binding yoke of colonialism disintegrated, interethnic and interreligious conflicts erupted. Independent Singapore's incarnation of the multiethnic colonial cocoon has broken open into a turbulent global environment, and Singapore's sustaining power as a thriving port-city remains questionable in the eyes of many Western commentators. Huntington (1996), nonetheless, saw in the Singapore model of multiethnicity an interesting case study that could avert the clash of civilisations.

There is a need to pause, reflect, and take stock of how plural societies have cooperated and coexisted, and of where international trade has encouraged transnational economic relations for the benefit of many. Colonial Singapore was a unique creation which took many hands, hearts, and minds to see to its successful fruition. Today's Singapore is a cosmopolitan experiment where multiracial and religious plurality have been intended to succeed; a seeming oasis of such heterogenic expressions. The colonial politics of multiculturalism and religious diversity, conversely, have fallen apart in other multiethnic former colonies like India, Myanmar, Malaysia, and Indonesia.

Throughout the 19th century, few Westerners talked in terms of the East-West divide because colonialism had triumphed and Western hegemony prevailed. It is from these first-hand, if limited, experiences with 'native' culture, that many Western concepts on cultural interpretation were derived. Donald Lach (1965) has argued that the Western age of exploration in the 16th century had led to the sense of cultural relativity because Europeans were for the first time witnessing foreign cultures in their native habitats. Laura Nader (2015, xviii) views intercultural observations as opening up "comparative consciousness", while Said (1979) has contended that the East-West exchanges during the Age of Colonialism created social distancing between a 'we' and a 'they'. In colonial Singapore, the Whites did not treat the Asian society as equals, partly because many of the locals were employed as their domestic helpers, as subordinates in offices, and labourers on plantations. The other perspective is that the British, with their long colonial sojourn in India, borrowed the caste system, and anointed themselves as high-caste while relegating everyone else to being half-caste, low-caste, or outcast.

After the Second World War and the demise of Western supremacy, the East-West fusion became complex, contradictory, and confusing. Echoing the French possibilist position that man might change all and be himself determined by nothing else, Barber (1988, 19) saw Singapore's East-West importance as being the product of human decisions: "A man-made sentinel dominating the narrow waters between the China Seas and the Indian Ocean — and thus between east and west, between Asia and Europe — Singapore in those carefree days was irresistible". On the ground, Enright (1969, 181) found the students in the university difficult to comprehend: "They combine the stoical inwardness of the East with the sociably relaxed exterior of the West. Westernly progressive, they approve of family planning; Easternly philoprogenitive, they approve of babies. In a Western way they believe in ideas and creeds, symposia and forums, in an Eastern way — they believe in survival".

The island colony provided a natural environment for cultural exchange in its unique way, certainly not the American "melting pot" cultural brew that Huntington (2004, 128–131) discussed, but an indigenous *rojak* (or local salad) of ethnic groups and religions. Every Western resident or visitor to Singapore described distinct ethnic groups and their seemingly peculiar cultures, traditions, and beliefs. Over the century-and-a-half of colonial rule, there was relatively little fusion of a Singaporean cultural identity that Europeans could talk about, but there was liberal praise for the way the various groups interacted and intermingled. For many Western visitors and residents, there was also the perception of an informal social identity. The Europeans, however, maintained their social distance from the Asian population, and hence never really understood how they lived, worshipped, and felt.

Writing on what he saw was the cusp of an Asian Renaissance, C. Northcote Parkinson (1963) described a "piston-like process" of world history by arguing that the decline of one civilisation creates a cultural vacuum that is filled by an adjacent civilisation. Specifically, he predicted in the impending rise of the East, through the Chinese and Indian civilisations, a challenge for the West and a time of great readjustment, adaptation, accommodation, and resistance. Pre-dating the popularisation of the Thucydides Trap, Parkinson (1963) had similar observations about the transition of global hegemonic power. His smug colonial Orientalist posture did not allow for acceptance of the "spirit of renascent Asia"; he felt instead that the West needed to learn the "secret of how to resist" (Parkinson 1963, 298). Ideas of world unity and universalism were not in the Raffles Professor's historical vocabulary; these he believed would lead to mental stagnation.

Indeed, at a time of concern that social development in the developed world seemed to be rendered stagnant by capitalism, Austrian economist Joseph Schumpeter's (1942) concept of 'creative destruction' (whereby new ideas could emanate from the destruction of old ones) was coined, not to end capitalism per se, but to break the stranglehold of the conservative capitalistic system for it no longer served either the developed or developing worlds. This book too maintains that we require greater globalisation, not nationalism; more accountable local politics; and more innovative information technologies to forge a revolutionary change in the current economic system. To use Alfred Kroeber's (1963, 137–144) argument that civilisations start with creativity which then rigidify into civilisational styles, Western-style capitalism has hardened into an organisational mould that has stifled the global economic system and paralysed the escalator momentum in progress and development. With reference to the Singapore context, can Western narratives about its colonial development provide the Lion City with lessons about embracing change and not being complacent with established patterns?

Parkinson's (1963) argument, however, has not so far been quite translated into historical reality. The duration of Western hegemony over 500 years, beginning with the Portuguese and Spanish global expansion, has created a Western mindset or Western thesis around the world, diffused through the adoption of Western languages, culture, and science. Malaysian politician Anwar Ibrahim (1996, 45) in writing about *The Asian Renaissance*, has noted that five centuries have changed little in the East-West equation, with the divide remaining between the "powerful and the marginalised". This was the subtext of Francis Fukuyama's (1992) 'end of history' idea that the Western thesis remains globally dominant and unchallenged. If Singapore in colonial times maintained itself as a city of change and modernisation, a place ahead of its regional neighbours, it underscored Fukuyama's thesis. Modernity in colonial Singapore arrived from the West. Fast forward to the 21st century, and Fukuyama's thesis may yet be challenged. As one Asian journalist has observed in hyper-developed Singapore, "Modernity now begins in the East and flows West" (Khanna 2016, xxi).

It was only in the 20th century that Western dominance was shattered by the rise of Japan, especially its symbolic if transient victory over Singapore as the iconic edifice of British military prowess. It left a bitter aftertaste for many Britons, a defeat which till today has been hard to swallow. Close after Japan's rise has been China's expanding influence, first under communism and now under that regime's version of state capitalism. The discomfort with China among Westerners was revealed in derogatory slogans and images about the inscrutable East, the Yellow Peril, the Third China (the Chinese diaspora), and the diabolical fictional criminal mastermind Fu Manchu. Today it is reflected in perceptions of China's growing political, economic, and military threat.

Nevertheless, Dennis Bloodworth, the long-time Singapore resident who was privy to its cultural mix, had a more positive, nuanced view of East-West competition. Ending his book about the region, *An Eye for the Dragon* (1970), which he based on his assignments in Singapore from 1954 to 1970, and underscoring his own mixed marriage, the British correspondent saw the East-West interplay resulting in a happy union:

> In this context, the flirting and prying and filching and cannibalising that make up the latest, slightly obscene chapter in the long, brutal story of interplay between East and West must be welcomed. It may be the prelude to a respectable and responsible relationship. For the most dangerous liaisons of the past often lead to the safest marriages of the future (Bloodworth 1970, 384).

The perennial see-saw of East-West relations over history remains an intellectual comfort to historians supportive of Western supremacy, but the existing geopolitical relations at any time define the intricate historical processes of change and stagnation, peace and revolution, stability and fermentation. Small colonies like Singapore were relatively stable under colonial rule, and the prosperity of Singapore's free port seemed guaranteed under British hegemony. Singapore's Western traders, merchants, and entrepreneurs were opportunistic capitalists and their public commentaries and debates centred on the entrepôt's economic viability. However, like the diverse immigrant Asian population, the European visitors saw their Singapore sojourn as transient, an occasion to make their fortunes, after which they would return home as wealthy pensioners.

Despite the current global geopolitical turmoil and the rise of unpredictable personality politics (Savage 2019), Graham Allison (2017) wonders whether we are ringside observers and actors to the recurring Thucydides Trap that has emerged 16 times in history, and in its present form between the prevailing American and rising Chinese hegemons. The US-China tussle is undergirded by an East-West conflict, which has historically been one of three meta-geographical themes, the other two being the concerns with continents and nation-states. Small states like Singapore are likely to be victims or beneficiaries of great power conflict. In the 19th century, Singapore was on the winning side of the East-West competition. In the 21st century, it has an uncertain and ambivalent role in the Orient-Occident contest.

Is Singapore's sustainability going to reflect its domestic leadership and political ability, or the external geopolitical environment? In analysing European hegemony in the 13th and 14th centuries, Janet Abu-Lughod (1989, 368–372) debunked the clichéd 'rise and fall' of nations, empires, and civilisations, and postulated a "theory of systemic change" (i.e., technological change; connections leading to system declines) that better explains system decay and growth, and the complex interrelationships of independent variables, vectors, and so forth. Singapore's unique location will remain the same, but one wonders if the ever-changing external environment will create viable reorganisations, revitalisations, corrections, and integrations for Singapore to remain relevant as a player in regional and international affairs.

Singapore's foundation and development must be seen in a regional context. The city-state remains a continuation of the flourishing Sri Vijayan empire of the seventh and eighth centuries, the Singapura of the 14th century, and even heir to the Malaccan emporium of the 15th and 16th centuries. The one constant among these flourishing trading polities had been location in the Straits of Malacca, which served as a funnel of maritime traffic between the Indian Ocean and South China Sea. The regional geographer E. H. G. Dobby (1973, 146) noted the "centrifugal" role of the straits, representing the "climax of routes and relations" for 20th-century Singapore as it did for Palembang, Malacca, Jakarta, and Penang in previous periods of history. Sunil Amrith's (2013, 85) illuminating book *Crossing the Bay of Bengal* echoes Dobby's strategic view of the straits over the centuries, when he argues that the "narrow point" of the Straits of Malacca was a prized location in the contest between empires. Particular rulers and administrations should also be credited with the success stories of these polities. Is independent Singapore a product of a metamorphosis, a marriage of old traditions and new expressions, or a revolution, a break with its Indianised and colonial past?

VII. Raffles' Vision, Lee's Audacious Impact

Singapore, the Lion City, has become a singular success story since its independence in 1965. Many interpretations and reasons for this have been put forth. Donald Moore posited that the Singapore story has been anchored by two personalities, Sir Stamford Raffles and Lee Kuan Yew. Raffles founded the British colony and Lee is the father of the independent nation-state. Both had many things in common; both were pragmatists, linguists, and visionaries. They believed in the value of education, and were themselves erudite and well-read. They had astute geopolitical views. Most of all, they had a deep belief and passion about Singapore. Both were men of their times, who faced incredible challenges to seeing the success of *their* Singapore. Yet, their relationship to and management of Singapore differed. While Raffles attributed his choice of Singapore to Malay culture and history, the post-war Western commentators on Singapore such as Enright, Bloodworth, Parkinson, and C. P. Fitzgerald would credit the culture and enterprise of the dominant Chinese population as being key to Singapore's success.

Raffles founded Singapore on the back of a rising global hegemon. In this sense, he had the relatively easy task of planting the flag in a field with a strategic location where the British had already held much global sway. His masters in Calcutta and London, with their appetites for territory, were ready to pounce on a good idea, and spent little time debating Raffles' proposal and audacious moves on Singapore. Without knowledge of the *Sejarah Melayu*, Raffles would never have understood the pivotal role which Singapore had played in the transfer of power from Sri Vijaya-Palembang to Malacca. Singapore came alive for Raffles through the authors of the Malay classic. He plotted his acquisition of Singapore. Gambling his career to obtain it for the company, he took a bold decision and was determined to see it through. His idea was an almost single-handed endeavour. The subsequent legacy of the island's rapid development in the 19th century must, however, be attributed to its Residents and governors, civil servants, professionals, entrepreneurs, and the general working population.

One might ask what Lee inherited from British colonialism that gave rise to Singapore's astounding success in the postcolonial era. Two areas come to mind. The first is the overt legacy of forerunner institutions and policies which were handed down. These included the civil service, the institutions of law and order, urban planning, public housing and health, an educational system, an established defence infrastructure, and an economic system built around Singapore's importance as an international emporium, port, and trading centre. These were common features which Western sojourners perpetually narrated and shared. Singapore was a model colonial city; cosmopolitan, full of life, vigour, and commercial activity. It was at the same time also a place which put on a vulgar display of materialism, money-making, and life in the fast lane.

The second inheritance is less visible and direct, but ideologically the more powerful factor in understanding postcolonial developmental debates. What made Singapore's success almost miraculous in the eyes of Western academics, politicians, correspondents, government officials, and industrial titans is how the PAP government pulled off the psychological coup of turning Singapore around from being a dependency of Britain to a shining example of self-governed rapid development. The accomplishment of this within one generation is narrated by Lee (2000) in his book.

Under both colonialism and indigenous independent rule, the quest was to create states in the tropics that were similar to those of the Western developed nations. Singapore was an example of experimentation through colonial education and a parallel vernacular education system, provided for example by Christian mission schools and Chinese clan associations. The chief problem with the quest was that many colonial masters believed that colonial rule had to be the 'vanguard' of the process, hence the reluctance of Spanish, French, and Dutch colonialists in the region to give up that rule. Moreover, colonial rule for the most part would fail to create successful indigenous states.

Against this background, the post-war years created a whole body of social science debates, explanations, and prescriptions, as seen through the writings like Walt Rostow, Clifford Geertz, and Anne Booth, discussing why Third World states were failing to develop. Reading through these academic theses, one might conclude that Third World states could not break through the scaffolding of political, social, cultural, and economic impediments to rise to developed status. Given all these supposed obstacles, Singapore's attainment of First World status to become a poster child for emulation has been all the more surprising.

The Singapore which was dropped into Lee's hands was a product of extraneous circumstances and fraught with challenges. When Raffles founded Singapore, Britain was in the ascendant as a global power. Lee inherited Singapore at the end of that power. He quickly aligned his country to the new American global hegemon, making it Singapore's surrogate security custodian.

Raffles was an absentee manager of Singapore and had to accept that without William Farquhar and Crawfurd, the first two Residents of Singapore, his aspirations for the great entrepôt would never have been realised. Lee on the other hand was a resident leader who marshalled a diverse group of like-minded colleagues to lay the foundations of independent Singapore. Lee was an indefatigable leader who believed in its stability and sustainability. Whereas the rising fortunes of colonial Singapore had passed from Raffles through the hands of many British rulers with different personal agendas and leadership abilities, Lee's Singapore became a success story within 50 years of his lifetime. One might add that Singapore's fortunes have built on the actions of a third person who had a vision of its place in the region. Sang Nila Utama gave Tumasik its first window of regional success as an experimental trading centre; Stamford Raffles saw the geopolitical potential of colonial Singapore as a great trading port; and Lee Kuan Yew had the verve and determination to make an independent city-state a reality.

While modern Singapore's fame and viability have relied on percipient leadership, a talented and hardworking heterogeneous population, and an ever-changing external environment that has been adeptly managed for the city's benefit, what has not changed since Tumasik is its location. If the Portuguese apothecary Tomé Pires (1944) called 16th-century Malacca the "gullet of the world", then Singapore in the 19th century was Asia's gullet. But the global gullet over the longer term must be the entire Straits of Malacca, which has sponsored thriving ports from Ptolemy's Kataha (Kedah) to Palembang, Jambi, Pedir, Aceh, Malacca, Penang, and Singapore.

Raffles had conceived of, and Lee operationalised, modern Singapore's success and sustainability. The fate of neither the colonial city nor city-state was decided by nature. Raffles and Lee believed in the power of free choice, independent human decision, and were optimistic about Singapore's future. As Moore and his wife Joanna (1969, 1) wrote in their book *The First 150 Years of Singapore*, "Raffles, a beacon of almost blinding light at the beginning, pointing the way; Lee Kuan Yew, successor in a world not even Raffles, for all his vision, could have recognized, today".

Judged against the dismal record of city-states in history, Singapore's recent 50th anniversary of independence and 200th anniversary of Raffles' founding have had mixed reception. Singapore once rode the crest of British naval power and global hegemony, but the situation is different in the 21st century. The city-state has now to sustain itself on a delicate balance within a newly emerging multipolar world, when the region is undergoing political and economic change, and a wave of religious extremism threatens its multicultural matrix and religious heterogeneity. The window of the world is fraught with political insecurity and economic uncertainty.

While this book has focused on the documented past of Singapore, one would find in it relevant themes for the present and possible future outcomes. The temporal unity through which Singapore's Western narratives might be viewed is the Sanskrit term *trikalam*, literally 'three times', referring to the past, present, and future. Some historians might scoff at the idea of history repeating itself, as purists like to believe that all events are unique. Nonetheless as Toynbee (1971, 44) stated: "the repetitive element in history reveals itself as an instrument for freedom of creative action, and not as an indication that God and man are the slaves of fate". Few historians talk about patterns and lawful orders in history. Frederick Teggart, the Berkeley intellectual who founded its sociology department, took a brave stab at underscoring a more lawful order of history which entailed its scientific understanding as the result of given conditions, as opposed to its being simply a series of accidents. He titled his book *Theory and Processes of History* (Teggart 1962).

The reflections emerging from the Singapore historical narrative demonstrate three facets of colonial rule. Firstly, from the founding of Singapore, the political elites co-opted prominent White and Asian residents to lead various institutions and committees. The expertise of various groups such as bureaucrats, naturalists, doctors, missionaries, architects, lawyers, militia, bankers, businessmen, and traders was called upon, which gave some credence to the view that the colonial city was not run on a purely top-down decision-making system. This power-sharing relationship, however, varied from Resident to Resident and governor to governor.

Secondly, with the absence of elections and a democratic system, the Western perceptions of Singapore that emerged from all walks of life had to function as the available source of continuous feedback to the power elites and bureaucrats. The openness of this feedback through newspaper columns, books, journal articles, government reports, diaries, and academic studies has enabled researchers to view from hindsight the challenges and issues confronting the colony at various points. It has shown that perceptions were at times erroneous and at others percipient and constructive.

Thirdly, the momentum of Singapore's development was a product of both internal and external factors, given that the colonial entrepôt was also reliant on the external geopolitical and geo-economic environment. At the end of the day, the authorities had to ensure that the city was sustainable. With no domestic natural resources, as European residents and visitors repeatedly observed, Singapore relied heavily on its hinterland. Yet it seems a misconception that Singapore as the regional trading port had nothing of itself to offer. It served rather as an interchange of goods and services, a place for processing natural resources, a market where merchants were comfortable with exchanging their products through barter trading or monetary terms.

Singapore today requires a paradigm shift in thinking because the city-state faces new externalities. Global power is rapidly moving from West to East: a new economic and political system has arisen because of globalisation, the digitised information system has created a 24/7 operational sphere, and climate change has made environmental sustainability a national prerequisite. The question is whether cities and city-states will thrive better under the new global political, technological, and environmental paradigm shift when they had failed in earlier centuries. What the colonial era has taught us are three fundamental lessons: (1) change is an inevitable aspect of the life of societies and states which we must prepare for; (2) no matter how much comfort one gets accustomed to, never become complacent and overconfident; and (3) continually invest in oneself rather than depend on others to meet challenges ahead.

What Raffles and British colonialism did was to broaden Singapore's storyline from that of a surrogate entity in the *Alam Melayu* to one of a cosmopolitan but predominantly Chinese city on a global stage. Similarly, Western historians and colonial administrators have continually recounted Singapore's importance in the narrative of the Malay World. European sojourners in their accounts of regional travels kept alive Singapore's historic significance from classical times. While the hard evidence for this significance might seem sparse, the legends, myths, and folk history of the Lion City resonate among the region's *rakyat* or 'little people'. Unfortunately, neither current governments nor other politicians in Malaysia and Indonesia are inclined to acknowledge Singapore's historical interlude in the predominantly Malay region. The present-day Chinese dominance in Singapore creates for the neighbouring Malay political classes contingent history that deflects from the veracity of Singapore's role in the Malay World. Nonetheless, Singapura loomed "large in the social memories" of 16th- and 17th-century Malays because, as local historians assert, "it was on Singapura that the divine origins of the raja and the right to rule the Malay people was first enacted" (Kwa, Heng, and Tan 2009, 62).

In celebrating the 100th anniversary of Raffles' founding, the British administrators and European residents organised multifaceted activities to commemorate the momentous occasion. A two-volume tome of contributions was published to mark the event, titled *One Hundred Years of Singapore*. A chapter by Walter Makepeace (1921d) presented a thumbnail sketch of most of the Europeans who had made Singapore in its first century. It is a pity that in this entire written record, only the European efforts were saluted while there was complete silence on the Asian inputs and personalities. This was in many ways a biased tribute to British administration and colonialism. The many unnamed and unknown other hands and hearts that contributed to Singapore's development will unfortunately remain forgotten. The last chapter, recording the centenary day festivities, was upbeat about the future. The writer, Gilbert Brooke (1921b, 585), concluded:

> The first century of its history, now ended, has been a long romance, and Singapore stands on the threshold of an unknown future pregnant with potential prosperity. We can but hope that she dreams and efforts of the past will prove to be an inspiration and stimulus to those who, during the coming centuries, will shape the destinies of the land which lay so near the heart of its great founder — SIR THOMAS STAMFORD RAFFLES.

With the republic now having passed the bicentennial of modern Singapore, the founding fathers and mothers of the independent Lion City would want the contributions of everyone to be recognised as part of its inclusive and unexpected development:

> A nation is great not by its size alone. It is the will, the cohesion, the stamina, the discipline of the people and the quality of their leaders which ensure it an honourable place in history (Moore and Moore 1969, 702).

Singapore in the next 50 years is a challenging proposition. The city-state in order to survive and thrive cannot ride on the coat-tails of the flying geese formation of more developed countries. It has to forge ahead and be inventive. As a fledgling developed state, it has to stand on its own feet and compete with the best in the world. This is going to be difficult at a time of changing hegemonies, nationalistic expressions, climate change challenges, and the hyper-accountability demanded by the IT revolution. Is the Singapore cultural, economic, and political ecosystem ready to withstand the global challenge and be an independent, creative force in regional and world affairs? Is Singapore's domestic political and intellectual scaffolding strong enough to lead rather than simply follow trends? Has it fostered a resilient society that can throw up innovative ideas, nurture creative leaders, and cultivate a self-sustaining stable political system? The future is open-ended with many black swan scenarios and many seemingly predictable outcomes.

Glossary

adat
In the Malay World, the term *adat* commonly refers to local custom. Hence, in land tenure, one sees inheritance rights concerning land that are based on local custom, and such land is deemed customary land. In Singapore, the occupancy of land by Malays was often based on *adat*. When the British bought over Singapore, they introduced a land tenure system based on Roman laws.

Alam Melayu
The Malay World. Its ambit was taken as the geographical realm of much of insular Southeast Asia, which was considered to include the area covered by modern Indonesia, Singapore, Malaysia, Brunei, southern Thailand, and the southern Philippines. This area was where the lingua franca was essentially any of the dialect variations of Malay.

amok
The term for individual Malay men who go momentarily berserk; running out of control and killing people. The Western view was that those who ran *amok* were on a suicidal trip.

atap
The leaves from the nipah palm (*Nypa fruticans*) were widely used in Southeast Asia for thatching the roofs of native houses. Hence, the houses

were often called *atap* houses. In some parts of the region besides Singapore, different palm leaves were used for thatch roofs. A common type was the sugar palm (*Arenga pinnata*) found on the roofs of Batak houses in Sumatra.

ayah
Ayahs were Asian women employed by early White settlers as babysitters in their homes. Most of the first *ayahs* were Indian. Over time the term came to refer to the helpers in the general hospital dealing with non-medical activities.

batu hidup
In Malay, the term refers to a living stone or rock. For much of their prehistory and history, the Malays were animist in their beliefs. Hence, they saw rocks and stones as living entities. After the arrival of Islam, such animist beliefs died down among Malay Muslims. In the past, *batu hidup* were revered as *keramats*.

Belle Époque
At the time when high colonialism was gaining deep inroads into various colonies, Europe and the US were also at their economic apogees. The *Belle Époque* often delineates the period of the Western economic and cultural heights between 1880 to 1914. Specifically, the French refer to *la Belle Époque* as 'the beautiful epoch' that was defined by optimism, economic prosperity, peace in the Western hemisphere, colonial expansion, technological innovation, and cultural and artistic development. This was for the West the golden age of civilisation and it transmitted to colonies in Southeast Asia, including Singapore, the sense of Western confidence and its superiority complex, as well as the cultural divergence between Whites and native societies.

Bukit Larangan
The site of the royal residence of the kings of Tumasik in the 13th to 14th centuries would over time be referred to by the Malay population as Bukit Larangan or 'forbidden hill'. It had originally been forbidden as a mark of respect for its royal aura. However, the Malays also came to believe the place to be haunted, hence one's being forbidden to go there. In colonial times it was called Fort Canning Hill or Government Hill.

bumboat
A generic term for small boats transferring goods or passengers between oceangoing ships and the shore. In Singapore, the term applied specifically to local cargo boats that for decades plied its rivers for these purposes. Singapore River *tongkangs* or *twakows* (wide-bodied, flat-bottomed barges or lighters for the transportation of traded goods) were in this category. More recently, with tourist traffic along the Singapore River, passenger boats are also being referred to as bumboats.

Cellates
A common term used to refer to the roving *orang laut* in the straits around Singapore.

chandi
The *chandi* is associated with the Hindu-Buddhist architectural ruins found in Java and Bali. There are many theories about *chandis*. Some believe they are graves or memorials to important *devarajas* (god-kings) of past Javanese kingdoms. Others see them as purely religious artefacts for reverence and worship.

chettiar
Since the days of Thomas Stamford Raffles, Indian moneylenders called *chettiars* had been part of Singapore's economic ecosystem. Given that there were few banks, they provided much of the funding for various activities and developments, notably for the local population. Up to the early 1970s, the *chettiars* were found especially along Market Street. They complemented the banks in Raffles Place with small loans to individuals that required no collaterals but involved high interest rates. Despite the informality of their moneylending activities, *chettiars* were in some ways institutionalised in the Market Street-Raffles Place business district.

Chuliah/Chulia
The term *Chuliah* is based on a geographical, ethnic region in southern India. The Chuliahs were a diaspora found in various parts of Southeast Asia — Myanmar, the Malay Peninsula, Singapore, and Indonesia. Just as the term *Kling* referred to people from the district of Kalinga in India, that of *Chuliah* referred similarly to a specific area of Indian outmigration. In Singapore, Chulia Street signified generally the concentration of Indians

around Raffles Place, which included Hindu *chettiars* and Indian Muslims.

daulat

Though *daulat* refers to magic by Malay Muslim sultans, the idea of the spiritual prowess of royalty in the Malay World originates from the earlier Indian concept of spiritual power wielded by the *devarajas* (god-kings). While in the Islamic tradition no human being is considered a divine person, the notion of *daulat* still gave sultans an aura of magical power that they could wield at will.

devaraja

The concept of *devaraja* refers to the god-king (*deva* meaning god, and *raja*, king). The idea was first introduced in ancient Cambodia in the ninth century AD by Jayavarman II, founder of the Khmer empire of Angkor. For centuries, the cult provided the religious basis for the royal authority of the Khmer kings. It gave Cambodian kings supernatural power over their subjects, who worshipped them as deities. The idea of *devaraja* is closely associated with Indianisation and its spread in Southeast Asia, which covered both the mainland and the island world.

five-foot way

One of the defining characteristics of the Singapore shophouse since its inception in the early 19th century was the provision of covered common pedestrian walkways which were colloquially termed five-foot ways, or what the Malays called *lima kaki*. Such covered walkways are only found in Singapore and the Malay Peninsula and nowhere else in Southeast Asia. The five-foot way was meant to provide a sheltered walkway against the unpredictable tropical weather of heavy rainfall and unbearable sunshine. As a result of these five-foot ways, in the 19th century there were riots that took place between shopkeepers who used the passageways as extensions of their shops, and pedestrians, who needed to walk through the five-foot ways.

gambier

Gambier (*Uncaria gambir*) was a widespread commercial crop that was found in the 18th and 19th centuries in Indonesia's Riau Archipelago, the Malay Peninsula, and Singapore. It was used as a tanning agent, a brown dye, a food additive, and as herbal medicine. The peak of Singapore's gambier trade was between the 1830s and 1850s, when demand was driven by the British dyeing and leather-tanning industries. It was initially used as medicine and chewed with betel. Also known as pale catechu, white catechu, or Japan Earth, it is often confused with other forms of catechu. The first Chinese gambier planters arrived in Singapore before Raffles and had colonised Pearl's Hill. After Raffles' arrival, gambier became a commercially viable crop in Singapore because the colonial administration could not police the island's land tenure system. The gambier industry needed vast amounts of timber for firewood to boil the plant for processing, and given the large available areas of forest, deforestation was massive in Singapore.

gamelan
The *gamelan* is a musical orchestra used in Java and Bali. It comprises many instruments that are made essentially of brass, which gives a metallic sound to music. Wherever Javanese-influenced cultural dances, music, and theatre are performed in the Malay World, one finds a *gamelan* underpinning these performances.

gharry
A 19th-century reference to horse-drawn carriages which were used as the means of transportation by Westerners. The term *gharry* was mainly employed in the British colonies in India, Burma, Malaya, and Singapore. In India, the locals who manned the carriages were referred to as *gharry-wallahs*.

high colonialism
The period of high colonialism is often taken by Western historians of Southeast Asia as being between 1870 to 1940. Given the varied colonial experiences in the region (Portuguese, Spanish, Dutch, French, and British), there were differing time periods of engagement in colonies. In general, however, the high colonial period encompassed four factors. (1) This was the era when Western activity went from pinprick colonialism to territorial expansion that gave colonial powers vast control under the land tenure systems of their imperial colonies, road and railway transport systems, and port expansions. (2) It was when the Western capitalistic expansion was at its zenith in terms of trade, plantation activities, mining, and the monetisation of the colonial economy. (3) Western powers also moved to colonise native cultures through education, Western language,

Christian proselytisation, and urban planning. (4) Finally and ironically, during this period of colonial consolidation and landscape transformation, the seeds of anti-colonialism were nurtured. Later, the Japanese Occupation provided the catalyst for what would become a groundswell of stirrings for independence.

Indian Archipelago/East Indies
For most of the 2,000 years during which Westerners have referred to Southeast Asia in texts and maps, the region has been subsumed under the umbrella of India. Hence, its place names often related to India. This originated from Ptolemy's first-century atlas in which Southeast Asia was referred to as 'India beyond the Ganges'. In short, the region never had an identity of its own until the late 19th century; Western historians often referred to it as Greater India or Further India.

istana
A Malay term for the palace of a sultan or raja, or the residence of the highest-ranking official of a community in a place. In Singapore, with Raffles signing the treaty with the eldest son of the sultan of Riau, an *istana* was built in Kampong Glam for the sultan. Known as the Istana Kampong Glam, the building erected by George Coleman in 1840 has become a symbol of Malay royalty in Singapore. After independence, the Singapore government turned the British governor's residence into the President's Istana.

joss/josh house
In the early 19th century, Westerners referred to Chinese temples in Singapore as joss or josh houses. These terms came about because the Chinese use joss sticks in their worship rituals.

kampong/kampung/campong/compong
The term *kampong* is commonly used in Southeast Asia, both in the Malay World, as well as in Cambodia, Thailand, and Vietnam. It often means a rural village, a nucleated settlement found in peasant agricultural areas. In Cham areas in Cambodia and Vietnam, the reference to *kampongs* or *compongs* is quite common, as with Kampong Cham in Cambodia. Though it is commonly viewed as a physical entity, a *kampong* can also have sociological and cultural connotations. In Singapore, most of the early Malay *kampongs* were essentially fishing villages along the coastline or riverine areas.

kebun

A Malay term for a garden. Malay houses were known for often being fronted by gardens, as they had a cultural liking for flowers, vegetables, and vegetation that surrounded their dwellings. In colonial Singapore, Malays and Indians were commonly employed by Westerners as gardeners, whom they also called *kebuns* (derived from the Malay terms for gardener, *pekebun* or *tukang kebun*), to tend to their house-and-garden homes.

keramat/kramat

A *keramat*, or *kramat*, is a sacred place in the Malay World. It could be a grave site, such as the Keramat Iskandar Shah in Fort Canning, or even a tree, like the Keramat Radin Mas which is a grave buried within a banyan tree. The banyan tree is often taken in the region's animistic beliefs as being sacred. A *keramat* sometimes expresses the syncretic fusion of prehistoric animistic worship and Islamic influences.

Kling

A colloquial term referring in general to the southern Indians, said to originate from the name given to Indians from Kalinga. Chulia Street was originally called Kling Street. The Indians, however, felt the name *Kling* was derogatory and Kling Street was renamed Chulia Street.

kraton

The *kraton* in Java and Bali is the royal enceinte of the sultan or raja, where the royal palace, the royal temple, and the king's assembly hall are located. One of the best preserved *kratons* is found in Yogyakarta where an active sultan still conducts his royal ceremonies and rituals. The *kraton* is often seen as a place of spiritual and political power.

kris

The Malay *kris*, or *keris*, is a distinctive, asymmetrical dagger originally from Indonesia and now ubiquitous throughout the Malay World. The wavy curves popularly associated with *kris* blades can be fatal for anyone who has been stabbed with them. The *kris* has symbolic significance. Both weapon and spiritual object, the *kris* is considered to possess magical powers. The earliest known examples go back to the 10th century and most probably spread from the island of Java throughout Southeast Asia.

mandala

This is the magical symbol of a circle enclosed in a square. It is found in Tantric Buddhism and can be seen as spatially manifested in Indianised capitals in Southeast Asia. The Buddhist *chandi* of Borobudur is a good representation of the mandala. Many of the cosmic kingdoms of Southeast Asia, including Tumasik, were based on mandala symbolism.

masuk Melayu

The expression *masuk Melayu* literally means 'to enter into Malayness' or 'become Malay', and refers to someone adopting a Malay identity. The Malay community is seen as being able to assimilate non-Malays if the latter practise three basic components of Malay identity: (1) speaking Malay; (2) behaving like Malays in terms of dress, eating, and other cultural behaviours; and (3) being Muslim. The early Chinese residents in Malacca and Penang fulfilled two of these components but became known as Peranakan because they did not convert to Islam.

Melayu

The term *Melayu* refers to the Malay peoples of Sumatra and the Malay Peninsula. It was originally a Javanese reference which was not very complimentary. The Javanese used *Melayu* to denote a fugitive or an exile. For culturally diverse Indonesia, the Malay is one of its 150 ethnic groups.

mission civilisatrice

One of the colonial crusades, engaged in especially by the French, was the *mission civilisatrice* with its sense of national calling to bring enlightenment to the colonies; in the case of Southeast Asia, these were in French Indo-China. As colonial expansion took place from the late 15th century onwards, what would come to be called the *mission civilisatrice* provided a political rationalisation for both military intervention and colonisation based on the modernisation and Westernisation of indigenous peoples. This was translated as French education, the promotion of the French language, and the bringing of French culture (the visual and performing arts, and literature) and Christianity to native peoples. Unlike the British in general, the French believed that they could 'civilise' these peoples to behave in accordance with French culture. The French *mission civilisatrice* was implemented in its entirety in the last quarter of the 19th century and continued till the end of colonialism. The Spanish *misión civilizadora* and Portuguese *missão civilizadora* underscored similar objectives in their respective colonial domains.

Mount Meru
In both the Hindu and Buddhist religions, the world revolves round a sacred mountain. Among the Hindus, the mountain is referred to as Mahameru and among the Buddhists, it is called Sumeru. Mount Meru is the abode of the gods. Geographically speaking, one may correlate it to the Himalayan mountains north of India. Hence, the waters of the holy river Ganges, which is believed to have its source in Mount Meru, are viewed by Hindus as sacred.

negara
In a broad sense, the Malays refer to a *negara* as a state with rather ambiguous borders. In the history of the region, a *negara* would expand and contract depending on the ruler (i.e. *devaraja*, sultan, or raja) in power.

orang laut
The term means the 'people of the sea'. They were a distinct group who lived on boats in the Malay Archipelago, ranging from the Andaman Islands to the Riau Archipelago. David Sopher referred to them as the 'sea nomads' and others called them the 'sea gypsies'.

orang puteh
The reference in Malay to 'White people'.

padang
A *padang* is an open field which is commonly found in Indonesia and Malaysia. Before the time of assembly halls, the *padang* was the area where people gathered. Coming from Bencoolen or Bengkulu in Sumatra, Raffles was familiar with the local importance of a *padang*. Ironically, the Padang in Singapore was located in the north side or European sector of the colonial town rather than in the Asian sector. In the early 19th century, Europeans used horse carriages to drive around the Padang for fresh air. Singapore's Padang has come to be associated with many important national occasions, parades, and celebrations.

pasar
Malay term for a local 'wet' market. In the Malay Archipelago, a *pasar* could be permanent in one location or appear cyclically, in certain places on particular days. The *pasar* generally was a venue where produce gathered by farmers would be sold. In the early days, the produce could be exchanged on a barter basis.

passisir
The term *passisir* was used in the 16th century to define the series of trading towns on the north coast of Java, from Gresik to Surabaya. The *passisir* towns were the fountainhead of Islamic diffusion into Java, and hence carried a mixed culture. Since the Hindu-Buddhist agrarian civilisations in inland Java had no place for traders or merchants, the adoption of Islam by the *passisir* traders gave them a new cultural and elevated identity.

Peranakan
The Peranakans, known colloquially as *Nonya Baba*, were the Straits-born Chinese who adopted elements of Malay culture and behaviour. The Peranakans had their origins in Malacca when Chinese traders and merchants intermarried with Malay women and created a new fused cultural identity. Peranakans were also found in Penang and parts of Indonesia. Many of these people, especially from Malaya, came to Singapore when it was established in 1819.

permatang
A *permatang* is a common man-made physical feature found especially in rice fields, where it is the ridge that divides the flooded field. In most agrarian rice areas, the *permatang* serves as a walkway for farmers to get from one place to another.

raja
A term for a king, used especially in the Malay World.

rakyat
A common Malay term that refers to people or the common masses. Sometimes the reference deals with what is called colloquially the 'little people'.

sampan
A small wooden boat that is manned by one rower. Before bridges were built across the Singapore River, there were many points along the river where *sampans* ferried people from the north to the south side of Singapore town. One of the areas where *sampans* were used till the late 1960s was between Alkaff Quay (the Havelock Road area) and the godowns at Clarke Quay.

sarong
An outfit that is in widespread use from India to Oceania. In various parts of this area, males and females wear what is sometimes called a 'tubular skirt' around their waist. In the Malay World it is referred to as *sarong*; in India such outfits are called *dhoti*; in Myanmar, as *longyi*; in the Pacific Islands they are called *lavalava* or *pareau*; and in Fiji, wrap-around *sulu*.

shophouse
Singapore had a unique distinction of developing the ubiquitous shophouse which served multiple functions including residence, retailing, wholesaling, and cottage manufacturing. Up to the 1960s, the shophouse accommodated over 60 per cent of Singapore's population in the Central Area which was covered by the original 1822 Raffles Town Plan. With urban renewal, the shophouse has now become a major conservation entity in many parts of Singapore such as Kampong Glam, Chinatown, Little India, and Syed Alwi Road.

Singapura (Singapore)
In Sanskrit, the name means a 'lion city'. The *Sejarah Melayu* or *Malay Annals* provide the best written documentation of how Singapore got its name. Most historians believe this account of Singapore's toponymic is wrapped in local myth and folklore. The 16th-century Portuguese historians, travellers, and officials also provided various interpretations of Singapore's name, quite different from that of the *Sejarah Melayu*. The name *Lion City* was not only used for Singapore but for other kingdoms in the region — in Vietnam, Thailand, and Indonesia. Even the location of Singapore was not well defined. In the 16th and 17th centuries, Western cartographers sited it in various locations in southern Johore.

temenggong
A prime minister; someone in charge of the fiefdom of a ruler. In Singapore, the *temenggong*'s jurisdiction was a sort of fief for the sultan of Riau. When Raffles landed in Singapore, he had to sign a treaty with both the *temenggong* (resident at the Singapore River) and the eldest son of the Sultan of Riau (resident at Kampong Glam).

toa poh* and *sio poh
The references in the Chinese Hokkien dialect to Singapore's 'big town' (*toa poh*, Chinatown) and 'small town' (*sio poh*, the Western town). The colloquial names were a dig at the colonial demarcation of the administrative centre on the north side of the river and the residential area of the native population on the south side. The Chinese thus considered Chinatown as the big town and the colonial administrative town as the small town.

towkay
Hokkien reference to a wealthy Chinese businessman. Over time, *towkay* became a universal expression in Singapore denoting someone who is rich, or simply a boss, or business-owner.

tuan/tuan besar
References by the native Malay population to White persons holding superior roles. *Tuan* is often taken as 'sir'. The term *tuan besar* means a 'big *tuan*' or 'big sir', usually a head of an organisation or administration.

Tumasik/Temasek
The proposed old name for Singapore. The *orang laut* used the term *tasikor* to refer to the sea. Hence, one understanding of the origins of the name *Tumasik* is that it is derived from the *orang laut* reference to the sea. Mentions of Tumasik appear in Javanese historical documents as well as Chinese cartographic and travellers' accounts. Ironically, there is only one eyewitness account of what Tumasik was in the 14th century and it comes from a lesser-known Chinese traveller, Wang Dayuan.

Ujong Tanah
Since the 13th century, itinerant traders in the thalassic kingdoms as well as *orang laut* used to refer to Singapore Island as Ujong Tanah, which in Malay means the 'farthest land', as seen from the perspective of the Asian continent.

vanua

Vanua is a common reference in the precolonial (Austronesian; Indianised) society of the Malay World, to three elements of spirit, place, and human beings, which define the complex fusion of the cultural, physical, and social dimensions of a locality. The term *vanua* thus implies that people in this area have a sense of belonging and identity that is bound up generally in the founding ancestors of the ethnic group.

wayang/wayang kulit

Wayang is a colloquial term in the Malay World for a theatre-type play activity, ranging from shadow puppetry to human performances involving dance and drama. The term *wayang* is also often used in Singapore to define Chinese street opera, which was popular at certain times of the Chinese cultural calendar such as the Lunar New Year or Seventh Ghost Month. While it is common for the generic term *wayang* to apply to Chinese street opera, the Malays have more specific references to their own performances. Their most popular *wayang* in Malaysia, Indonesia, and southern Thailand is the *wayang kulit* or 'shadow play'.

wet market

A colloquial term for a market which sells a wide variety of foods, especially fresh produce that includes meat (chicken, duck, beef, mutton, pork), vegetables, and sea produce (fish, squid, prawns, crabs, clams). In Chinese, the wet market refers to a market selling perishable goods. The name is an expression of messiness; wet markets tend not to have dry floors. In the past, wet markets in Singapore were open air and were only later housed in covered areas. Due to the multiracial population vendors sold various culturally specific produce that catered to Chinese, Malay, Indian, and European preferences.

REFERENCES AND SELECTED BIBLIOGRAPHY

Abu-Lughod, Janet L. 1989. *Before European Hegemony: The World System A.D. 1250–1350*. New York: Oxford University Press.
Adams, Arthur. 1848. *Notes from a Journal of Research into the Natural History of the Countries Visited during the Voyage of H.M.S. Samarang under the Command of Captain Sir Edward Belcher, C.B., F.R.A.S.* London: Reeve, Benham, and Reeve.
Alatas, Syed Hussein. 1971. *Thomas Stamford Raffles, 1781–1826: Schemer or Reformer? An account of his political philosophy and its relation to the Massacre of Palembang, the Banjarmasin Affair, and some of his views and legislations, during his colonial career in Java, Sumatra, and Singapore*. Sydney: Angus and Robertson.
Allen, Louis. 1977. *Singapore 1941–1942*. London: Davis-Poynter.
Allison, Graham. 2017. *Destined for War: Can America and China Escape Thucydides's Trap?* New York: Houghton Mifflin Harcourt.
Amrith, Sunil S. 2013. *Crossing the Bay of Bengal: The Furies of Nature and the Fortunes of Migrants*. Cambridge, MA: Harvard University Press.
Andaya, Barbara Watson. 2019. Recording the Past of 'Peoples without History': Southeast Asia's Sea Nomads. *Asian Review* 32 (1): 5–33.
Andaya, Barbara Watson, and Leonard Y. Andaya. 2015. *A History of Early Modern Southeast Asia, 1400–1830*. Cambridge: Cambridge University Press.
Anderson, Benedict. 1991. *Imagined Communities: Reflections on the Origin and Spread of Nationalism*. London; New York: Verso.
Anderson, Isabel. 1934. *In Eastern Seas: With a Visit to Insulinde and the Golden Chersonese*. Boston: Bruce Humphries.

Anderson, John. 1824. *Political and Commercial Considerations Relative to the Malayan Peninsula, and the British Settlements in the Straits of Malacca*. Prince of Wales Island: Printed under the Authority of Government by William Cox.

Anderson, Kurt. 2017. *Fantasyland: How America Went Haywire, A 500-Year History*. New York: Random House.

Anderson, Patrick. 1955. *Snake Wine: A Singapore Episode*. London: Chatto & Windus.

Anwar, Ibrahim. 1996. *The Asian Renaissance*. Singapore: Times Books International.

Appiah, Kwame Anthony. 2006. *Cosmopolitanism: Ethics in a World of Strangers*. New York: W. W. Norton.

Architectural Restoration Consultants. n.d. *Mount Washington*. Unpublished manuscript. Singapore.

Armstrong, John. 2010. *In Search of Civilization: Remaking a Tarnished Idea*. London: Penguin Books.

Arrighi, Giovanni. 2010. *The Long Twentieth Century: Money, Power and the Origins of Our Times*. London: Verso.

Ashcroft, Bill, Gareth Griffiths, and Helen Tiffin. 1998. *Post-Colonial Studies: The Key Concepts*. London: Routledge.

Baker, Jim. 2005. *The Eagle in the Lion City: America, Americans and Singapore*. Singapore: Landmark Books.

Balestier, J. 1848. View of the State of Agriculture in the British Possessions in the Straits of Malacca. *Journal of the Indian Archipelago and Eastern Asia* 2 (3): 139–150.

Barber, Noel. 1971. *The War of the Running Dogs: How Malaya Defeated the Communist Guerrillas, 1948–60*. London: Collins.

———. 1978. *The Singapore Story: From Raffles to Lee Kuan Yew*. London: Fontana.

———. 1988. *Sinister Twilight: The Fall of Singapore*. London: Arrow Books.

Barendse, R. J. 2002. *The Arabian Seas: The Indian Ocean World of the Seventeenth Century*. New Delhi: Vision Books.

Barley, Nigel, ed. 1999. *The Golden Sword: Stamford Raffles and the East*. London: British Museum Press.

Barnard, Timothy P. 2016. *Nature's Colony: Empire, Nation and Environment in the Singapore Botanic Gardens*. Singapore: NUS Press.

———, ed. 2004. *Contesting Malayness: Malay Identity Across Boundaries*. Singapore: Singapore University Press.

Barrow, John. 1806. *A Voyage to Cochinchina, in the years 1792 and 1793: Containing a general view of the valuable productions and the political importance of this flourishing kingdom; and also of such European settlements as were visited on the voyage: with sketches of the Manners,*

Character, and Condition of their several inhabitants. To which is annexed An Account of a Journey, made in the years 1801 and 1802, to the residence of the chief of the Booshuana Nation, being the remotest point in the interior of Southern Africa to which Europeans have hitherto penetrated. The facts and descriptions taken from a manuscript journal. With a chart of the route. London: T. Cadell and W. Davies.

Bartley, W. 1982. The Population of Singapore in 1819. In *Singapore 150 Years*, edited by Mubin Sheppard, p. 117. Published for the Malaysian Branch of the Royal Asiatic Society. Singapore: Times Books International.

Barzini, Luigi. 1984. *The Europeans*. New York: Penguin Books.

Bastin, J. S. 1960. *The Western Element in Modern Southeast Asian History*. Papers on Southeast Asian Subjects, No. 2. Kuala Lumpur: Department of History, University of Malaysia.

———. 1965. Introduction. In *Political and Commercial Considerations Relative to the Malayan Peninsula and the British Settlements in the Straits of Malacca*, by John Anderson, pp. 1–10. Singapore: MBRAS.

———. 2019. *Sir Stamford Raffles and Some of His Friends and Contemporaries: A Memoir of the Founder of Singapore*. Singapore: World Scientific.

Begbie, P. J. 1834. *The Malayan Peninsula: Embracing Its History, Manners and Customs of the Inhabitants, Politics, Natural History &c. from its earliest Records*. Madras: Vepery Mission Press.

Benda, Harry J., and John A. Larkin. 1967. *The World of Southeast Asia: Selected Historical Readings*. New York: Harper & Row.

Benjamin, Geoffrey. 2002. On Being Tribal in the Malay World. In *Tribal Communities in the Malay World: Historical, Cultural and Social Perspectives*, edited by Geoffrey Benjamin and Cynthia Chou, pp. 7–76. Leiden: IIAS; Singapore: ISEAS.

Benjamin, Geoffrey, and Cynthia Chou, eds. 2002. *Tribal Communities in the Malay World: Historical, Cultural and Social Perspectives*. Leiden: IIAS; Singapore: ISEAS.

Bennett, George. 1834. *Wanderings in New South Wales, Batavia, Pedir Coast, Singapore, and China; Being the Journal of a Naturalist in those Countries, during 1832, 1833, and 1834*, vol. 2. London: Richard Bentley.

Berdoulay, Vincent. 1974. The Emergence of the French School of Geography (1870–1914). Unpublished PhD diss. Berkeley: Department of Geography, University of California.

Berry, Graham. 2015. *From Kilts to Sarongs: Scottish Pioneers of Singapore*. Singapore: Landmark Books.

Berry, Linda. 1982. *Singapore's River: A Living Legacy*. Singapore: Eastern Universities Press.

Bird, Isabella L. [Mrs. Bishop]. 1883. *The Golden Chersonese and the Way Thither*. New York: G. P. Putnam's Sons.

Blagden, C. O. 1921. Singapore Prior to 1819. In *One Hundred Years of Singapore: Being Some Account of the Capital of the Straits Settlements from its Foundation by Sir Stamford Raffles on the 6th February 1819 to the 6th February 1919*, vol. 1, edited by Walter Makepeace, Gilbert E. Brooke, and Roland St. J. Braddell, pp. 1–5. London: John Murray.

Blaut, J. M. 1953. The Economic Geography of a One-Acre Farm in Singapore: A Study in Applied Microgeography. *Journal of Tropical Geography* (1): 37–48.

Bleackley, Horace. 1928. *A Tour in Southern Asia: (Indo-China, Malaya, Java Sumatra, and Ceylon, 1925–1926)*. London: John Lane The Bodley Head.

Bloodworth, Dennis. 1970. *An Eye for the Dragon: Southeast Asia Observed: 1954–1970*. New York: Farrar, Straus and Giroux.

———. 1986. *The Tiger and the Trojan Horse*. Singapore: Times Books International.

Bogaars, G. E. 1982. The Effect of Opening the Suez Canal on the Trade and Development of Singapore. In *Singapore 150 Years*, edited by Mubin Sheppard, pp. 220–264. Published for the Malaysian Branch of the Royal Asiatic Society. Singapore: Times Books International.

Booth, Anne. 1998. *The Indonesian Economy in the Nineteenth and Twentieth Centuries: A History of Missed Opportunities*. New York: St. Martin's Press.

Bowen, John R. 1983. Cultural Models for Historical Genealogies: The Case of the Melaka Sultanate. In *Melaka: The Transformation of a Malay Capital, c. 1400–1980, Volume One*, edited by Kernial Singh Sandhu and Paul Wheatley, pp. 162–179. Kuala Lumpur: Oxford University Press.

Bowring, Philip. 2019. *Empire of the Winds: The Global Role of Asia's Great Archipelago*. London: I. B. Tauris.

Braddell, Roland. 1921a. A Short History of the Colony. In *One Hundred Years of Singapore: Being Some Account of the Capital of the Straits Settlements from its Foundation by Sir Stamford Raffles on the 6th February 1819 to the 6th February 1919*, vol. 1, edited by Walter Makepeace, Gilbert E. Brooke, and Roland St. J. Braddell, pp. 12–31. London: John Murray.

———. 1921b. The Good Old Days. In *One Hundred Years of Singapore: Being Some Account of the Capital of the Straits Settlements from its Foundation by Sir Stamford Raffles on the 6th February 1819 to the 6th February 1919*, vol. 2, edited by Walter Makepeace, Gilbert E. Brooke, and Roland St. J. Braddell, pp. 465–524. London: John Murray.

———. 1935. *The Lights of Singapore*. London: Methuen.

Braddell, T. 1855. Notes on the Chinese in the Straits. *Journal of the Indian Archipelago and Eastern Asia* 9 (2): 109–124.

Braudel, Fernand. 1972. *The Mediterranean and the Mediterranean World in the Age of Philip II*, vol. 1. Translated by Siân Reynolds. New York: Harper & Row, 1972–1973.

———. 1973. *The Mediterranean and the Mediterranean World in the Age of Philip II*, vol. 2. Translated by Siân Reynolds. New York: Harper & Row, 1972–1973.

———. 1981. *The Structures of Everyday Life: The Limits of the Possible*. Vol. 1 of *Civilization and Capitalism, 15th–18th Century*. Translated by Siân Reynolds. New York: Harper & Row, 1981–1984.

———. 1982. *The Wheels of Commerce*. Vol. 2 of *Civilization and Capitalism, 15th–18th Century*. Translated by Siân Reynolds. New York: Harper & Row, 1981–1984.

Brooke, Gilbert E. 1921a. Botanic Gardens and Economic Notes. In *One Hundred Years of Singapore: Being Some Account of the Capital of the Straits Settlements from its Foundation by Sir Stamford Raffles on the 6th February 1819 to the 6th February 1919*, vol. 2, edited by Walter Makepeace, Gilbert E. Brooke, and Roland St. J. Braddell, pp. 63–78. London: John Murray.

———. 1921b. The Centenary Day and Its Celebration. In *One Hundred Years of Singapore: Being Some Account of the Capital of the Straits Settlements from its Foundation by Sir Stamford Raffles on the 6th February 1819 to the 6th February 1919*, vol. 2, edited by Walter Makepeace, Gilbert E. Brooke, and Roland St. J. Braddell, pp. 570–585. London: John Murray.

Brooke, James. 1848. *Narrative of Events in Borneo and Celebes, Down to the Occupation of Labuan: From the Journals of James Brooke, Esq. Rajah of Sarāwak, and Governor of Labuan. Together with a Narrative of the Operations of H.M.S. Iris. By Captain Rodney Mundy*. 2 vols. London: John Murray.

Brown, C. C., trans. 1952. Sějarah Mělayu or 'Malay Annals': A Translation of Raffles MS 18. In *Journal of the Malayan Branch Royal Asiatic Society* 25, Pts. 2 and 3.

———, trans. 1982. Temasek and Singapura: An Extract from the Malay Annals. In *Singapore 150 Years*, edited by Mubin Sheppard, pp. 32–40. Published for the Malaysian Branch of the Royal Asiatic Society. Singapore: Times Books International.

Brown, Edwin A. 2007. *Indiscreet Memories: 1901 Singapore through the Eyes of a Colonial Englishman*. Singapore: Monsoon Books.

Brown, Edwin A., and Mary Brown. 2015. *Singapore Mutiny: A Colonial Couple's Stirring Account of Combat and Survival in the 1915 Singapore Mutiny*. Singapore: Monsoon Books.

Buchanan, Iain. 1972. *Singapore in Southeast Asia: An Economic and Political Appraisal*. London: G. Bell.

Buchanan, Keith. 1967. *The Southeast Asian World: An Introductory Essay*. London: G. Bell.

Buckley, Charles Burton. 1902. *An Anecdotal History of Old Times in Singapore*. 2 vols. Singapore: Fraser & Neave.

———. 1965. *An Anecdotal History of Old Times in Singapore*. Kuala Lumpur: University of Malaya Press; New York: Oxford University Press.

Burbidge, F. W. 1880. *The Gardens of the Sun; or, A Naturalist's Journal on the Mountains and in the Forests and Swamps of Borneo and the Sulu Archipelago*. London: John Murray.

Burkill, I. H. 1935. *A Dictionary of the Economic Products of the Malay Peninsula*. 2 vols. Published for the Governments of the Straits Settlements and Federated Malay States. London: Crown Agents for the Colonies.

Bury, J. B. 1955. *The Idea of Progress: An Inquiry into its Origin and Growth*. New York: Dover Publications.

Butcher, John G. 2004. *The Closing of the Frontier: A History of the Marine Fisheries of Southeast Asia c. 1850–2000*. Singapore: ISEAS; Leiden: KITLV.

Calder, Kent E. 2016. *Singapore: Smart City, Smart State*. Washington, DC: Brookings Institution Press.

Cameron, Charlotte. 1924. *Wanderings in South-Eastern Seas*. London: T. Fisher Unwin.

Cameron, John. 1965. *Our Tropical Possessions in Malayan India: Being a Descriptive Account of Singapore, Penang, Province Wellesley, and Malacca: Their Peoples, Products, Commerce, and Government*. Kuala Lumpur: Oxford University Press.

Carlos, A. H. 1921a. The Eurasians of Singapore. In *One Hundred Years of Singapore: Being Some Account of the Capital of the Straits Settlements from its Foundation by Sir Stamford Raffles on the 6th February 1819 to the 6th February 1919*, vol. 1, edited by Walter Makepeace, Gilbert E. Brooke, and Roland St. J. Braddell, pp. 363–374. London: John Murray.

———. 1921b. The Chinese of Singapore. In *One Hundred Years of Singapore: Being Some Account of the Capital of the Straits Settlements from its Foundation by Sir Stamford Raffles on the 6th February 1819 to the 6th February 1919*, vol. 1, edited by Walter Makepeace, Gilbert E. Brooke, and Roland St. J. Braddell, pp. 374–376. London: John Murray.

Castells, Manuel. 2010. *End of Millennium*. Vol. 3 of *The Information Age: Economy, Society, and Culture*. West Sussex: Wiley-Blackwell.

Chandra, Satish, and Prabha R. Himanshu, eds. 2013. *The Sea, Identity and History: From the Bay of Bengal to the South China Sea*. Singapore: ISEAS; New Delhi: Manohar.

Cheng, Lim Keak. 1995. *Geographic Analysis of the Singapore Population*, Census of population, 1990, monograph no. 5. Singapore: Department of Statistics, Ministry of Trade & Industry.

Chew, Ernest C. T., and Edwin Lee, eds. 1991. *A History of Singapore*. New York: Oxford University Press.

Chong, Terence, ed. 2010. *Management of Success: Singapore Revisited*. Singapore: Institute of Southeast Asian Studies.

Chou, Cynthia. 2013. Space, Movement and Place: The Sea Nomads. In *The Sea, Identity and History: From the Bay of Bengal to the South China Sea*, edited by Satish Chandra and Himanshi Prabha Ray, pp. 41–66. Singapore: ISEAS; New Delhi: Manohar.

Clark, Steve. 2017. Isabella Bird, Rudyard Kipling, and the 'Bandobast' of East Asian Travel. *Studies in Travel Writing* 21 (1): 76–91. Accessed June 28, 2019, https://doi.org/10.1080/13645145.2017.1303919

Clegg, Jenny. 1994. *Fu Manchu and the 'Yellow Peril': The Making of a Racist Myth*. Stoke-on-Trent: Trentham.

Clifford, Hugh C. 1897. *In Court and Kampong: Being Tales & Sketches of Native Life in the Malay Peninsula*. London: Grant Richards.

———. 1916. *The Further Side of Silence*. Garden City, NY: Doubleday, Page.

———. 1929. *Bush-Whacking and Other Asiatic Tales and Memories*. London: W. Heinemann.

———. 1983. Life in the Malay Peninsula: As It Was and Is. In *Honourable Intentions: Talks on the British Empire in South-East Asia delivered at the Royal Colonial Institute, 1874–1928*, edited by Paul H. Kratoska, pp. 224–256. Singapore: Oxford University Press.

Coclanis, Peter A. 2006. *Time's Arrow, Time's Cycle: Globalization in Southeast Asia over la Longue Durée*, The Raffles Lecture Series. Singapore: Institute of Southeast Asian Studies.

Coedès, G. 1968. *The Indianized States of Southeast Asia*. Translated by Susan Brown Cowing and edited by Walter F. Vella. Canberra: Australian National University Press.

Cohn, Bernard S. 1996. *Colonialism and Its Forms of Knowledge: The British in India*. Princeton, NJ: Princeton University Press.

Collingwood, Cuthbert. 1868. *Rambles of a Naturalist on the Shores and Waters of the China Sea: Being Observations in Natural History During a Voyage to China, Formosa, Borneo, Singapore, etc., Made in Her Majesty's Vessels in 1866 and 1867*. London: John Murray.

Conrad, Joseph. 1974. *Youth; Heart of Darkness; The End of the Tether: Three Stories by Joseph Conrad*. London: J. M. Dent.

Cook, J. A. Bethune. 1918. *Sir Thomas Stamford Raffles, Kt. LL. D, F.R.S., Founder of Singapore, 1819, and Some of His Friends and Contemporaries*. London: Arthur H. Stockwell.

Cornish, Vaughan. 1983. Singapore and Naval Geography. In *Honourable Intentions: Talks on the British Empire in South-East Asia delivered at the Royal Colonial Institute 1874–1928*, edited by Paul H. Kratoska, pp. 382–400. Singapore: Oxford University Press.

Coupland, R. 1934. *Raffles, 1781–1826*. London: Oxford University Press.

Cox, C. B. 1974. Introduction. In *Youth; Heart of Darkness; The End of the Tether: Three Stories by Joseph Conrad*, by Joseph Conrad, pp. vii–xxii. London: J. M. Dent.

Crawfurd, John. 1820. *History of the Indian Archipelago. Containing an Account of the Manners, Arts, Languages, Religions, Institutions, and Commerce of its Inhabitants*. 3 vols. Edinburgh: Archibald Constable.

———. 1830. *Journal of an Embassy from the Governor-General of India to the Courts of Siam and Cochin China; Exhibiting a View of the Actual State of those Kingdoms*. 2 vols. London: Henry Colburn and Richard Bentley.

———. 1834. *Journal of an Embassy from the Governor General of India to the Court of Ava, with an Appendix, Containing a Description of Fossil Remains, by Professor Buckland and Mr. Clift*. 2 vols. London: Henry Colburn.

———. 1849. Agriculture of Singapore. *Journal of the Indian Archipelago and Eastern Asia* 3 (8): 508–511.

———. 1856. *A Descriptive Dictionary of the Indian Islands and Adjacent Countries*. London: Bradbury & Evans.

Cross, William. 1921. Stamford Raffles, the Man. In *One Hundred Years of Singapore: Being Some Account of the Capital of the Straits Settlements from its Foundation by Sir Stamford Raffles on the 6th February 1819 to the 6th February 1919*, vol. 1, edited by Walter Makepeace, Gilbert E. Brooke, and Roland St. J. Braddell, pp. 32–68. London: John Murray.

Dalton, Clive. 1937. *A Child in the Sun*. London: Eldon Press.

Dalton, J. 1837. Mr. Dalton's Journal of a Voyage from Singapore to Coti. In *Notices of the Indian Archipelago, and Adjacent Countries: Being a Collection of Papers Relating to Borneo, Celebes, Bali, Java, Sumatra, Nias, the Philippine Islands, Sulus, Siam, Cochin China, Malayan Peninsula, etc.*, edited by J. H. Moor, pp. 30–35. Singapore.

Danvers, Frederick Charles. 1888. *Report to the Secretary of State for India in Council on the Records of the India Office*. London: Her Majesty's Stationery Office.

Davidson, G. F. 1846. *Trade and Travel in the Far East; or, Recollections of Twenty-One Years Passed in Java, Singapore, Australia, and China*. London: Madden and Malcolm.

de Blij, Harm. 2009. *The Power of Place: Geography, Destiny, and Globalization's Rough Landscape*. Oxford; New York: Oxford University Press.

de Bruyn Kops, G. F. 1854. Sketch of the Rhio-Lingga Archipelago. *Journal of the Indian Archipelago and Eastern Asia* 8 (5): 386–402.

———. 1855. Sketch of the Rhio-Lingga Archipelago. *Journal of the Indian Archipelago and Eastern Asia* 9 (1): 96–108.

de Koninck, Rodolphe. 1992. *Singapore: An Atlas of the Revolution of Territory*. Montpellier: GIP Reclus; La Documentation française.

de Koninck, Rodolphe, Julie Drolet, and Marc Girard. 2008. *Singapore: An Atlas of Perpetual Territorial Transformation*. Singapore: NUS Press.

de Souza, Dudley. 1994. Singapore. In *Traveller's Literary Companion to Southeast Asia*, edited by Alastair Dingwall, pp. 252–292. Brighton: In Print Publishing.

de Wit, H. C. D. 1959. Georgius Everhardus Rumphius. In *Rumphius Memorial Volume*, edited by H. C. D. de Wit, pp. 1–26. Baarn: Uitgeverij en Drukkerij Hollandia NV.

Dennys, N. B. 1894. *A Descriptive Dictionary of British Malaya*. London: "London and China Telegraph" Office.

Diamond, Jared. 2019. What We Gain or Lose in Cities. *National Geographic* (April): 17–18.

Dikötter, Frank. 2010. *Mao's Great Famine: The History of China's Most Devastating Catastrophe, 1958–1962*. London; Oxford: Bloomsbury Publishing.

Dobby, E. H. G. 1940. Singapore: Town and Country. *Geographical Review* 30 (1): 84–109.

———. 1973. *Southeast Asia*. London: University of London Press.

Doggett, Marjorie. 1957. *Characters of Light: [A Guide to the Buildings of Singapore]*. Singapore: Donald Moore.

Doran, Christine. 2016. Popular Orientalism: Somerset Maugham in Mainland Southeast Asia. *Humanities* 5 (13): 1–9.

Drabble, J. H. 1983. The Rubber Industry in Melaka. In *Melaka: The Transformation of a Malay Capital, c. 1400–1980, Volume One*, edited by Kernial Singh Sandhu and Paul Wheatley, pp. 568–588. Kuala Lumpur: Oxford University Press.

Drysdale, John. 1984. *Singapore: Struggle for Success*. Singapore: Times Books International.

Duara, Prasenjit. 1995. *Rescuing History from the Nation: Questioning Narratives of Modern China*. Chicago: University of Chicago Press.

Dyer, Colin. 2017. Three French Accounts of Nineteenth-Century Singapore and Penang. *Journal of the Malaysian Branch of the Royal Asiatic Society* 90, Pt. 2 (313): 97–116.

Earl, George Windsor. 1837. *The Eastern Seas, or, Voyages and Adventures in the Indian Archipelago, in 1832-33-34, Comprising a Tour of the Island of Java — Visits to Borneo, the Malay Peninsula, Siam, etc; Also an Account of the Present State of Singapore, with Observations on the Commercial Resources of the Archipelago*. London: Wm. H. Allen.

Enright, D. J. 1969. *Memoirs of a Mendicant Professor*. London: Chatto & Windus.

Eredia [Erédia], Godinho de. 1997. *Eredia's Description of Malaca, Meridional India, and Cathay*. [*Malaca, L'Inde Méridionale et le Cathay*]. Translated by J. V. Mills. Kuala Lumpur: MBRAS.

Fanon, Frantz. 2004. *The Wretched of the Earth*. Translated by Richard Philcox. New York: Grove Press.

Fell, R. T. 1988. *Early Maps of South-East Asia*. Singapore: Oxford University Press.

Fernández-Armesto, Felipe. 1995. *Millennium: A History of Our Last Thousand Years*. London: Bantam.
——. 2001. *Civilizations: Culture, Ambition, and the Transformation of Nature*. New York: Touchstone.
Finlayson, George. 1826. *The Mission to Siam and Hue, the Capital of Cochin China, in the Years 1821–2, from the Journal of the Late George Finlayson; with a Memoir of the Author by Sir Thomas Stamford Raffles*. London: John Murray.
Firbank, L. T. 1985. A History of Fort Canning. *China Society 35th Anniversary Journal*: 17–28.
Firmstone, H. W. 1905. Chinese Names of Streets and Places in Singapore and the Malay Peninsula. *Journal of the Straits Branch of the Royal Asiatic Society* (42): 53–208.
Fitch, George Hamlin. 1913. *The Critic in the Orient*. San Francisco: Paul Elder.
Fitzgerald, C. P. 1965. *The Third China: The Chinese Communities in South-East Asia*. Melbourne: F. W. Cheshire.
Flannery, Tim. 2005. *The Weather Makers: The History & Future Impact of Climate Change*. New York: Atlantic Monthly Press.
Flower, Raymond. 1984. *Raffles: The Story of Singapore*. Singapore: Eastern Universities Press.
Foran, W. Robert. 1985. A Most Amazing Adventure. In *Travellers' Tales of Old Singapore*, edited by Michael Wise with Mun Him Wise, pp. 227–231. Singapore: Times Books International.
Forster, E. M. 1924. *A Passage to India*. London: Edward Arnold.
Frank, Andre Gunder. 1998. *ReORIENT: Global Economy in the Asian Age*. Berkeley: University of California Press.
Freitag, Ulrike. 2002. Arab Merchants in Singapore: Attempt of a Collective Biography. In *Transcending Borders: Arabs, Politics, Trade and Islam in Southeast Asia*, edited by Hubb de Jonge and Nico Kaptein, pp. 109–142. Leiden: KITLV Press.
Frey, Marc, and Nicola Spakowski, eds. 2016. *Asianisms: Regionalist Interactions & Asian Integration*. Singapore: NUS Press.
Frost, Mark Ravinder, and Yu-Mei Balasingamchow. 2009. *Singapore: A Biography*. Singapore: Editions Didier Millet.
Fukuyama, Francis. 1992. *The End of History and the Last Man*. New York: Free Press.
——. 2018. *Identity: The Demand for Dignity and the Politics of Resentment*. New York: Farrar, Straus and Giroux.
Furnivall, J. S. 1948. *Colonial Policy and Practice: A Comparative Study of Burma and Netherlands India*. Cambridge: Cambridge University Press.
Geertz, Clifford. 1963. *Peddlers and Princes: Social Development and Economic Change in Two Indonesian Towns*. Chicago: University of Chicago Press.

———. 1971. *Agricultural Involution: The Processes of Ecological Change in Indonesia.* Berkeley: University of California Press.

Ghesquière, Henri. 2007. *Singapore's Success: Engineering Economic Growth.* Singapore: Thomson Learning.

Gibson-Hill, C. A. 1954. Singapore: Notes on the History of the Old Strait, 1580–1850. *Journal of the Malayan Branch of the Royal Asiatic Society* 27, Pt. 1 (165): 163–214.

———. 1959. George Samuel Windsor Earl. *Journal of the Malayan Branch of the Royal Asiatic Society* 32, Pt. 1 (185): 105–153.

———. 1982. The Orang Laut of Singapore River and the Sampan Panjang. In *Singapore 150 Years*, edited by Mubin Sheppard, pp. 121–134. Published for the Malaysian Branch of the Royal Asiatic Society. Singapore: Times Books International.

Glacken, Clarence J. 1967. *Traces on the Rhodian Shore: Nature and Culture in Western Thought from Ancient Times to the End of the Eighteenth Century.* Berkeley: University of California Press.

Glendinning, Victoria. 2012. *Raffles and the Golden Opportunity.* London: Profile Books.

Goh, C. B. 1998. Creating a Research and Development Culture in Southeast Asia: Lessons from Singapore's Experience. *Southeast Asian Journal of Social Science* 26 (1): 49–68.

Gunn, Geoffrey C. 2011. *History Without Borders: The Making of an Asian World Region, 1000–1800.* Hong Kong: Hong Kong University Press.

Hack, Karl, and Jean-Louis Margolin. 2010. Singapore: Reinventing the Global City. In *Singapore from Temasek to the 21st Century: Reinventing the Global City*, edited by Karl Hack and Jean-Louis Margolin, with Karine Delaye, pp. 3–36. Singapore: NUS Press.

Hack, Karl, and Jean-Louis Margolin, with Karine Delaye, eds. 2010. *Singapore from Temasek to the 21st Century: Reinventing the Global City.* Singapore: NUS Press.

Hahn, Emily. 1946. *Raffles of Singapore.* New York: Doubleday.

Hale, Richard E. 2016. *The Balestiers: The First American Residents of Singapore.* Singapore: Marshall Cavendish.

Hall, D. G. E. 1968. *A History of Southeast Asia.* London: Macmillan.

Hall, Kenneth R. 2011. *A History of Early Southeast Asia: Maritime Trade and Societal Development, 100–1500.* Lanham, MD: Rowman & Littlefield.

Hamilton, Alexander. 1727. *A New Account of the East Indies, Being the Observations and Remarks Of Capt. Alexander Hamilton, Who spent his Time there From the Year 1688, to 1723. Trading and Travelling, by Sea and Land, to most of the Countries and Islands of Commerce and Navigation, between the Cape of Good-hope, and the Island of Japon.* 2 vols. Edinburgh: John Mosman.

Hancock, T. H. H., and C. A. Gibson-Hill. 1954. *Architecture in Singapore*. Singapore: Singapore Art Society.

Hanitsch, R. 1982. Letters of Nathaniel Wallich Relating to the Establishment of Botanical Gardens in Singapore. In *Singapore 150 Years*, edited by Mubin Sheppard, pp. 155–165. Published for the Malaysian Branch of the Royal Asiatic Society. Singapore: Times Books International.

Harper, T. N. 1999. *The End of Empire and the Making of Malaya*. Cambridge: Cambridge University Press.

Harrison, Brian. 1954. *South-East Asia: A Short History*. London: Macmillan.

Hart, John Fraser. 1975. *The Look of the Land*. Englewood Cliffs, NJ: Prentice-Hall.

Harvey, David. 1973. *Social Justice and the City*. Baltimore, MD: Johns Hopkins University Press.

Hedges, Chris. 2018. *America: The Farewell Tour*. New York: Simon & Schuster.

Heine-Geldern, Robert. 1942. Conceptions of State and Kingship in Southeast Asia. *Far Eastern Quarterly* 2 (1): 15–30.

Hendley, Charles M. 1985. Strangers at Singapore. In *Travellers' Tales of Old Singapore*, edited by Michael Wise with Mun Him Wise, pp. 191–193. Singapore: Times Books International.

Herman, Arthur. 1997. *The Idea of Decline in Western History*. New York: Free Press.

Hill, A. H., trans. 1982. The Founding of Singapore Described by 'Munshi Abdullah'. In *Singapore 150 Years*, edited by Mubin Sheppard, pp. 94–111. Published for the Malaysian Branch of the Royal Asiatic Society. Singapore: Times Books International.

Hill, R. D. 1977. The Vegetation Map of Singapore: A First Approximation. *Journal of Tropical Geography* 45: 26–33.

Hobson, John M. 2004. *The Eastern Origins of Western Civilisation*. Cambridge: Cambridge University Press.

Hoefer, H. 1977. Meeting the Singaporean. In *Southeast Asia and the Germans*, edited by anon., pp. 248–259. Tübingen; Basle: Horst Erdmann Verlag; Bonn: Inter Nationes.

Hooi, C. 1985. Singapore in February 1819. *China Society 35th Anniversary Journal*: 8–12.

Hornaday, William T. 1885. *Two Years in the Jungle: The Experiences of a Hunter and Naturalist in India, Ceylon, the Malay Peninsula and Borneo*. New York: Charles Scribner's Sons.

Hose, Charles. 1927. *Fifty Years of Romance and Research, or, A Jungle-wallah At Large*. London: Hutchinson.

Hsü, Yün-Ts'iao. 1982. Singapore in the Remote Past. In *Singapore 150 Years*, edited by Mubin Sheppard, pp. 1–9. Published for the Malaysian Branch of the Royal Asiatic Society. Singapore: Times Books International.

Humphrey, John W. 1985. *Geographic Analysis of Singapore's Population*, Census Monograph No. 5. Singapore: Department of Statistics.
Huntington, Samuel P. 1996. *The Clash of Civilizations and the Remaking of World Order*. New York: Simon & Schuster.
———. 2004. *Who Are We? The Challenges to America's National Identity*. New York: Simon & Schuster.
Innes, Emily. 1885. *The Chersonese with the Gilding Off*. 2 vols. London: Richard Bentley.
Jackson, J. C. 1967. Tapioca: The Plantation Crop Which Preceded Rubber in Malaya. *Malaysia in History* 10 (2): 13–24.
Jackson, John Brinckerhoff. 1984. *Discovering the Vernacular Landscape*. New Haven; London: Yale University Press.
Jacobs, Jane. 1961. *The Death and Life of Great American Cities*. New York: Vintage Books.
Jacobs, Jane M. 1996. *Edge of Empire: Postcolonialism and the City*. London: Routledge.
Jagor, Fedor. 1977. Singapore — 120 Years Ago. In *Southeast Asia and the Germans*, edited by anon., pp. 23–37. Tübingen; Basle: Horst Erdmann Verlag; Bonn: Inter Nationes.
Jayapal, Maya. 1992. *Old Singapore*. Singapore: Oxford University Press.
Kaplan, Robert D. 2012. *The Revenge of Geography: What the Map Tells Us about Coming Conflicts and the Battle against Fate*. New York: Random House.
Kaye, Barrington. 1960. *Upper Nankin Street Singapore: A Sociological Study of Chinese Households Living in a Densely Populated Area*. Singapore: University of Malaya Press.
Keppel, Henry. 1853. *A Visit to the Indian Archipelago, in H. M. Ship Maeander; with Portions of the Private Journal of Sir James Brooke*. 2 vols. London: Richard Bentley.
Khanna, Parag. 2016. *Connectography: Mapping the Future of Global Civilization*. New York: Random House.
Kipling, Rudyard. 1899a. *Ballad of East and West*. New York: M. F. Mansfield and A. Wessels.
———. 1899b. Ballads. In *Departmental Ditties, Ballads and Barrack Room Ballads*. Toronto: George N. Morang; New York: Doubleday & McClure.
———. 1900. *From Sea to Sea and Other Sketches: Letters of Travel*, vol. 1. London: Macmillan.
———. 1934. *Verse, Inclusive Edition, 1885–1932*. Garden City, NY: Doubleday, Doran.
Kolbert, Elizabeth. 2014. *The Sixth Extinction: An Unnatural History*. London: Bloomsbury.
Kotkin, Joel. 2006. *The City: A Global History*. New York: Modern Library.

Kozok, Uli. 2015. *A 14th Century Malay Code of Laws: The Nitisarasamuccaya.* Singapore: Institute of Southeast Asian Studies.

Kratoska, Paul H., ed. 1983. *Honourable Intentions: Talks on the British Empire in South-East Asia delivered at the Royal Colonial Institute, 1874–1928.* Singapore; New York: Oxford University Press.

Kroeber, A. L. 1963. *Anthropology: Culture Patterns & Processes.* New York: Harbinger Books.

Kwa, Chong Guan. 2010. Singapura as a Central Place in Malay History and Identity. In *Singapore from Temasek to the 21st Century: Reinventing the Global City*, edited by Karl Hack and Jean-Louis Margolin, with Karine Delaye, pp. 133–154. Singapore: NUS Press.

Kwa, Chong Guan, Derek Heng, and Tan Tai Yong. 2009. *Singapore: A 700-Year History.* Singapore: National Archives of Singapore.

Lach, Donald F., [and Edwin J. van Kley]. 1965–1993. *Asia in the Making of Europe.* 3 vols. Chicago; London: University of Chicago Press.

Le May, Reginald. 1956. *The Culture of South-East Asia: The Heritage of India.* London: George Allen & Unwin.

Lee, Edwin. 2008. *Singapore: The Unexpected Nation.* Singapore: ISEAS.

Lee, Kuan Yew. 1998. *The Singapore Story: Memoirs of Lee Kuan Yew.* Singapore: Times Editions; Singapore Press Holdings.

———. 2000. *From Third World to First: The Singapore Story, 1965–2000: Singapore and the Asian Economic Boom.* New York: HarperCollins.

Leong, Foke Meng. 2004. Early Land Transactions in Singapore: The Real Estates of William Farquhar (1774–1839), John Crawfurd (1783–1868), and Their Families. *Journal of the Malaysian Branch of the Royal Asiatic Society* 77 (1): 23–42.

Levathes, Louise. 1994. *When China Ruled the Seas: The Treasure Fleet of the Dragon Throne, 1405–1433.* New York; Oxford: Oxford University Press.

Lewis, Martin W., and Kären E. Wigen. 1997. *The Myth of Continents: A Critique of Metageography.* Berkeley: University of California Press.

Leyden, John, trans. 2009. *John Leyden's Malay Annals.* Kuala Lumpur: JMBRAS.

Li, Chung Chu. 1985. Greater Town. In *Travellers' Tales of Old Singapore*, edited by Michael Wise with Mun Him Wise, pp. 133–136. Singapore: Times Books International.

Li, Jin. 2012. *Cultural Foundations of Learning: East and West.* Cambridge: Cambridge University Press.

Lieberman, Victor. 2003. *Strange Parallels: Southeast Asia in Global Context, c. 800–1830. Volume 1: Integration on the Mainland.* New York: Cambridge University Press, 2003–2009.

———. 2009. *Strange Parallels: Southeast Asia in Global Context, c. 800–1830. Volume 2: Mainland Mirrors: Europe, Japan, China, South Asia, and the Islands.* New York: Cambridge University Press, 2003–2009.

Lim, Chung Tat. 2013. *University of Malaya 1949 to 1985: Its Establishment, Growth and Development.* Kuala Lumpur: University of Malaya Press.

Lim, Irene. 2003. *Sketches in the Straits: Nineteenth-century Watercolours and Manuscript of Singapore, Malacca, Penang and Batavia by Charles Dyce.* Singapore: NUS Museums; National University of Singapore.

Lim, Rosemary. 2008. *An Irish Tour of Singapore.* Singapore: Two Trees.

Lin, Justin Yifu. 1995. The Needham Puzzle: Why the Industrial Revolution Did Not Originate in China. *Economic Development and Cultural Change* 43 (2): 269–292.

Little, Robert. 1848a. On the Habitual Use of Opium in Singapore. *Journal of the Indian Archipelago and Eastern Asia* 2 (1): 1–79.

———. 1848b. An Essay on Coral Reefs as the Cause of Blakan Mati Fever and of the Fevers in Various Parts of the East. Part I. *Journal of the Indian Archipelago and Eastern Asia* 2 (6): 449–494.

———. 1848c. An Essay on Coral Reefs as the Cause of Blakan Mati Fever, and of the Fevers in Various Parts of the East. Part II. *Journal of the Indian Archipelago and Eastern Asia* 2 (9): 571–602.

———. 1849a. An Essay on Coral Reefs as the Cause of Blakan Mati Fever and of the Fevers in Various Parts of the East. Part III. *Journal of the Indian Archipelago and Eastern Asia* 3 (9): 413–444.

———. 1849b. Diseases of the Nutmeg Tree. *Journal of the Indian Archipelago and Eastern Asia* 3 (10): 678–681.

Lockard, Craig A. 2009. *Southeast Asia in World History.* Oxford; New York: Oxford University Press.

Lockhart, R. H. Bruce. 1936. *Return to Malaya.* London: Putnam.

Logan, J. R., ed. 1847a. The Present Condition of the Indian Archipelago. *Journal of the Indian Archipelago and Eastern Asia* 1 (1): 1–21.

———. 1847b. The Orang Biduanda Kallang of the River Pulai in Johore. *Journal of the Indian Archipelago and Eastern Asia* 1 (5): 299–302.

———. 1847c. The Orang Seletar. *Journal of the Indian Archipelago and Eastern Asia* 1 (5): 302–304.

———. 1849. Malay Amoks and Piracies: What Can We Do to Abolish Them? *Journal of the Indian Archipelago and Eastern Asia* 3 (7): 463–467.

———, ed. 1854a. Notices of Singapore. *Journal of the Indian Archipelago and Eastern Asia* 8 (1): 97–111.

———, ed. 1854b. Notices of Singapore. *Journal of the Indian Archipelago and Eastern Asia* 8 (3) 329–348.

———, ed. 1855. Notices of Singapore. *Journal of the Indian Archipelago and Eastern Asia* 9 (4): 442–482.

Long, Nicholas J. 2013. *Being Malay in Indonesia: Histories, Hopes and Citizenship in the Riau Archipelago.* Singapore: NUS Press; Copenhagen: NIAS Press.

Lornie, James. 1921. Land Tenure. In *One Hundred Years of Singapore: Being Some Account of the Capital of the Straits Settlements from its Foundation by Sir Stamford Raffles on the 6th February 1819 to the 6th February 1919*, vol. 1, edited by Walter Makepeace, Gilbert E. Brooke, and Roland St. J. Braddell, pp. 301–314. London: John Murray.

Lovejoy, Arthur O. 1936. *The Great Chain of Being: A Study of the History of an Idea*. Cambridge, MA: Harvard University Press.

Lovelock, James. 2015. *A Rough Ride to the Future*. London: Penguin Books.

Low, Hugh. 1968. *Sarawak: Its Inhabitants and Productions*. London: Frank Cass.

Low, James. (1836) 1972. *The British Settlement of Penang*. Reprint, Singapore: Oxford University Press.

Lowe, Keith. 2017. *The Fear and the Freedom: How the Second World War Changed Us*. London: Viking.

Lynch, Kevin. 1972. *The Image of the City*. Cambridge, MA; London: M.I.T. Press.

Mackerras, Colin. 1999. *Western Images of China*. Hong Kong; New York: Oxford University Press.

Mahizhnan, Arun, and Lee Tsao Yuan, eds. 2002. *Singapore: Re-engineering Success*. Published for the Institute of Policy Studies. Singapore: Times Academic Press.

Makepeace, Walter, ed. 1907. *Handbook to Singapore with Map*. By G. M. Reith and revised by Walter Makepeace. Singapore: Fraser and Neave.

———. 1921a. The Port of Singapore. In *One Hundred Years of Singapore: Being Some Account of the Capital of the Straits Settlements from its Foundation by Sir Stamford Raffles on the 6th February 1819 to the 6th February 1919*, vol. 1, edited by Walter Makepeace, Gilbert E. Brooke, and Roland St. J. Braddell, pp. 578–592. London: John Murray.

———. 1921b. The Machinery of Commerce. In *One Hundred Years of Singapore: Being Some Account of the Capital of the Straits Settlements from its Foundation by Sir Stamford Raffles on the 6th February 1819 to the 6th February 1919*, vol. 2, edited by Walter Makepeace, Gilbert E. Brooke, and Roland St. J. Braddell, pp. 166–234. London: John Murray.

———. 1921c. Institutions and Clubs. In *One Hundred Years of Singapore: Being Some Account of the Capital of the Straits Settlements from its Foundation by Sir Stamford Raffles on the 6th February 1819 to the 6th February 1919*, vol. 2, edited by Walter Makepeace, Gilbert E. Brooke, and Roland St. J. Braddell, pp. 278–319. London: John Murray.

———. 1921d. Concerning Known Persons. In *One Hundred Years of Singapore: Being Some Account of the Capital of the Straits Settlements from its Foundation by Sir Stamford Raffles on the 6th February 1819 to the 6th February 1919*, vol. 2, edited by Walter Makepeace, Gilbert E. Brooke, and Roland St. J. Braddell, pp. 416–464. London: John Murray.

Makepeace, Walter, Gilbert E. Brooke, and Roland St. J. Braddell, eds. 1921. *One Hundred Years of Singapore: Being Some Account of the Capital of the Straits Settlements from its Foundation by Sir Stamford Raffles on the 6th February 1819 to the 6th February 1919*. 2 vols. London: John Murray.

Malayanisation Commission. 1956. *Final Report of the Malayanisation Commission*. Singapore: Government Printing Office, by F. S. Horslin.

March, Andrew L. 1974. *The Idea of China: Myth and Theory in Geographic Thought*. London: David & Charles.

Marriott, Hayes. 1911. *Report on the Census of the Colony of the Straits Settlements, Taken on the 10th March, 1911*. Singapore: Government Printing Office.

Marsden, William. (1783) 1811. *The History of Sumatra: Containing an Account of the Government, Laws, Customs, and Manners of the Native Inhabitants, with a Description of the Natural Productions, and a Relation of the Ancient Political State of that Island*. London: J. M' Creery.

Maugham, W. Somerset. 1951. *The Complete Short Stories of Somerset Maugham*, vol 1. Melbourne: William Heinemann.

———. 1993. *Far Eastern Tales*. London: Mandarin.

———. 2000. *More Far Eastern Tales*. London: Vintage Books.

Maxwell, W. E. 1982. The Founding of Singapore. In *Singapore 150 Years*, edited by Mubin Sheppard, pp. 77–86. Published for the Malaysian Branch of the Royal Asiatic Society. Singapore: Times Books International.

McGee, Terry. 1976. Beach-Heads and Enclaves: The Urban Debate and the Urbanization Process in Southeast Asia since 1945. In *Changing Southeast Asian Cities: Readings on Urbanization*, edited by Y. M. Yeung and C. P. Lo, pp. 60–75. London: Oxford University Press.

McGregor, Richard. 2018. *Asia's Reckoning: The Struggle for Global Dominance*. London: Penguin Books.

McKie, Ronald C. H. 1942. *This Was Singapore*. Sydney: Angus & Robertson.

Medhurst, Walter H. 1983. British North Borneo. In *Honourable Intentions: Talks on the British Empire in South-East Asia delivered at the Royal Colonial Institute 1874–1928*, edited by Paul H. Kratoska, pp. 91–124. Singapore: Oxford University Press.

Miksic, John N. 1985. *Archaeological Research on the "Forbidden Hill" of Singapore: Excavations at Fort Canning, 1984*. Singapore: National Museum.

———. 2004. 14th-Century Singapore: A Port of Trade. In *Early Singapore: 1300s–1819: Evidence in Maps, Text and Artefacts*, edited by John N. Miksic and Cheryl-Ann Low Mei Gek, pp. 41–54. Singapore: Singapore History Museum.

———. 2010. Temasik to Singapura: Singapore in the 14th to 15th Centuries. In *Singapore from Temasek to the 21st Century: Reinventing the Global City*, edited by Karl Hack and Jean-Louis Margolin, with Karine Delaye, pp. 103–132. Singapore: NUS Press.

———. 2013. *Singapore & the Silk Road of the Sea 1300–1800*. Singapore: NUS Press; National Museum of Singapore.

Miksic, John N., and Cheryl-Ann Low Mei Gek, eds. 2004. *Early Singapore, 1300s–1819: Evidence in Maps, Text and Artefacts*. Singapore: Singapore History Museum.

Miller, H. Eric. 1941. Extracts from the Letters of Col. Nahuijs. *Journal of the Malayan Branch of the Royal Asiatic Society* 19, Pt. 2 (139): 169–209.

———. 1982. Letter from Col. Nahuijs, 1824. In *Singapore 150 Years*, edited by Mubin Sheppard, pp. 166–173. Published for the Malaysian Branch of the Royal Asiatic Society. Singapore: Times Books International.

Milner, Anthony. 2003. *Region, Security and the Return of History*. Published for the Department of History, National University of Singapore. Singapore: Institute of Southeast Asian Studies.

———. 2004. Afterword: A History of Malay Ethnicity. In *Contesting Malayness: Malay Identity Across Boundaries*, edited by Timothy P. Barnard, pp. 241–257. Singapore: Singapore University Press.

Mokyr, Joel. 2017. *A Culture of Growth: The Origins of the Modern Economy*. Princeton, NJ: Princeton University Press.

Montgomerie, W. 1855. Report upon the Present State of the Honourable Company's Botanical Garden at Singapore, 1st February 1827. *Journal of the Indian Archipelago and Eastern Asia* 9 (1): 62–65.

Moor, J. H. 1837. *Notices of the Indian Archipelago, and Adjacent Countries: Being a Collection of Papers Relating to Borneo, Celebes, Bali, Java, Sumatra, Nias, the Philippine Islands, Sulus, Siam, Cochin China, Malayan Peninsula, etc*. Singapore.

Moore, Donald. 1953. *Far Eastern Agent; or, The Diary of an Eastern Nobody*. London: Hodder and Stoughton.

———. 1955. *We Live in Singapore*. London: Hodder & Stoughton.

———. 1975. *The Magic Dragon: The Story of Singapore*. St. Albans, Hertfordshire: Panther Books.

Moore, Donald, and Joanna Moore. 1969. *The First 150 Years of Singapore*. Singapore: Donald Moore Press in association with the Singapore International Chamber of Commerce.

Morris, Desmond. 2002. *Peoplewatching: The Desmond Morris Guide to Body Language*. London: Vintage.

Multatuli. 1995. *Max Havelaar, or, The Coffee Auctions of the Dutch Trading Company*. Translated by Roy Edwards. London: Penguin Books.

Mumford, Lewis. 1970. *The Culture of Cities*. New York: Harcourt, Brace.

Myrdal, Gunnar. 1968. *Asian Drama: An Inquiry into the Poverty of Nations*. 3 vols. New York: Pantheon Books; Twentieth Century Fund.

Nader, Laura, ed. 2015. *What the Rest Think of the West: Since 600 AD*. Berkeley: University of California Press.

Nas, Peter J. M., and Welmoet Boender. 2002. The Indonesian City in Urban Theory. In *The Indonesian Town Revisited*, edited by Peter J. M. Nas, pp. 3–17. Singapore: ISEAS.

Needham, Joseph. 1954. *Science and Civilisation in China. Volume 1: Introductory Orientations*. Cambridge: Cambridge University Press, 1954–.

Newbold, T. J. 1839. *Political and Statistical Account of the British Settlements in the Straits of Malacca viz. Pinang, Malacca, and Singapore; with a History of the Malayan States on the Peninsula of Malacca*. 2 vols. London: John Murray.

Nirmala, Murugaian. 2018. *Journeys: Tamils in Singapore, 1800–Present*. Singapore: Straits Times Press.

O'Connor, Richard A. 1983. *A Theory of Indigenous Southeast Asian Urbanism*, Research Notes and Discussions Paper No. 38. Singapore: ISEAS.

Ommanney, F. D. 1960. *Eastern Windows*. London: Longmans.

Ooi, Jin-Bee, and Chiang Hai Ding, eds. 1969. *Modern Singapore*. Singapore: University of Singapore.

Ooi, Kee Beng. 2015. *The Eurasian Core and Its Edges: Dialogues with Wang Gungwu on the History of the World*. Singapore: Institute of Southeast Asian Studies.

Orwell, George. 1935. *Burmese Days*. London: Victor Gollancz.

Osborn, Sherard, ed. 1857. *The Discovery of the North-west Passage by H.M.S. "Investigator,": Capt. R. M'Clure, 1850, 1851, 1852, 1853, 1854*. London: Longman, Brown, Green, Longmans, & Roberts.

———. 1987. *The Blockade of Kedah in 1838: A Midshipman's Exploits in Malayan Waters*. Singapore: Oxford University Press.

Osterhammel, Jürgen. 2014. *The Transformation of the World: A Global History of the Nineteenth Century*. Translated by Patrick Camiller. Princeton, NJ: Princeton University Press.

———. 2018. *Unfabling the East: The Enlightenment's Encounter with Asia*. Translated by Robert Savage. Princeton, NJ: Princeton University Press.

Ota, Atsushi. 2010. The Business of Violence: Piracy around Riau, Lingga, and Singapore, 1820–40. In *Elusive Pirates, Pervasive Smugglers: Violence and Clandestine Trade in the Greater China Seas*, edited by Robert J. Antony, pp. 127–141. Hong Kong: Hong Kong University Press.

Owen, G. P. 1921. A Century of Sport. In *One Hundred Years of Singapore: Being Some Account of the Capital of the Straits Settlements from its Foundation by Sir Stamford Raffles on the 6th February 1819 to the 6th February 1919*, vol. 2, edited by Walter Makepeace, Gilbert E. Brooke, and Roland St. J. Braddell, pp. 320–380. London: John Murray.

Oxley, T. 1848. Some Account of the Nutmeg and Its Cultivation. *Journal of the Indian Archipelago and Eastern Asia* 2 (10): 641–660.

———. 1849. The Zoology of Singapore. *Journal of the Indian Archipelago and Eastern Asia* 3 (9): 594–597.

Parkinson, C. Northcote. 1963. *East and West*. Boston: Houghton Mifflin.
Pearson, H. F. 1955. *People of Early Singapore*. London: University of London Press.
———. 1982. Lt. Jackson's Plan of Singapore. *Singapore 150 Years*, edited by Mubin Sheppard, pp. 150–154. Published for the Malaysian Branch of the Royal Asiatic Society. Singapore: Times Books International.
Percival, A. E. 1977. Appendix II — The Strategical Problems of Singapore. In *Singapore 1941–1942*, by Louis Allen, pp. 272–287. London: Davis-Poynter.
Perry, John Curtis. 2017. *Singapore: Unlikely Power*. New York: Oxford University Press.
Phuah, Millie. 2019. The Man Who Would Be Sultan — Tengku Sri Indra. *Passage* (May/June): 6–7.
Pilon, Maxime, and Danièle Weiler. 2011. *The French in Singapore: An Illustrated History (1819–Today)*. Singapore: Editions Didier Millet.
Pires, Tomé. 1944. *The Suma Oriental of Tomé Pires: An Account of the East, from the Red Sea to Japan, Written in Malacca and India in 1512–1515, and, the Book of Francisco Rodrigues, Rutter of a Voyage in the Red Sea, Nautical Rules, Almanack and Maps, Written and Drawn in the East before 1515*. Translated and edited by Armando Cortesão. London: Hakluyt Society.
Planning Department, Ministry of National Development. 1985. *Revised Master Plan 1985: Report of Survey*. Singapore.
Poh, Soo Kai, Tan Jing Quee, and Koh Kay Yew, eds. 2010. *The Fajar Generation: The University Socialist Club and the Politics of Postwar Malaya and Singapore*. Petaling Jaya: Strategic Information and Research Development Centre.
Poivre, Pierre. 1769. *Travels of a Philosopher; or, Observations on the Manners and Arts of Various Nations in Africa and Asia*. London: T. Becket.
Pollock, Sheldon. 2006. *The Language of the Gods in the World of Men: Sanskrit, Culture, and Power in Premodern India*. Berkeley; Los Angeles: University of California Press.
Polo, Marco. 1871. *The Book of Ser Marco Polo, the Venetian, Concerning the Kingdoms and Marvels of the East*. 2 vols. Translated and edited by Henry Yule. London: John Murray.
Pomeranz, Kenneth. 2000. *The Great Divergence: China, Europe, and the Making of the Modern World Economy*. Princeton, NJ: Princeton University Press.
Population Reference Bureau. 1987. *World Population Data Sheet*. Washington, DC.
Prapañca, Mpu. 1995. *Deśawarnana (Nagarakrtagama)*. Translated by Stuart Robson. Leiden: KITLV Press.

Pratt, Ambrose. 1931. *Magical Malaya*. Melbourne: Robertson & Mullens.
Price, H. 1921. Rubber and Rubber Planting. In *One Hundred Years of Singapore: Being Some Account of the Capital of the Straits Settlements from its Foundation by Sir Stamford Raffles on the 6th February 1819 to the 6th February 1919*, vol. 2, edited by Walter Makepeace, Gilbert E. Brooke, and Roland St. J. Braddell, pp. 88–91. London: John Murray.
Ptolemy, Claudius. 1932. *Geography of Claudius Ptolemy*. Translated and edited by Edward Luther Stevenson. New York: New York Public Library.
Purcell, Victor. 1962. *The Revolution in Southeast Asia*. London: Thames and Hudson.
———. 1965. *The Chinese in Southeast Asia*. London: Oxford University Press.
Pye, Lucian W. 1972. *China: An Introduction*. Boston: Little Brown.
Rabb, Theodore K. 2006. *The Last Days of the Renaissance & the March to Modernity*. New York: Basic Books.
Raffles, Sophia. 1830. *Memoir of the Life and Public Services of Sir Thomas Stamford Raffles, F.R.S. etc., Particularly in the Government of Java, 1811–1816, and of Bencoolen and its Dependencies, 1817–1824; with Details of the Commerce and Resources of the Eastern Archipelago, and Selections from his Correspondence*. London: John Murray.
Raffles, Thomas Stamford. 1816. On the Maláyu Nation: With a Translation of Its Maritime Institutions. *Asiatick Researches* 12: 102–158.
———. (1817) 1830. *The History of Java*. 2 vols. London: John Murray.
Ratzel, Friedrich. 1898. *The History of Mankind*, vol. 1. Translated by A. J. Butler. London: Macmillan.
Redfern, James. 1985. Chinks, Drinks and Stinks. In *Travellers' Tales of Old Singapore*, edited by Michael Wise with Mun Him Wise, pp. 170–173. Singapore: Times Books International.
Reed, Robert Ronald. 1978. *Colonial Manila: The Context of Hispanic Urbanism and Process of Morphogenesis*. Berkeley: University of California Press.
Regnier, Philippe. 1992. *Singapore: City-State in South-East Asia*. Kuala Lumpur: S. Abdul Majeed.
Reid, Anthony. 1988. *Southeast Asia in the Age of Commerce 1450–1680. Volume One: The Lands below the Winds*. Chiang Mai: Silkworm Books, 1988–1993.
———. 1993. *Southeast Asia in the Age of Commerce 1450–1680. Volume Two: Expansion and Crisis*. Chiang Mai: Silkworm Books, 1988–1993.
———. 2000. *Charting the Shape of Early Modern Southeast Asia*. Singapore: ISEAS; Chiang Mai: Trasvin.
———. 2010. Singapore between Cosmopolis and Nation. In *Singapore from Temasek to the 21st Century: Reinventing the Global City*, edited by Karl Hack and Jean-Louis Margolin, with Karine Delaye, pp. 37–54. Singapore: NUS Press.

Reid, Anthony, and David Marr. 1979. *Perceptions of the Past in Southeast Asia*. Published for the Asian Studies Association of Australia. Singapore: Heinemann Educational Books.

Reith, G. M. 1892. *Handbook to Singapore, With Map and a Plan of the Botanical Gardens*. Singapore: Singapore and Straits Printing Office.

Reynolds, Craig J. 2008. The Professional Lives of O. W. Wolters. In *Early Southeast Asia: Selected Essays*, edited by Craig J. Reynolds, pp. 1–38. Ithaca, NY: Southeast Asia Program Publications, Cornell University.

Ridley, H. N. 1904. The Orang Laut of Singapore. *Journal of the Straits Branch of the Royal Asiatic Society* (41): 129–130.

Robequain, Charles. 1958. *Malaya, Indonesia, Borneo, and the Philippines*. Translated by E. D. Laborde. London: Longmans.

Rostow, W. W. 1959. The Stages of Economic Growth. *Economic History Review* 12 (1): 1–16.

Ryan, N. J. 1962. *The Cultural Heritage of Malaya*. Kuala Lumpur: Longman Malaysia.

Sahlins, Marshall. 1974. *Stone Age Economics*. London: Tavistock Publications.

Said, Edward W. (1978) 1979. *Orientalism*. New York: Vintage Books.

———. 1994. *Culture and Imperialism*. London: Vintage Books.

Sandhu, Kernial Singh, and Paul Wheatley. 1983a. *Melaka: The Transformation of a Malay Capital, c. 1400–1980*. 2 vols. Kuala Lumpur; New York: Oxford University Press.

———. 1983b. The Name Melaka. In *Melaka: The Transformation of a Malay Capital, c. 1400–1980, Volume One*, edited by Kernial Singh Sandhu and Paul Wheatley, pp. viii–ix. Kuala Lumpur; New York: Oxford University Press.

———. 1983c. The Historical Context. In *Melaka: The Transformation of a Malay Capital, c. 1400–1980, Volume One*, edited by Kernial Singh Sandhu and Paul Wheatley, pp. 3–69. Kuala Lumpur; New York: Oxford University Press.

———, eds. 1989. *Management of Success: The Moulding of Modern Singapore*. Singapore: Institute of Southeast Asian Studies.

Santos, Milton. 1979. *The Shared Space: The Two Circuits of the Urban Economy in Underdeveloped Countries*. Translated by Chris Gerry. London: Methuen.

Savage, Victor R. 1984. *Western Impressions of Nature and Landscape in Southeast Asia*. Singapore: Singapore University Press.

———. 1992. Landscape Change: From Kampong to Global City. In *Physical Adjustments in A Changing Landscape: The Singapore Story*, edited by Avijit Gupta and John Pitts, pp. 5–31. Singapore: Singapore University Press.

———. 1997. Singapore's Garden City: Translating Environmental Possibilism. In *City and the State: Singapore's Built Environment Revisited*, edited by Ooi Giok Ling and Kenson Kwok, pp. 187–202. Singapore: Oxford University Press.

———. 2003. Changing Geographies and the Geography of Change: Some Reflections. *Singapore Journal of Tropical Geography* 24 (1): 61–85.

———. 2004. Human-Environment Relations: Singapore's Environmental Ideology. In *Imagining Singapore*, edited by Ban Kah Choon, Anne Pakir, and Tong Chee Kiong, pp. 187–217. Singapore: Eastern Universities Press.

———. 2019. Afterword — China's Ascendency: ASEAN States Belt Up and Adapt for the Geopolitical Roller Coaster Ride. In *China and Southeast Asia in the Xi Jinping Era*, edited by Alvin Cheng-Hin Lim and Frank Cibulka, pp. 205–224. New York: Lexington Books.

Savage, Victor R., and Lily Kong. 1995. Hugh Clifford and Frank Swettenham: Environmental Cognition and the Malayan Colonial Process. In *The Writer as Historical Witness: Studies in Commonwealth Literature*, edited by Edwin Thumboo and Thiru Kandiah, pp. 409–425. Singapore: UniPress.

Schama, Simon. 1987. *The Embarrassment of Riches: An Interpretation of Dutch Culture in the Golden Age*. New York: Vintage Books.

Schumpeter, Joseph A. 1942. *Capitalism, Socialism, and Democracy*. New York; London: Harper.

Scientific American. 2016. When Did the Anthropocene Begin? *Scientific American* 315 (3): 36–37.

Shamsul, A. B. 2004. A History of an Identity, An Identity of a History: The Idea and Practice of 'Malayness' in Malaysia Reconsidered. In *Contesting Malayness: Malay Identity Across Boundaries*, edited by Timothy P. Barnard, pp. 135–148. Singapore: Singapore University Press.

Shan, Weijian. 2019. *Out of the Gobi: My Story of China and America*. Hoboken, NJ: John Wiley.

Shennan, Margaret. 2015. *Out in the Midday Sun: The British in Malaya 1880–1960*. Singapore: Monsoon Books.

Sheppard, Mubin, ed. 1982. *Singapore 150 Years*. Published for the Malaysian Branch of the Royal Asiatic Society. Singapore: Times Books International.

Sherry, Norman. 1966. *Conrad's Eastern World*. Cambridge: Cambridge University Press.

Sidney, R. J. H. 1926. *Malay Land "Tanah Malayu": Some Phases of Life in Modern British Malaya*. London: Cecil Palmer.

Simmons, I. G. 2008. *Global Environmental History: 10,000 BC to AD 2000*. Edinburgh: Edinburgh University Press.

Simms, Jacqueline, ed. 1990. *Life by Other Means: Essays on D. J. Enright*. Oxford; New York: Oxford University Press.

Singapore Chronicle. 1825. Journal of a Voyage Round the Island of Singapore. *Singapore Chronicle* (November).

Singapore Free Press. 1849. The Statistics of Nutmegs. *Journal of the Indian Archipelago and Eastern Asia* 3 (1): iii–vii.

Singapore Rediscovered: A Visual Documentation of Early Singapore. 1983. Singapore: National Museum.

Skeat, W. W., and H. N. Ridley. 1900. The Orang Laut of Singapore. *Journal of the Straits Branch of the Royal Asiatic Society* (33): 247–250.

———. 1982. The Orang Laut of Singapore. In *Singapore 150 Years*, edited by Mubin Sheppard, pp. 118–120. Published for the Malaysian Branch of the Royal Asiatic Society. Singapore: Times Books International.

Skott, Christina. 2010. Imagined Centrality: Sir Stamford Raffles and the Birth of Modern Singapore. In *Singapore from Temasek to the 21st Century: Reinventing the Global City*, edited by Karl Hack and Jean-Louis Margolin, with Karine Delaye, pp. 155–184. Singapore: NUS Press.

Slametmuljana. 1976. *A Story of Majapahit.* Singapore: Singapore University Press.

Smith, Monica L. 2019. *Cities: The First 6,000 Years.* London: Simon & Schuster.

Smith, P. D. 2012. *City: A Guidebook for the Urban Age.* London: Bloomsbury.

Song, Ong Siang. (1923) 1967. *One Hundred Years' History of the Chinese in Singapore.* Reprint, Singapore: University of Malaya Press.

Sopher, David E. 1965. *The Sea Nomads: A Study Based on the Literature of the Maritime Boat People of Southeast Asia.* Singapore: Government Printer.

Southeast Asia and the Germans. 1977. Tübingen; Basle: Horst Erdmann Verlag; Bonn: Inter Nationes.

Spencer, Nick. 2016. *The Evolution of the West: How Christianity Has Shaped Our Values.* London: SPCK.

Stark, Rodney. 2005. *The Victory of Reason: How Christianity Led to Freedom, Capitalism, and Western Success.* New York: Random House.

Steadman, John M. 1969. *The Myth of Asia: A Refutation of Western Stereotypes of Asian Religion, Philosophy, Art and Politics.* New York: Simon & Schuster.

Strabo. 1917–1932. *The Geography of Strabo.* 8 vols. Translated by Horace Leonard Jones. London: William Heinemann; New York: G. P. Putnam's Sons.

Suryadinata, Leo. 2004. *Chinese and Nation-building in Southeast Asia.* Singapore: Marshall Cavendish Academic.

Swettenham, Frank Athelstane. 1895. *Malay Sketches.* London: John Lane.

Tamney, Joseph B. 1996. *The Struggle over Singapore's Soul: Western Modernization and Asian Culture.* Berlin; New York: Walter de Gruyter.

Tan, Tony K. J., and S. A. Tan. 1984. Changing Trends in Singapore's Public Housing Development. In *Proceedings of 3rd Symposium on Our Environment*, edited by Koh Lip Lin and Hew Choy Sin, pp. 16–23. Singapore: Faculty of Science, NUS.

Tate, D. J. M. 1971. *The Making of Modern South-East Asia. Volume 1: The European Conquest.* Kuala Lumpur: Oxford University Press, 1971–1979.
Taylor, Edmond. 1947. *Richer by Asia.* Boston: Houghton Mifflin.
Taylor, Nigel P. 2014. The Environmental Relevance of the Singapore Botanic Gardens. In *Nature Contained: Environmental Histories of Singapore*, edited by Timothy P. Barnard, pp. 115–137. Singapore: NUS Press.
Teggart, Frederick J. 1962. *Theory and Processes of History.* Berkeley; Los Angeles: University of California Press.
Teo, Siew Eng, and Victor R. Savage. 1991. Singapore Landscape: A Historical Overview of Housing Image. In *A History of Singapore*, edited by Ernest C. T. Chew and Edwin Lee, pp. 312–338. Singapore: Oxford University Press.
Theroux, Paul. 1973. *Saint Jack: A Novel.* Boston: Houghton Mifflin.
Thomson, John Turnbull. 1847. Remarks on the Sletar and Sabimba Tribes. *Journal of the Indian Archipelago and Eastern Asia* 1 (5): 341–352.
———. 1849a. General Report on the Residency of Singapore, Drawn Up Principally with a View of Illustrating its Agricultural Statistics. *Journal of the Indian Archipelago and Eastern Asia* 3 (10): 618–628.
———. 1849b. General Report of [on] the Residency of Singapore, Drawn Up Principally with a View of Illustrating its Agricultural Statistics. *Journal of the Indian Archipelago and Eastern Asia* 3 (12): 744–755.
———. 1850a. General Report on the Residency of Singapore, Drawn Up Principally with a View of Illustrating its Agricultural Statistics: Fruit Trees. *Journal of the Indian Archipelago and Eastern Asia* 4 (3): 134–143.
———. 1850b. General Report on the Residency of Singapore, Drawn Up Principally with a View of Illustrating its Agricultural Statistics. *Journal of the Indian Archipelago and Eastern Asia* 4 (5): 206–219.
———. 1865. *Some Glimpses into Life in the Far East.* London: Richardson.
———. 1984. *Glimpses into Life in Malayan Lands.* Singapore: Oxford University Press.
Tinsley, Bonnie. 1983. *Singapore Green: A History and Guide to the Botanic Gardens.* Singapore: Times Books International.
Toynbee, Arnold. 1971. *Civilization on Trial and The World and the West.* New York: Meridian Books.
———. 1972. *A Study of History.* London: Oxford University Press; Thames and Hudson.
———. 1976. *Mankind and Mother Earth: A Narrative History of the World.* New York: Oxford University Press.
Turnbull, C. Mary. 1977. *A History of Singapore 1819–1975.* Kuala Lumpur: Oxford University Press.
———. 1983. Melaka under British Colonial Rule. In *Melaka: The Transformation of a Malay Capital, c. 1400–1980, Volume One*, edited by Kernial Singh

Sandhu and Paul Wheatley, pp. 242–296. Kuala Lumpur: Oxford University Press.

———. 1989. *A History of Malaysia, Singapore and Brunei*. Sydney: Allen & Unwin.

Tyers, Ray. 1976. *Singapore Then & Now*. Singapore: University Education Press.

van Cuylenburg, John Bertram. 1982. *Singapore: Through Sunshine and Shadow*. Singapore: Heinemann Asia.

van Dijk, C. 2002. Colonial Fears, 1890–1918: Pan-Islamism and the Germano-Indian Plot. In *Transcending Borders: Arabs, Politics, Trade and Islam in Southeast Asia*, edited by Huub de Jonge and Nico Kaptein, pp. 53–89. Leiden: KITLV Press.

van Leur, J. C. 1955. *Indonesian Trade and Society: Essays in Asian Social and Economic History*. Published for the Royal Tropical Institute — Amsterdam. The Hague; Bandung: W. van Hoeve.

Vickers, Adrian. 2004. 'Malay Identity': Modernity, Invented Tradition, and Forms of Knowledge. In *Contesting Malayness: Malay Identity Across Boundaries*, edited by Timothy P. Barnard, pp. 25–55. Singapore: Singapore University Press.

Wade, Geoff. 2000. The Southern Chinese Borders in History. In *Where China Meets Southeast Asia: Social & Cultural Change in the Border Regions*, edited by Grant Evans, Christopher Hutton, and Kuah Khun Eng, pp. 28–50. Singapore: ISEAS.

Wake, C. H. 1983. Melaka in the Fifteenth Century: Malay Historical Traditions and the Politics of Islamization. In *Melaka: The Transformation of a Malay Capital, c. 1400–1980, Volume One*, edited by Kernial Singh Sandhu and Paul Wheatley, pp. 128–161. Kuala Lumpur: Oxford University Press.

Wallace, Alfred Russel. 1863. On the Physical Geography of the Malay Archipelago. *Journal of the Royal Geographical Society* 33: 217–234.

———. 1869. *The Malay Archipelago: The Land of the Orang-Utan, and the Bird of Paradise. A Narrative of Travel, with Studies of Man and Nature*. New York: Harper.

———. 1878. *Tropical Nature, and Other Essays*. London: Macmillan.

———. 2015. *Alfred Russel Wallace: Letters from the Malay Archipelago*. Edited by John van Wyhe and Kees Rookmaaker. Oxford: Oxford University Press.

Wallerstein, Immanuel. 1983. *Historical Capitalism*. London: Verso.

———. 2011a. *The Modern World-System I: Capitalist Agriculture and the Origins of the European World-Economy in the Sixteenth Century*. Berkeley: University of California Press.

———. 2011b. *The Modern World-System II: Mercantilism and the Consolidation of the European World-Economy, 1600–1750*. Berkeley: University of California Press.

———. 2011c. *The Modern World-System III: The Second Era of Great Expansion of the Capitalist World-Economy, 1730s–1840s*. Berkeley: University of California Press.

Walling, R. N. 1985. An Eastern Petticoat Lane. In *Travellers' Tales of Old Singapore*, edited by Michael Wise with Mun Him Wise, pp. 223–224. Singapore: Times Books International.

Wang, Gungwu. 1979. Introduction: The Study of the Southeast Asian Past. In *Perceptions of the Past in Southeast Asia*, edited by Anthony Reid and David Marr, pp. 1–8. Published for the Asian Studies Association of Australia. Singapore: Heinemann Educational Books.

Warraq, Ibn. 2007. *Defending the West: A Critique of Edward Said's Orientalism*. Amherst, NY: Prometheus Books.

Warren, James F. 2003. *Rickshaw Coolie: A People's History of Singapore, 1880–1940*. Singapore: NUS Press.

Weidenbaum, Murray L., and Samuel Hughes. 1996. *The Bamboo Network: How Expatriate Chinese Entrepreneurs Are Creating a New Economic Superpower in Asia*. New York: Martin Kessler Books.

Weld, Frederick A. 1983. The Straits Settlements and British Malaya. In *Honourable Intentions: Talks on the British Empire in South-East Asia delivered at the Royal Colonial Institute 1874–1928*, edited by Paul H. Kratoska, pp. 43–90. Singapore: Oxford University Press.

Wheatley, Paul. 1954. Land Use in the Vicinity of Singapore in the 1830s. *Malayan Journal of Tropical Geography* 2: 63–66.

———. 1961. *The Golden Khersonese: Studies in the Historical Geography of the Malay Peninsula before A.D. 1500*. Kuala Lumpur: University of Malaya Press.

———. 2008. *The Origins and Character of the Ancient Chinese City. Volume II: The Chinese City in Comparative Perspective*. New York: Routledge.

Whitehead, John. 1893. *Exploration of Mount Kina Balu, North Borneo*. London: Gurney and Jackson.

Wilkes, Charles. 1845. *Narrative of the United States Exploring Expedition. During the Years 1838, 1839, 1840, 1841, 1842*, vol. 5. Philadelphia: Lea & Blanchard, 1845–1861.

———. 1984. *The Singapore Chapter of the Narrative of the United States Exploring Expedition. During the Years 1838, 1839, 1840, 1841, 1842*. Singapore: Antiques of the Orient.

Wilson, Dick. 1972. *The Future Role of Singapore*. Published for the Royal Institute of International Affairs. London: Oxford University Press.

———. 1975. *East Meets West: Singapore*. Singapore: Times Printers.

Winichakul, Thongchai. 1994. *Siam Mapped: A History of the Geo-Body of a Nation*. Chiang Mai: Silkworm Books.

Winstedt, Richard O. 1953. *The Malays: A Cultural History.* London: Routledge & Paul.
———. 1962. *A History of Malaya.* Singapore: Marican.
Wise, Michael, with Mun Him Wise, eds. 1985. *Travellers' Tales of Old Singapore.* Singapore: Times Books International.
Wittfogel, Karl A. 1957. *Oriental Despotism: A Comparative Study of Total Power.* New Haven: Yale University Press.
Wolf, Eric R. 1982. *Europe and the People Without History.* Berkeley: University of California Press.
Wolters, O. W. 1967. *Early Indonesian Commerce: A Study of the Origins of Srivijaya.* Ithaca, NY: Cornell University Press.
———. 1970. *The Fall of Srivijaya in Malay History.* Ithaca, NY: Cornell University Press.
———. 1999. *History, Culture, and Region in Southeast Asian Perspectives.* Ithaca, NY: Southeast Asia Program Publications, Cornell University; Singapore: Institute of Southeast Asian Studies.
Wood, Ellen Meiksins. 2002. *The Origin of Capitalism: A Longer View.* London: Verso.
Wright, H. R. C. 1958. The Moluccan Spice Monopoly, 1770–1824. *Journal of the Malayan Branch Royal Asiatic Society* 31 (4): 1–127.
Wright, Nadia H. 2003. *Respected Citizens: The History of Armenians in Singapore and Malaysia.* Middle Park, Victoria: Amassia Publishing.
———. 2017. *William Farquhar and Singapore: Stepping out from Raffles' Shadow.* Penang, Malaysia: Entrepot Publishing.
Wurtzburg, C. E. 1954. *Raffles of the Eastern Isles.* London: Hodder and Stoughton.
Yeo, K. W., and A. Lau. 1991. From Colonialism to Independence, 1945–1965. In *A History of Singapore*, edited by Ernest C. T. Chew and Edwin Lee, pp. 117–153. New York: Oxford University Press.
Yeoh, Brenda S. A. 1996. *Contesting Space, Power Relations and the Urban Built Environment in Colonial Singapore.* Kuala Lumpur: Oxford University Press.
You, Poh Seng. 1967. The Population of Singapore 1966: Demographic Structure, Social and Economic Characteristics. *Malayan Economic Review* 12 (2): 59–96.
Young, Adam J. 2005. Roots of Contemporary Maritime Piracy in Southeast Asia. In *Piracy in Southeast Asia: Status, Issues, and Responses*, edited by Derek Johnson and Mark Valencia, pp. 1–33. Leiden: IIAS; Singapore: ISEAS.
Yvan. 1855. *Six Months among the Malays; and A Year in China.* London: James Blackwood; Paternoster Row.

Zangger, Andreas. 2013. *The Swiss in Singapore*. Singapore: Editions Didier Millet.

Zukin, Sharon. 2006. David Harvey on Cities. In *David Harvey: A Critical Reader*, edited by Noel Castree and Derek Gregory, pp. 102–120. Malden, MA: Blackwell.

INDEX

A
Abdul Rahman, Temenggong, 108, 404
Abu-Lughod, Janet, 354
Adams, Arthur, 129
adat, 96–97, 109, 137, 271
Addenbrooke, Col., 98
agriculture
    betel vine (*sirih*), 137
    cash crops, 22
    gambier (Chinese), 120, 143–145, 396
    gutta percha (*getah*), 129
    impacts on vegetation, 139
    labour cost, 136
    land tenure system, 137
    Malakoff Plantation Company, 147
    market gardening (Chinese), 148
    plantations, 140
    rubber (*caoutchouc*), 129, 146–147
    spices (nutmeg, pepper), 37, 92, 137, 140–141, 184
    tropical fruit, 145

Alam Melayu, 5, 16, 52–53, 61–63, 65, 67–68, 71, 73, 91, 261, 263, 266, 339, 359
    Boyanese, 177
    Bugis, 271–272
    definition, 135
    Javanese, 177
    Melayu Nation, (*see also* Malays)
    Minangkabaus, 268
Alatas, Syed Hussein, 85–86, 96, 105
    Raffles' imperialist ideology, 86
Albuquerque, Alfonso de, 56
Allison, Graham, 314, 349, 353
Almeida, Jose (Joaquim) d', 140, 142
Amrith, Sunil, 354
Anderson, Benedict, 30, 253, 305, 319, 321
    imagined communities, 251
    three factors legitimising colonies, 30, 38
    print capitalism, 30
Anderson, Isabel, 81, 178, 181, 183
Anderson, John, 89, 195

Anderson, Patrick, 47, 121, 183, 200–201, 204–205, 219–220, 244, 255–258, 260, 262, 270, 272, 274–275, 277, 303, 307
Anglo-Dutch Treaty, 1824, 10, 100
Anthropocene, 117
anti-colonialism, 313, 368
Anwar, Ibrahim, 352
Appiah, Kwame, 253
Arabs, 108, 111, 181, 197, 232, 253, 255, 263, 267, 282–283, 299, 332, 335
    Arab Street, 183
    fringe Westernisation, 282
    Hadhrami Arabs (from Hadhramaut), 283
    Moors, 262, 283
    "unhealthy Arabisation", 283
Armenians, 14, 31, 104, 107, 166, 214, 232, 255
    Sarkies brothers, 214, 342
Arrighi, Giovanni, 32, 90, 231, 338
Asian Town (*see* Chinatown), 106, 179–182
    location, 4, 5, 11, 21
    description, 21, 106, 180, 343
Aurea Khersonese/Golden Chersonese, 37, 59

B

Baker, Jim, 14, 289
Balasingamchow, Yu-mei, 16
Balestier, Maria & Joseph, 43, 100, 107, 112, 129, 140–144, 146, 183, 200, 212, 216, 226–227, 233–234, 236, 238–239, 255, 257, 274, 277, 285, 287, 330, 342, 344
Barber, Noel, 8, 41, 83, 179, 183, 197, 199–200, 235, 240, 260, 317, 336, 350
Barendse, R.J., 6, 82, 85, 334
Barros, João de, 56, 61, 266

Barrow, John, 27, 186
Barzini, Luigi, 31
Bastin, John, 19, 35–36, 40, 56, 92, 97, 102, 191
Begbie, Peter, 70, 144, 189–191
Belle Époque, 34, 394
Bencoolen, 84, 88–89, 92, 100, 109, 120, 123, 136–137, 140, 177, 269
Benda, Harry J., 5
Benjamin, Geoffrey, 53
Bennett, George, 139, 141, 143–144, 230, 240
Berry, Graham, 14
Bird, Isabella, 43, 92, 123–124, 128, 135, 180, 185, 200, 215, 237, 257–259, 266, 273, 276, 296
Blaut, J.M., 145
Bleackley, Horace, 39, 176, 184, 188, 191–192, 196, 199, 208, 219, 247, 267–268, 276–277, 300
Bloch, Marc, 19
Bloodworth, Dennis, 17, 307, 312–318, 353, 355
Boat Quay, 105, 198
Booth, Anne, 229, 291–292, 356
Botanic Gardens, Singapore, 129, 139–140, 146, 348
    Fort Canning, 1822, 339, 348
    Montgomerie, William, 108, 139
    Superintendents (Burkill, Murton, Ridley), 139–140
    Tanglin, 140, 348
Boustead, 43, 148, 232, 342
Bowen, John, 68
Bowring, Philip, 37, 60, 67
Braddell, Roland, 3, 13, 62, 71, 73, 84, 109, 124, 212–216, 219, 237, 256, 260, 263–265, 276–277, 344
Braudel, Fernand, 45–46, 52, 93, 227–228

British power, 40, 100, 110, 296, 312
  divide and rule, 105, 177
  spatial apartheid, 104–105, 206
  spatial dualism, 343
Brooke, Gilbert, 13, 138, 360
Brooke, James, 89, 94, 126–127, 130, 222–223, 265, 297
Brown, C.C., 57–58, 70
Brown, Mary & Edwin, 43, 300
Buchanan, Iain, 231, 307
Buchanan, Keith, 304–306, 321
Buckley, Charles Burton, 13, 84–85, 90, 101, 131, 133, 135, 142–143, 212, 221–222, 238–239, 275
Bugis Street, 164, 200–202, 204, 207, 317, 343
Buitenzorg Botanical Gardens, 140, 348
Bukit Larangan, 72, 197
Burbidge, Frederick, 216
Burkill, Henry, 139–140
Butterworth, William, 34, 148, 237–238, 297

C

Calder, Kent, 15
Cameron, John, 112, 122, 130, 132, 134, 139, 146, 188, 196, 212, 226, 229, 234–235, 238–240, 334, 344
capitalism, 93–94, 232, 246–247
  colonial-capitalist relationship, 321
  definition, 93
  van Leur, 93, 232–233, 349
Carlos, A. H., 191
Carnie, Neil Martin, 133
cartography, 11, 38, 341
  see Benedict Anderson
  documentation in cartography, 11–12
  Singapore records, 39
  surveys of the colony, 38

Castells, Manuel, 30, 90, 223
Cellates (Straits people), 65, 395
Central Business District (CBD), 190, 198, 231
  see Commercial Square/Raffles Place
  see Kampong Gelam
  see land tenure
Change Alley, 163, 196–198, 207, 213
chettiar, 199
Chiang, Hai Ding, 14–15
Chinatown, 107, 162, 180–187, 191–195, 207, 276–277
  see Barrington Kaye
  characteristic, 256
  communal living, 107
  economic specialization, 195–196
  five-foot ways, 195–196, 396
  see Simpson Report
  shophouse, 178, 193–195, 206, 403
  slums, 188, 192, 194
  street scenes, 192
  toa poh, 182, 192, 404
  tuberculosis, 195
  Upper Nankin Street, 46, 193–194
Chinese, 272–280
  bamboo network, 315
  burial grounds, 105, 107
  Chinese High School, 317
  city, 11, 33, 276–277, 323
  cultural profiling, 272–274
  demography, 252, 257
  diaspora, 17
  domestic 'boys', 22, 256–258, 275, 330–331, 345, 350
  English-educated and Chinese-educated, 279, 285, 307, 311, 315, 323
  entrepreneurship, 280
  funerals (*see* Sago Lane), 287

joss house, 188, 398
New Year, 29, 188
Straits Chinese British Association, 273
Straits Chinese (Peranakans), 273, 300, 316, 402
towkays, 147–148, 171, 200, 207, 238, 245–246, 257, 277–278, 280, 331, 334, 339, 404
wayang, 83, 188, 257, 405
Chong, Terence, 15
Chuliah/Chulia, 280–281
Cities of Light, 216
   characters of light, 217
city
   Chinese city, 11
   definition, 93, 225, 246
   model city, 255
   streets, 213
   sustainability, 344
   see urban morphology
Clarke, Sir Andrew, governor, 38
Clifford, Hugh, 34, 45, 94, 96, 237, 260, 267–268, 296–299
Coclanis, Peter, 41, 339
Coèdes, George, 227–228, 339
Cohn, Bernard S., 260, 284–285, 297, 332, 334
   colonial knowledge, 260, 285, 297, 334
Cold War, 18–19, 22, 305, 312, 316, 319, 322
Coleman, George, 221
Collingwood, Cuthbert, 124–125, 129, 133–134, 139, 141–142, 144, 146, 180, 194, 218, 244, 265, 274, 281–282
colonial city, 101–102, 104, 106, 111, 212
   definition, 93
   divide and rule, 105
   Spanish grid cities, 103

colonialism
   administrator-scholars, 35–36, 38, 61, 87–88, 90, 92–97, 101, 139, 260, 289–290, 307, 322, 359
   East-West debate, 8, 295, 305, 308, 317, 319
   evaluations, 129, 141, 298, 316
   high colonialism, 34, 37, 290, 397
   impact/influence of Western civilization, 47, 76, 226, 304, 334
   migrant policies, 27
   philosopher-administrators, 84, 92–93
   Royal Colonial Institute, 296
   Singapore experiment, 48, 90, 119
Commercial Square (Raffles Place), 111, 190, 197–198
   commercial hub, 198, 214
   firm-centred economy, 196, 198, 338
communism, 279, 305, 352
Conrad, Joseph, 35, 119, 178–179, 214–215, 236, 303, 336, 343
cosmic symbolism, Hindu-Buddhist, 61, 339
cosmopolitan population, 44, 159, 253
   definition, 253
Coupland, R., 84, 88–89
Coward, Noel, 214, 289
Crane, Thomas Owen, 131, 140
Crawfurd, John, 9, 11, 13, 61, 81, 86–87, 89, 92–96, 100, 103, 105–106, 111, 120, 130, 137–138, 141, 145–146, 148, 181, 212, 225–226, 228–231, 234, 236–237, 241–242, 272–274, 289–290, 296, 342, 356
Cricket Club, 206
Cross, Rev. William, 38, 90, 100, 110, 113, 203, 340

Crown Colony, British, 10, 228, 237, 336
culture
    comparative consciousness, 350
    cultural distancing, 284–287, 331, 350
    cultural relativity, 287, 350
Culture System (*cultuurstelsel*), Java, 140, 147, 230, 304

D
Dalrymple, A., 89
Dar al-Islam (House of Islam), 74
Davidson, G.F., 126, 132–133, 141, 228–229, 254, 271
de Blij, Harm, 192, 225
    mobal, 225, 246
    power of place, 192
de Erédia, Emanuel Godinho, 59
    map of 'Sincapura' 1604, 11
de Koninck, R., 344
de Souza, Dudley, 220
death houses (*see* Sago Lane)
Dekker, Eduard, 304
Delaye, Karine, 16, 52
Demang Lebar Daun, 57–58, 62–63, 72
Dennys, Nicholas, 13, 56, 60–61, 81, 142, 146, 199, 225, 230, 256, 264, 336
Design Earth, 128, 335
Diamond, Jared, 327
Dikötter, Frank, 317
Dobby, E.H.G., 47, 230, 313–314, 354
    colonial speech, 47
Doggett, Margorie & Victor, 217–218
Dragon's Teeth Gate (*see Lung ya men*), 55, 124
Drysdale, John, 15, 147, 236, 248, 287–288, 307, 313–314
dual economy (*see* Geertz and Santos)
    firm-centred, 196, 198, 338
    pasar/bazaar, 196, 198, 402
Duara, Prasenjit, 15, 52
    contingent history, 15, 52, 359
Dunlop, 148
Dutch, 37, 45, 75, 80–83, 85, 88, 99–101, 137, 140, 144, 147, 229, 348
    ascendancy, 83
    cultuurstelsel (Culture System)
    Dutch (VOC), 80–81
    Java-centric policy, 229
Dyce, Charles Andrew, 12

E
Earl, George Windsor, 101, 112, 138, 140, 176, 181, 226, 255–256, 268, 271–272, 281
East India Company (EIC), 4, 17–19, 22, 76, 79, 81–83, 85, 90, 106, 131, 221, 247, 252, 296
East-West oscillations, 17, 20, 36, 37, 92, 215, 254, 286, 295, 308, 311, 318, 319, 330, 333–334, 336, 348–350, 352–353
    Parkinson's hypothesis, 62, 344
education
    Institution/Raffles Institution, 98, 102, 104, 246
    see mission civilisatrice
Enright, D.J., 18, 28, 47, 219, 245, 307–315, 332, 334, 351, 355
    Affair, 22
    authors on, 86, 95–96, 110
    cultural spring cleaning, 47, 309
    English-educated vs Chinese educated, 307, 311, 315, 323
    hybrid culture, 311
    national culture, 310
    types of writers, 28
    yellow culture, 18, 47, 308–310
environmental determinism, 95, 119, 122–123, 265, 290, 292, 296

Eurasians, 217, 235, 253, 256, 273, 284, 299–300, 309, 311
British views, 240
'others' category, 253, 267
population, 6, 122
Singapore Recreation Club, 235
Eurocentrism, 101, 286, 333
European/s: definition, 5–8, 14, 18, 21
European exceptionalism (*see* Lieberman)
European Town 21, 87, 103, 106, 166, 176, 179–182, 188, 343
description, 106, 176, 181
graveyards, Fort Canning Hill, 107
grid-like layout, 106
location, 176
population density, 107, 195
sio poh, 182, 404
exchange hour, 238–239, 345

F
Fajar Generation, 313
Fame (ship), 113
Fanon, Frantz, 104
Farquhar, William, 17, 85–87, 94, 100, 102–103, 108, 110, 120, 125, 148, 197–198, 231, 233, 356
Fernández-Armesto, Felipe, 67, 346–347
First World War, 299–300
Fitch, George, 254
Fitzgerald, C.P., 279, 305, 312, 314–315, 355
five-foot way, 195–196
Flower, R., 79, 80, 202, 214
Foran, R., 184
Forster, E.M., 304
Fort Canning Hill (*Bukit Larangan*), 20, 60, 66, 72, 189, 197, 222, 339, 348, 394

Franklin, James, 11
Freitag, U., 282, 283
Frost, Mark R., 16
Fukuyama, Francis, 87, 235, 352
end of history, 352
identity politics, 87
megalothymia, 235
Fu Manchu, 280, 352
Furnivall, J.S., 225, 252–253
plural societies, 48, 252, 305, 350

G
Gajah Mada, 65
gambier, 120, 143–145 *see* agriculture
Geertz, Clifford, 147, 198, 291, 338, 356
agricultural involution, 291
Japan and Java comparison, 291
pasar-firm centred economy, 196, 198, 291, 338, 356, 402
Ghesquière, Henri, 15
Gibson-Hill, C.A., 125, 189, 264
Glacken, Clarence, 118, 123
Glendinning, Victoria, 79, 85, 88
Government Hill (*see* Fort Canning Hill), 98
Grand Hotel de l'Europe, 39, 166, 179, 213, 219, 282, 343
Gunn, Geoffrey, 90
Eurasian Exchange, 91
Guthrie, 43, 147, 232, 342

H
Hack, Karl, 16, 52
Hahn, Emily, 90, 103
Hale, Richard, 43, 200, 226, 257, 274, 275, 277, 286–288
Hall, D.G.E., 231, 233

Hall, Kenneth, 65
Hamilton, Capt. Alexander, 80–81
Hancock, T.H.H., 189
Harper, Timothy, 36
Harrisons & Crosfield, 148
hawkers
    street culture, 207
    travelling kitchens, 184
Hedges, Chris, 299
Heine-Geldern, Robert, 339
Heng, Derek, 16
Herman, Arthur, 289–290
Hikayat Abdullah, 84
Hill, A., 197–198
Hill, Ronald, 131, 184
history
    contingent history, 52
    cross-sectional history, 7, 32, 43, 45, 338
    ecumenical age, 82
    historical processes, 5, 13
    longue durée, 52
    metanarrative, 36
    narrative historical geography, 12, 28–29, 329
Hornaday, William, 128, 180–181, 183, 195, 198, 218–219, 254
Hose, Charles, 89
Howell, E.F., 262
Hsu Yun Ts'iao, 56
Hughes, Samuel, 315
human-nature relationships, 117, 119, 147
Huntington, Samuel, 23–24, 319, 349–351

I
imageability, 22, 187, 211, 213, 225, 330, 342
    definition/concept, 5, 213
    Kevin Lynch, 22
    landscapes, 43

Singapore manifestations, 22, 175, 178, 187–188, 200, 213–215, 310–311
India Extra Gangem (India beyond the Ganges), 59
India Intra Gangem (India within the Ganges), 59
Indians, 280–282
    chettiars, 199, 280, 395
    cultural profiling, 284
    employment, 275
    Klings/Chuliahs, 255, 257, 261, 280–282, 288, 395
    physical description, 282
Innes, Emily, 237, 259
Iskandar Shah, 62, 66, 74–76
istana, 105, 108–109, 155, 177

J
Jackson, John Brinkerhoff, 29, 45, 180, 188, 215, 217, 222
Jackson Plan 1822, 12, 46, 105, 106, 221, 337
Jacobs, Jane, 186
Jacobs, Jane M., 37
Jagor, Fedor, 180, 184, 256–257
James Franklin's Plan (1830), 11, 38
Japanese
    occupation, 10, 46–47, 172, 280, 295, 299–300, 302–303
    vice trade, 296, 298, 317
Java
    land tenure system (*adat*), 96–97, 109, 137
Jews, 104, 181, 197, 232, 255
joss/josh house, 188, 398

K
Kampong Gelam/Glam, 12, 105–106, 108, 176–177, 183, 197–198, 216, 331, 398
    Istana, 108, 177, 398

Sultan Ali, 331
Sultan of Singapore, 109, 331
kampong/kampung/campong/ compong, 103–104, 208, 269
Kaplan, Robert D., 340
Kaye, Barrington, 46, 193–195
Keppel, Henry, 284
Keppel Harbour, 125, 133, 161, 189–190, 223
Khanna, Parag, 341, 352
keramat, 66, 70, 107, 134, 399
Kipling, Rudyard, 17, 35, 119, 214–215, 219, 221, 224, 254, 277, 303, 305
Kotkin, Joel, 327–328, 334, 344
kraton, 61, 399
Kratoska, Paul, 296
Kroeber, Alfred, 352
Kwa, Chong Guan, 16, 52, 63, 69, 359

L
labour
  employment, 177
  wages, 194, 239, 258, 274
Lach, Donald, 33, 55–56, 65–67, 350
land tenure system, 96–97, 109–112, 137, 143, 329–330, 347–348
  adat, 96–97, 109, 137, 271, 393
  British law, 62, 110
  Crown land, 110
landscape
  cultural, 10, 29, 34, 106, 135, 211, 216, 221–224, 337
  functional, 207
  sense, 182–183, 192, 204
  see vernacular
Lauvergne, Barthélemy, 12
Le May, Reginald, 71, 281
Lee, Edwin, 14, 17, 318–319

Lee Kuan Yew, 15–17, 23, 292, 311–314, 319, 327, 341, 354–357
legibility, 183, 200, 213, 221, 330
  amorphous city, 220
  chaotic landscape, 21, 181, 185, 207, 218, 312
Levathes, Louise, 74
Lewis & Wigen, 254
Leyden, John, 56–58, 97
Li, Jen, 297, 311, 334
Lieberman, Victor, 32, 251, 304, 328, 332–333
  European exceptionalism, 286, 328, 333
Lim, Rosemary, 14
Lion City (*see* Singapura, Tumasik), 4, 7, 9, 11–12, 17, 20, 27–28, 36, 42, 51–56, 58–76, 98, 125, 180, 182, 184, 191, 211–212, 217, 223, 225, 237, 252, 254, 284, 307, 339, 342, 348–349, 352, 354, 359–360, 403–404
Little, Robert, 130–131, 135, 140, 200, 212, 242–243
Lockard, Craig, 74
Lockhart, Bruce, 183, 203–204, 245, 262, 270–271, 278, 299, 301, 311
Logan, James, 84, 180, 212, 243, 264, 270, 275, 338
Long, Nicholas, 53, 68, 271
Lornie, James, 110
Lovejoy, Arthur, 28
Lovelock, James, 322
Lowe, Keith, 8, 302–303
Low, James, 137
Lumsdaine, James, 104, 137
Lung Ya Men/Longya men (Dragon's Teeth Gate), 55, 60, 125
Lynch, Kevin, 22, 213, 221

M

Macassar, 82, 229
MacDonald, Malcolm, 215, 225, 236, 254, 259–260, 287–288, 292
Mackerras, Colin, 316
Mahizhnan, Arun, 15
Majapahit empire, 52–53 55, 59–60, 62–65, 68, 70, 72, 75
    golden age, 63
Makepeace, Walter, 13, 230, 238, 360
Malacca
    Iskandar Shah, 62, 66, 74–76
    origin, 64, 66
    Sikandar Shah (Xaquem Darxa), 66
    Sultanate, 16, 20, 52–53, 56, 63–64, 68–69, 74–76
    symbolic links, 27
    Undang-undang Melaka, 74, 97
malaria, 46, 119, 123, 126, 130–132
    Dr Little's theory, 131
Malay Annals (*see* Sejarah Melayu), 20, 53, 55, 58, 97
Malay Archipelago, 36, 76, 91, 126–127, 132, 141, 179, 211, 229, 233, 243, 255, 261, 296, 341, 348
Malays, 263–272
    adat (customary rights), 96–97, 109, 271, 393
    beliefs, practices, 268
    character, 263
    cultural identity/profiling, 5, 271
    fugitive, an exile, 266
    kampong culture, 269, 398
    language, 264
    lazy native, 268
    Malaiur, 71
    masuk Melayu, 177, 264, 400
    Malayophilia, 268
    Melayu Nation, 97
    mythology, 20, 53
    population 268–279
    Sultan of Singapore, 10, 109, 331
    Tanah Melayu, 68, 264, 267
    Telok Blangah, 108
Malay World (see *Alam Melayu*)
Malayan Emergency, 317
Malayanisation Report, 22, 47
Malaysia, 322, 323
March, Andrew, 312, 344
Margolin, Jean-Louis, 16, 52
Marr, David, 5, 40
Marriot, Hayes, 254
Marsden, William, 84, 92–94, 96, 101, 260, 263, 265, 296
Marshall, David, 310
Maugham, W. Somerset, 35, 214–215, 219, 261, 303–304
McGee, Terry, 345
McKie, Ronald, 184–185, 196, 203
merlion, 11
Miksic, John, 16, 56, 62–63, 67, 75
Miller, Eric, 82
Milner, Anthony, 98, 263
mission civilisatrice, 95, 101–102, 243, 286, 290, 298, 309–312, 314–315, 321, 340, 347, 400
Mokyr, Joel, 8, 91, 297, 320, 333
Montgomerie, William, 108, 139–140, 142, 146
Moore, Donald, 8, 14, 16, 79, 113–114, 185, 188, 196, 200, 204–206, 208, 215, 218, 225, 231, 254, 259–260, 277, 289, 292, 302, 312–313, 329–330, 334, 338, 342, 354, 357, 360
Moor, John Henry, 12, 144
Mount Meru, 72, 74
Movement poet, 28
Morris, Desmond, 35
Mpu Prapañca, 60
Mumford, Lewis, 175

Munshi, Abdullah, 84, 96, 198
Myrdal, Gunnar, 304

N
Nader, Laura, 42, 350
Nagarakretagama (*Desawarnana*), 55, 60, 65–66
Nahuijs, Col., 82, 99, 105–106, 239–240
narrative
    historical-geography, 12, 28–29, 329
    metanarratives, 36
    roadside, 186–189
nationalism, 318
Needham, Joseph, 291
Newbold, Thomas, 70, 100, 141, 227, 233, 264, 342
newspapers, Singapore, 30
    Eastern Daily Mail, 30
    Singapore Chronicle, 30
    The Malaya Tribune, 30
    The Singapore Free Press, 30
    The Straits Times, 30
Notices, 12, 47, 241, 328

O
O'Connor, Richard, 87, 177
Ommanney, F.D., 192, 201, 244
Ooi, Jin Bee, 14–15
opium smoking, trade (*see* vices)
orang laut (sea nomads), 11, 53–54, 66, 73, 96, 109, 125, 140, 143, 150, 177, 252, 264, 266–267, 269, 332, 401
    Orang Gelam, 269
    Orang Geylang, 54
    Orang Kallang, 54, 269
    Orang Seletar, 54, 269
    Orang Suku Laut, 54
    tanah saya, 54
    tempat saya, 54

orang puteh, 39, 272, 288, 296–299
oriental despotism, 18, 95, 306
Orchard Road, 135, 138–139, 146, 156, 159, 200, 208, 219, 253
    Tuan's street, 208, 404
Orwell, George, 304, 327
Osborn, Sherard, 180, 187, 190–191, 276
Osterhammel, Jürgen, 32, 34, 37, 45, 51, 88, 216, 246, 286, 299, 333, 342
    fabled Orient, 51, 246
    unfabling of the East, 51, 246
    Western identity, 286
Oxley, Thomas, 130, 133, 135, 140, 212, 242

P
padang, 87, 150, 343, 401
Palembang, 20, 57, 62–64, 66, 69–71, 75–76, 263, 266, 354, 357
Parameswara, 65–68, 74–76
Parkinson, C. Northcote, 17, 47, 307, 312, 351–352, 355
pasar-bazaar economy, 196, 198, 402
passisir culture, Java, 76, 271, 402
Penang (Prince of Wales Island), 10, 88–89, 99, 129, 136–137, 141, 170, 185, 269, 316, 342, 354
People's Action Party (PAP), 18, 279, 307, 311, 312, 322, 337
Peranakans (*Nonya Baba*), 170, 177, 272–273, 300, 316, 355, 402
perceptions, western, 5–7, 10, 17–18, 20, 27–48, 79, 104, 120, 131–132, 192, 279–280, 322
    definition, 4, 27–31
    etic approach, 42
Percival, Lt. Gen. Arthur, 41
Perry, John Curtis, 16
Pilon, Maxine, 14
Pires, Tomé, 62, 66, 266, 357
plantations (*see* agriculture)

plural society, 251–292
　cosmopolitan identity, 252
　dual cultural identity, 252
　ethnic characteristics, 260–283
　ethnic diversity, 253–254, 258
　imagined communities, 251
　multiculturalism, 33, 253
　polyglot societies, 254–256
Poivre, Pierre, 265
Polo, Marco, 37, 59, 71
Pollock, Sheldon, 8, 58, 74, 113, 297, 320, 333, 339, 345
Pomeranz, Kenneth, 8, 91, 113, 297, 320, 333, 345
population
　1824 census, 43
　census, 38
　ethnic profile, 271
　gender imbalance, 256–257
　living conditions, 46
Portuguese, 31, 54, 56, 59, 62, 66, 70, 118, 147, 232, 235, 266, 352, 357
possibilism, environmental, 296, 346–347
Pratt, Ambrose, 178, 181, 183–184, 195, 200, 215, 223
primate city, 17
prostitution, 22, 202–203, 240, 244, 256
　karayuki-san, 203
　see vices
Ptolemy, Claudius, 37, 59, 357
Pulau Ujong, 55–56
Purcell, Victor, 18, 273, 304–305
Pye, Lucien, 316

Q
Queen Victoria, 3, 88, 107, 237

R
Raffles Collection, 83, 113
Raffles College, 46, 89

Raffles Hotel, 89, 202, 213–215, 219
Raffles Museum, 38, 89
Raffles Place, 104, 111, 163, 190, 196–200, 231 (*see* Commercial Square)
Raffles, Thomas Stamford, 3, 21, 79–89, 92, 112, 151, 354–361
　colonial political rule, 33
　factory, principles of, 38
　History of Java, 80, 88, 91, 93
　Land Allocation Committee, 103–104, 108, 110
　Raffles MS No 18, 56
　1822 Raffles Town Plan, 12, 21, 43, 46, 105, 175–176, 178, 189, 197–199, 206, 220
　Singapore child, 21, 84
　Town Plan Committee, 103
Ratzel, Friedrich, 263
Redfern, James, 188
red-light areas, 201–204, 331
　Desker Road, 202, 207
　Lavender Street, 202
　Malabar Street, 203
　Malay Street, 204, 262
　Middle Road, 203, 262
　Sago Lane, 202, 204, 206–207
Regnier, Philippe, 248, 279
Reid, Anthony, 5, 56, 91, 179, 228
Reith, G.M., 13
Reynolds, Craig, 52, 268
Ridley, Henry N., 134–135, 146, 264
Robequain, Charles, 81, 231
Romanticism (*see* Western civilisation)
Ross, Ronald, 131–132
Rostow, Walt, 291, 356
Ryan, N.J., 320

S
Sago Lane, 165, 202, 204–207
　death houses, 204–206

Said, Edward, 6, 37, 92, 176, 236, 284, 288, 291, 297, 304, 330, 349
  imperialism, 37
  Orientalism, 38
  'we' and 'they', 6, 20, 22, 38, 92, 176, 284–289, 291, 307
Sailendras, 71
Sailors' Home, 179, 215, 343
Sandhu, Kernial, 15, 64, 266
Sang Nila Utama, 11, 57, 75, 357
Sanskrit, 58–59, 62, 74, 339
Santos, Milton, 198
Sarkies brothers, 214, 342
Savage, Victor R., 12, 46–47, 96, 130, 237, 270, 292, 296
Scandal Point, 239, 345
Schama, Simon, 45
Schumpeter, Joseph, 351
Scott, William, 34, 140, 145–146
Second World War, 8, 22, 46, 217, 240, 259, 279–280, 295, 300–304, 307, 313, 317, 330, 333, 345, 350
Sejarah Melayu, (see *Malay Annals*), 20–21, 53, 55–58, 62–64, 66, 68–70, 72, 81, 355
  The Dynasty of Melayu, 55
  Singapore mythology, 56
Sepoy uprising, 7–11
Shan, Weijian, 317
shophouse, 46, 107, 159, 178, 187, 193–196, 207
Sidney, R.J.H., 178, 183, 185, 187, 191–192, 199, 223, 232, 258
Simpson Report, 46, 195, 246
Simpson, W.J., 195
Singapore
  Agricultural and Horticultural Society, 142
  archetypal colonial city, 340
  'Black Hole' of Singapore history, 60
  British military base, 41
  evolutionary and revolutionary change, 46
  immigrants, 8
  laboratory, tropical, 346–348
  location, 5, 11
  Malay town (1824), 267
  Master Plan (1958), 337
  model colonial city, 355
  mythical origin/history, 11, 57–58
  primate city of Malaya, 17, 37–38
  Raffles' founding, 20, 52
  security and defence, 37, 110, 233, 340
  socialist system, 306–307
  toponyms, 53–60
Singapore economy
  cottage industries, 218, 231
  department stores (Whiteaway, John Little & Co, Robinson & Co), 199
  East-West trade, 36, 114
  entrepôt, 22, 33, 37, 40–41, 44, 98–101, 224–225
  free trade/port, 98, 100
  labour costs, 330, 338
  regional loci, 231
  trading products, 226
Singapore geobody, 331
Singapore River, 181, 189–191, 197, 343
  dividing line, 189
  Elgin Bridge, 190
  port, 226–228
Singapura (Singapore), 4, 11, 20, 51–56, 58–76, 98, 125, 339, 354, 359
Singapura-Tumasik, 403
  see *Alam Melayu*
  cosmic kingdom, 73

Iskandar Shah, 66, 70, 74–76
Keramat Iskandar Shah, 66, 70
magical stones, 70–71
mountain symbolism: Bukit
  Larangan, 72, 394
myths and fables, 62, 70, 359
negara, 69, 401
Pulau Ujong, 55–56
Sang Nila Utama, 75
toponymics, 53, 55–60
trade emporium, 64, 91
Ujong Tanah, 55, 404
Singapore urban biography, 43
Skeat, W.W., 264, 269
Slametmuljana, 60, 65–66, 72
Smith, Monica, 246
Solon of Java, 88
Song, Ong Siang, 13, 273
Sopher, David, 54, 264, 269
Spencer, Nick, 42
Sri Tri Buana, 57–58, 63–64, 72, 75–76
Sri Vijaya, 69, 354
  alliance model/descent model, 68–69
  Bukit Seguntang Mahameru, 20, 71–72, 75–76
    empire, 4, 20, 53, 57, 59, 62–64, 67, 72
  negara, 69, 401
Steadman, John, 33, 37, 182
stereotyping native, 22, 29, 31
Straits of Malacca, 5, 9, 20, 54, 64, 68, 73–74, 81, 340, 354, 357
Straits Settlements, 10, 185, 237, 247, 273, 276, 305, 336
style of civilization, 352
swamps, 126, 129, 131–132
Swettenham, Frank, 267–268
Syonan-to (Light of the South), 217, 302

T
Tamney, Joseph, 44, 225
Tan, Tai Yong, 16
Tanglin Club (*see* White society)
Taylor, Edmond, 298
Taylor, Nigel, 146
Teggart, Frederick, 69, 332, 358
temenggong, 10, 82, 84–85, 96, 108–109, 176, 252, 269, 331
thalassic kingdom, 4–5, 9, 20, 51–52, 60–63, 73–76, 342
Theroux, Paul, 19, 47, 211, 244, 307
Third China, 279, 305
  Chinese High School, 317
  communism, 22–23, 305, 312–319
  supplementary China, 305
Thomson and MacDonald, 259
Thomson, John, 12–13, 34, 70–71, 84–85, 106–108, 122, 133–134, 138–139, 145, 176, 181, 221, 238–239, 243, 254, 259, 261, 267–268, 296–297
tiger, menace, 132–133
  human deaths, 21
  hunting, 134
  Rimaupore, 134
  tiger club, 134
  tiger spirits — *keramats*, 66, 70, 107, 399
Tinsley, Bonnie, 348
Toynbee, Arnold, 40, 346, 358
tropics
  ancient perceptions, 118–119
  definition, 118–119
  Singapore experiences, 119–121
  tropical climate, 121
  tropical diseases, 123
Tumasik/Temasek, 4–5, 9, 16, 20, 51–76, 82, 125, 177, 197, 334, 339–342, 357
Turnbull, C. Mary, 9, 14, 89, 113, 185–186, 217, 273, 302–303

U

Ujong Tanah (Farthest Land), 55, 59, 63, 68, 100, 104, 404
Upper Nankin Street (*see* Chinatown)
urban biography, Singapore, 43–44
urban morphology, 21, 28, 175–208
   definition, 175–179
   dual town: European and Asian, 21
   no historical landmarks, 179
   Raffles Town Plan, 1822, 12, 21, 43, 46, 105, 178
   shifting cultural landscapes, 221–224
   streets, 182–187
   undulating topography, 176

V

van Cuylenburg, John, 202, 203, 255, 262
van Dijk, C., 283
Van Dorth Hotel, 214–215
van Leur, Jacob Cornelius, 93, 226, 228, 233, 349
vanua, 72
van Otterloo, A., 190
vernacular landscape, 217–218
   concept, 29, 45, 140, 180, 188, 215, 217, 356
   see John Brinckerhoff Jackson
vice trade, 240–245
   gambling, 240–245
   liquor, 240–245
   opium, 240–245
   prostitution, 202–203, 240–245
Vickers, Adrian, 321
Vietnam War, 19, 280
Vitruvius, 130

W

wages, local employees, 194, 239
Wake, C.H., 64, 76, 271
Wallace, Alfred Russel, 21, 126–128, 132, 143, 145, 176, 211, 218, 243, 258, 273, 276, 278, 296, 337
   Bukit Timah species collection, 126–127
   longicornes (long-horned beetles), 127
Wallich, Nathaniel, 104, 120, 136, 139, 348
Walling, R., 197
Wang, Gungwu, 339
Wang Ta-yuan (Wang Dayuan), 55, 60, 68
Warraq, Ibn, 290
Warren, James, 224
Weidenbaum, Murray L., 315
Weiler, Danièle, 14
Western civilization
   definition, 346
   enlightenment, 335
   European exceptionalism, 333
   Industrial Revolution, 335
   Romanticism, 34, 335
Westerners
   definition, 31, 34
   European identity, 32
   resident population, 10
Whampoa, Hoo Ah Kay, 34, 171, 297, 335
Wheatley, Paul, 59, 64, 111, 125, 198
White society 179, 234–240
   Cameron, John, 238, 240, 334
   elite class, 236
   imperialist culture, 236
   living conditions, 240
   Scandal Point, 345
   Singapore Cricket Club, 206
   Tanglin Club, 206
   way of life, 247

Whitehead, John, 257–258, 278, 280
Wilkes, Charles, 29, 43, 177,
    187–188, 218, 224, 235, 256–257,
    261, 267
Wilson, Dick, 59, 331
Winichakul, Thongchai, 331
Winstedt, Richard, 53, 56, 226, 260
Wise and Wise, 218, 262, 276,
    284–285
Wittfogel, Karl, 18, 306
Wolters, Oliver M., 53, 58, 64,
    68–69, 75–76, 91, 266, 341
Wright, Nadia, 14, 85–87, 103, 120

Y
yellow culture, 18, 308–310
    definition, 308
    Enright, D.J., 47, 310
yellow peril, 18, 262, 280, 305
Yeoh, Brenda, 46, 336
Yvan, 108, 128, 183, 216, 257–258

Z
Zangger, Andreas, 14
Zheng He (Cheng Ho), 60, 67,
    74–75
zomia, watery, 269

www.ingramcontent.com/pod-product-compliance
Lightning Source LLC
Chambersburg PA
CBHW050525300426
44113CB00012B/1954